# THE GREAT BATTLES
# OF WORLD WAR II

# THE GREAT BATTLES OF WORLD WAR II

## BY HENRY MAULE

**Hamlyn**

London · New York · Sydney · Toronto

Published 1972 by The Hamlyn Publishing Group Limited
London · New York · Sydney · Toronto
Hamlyn House, Feltham, Middlesex, England

First impression

Phototypeset by Filmtype Services Limited,
Scarborough
Printed in Great Britain by Jarrold & Sons Ltd, Norwich

ISBN 0 600 72070 5

# Contents

# Foreword

To make a selection of great battles of the Second World War, the most enormous universal conflagration of all time, and to present them in a single book was obviously a formidable task. The immensity of any one battle, the vastness of the armies, fleets or air forces embroiled, did not necessarily qualify it for inclusion. What was important was the direct effect it had on the ultimate course of the war. To quote the advice that General of the Army Omar N. Bradley gave me from Washington: 'As you know, a relatively small and unspectacular engagement could have a far greater effect on subsequent history than a major campaign.'

Thus among the battles included here is the almost unknown one of Keren, which took place in East Africa early in 1941. Only nineteen British and Indian battalions stormed a supposedly impregnable mountain fortress defended by forty-two battalions of crack Italian and Colonial troops, yet it was a battle whose outcome had significant repercussions on the whole future course of the war. Had it not been a British victory, the Red Sea route to Egypt would have been blocked and there would have been no way of reinforcing the British Desert Army. With Rommel and his Afrika Korps already advancing across Libya, this would have meant the destruction of the British North African flank against Germany, a potential threat which forced Hitler to waste valuable time invading Greece and the Balkans, and fatally delayed his attack upon Russia. This precipitate attack had to defeat the Red Army utterly before the onset of the dreadful Russian winter if Germany were to be sure of winning the war.

Hitler and his High Command had always envisaged the Second World War as a swift succession of blitzkriegs in which first the Western Allies, then Russia, would be knocked out by lightning blows. The bitter seeds of the German failure to do this were sown by the British and Indian soldiers who fought and died with such valour at Keren.

Similarly, although Dunkirk climaxed a catastrophic Allied defeat after a brilliant German blitzkrieg campaign of near technical perfection, it meant that Britain was still in the war. And as long as Britain was in, Germany had to contend against a sea-power it could not match, and against a growing airpower which soon proved itself the master in the Battle of Britain. With increasing aid coming from the United States, the world's greatest industrial power, Hitler was compelled next to strike the blow at Russia. It was before his war industries were in top gear or his armed forces fully equipped – the outcome is history.

Every battle in this book will be found, like Keren, to have a deeper significance than any more huge and horrifying clash of multitudes of armed men and their awesome war machines. Each marked a turning point in the war which set the Allies firstly upon the precarious road out of defeat, then on to the triumphant highway to victory.

# 1. Dunkirk

As the dawn mists, promising the bliss of a lovely spring day, spread from the rivers of France across lush meadows and blossoming orchards on May 10, 1940, a terrible storm burst upon the land. After eight months of phoney war, just five weeks since British Prime Minister Neville Chamberlain's comfortable assertion, 'Hitler has missed the bus', the German blitzkrieg was launched upon the West.

The onslaught was made with 136 fully trained divisions, spearheaded by ten Panzer divisions with their 3,000 tanks and swarms of armoured cars, and by waves of heavy bombers, dive-bombers, fighters, paratroop-planes and gliders bearing shock-troops. The whole armed might of Nazi Germany was hurled against the French, British, Belgians and Dutch. Thanks to his peace pact with Stalin, Hitler only needed a scattering of troops to watch his Russian frontiers.

The German attack upon the West was made by three army groups. Army Group B, comprising 28 divisions under General Fedor von Bock, overran Holland and Belgium, although both countries were neutral, and thrust into France as the right wing of Hitler's invasion. Army Group A, comprising 44 divisions commanded by General Gerd von Rundstedt, attacked south of them from Aix-la-Chapelle to the River Moselle. This was to be the main attack. Army Group C, comprising 17 divisions under General Ritter von Leeb, pressed forward along the rest of the front from the Moselle down to Switzerland. Theirs was to be a containing attack against the Maginot Line, reputedly the finest fortress system ever built and believed by the French to be impregnable. There were a further 41 divisions in reserve.

The Allied formations facing this German force consisted of the French 1st Army Group under General Billotte, made up of 51 divisions which included 9 divisions of the British Expeditionary Force, and the French 2nd and 3rd Army Groups which totalled 43 divisions including reserves. The 1st Army Group stood along the French frontier from Longwy, at the northern end of the Maginot Line, to the Belgian frontier, and thence along this right up to the sea near Dunkirk. The Belgians and the Dutch had respectively 22 and 10 divisions forward of the Anglo–French positions, to spring to arms only if attacked. As both nations were anxious to keep out of the war, they were not fully mobilized. In the Maginot Line itself the French had nine divisions.

Including the Belgians and Dutch, there were 135 Allied divisions to contest the enemy's advance. So far as armoured divisions were concerned, the French had no less than six divisions with some 2,300 tanks, but most of these were

*Above* Winston Churchill, newly appointed prime minister, brings a new resolution to Britain. He told the House of Commons: 'I have nothing to offer but blood, toil, tears and sweat'

*Right* General Weygand (centre with sword), appointed Commander-in-Chief when France was facing defeat, with the British Commander Lord Gort (on his left)

lightly armoured, undergunned and scattered all over the front in small groups. The British, though pioneers of tank warfare, had yet barely completed the training and equipping of their first armoured division which, with its 328 tanks, was still in England.

The Germans had no compunction in suddenly subjecting neutral Holland, Belgium and Luxembourg to the fury of undeclared total war. Spearheaded by paratroops, saboteurs, dive-bombers and armoured Panzer divisions, 70 divisions under Bock and Rundstedt surged forward. The French and British put into effect Plan D – a plan drawn up by France's much-admired general, Gamelin, commander-in-chief of all the Allied forces. General Giraud's 7th French Army roared north-east to aid the Dutch, while the British and French divisions under General Billotte rolled rapidly across Belgium to challenge the enemy. They were to hold a line, broadly along the course of the River Dyle, from Antwerp on the coast, down through Louvain and Namur, and thence following the River Meuse down to the French frontier. The Belgians, meanwhile, were to hold a line well forward of this, along the Meuse and Albert Canal, for as long as they could. It was acknowledged that they could do no more than delay the enemy's advance.

The British had accepted Plan D with grave misgivings. In their view the advance to the Dyle should be delayed until it was certain the Belgians were indeed holding their forward line. If this was broken at the outset, the British and French should stand firm to await the first shock of battle on the French frontier, where strong defences linking the Maginot Line and the sea had been constructed since September, 1939. At the most, the British contended, they should move forward no farther than the line of the River Scheldt from the French frontier through Ghent to Antwerp. But they were tartly reminded, 'Is not Plan D the inspiration of General Gamelin, who drew up the orders for the great French victory of the Marne in the First World War?'

Neutral Belgium had not adequately fortified her frontier. Thus it had been overrun in many places even before Gamelin gave the signal to put Plan D into effect. Two hours before the German guns erupted, paratroops and glider-borne shock-troops had captured or destroyed vital fortifications, bridges, communication centres, headquarters and ammunition dumps in daring pre-dawn raids. Half the Belgian war-planes had been shattered on their airfields by surprise bombing. And, most important to the Germans and fatal to the Allies, three bridges across the Albert Canal had been captured intact.

In Holland German paratroopers had seized sluices that would have released an impassable water barrier across the flat lands. Yet, although vital defence points had been overwhelmed, the British and French rushed forward across Belgium, and by May 12 the first phase of Plan D had been carried out. But the line taken up was already in danger of being outflanked from the north.

The French High Command had expected the major German effort in the north and had concentrated accordingly. This rather served the purposes of the Germans for, farther south, they unleashed a vast armoured onslaught through the steep and densely wooded Belgian Ardennes. Bounded by the broad River Meuse, it was terrain that the French had deemed impossible for the tanks and guns of armoured divisions. Consequently they had manned the sector with inferior troops.

The Germans delivered their pulverizing punch at the shoulder joint of the Anglo–French left arm, as it swung from its pivot at Longwy towards them. By May 14 they had broken through at Sedan. General von Kleist's Army Group surged forward in awesome waves of tanks and armoured cars, guns, armoured troop-carriers and lorried infantry. They had a power and speed never before known in war. A terrible tide of fire-breathing armour rolled towards the defenders. Ahead of it, swarms of crook-winged Stuka dive-bombers blasted them with high explosive. There was something dreadfully personal about the steep plunge of the ugly black Stukas, howling down to bomb at low level and, at the instant of release, pulling out and up into a tearing climb. To scores of soldiers the attacks seemed to aim at each one personally. Inexperienced French troops began to crack. At the Meuse bridgehead, the German armour burst through with almost contemptuous ease.

Already sensing the ordeals ahead, Winston Churchill, newly elected Prime Minister of Britain, told the House of Commons defiantly,

'I have nothing to offer you but blood, toil, tears and sweat . . . You ask, what is our policy? I will say: It is to wage war, by sea, land and air, with all our might and all the strength that God gave

Hitler conferring with some of his commanders, specialists in armoured blitzkrieg. From right to left: General Guderian, Field-Marshal Von Bock and Field-Marshal Keitel

us; to wage war against a monstrous tyranny, never surpassed in the dark, lamentable catalogue of human crime. That is our policy. You ask what is our aim? I can answer in one word: It is victory, victory at all costs, victory in spite of terror, victory however long and hard the road may be. . .'

But at this moment victory was all for Hitler's iron columns from the Ardennes. They roared onwards, fanning out behind the French 9th Army, spreading confusion and terror and defeatism. Two more armoured divisions crossed the Meuse and broke through at Dinant. Early in the morning of May 15 Winston Churchill was amazed to receive a telephone call from the French Premier, Paul Reynaud, 'We are beaten, we have lost the battle'.

The French 9th Army had in fact completely disintegrated. A vast mass of enemy armour was

*Top* A formation of Stuka dive-bombers about to plunge down upón the battlefield. In the early days of the war they proved to be a terrifying weapon

*Left* A formation of Messerschmitt 110 fighter bombers flying over France

pouring through a gap 50 miles wide. The foremost Panzers were already 100 miles deep into France. Over wide areas before and around them terrified refugees were fleeing, choking the roads vital for the movement of Allied troops.

As catastrophe followed catastrophe in the south, the British army got to grips with the enemy in the north. The British soldiers and airmen plunged into the battle with a confidence and elan which augured well for the future.

By the end of May 15 the German 6th Army had not been able to make a single penetration in the Dyle defences.

Meanwhile the French 1st Army on the British right, though fighting bravely, had had a gap of 5,000 yards long torn in its front. On its left all was disaster: the Belgian Army was disintegrating fast, and the Dutch on the point of being overwhelmed. The Germans had bombed the civilian population, especially Rotterdam, to force the Dutch to surrender. The French 7th Army, which had moved into Holland so fast, recoiled as swiftly into the Antwerp defences. On May 15, the Dutch High Command capitulated. At 10 a.m. on May 16 Lord Gort, the British commander of the B.E.F., was ordered by General Billotte to begin a withdrawal.

With the Allied front torn apart to the north and the German armour surging deeper and deeper into France in the south, the B.E.F. and French 1st Army could only pull back to the next defensible line, the River Scheldt, where seven of the nine British divisions were heavily engaged. The Germans entered Brussels and Cambrai and bypassed St Quentin. On May 18 German Panzer divisions enveloped Amiens.

German armoured spearheads were already menacing the B.E.F.'s lines of communications. It was perfectly obvious: their objective was not Paris, but the Channel ports. It was equally disturbing that the French High Command was lost in indecision, and had not provided itself with a suitable force to counter-attack the swiftly swelling German salient.

Gort informed the anxious war cabinet in London that he might have to try to extricate the B.E.F. He was, however, instructed to march his troops south-west towards Amiens to join up with the main mass of French troops, understood to be on the line of the Somme. But by May 20 the position had further deteriorated. German armoured columns, having captured Amiens and Abbeville, had reached the Channel coast. Gort's army was cut off from its bases south of the Somme and thus deprived of much of its fighting efficiency. The war cabinet had second thoughts about the B.E.F. as recorded in a minute: 'The Prime Minister thought that as a precautionary measure the Admiralty should assemble a large number of small vessels in readiness to proceed to the ports and inlets on the French coast'. The Admiralty acted immediately. Operational control, 'should evacuation become necessary', was given to Vice-Admiral Sir Bertram Ramsay, flag officer commanding Dover. The contemplated operation was code-named Dynamo.

Although only a total of 36 oddly assorted vessels suitable for carrying troops were immediately available, a plan for the emergency evacuation of 'very large forces' was swiftly drawn up. It envisaged ferrying home 10,000 men per day from each of the ports of Calais, Boulogne and Dunkirk, with Zeebrugge, Ostend and Nieuport possibly employed in a similar fashion. 30 ferry boats including cross-Channel 'day tripper' vessels, 12 naval drifters and 6 small coasters were quickly mustered. Soon they were joined by 40 Dutch Schuits sheltering in British ports, which were requisitioned and manned by naval crews. From Harwich to Weymouth, sea-transport officers listed all suitable vessels up to 1,000 tons. A complete record was made of all shipping in British harbours likely to be suitable.

When the war began, the British had ten fighter squadrons of Hurricanes in France, as well as eight squadrons of single-engined Battle bombers (which soon earned the nickname 'flying coffins'), six squadrons of twin-engined Blenheim bombers and five squadrons of Lysander spotter planes. Air-Chief-Marshal Sir Hugh Dowding, head of Fighter Command, had insisted that 25 squadrons were the absolute minimum that must be kept at home to defend Britain. General Weygand, who succeeded Gamelin on May 19, implored Churchill to commit the whole of the R.A.F.'s fighter force to the battle of France, but Churchill replied, 'This is not the decisive point and this is not the decisive moment. That moment will come when Hitler hurls his Luftwaffe against Great Britain. If we can keep command of the air, and if we can keep the seas open, as we certainly shall keep them open, we will win it all back for you.'

When the German blitzkrieg commenced the French had less than 100 bombers, only 25 of them modern. Allied retaliatory bombing, therefore, was carried out by the suicidal, single-engined Battles and the twin-engined Blenheims of the R.A.F. They aimed mostly at bridges and road junctions forming bottlenecks, to slow the onrushing German columns. Meanwhile the British heavy bombers, which the R.A.F. were eager to employ in bombing the closely packed war industries of the Ruhr, were held back in Britain for fear of retaliatory raids on French cities. In his apprehension of a 'bombing war' Gamelin would not even give permission for the Battles and Blenheims to be sent out to attack enemy troops. In the end Air-Marshal Sir Arthur Barratt did this of his own initiative. The very first mission was a brutal example of what the slow, underarmed Battles could expect. There were not enough R.A.F. fighters to give them cover and many were shot down by machine-gun and small-arms fire. In one attack on German columns in the Ardennes, only one

of eight Battles returned.

By May 20 the objective of the spearheading German armoured columns was frighteningly clear: they were definitely swinging round north-westwards toward the sea. When they stormed on through burning Abbeville, the line of communications of the armies in the north, including the B.E.F., was irreparably cut. And, getting worse every hour, all the lines of retreat were choked with refugees. Since the First World War, the military and civilians alike had been taught that any future war would be limited to the holding of the impregnably fortified Maginot Line against the Germans. Nobody could think rationally now the front was shattered so easily, so completely. The whole French Army seemed to have collapsed like a pricked balloon once its front had been pierced.

The B.E.F. had no alternative but evacuation. One last determined counter-attack southwards was made, an attempt to break the line of German tanks that had scythed around to encircle them at Arras. But the French did not join

*Above* German tanks emerge from a forest in the Ardennes. It was here, at Sedan, that they made the fatal breakthrough

*Left* The devastation wrought by German bombers in Rotterdam

the counter-attack, and the only complete British armoured division had been landed at Cherbourg too late to join the B.E.F. except in dribs and drabs. Consequently two under-strength British divisions and a brigade of 65 worn infantry-support tanks found themselves fighting 400 tanks of the crack German 7th and 8th Armoured Divisions, under a general named Erwin Rommel, which were soon joined by another Panzer division and an S.S. division. But before they were forced to withdraw, the British inflicted heavy casualties and took 500 prisoners.

On May 25 Lord Gort knew for certain that the only thing to do was to get his army out of France – via Dunkirk. The Belgian Army, on his northern flank, had completely disintegrated,

and King Leopold was obviously about to surrender. This removed Zeebrugge, Ostend and Nieuport from the evacuation ports available. The burning question now was: could the B.E.F. reach the sea through a corridor 15 miles wide and 50 miles long before being completely encircled? And if so, would it be possible to evacuate it to England? The German intention with regard to the first problem was already apparent in General von Brauchitsch's order to von Rundstedt to 'lead the German 4th Army in the last act of the encirclement battle'. But the determination of the British counter-attack at Arras had done much to persuade the German commanders that caution was necessary. Von Rundstedt had no desire to launch his armour, unsupported by infantry and artillery, against such formidable foes.

As captured records show, Hitler agreed entirely to the halting of the armour. Infantry, artillery and the Luftwaffe could easily achieve the final destruction of the trapped B.E.F. Reichsmarschall Hermann Goering, comman-

*Opposite, top* German bicycle-borne infantry swarm into a Belgian town

*Left* In the wake of the bombers German soldiers, with grenades and machine pistols at the ready, enter a blitzed town

*Below, left* British machine-gunners left as a rear-guard await the onrush of German armour

der in chief of the Luftwaffe, had already urgently telephoned his Führer that this was a special job for the Luftwaffe. More than half of von Kleist's 1,250 tanks urgently needed repairs, and the terrain into which the British were withdrawing was marshy and criss-crossed by dykes – certainly no place for armour to fight unsupported.

When von Rundstedt received instructions from von Brauchitsch that his Panzers were to be switched to von Bock's Army Group B, to attack the British from the east, he ignored them. Not until May 26 did he order the 4th Army commander, von Kluge, to press forward. Meanwhile General-Major Jodl, Hitler's operations officer, had assured impatient panzer commanders, 'The war is already won. Why waste tanks doing what the Luftwaffe can do economically?'

However, it was not only von Rundstedt's halting of his Panzers for 40 hours on the high ground between Béthune and St Omer that prevented them getting to Dunkirk sooner. Along the coast between Dunkirk and Calais sluices had already been opened to inundate the surrounding flat terrain. Armoured columns which had reached the sea beyond Abbeville and moved fast up the coast toward the Channel ports were halted by a watery wilderness. Meanwhile, determined garrisons had been put into Boulogne and Calais, both directly threatened as early as May 21. Their orders were to fight to the death. First in Boulogne, some resolute British and French troops gave a ferocious account of themselves. Amidst a chaos of flaming ruins they were still undefeated when finally evacuated by sea. But in Calais French and British infantry did fight to the last man and the last round. The three terrible days and nights in which the heroes of Calais held out against overwhelming odds permitted defenders to be rushed

into position along the Gravelines water barrier, to secure the left flank of the retreating B.E.F.

The semicircular front on which the British army was fighting was some 90 miles around. The final collapse of the Belgians was permitting the enemy to swarm up to the coast at Ostend and down toward Nieuport. Gort ordered his Arras counter-attack force of two divisions to drive back as fast as they could to plug the gap left by the Belgians. At the same time he and Billotte's successor, General Blanchard, made a plan to stand and fight around a bridgehead at Dunkirk. The French were to hold from Gravelines to Bergues; the British would stand along a canal line from Bergues through Furnes to the sea at Nieuport. The whole perimeter was 128 miles long, 97 of which were held by the British.

Meanwhile, the German onslaught by land and air to destroy the trapped B.E.F. was already under way. Five of von Rundstedt's Panzer divisions were to advance to within 12 miles of the port to close the trap from the west and south-

west while von Bock's Army Group B was to surge in from the east and south-east. Von Rundstedt was to provide the anvil and von Bock, with his masses of infantry and artillery, the hammer. And from above the full fury of the Luftwaffe would be unleashed to blast the British to destruction or surrender.

Four British divisions and the entire French 1st Army, still 40 miles south around Lille, were menaced by massive armoured jaws threatening to close upon them before they could get through. But furious fighting held the trap open for two and a half days, until May 29, when nearly all the intended prey had gone. The fate of the B.E.F. had indeed hung in the balance throughout this terrible battle of May 26–28, from Comines to Ypres and northwards. But the Germans had met their match. It was the first undeniable proof that the British soldier was as good as the German soldier, and, when he could challenge on equal terms, would ultimately outfight him. It was important to know this fact.

*Above* A German column at rest along a French road, unconcernedly nose-to-tail because they know that the Luftwaffe has swept the skies clear of enemy planes

*Top left* This picture, taken by Rommel himself, demonstrates how contemptuously the advancing Germans treated captured French soldiers. They merely took their rifles away from them and told them to go home

*Left* A German Panzer column thrusts onwards through the French countryside

**Dunkirk**

While die-hard screens of General Alan Brooke's 2nd Corps held off the enemy, huge masses of transport and troops poured through to the Dunkirk beachhead. First into the town and down to the sandy beaches were the communication and administration troops and the headquarters staffs. Then, in increasing numbers, came the fighting men, as the defence perimeter was tightened to 58 miles for the stand at bay, while the evacuation was carried out. Meanwhile, five divisions of the French 1st Army held back seven German divisions at Lille for three days and nights, until their ammunition was exhausted.

Gort gave the final order for withdrawal into the bridgehead in the afternoon of May 28, when the first rescue ships were sliding into Dunkirk harbour. Along the front from Gravelines through Bergues and Furnes to Nieuport – a line that had to be held – British and French soldiers defied the enemy. On half-rations since May 23, with very little water, desperately short of ammunition and almost every other essential of warfare, almost without sleep, the British army had fought sternly and unyielding all the way back, compelled to retreat only by the collapse of their allies on both flanks. By May 30 all the divisions of the B.E.F., or what remained of them, were back within the perimeter, either holding it or awaiting evacuation. After their terrifying 300-mile rush through France, the iron columns of the Master Race had finally been halted – six miles from their objective! On the evening of May 26 the Admiralty had ordered Operation Dynamo to be put into action. That very night the first soldiers, non-combatant administrative troops, were brought back from Dunkirk.

Originally, the planners of Operation Dynamo had reckoned on the use of three French ports, and estimated that no more than 45,000 men were likely to be rescued in two days. To effect the miracle which now had to be performed, hundreds more boats were needed.

Admiralty officers were hurriedly despatched to search boatyards up the Thames and around the coast. They produced Thames tugs and pleasure steamers, barges, lighters, launches, yachts, fishing vessels, cabin cruisers and pleasure boats of all sorts and sizes. As soon as the evacuation had begun and there was no more possibility of secrecy, the Admiralty broadcast appeals to anyone with a likely boat to join the incredible armada. Weekend sailors and pleasure-craft owners came in their hundreds with their little vessels, from rivers and creeks and backwaters all over the south and south-east of England.

The Dunkirk armada sailed from six British ports – Sheerness, Margate, Ramsgate, Dover, Folkestone and Newhaven. Returning vessels also landed at Southend and Deal and even on some of the south-coast beaches. Sheerness, the most northern, at the mouth of the Medway, had for centuries been a naval port, and had good dockyard facilities accordingly. Margate, not strictly a harbour, had one narrow curving jetty and a lattice-work pleasure pier. Ramsgate, a true harbour, had two stout curving jetties enclosing its basin, while Dover had three enormous stone breakwaters protecting its harbour. Folkestone, in peacetime paired with Dover as a principal cross-channel port, had a 500-yard-long harbour pier; the most westerly port of Newhaven had a narrow stone-walled harbour. In the momentous days to come, rescuing warships and other sizeable vessels along with small craft in their hundreds were to shuttle between these ports and the flaming inferno that was Dunkirk.

As the Germans had captured Calais and Boulogne, only the harbour of Dunkirk – already heavily bombed and partly destroyed – remained, plus a few miles of wide sandy beaches towards the Belgian frontier. So long as there remained any workable section of the long mole jutting out to sea from the port, the destroyers of the Royal Navy could play the major role in rescuing the trapped army. But if the Luftwaffe commanded the skies, only the little ships that could get in close to the beaches would stand a chance.

When the first rescue ships arrived on May 26, the shore still held by the British–French force extended from Gravelines to Ostend. With the Belgian surrender on May 27 this strip of coast shrank to only 25 miles, from Nieuport to Mardyck. Two-thirds of the beaches lay between Dunkirk and Nieuport. Here were little seaside villages, all without harbour or jetty, nestling at the end of a good access road behind undulating dunes and sandy beaches. At low tide almost half a mile of firm sand was exposed, and not much farther out to sea an 800-yard-wide deep

Black smoke from burning oil tanks billows from Dunkirk. The plane in the foreground on the right is a Hudson reconnaissance aircraft of the R.A.F. pressed into service as a fighter in the desperate emergency

water channel ran parallel to the coast both east and west of Dunkirk, connecting with a channel from the port. Any vessel entering Dunkirk had to sail parallel and close to the coast for a considerable distance. All around this channel the waters were perilous with hidden shoals and currents, while in some places a maximum depth of two fathoms barred a passage to all but shallow-draft vessels. The most sinister fact of all was that, if enemy guns reached the coast, they could subject all shipping in the narrow channel to prolonged fire from which there could be no escape.

Dunkirk itself, an ancient fortress town, had been a port for a thousand years. By 1939 it had become the third port of France, a splendid modern harbour with seven large dock basins suitable for big ships, four dry docks and five miles of quays. The docks were set deep into the town itself, a dredged channel providing access for large vessels. A great pier and a mole protected the entrance from the powerful currents of the English Channel and the waves that pounded in from the North Sea.

Had all the port facilities been available, and had its exodus been unopposed, the B.E.F. could have escaped with all its equipment within a very few days. However, for more than two weeks Dunkirk had been subjected to an escalating fury of bombing. The docks were wrecked, the quays had been pounded to rubble, and more than half the town lay in smouldering ruins. The 1,400-yard-long East Mole remained for rescue vessels to pull alongside, but this mole was merely a spidery erection of timber piles topped by a narrow plank walkway on which men could go just three abreast. Its seawards end had a concrete substructure supporting a stumpy lighthouse. There were piles suitable for tying up to in an emergency, but the swirl of the powerful tides through these piles made it hazardous to bring a vessel alongside.

There could have been no better man in charge of the evacuation from Dunkirk than 57-year-old Vice-Admiral Ramsay. Operating from the Dynamo Room, cut deep into the chalk of the white cliffs of Dover, he and a staff of only 16 organized perhaps the most complex and hazardous sea manoeuvre in the world's history. Out among the shuttling shipping and the fury of gunfire and bombs, were Rear-Admiral W. F. Wake-Walker who was responsible for the Channel and Dunkirk waterways, Captain William Tennant who was responsible for the beaches and town, and Commander Jack Clouston who was responsible for embarkation from the vital East Mole.

These officers had been appointed and despatched with dramatic suddenness. The hawk-faced Captain Tennant indicated that he was senior naval officer in charge of embarkation by sticking on his helmet the letters S.N.O. cut from a cigarette packet's silver-paper lining. To assist him in the marshalling and embarkation of 300,000 men he had a mere 12 officers and 150 ratings of the Royal Navy. In answer to the Admiralty's urgent summons, naval officers and men from shore establishments and leave, from courses and from officer-training units, hurried from all over Britain to man the armada.

Vice-Admiral Ramsay set Operation Dynamo into action at 6.57 p.m. on Sunday May 26. That night, at 10.30 p.m., the first rescue ship returned with 1,312 men from base units.

The shortest route from Dunkirk to Dover, Route Z, lay within the range of German guns and was unusable. The next most direct route was the 55-mile Route X, but it was almost completely blocked by British minefields which would take days to sweep clear. Thus the only available route was Route Y. It was no less than 87 sea miles long, heading due east from Ramsgate to beyond the Kwinte Buoy, some 12 miles north of Ostend, then south-west to strike the Dunkirk channel near Bray-Dunes. The disadvantage of this route was that each crossing would take five and a half hours, instead of two, which exposed the rescue ships to the Luftwaffe that much longer.

On May 27, 7,669 men were brought back, most from the harbour and few from the beaches. The vulture flock of Stukas wheeled and plunged upon the port and beaches for nearly the whole day. The smoking air was rent by explosions and the roar of flames. Goering's Stukas, Heinkels and Dorniers dropped 15,000 high-explosive bombs, mostly 500-pounders, and 30,000 incendiaries. Over a thousand civilians lay beneath the ruins. The predicament of the scores of thousands of soldiers, crammed into the tiny bridgehead, seemed so desperate that the craggy, imperturbable Captain Tennant signalled back 'Evacuation tomorrow night is problematical'. He pleaded that every available craft should be sent to the beaches without delay, and although it was forbiddingly apparent that the Royal Navy would require every warship it possessed in the desperate fight to ward off the imminent invasion of Britain, one cruiser, eight destroyers and 26 vessels were despatched. Meanwhile, the R.A.F. threw every available fighter into the battle over Dunkirk.

It was on May 27 that the destroyers first acted as troop transports, although they had taken small numbers of men earlier. These lean, rakish ships were never meant to carry passengers and had little enough room for their own crews amongst the guns, ammunition, depth-charges and powerful engines. Most were elderly vessels built before attack from the air was even considered. Their decks were so laden with troops that they came back to Dover canted at fantastic angles, having by some miracle of seamanship zig-zagged, at high speed, through seas seething with shell-fire and bomb-blast, and all the time fighting back furiously with every gun.

Also, late that night on May 27, the little ship flotillas began to muster at Deal, Dover and Ramsgate, ready to move out into the darkness, while German E-boats, submarines and mine-layers set out from captured Dutch and Belgian ports to make the waters even more hazardous.

As the enemy, from air and sea, increasingly assailed Dunkirk and its approaches, the troops still holding open the overland escape corridor were stemming attacks from German infantry.

*Above* Admiral Sir Bertram Ramsay planned and master-minded 'Operation Dynamo', the evacuation from Dunkirk, from beginning to end

*Above right* Where there were no piers the British soldiers queued up in lines stretching out into the sea ready to be taken aboard rescue vessels. Many men stood for hours with water up to their chins

*Right* An improvised pier made of army lorries with a plank walk on top juts out into the sea to facilitate the embarkation of waiting troops

*Opposite, top* Although there was little chance of bringing down a German bomber, British soldiers on the beaches at Dunkirk kept firing their rifles at their attackers

*Opposite, bottom* A section of the beach at Dunkirk showing British and French troops waiting in orderly lines for the rescue boats to come in

The most crucial section of the front now was to the north, and it seemed as if nothing could stop the powerful German formations roaring through the gap left by the Belgian collapse and cutting the main road into Dunkirk. But General Bernard Montgomery, in a brilliant manoeuvre, extricated his division from the midst of the German 6th Army in Roubaix and made a 36-mile night march to bar the enemy's way by morning. Each one of his 600 vehicles had its differential casing coated with luminous paint and lit by a small lamp hidden beneath the tailboard; each driver had but to follow the vehicle in front. The route was posted with military police at every turn or crossroads likely to cause mistakes. The whole move was immaculately executed.

Next day, May 28, the beaches were used more successfully. Little boats that had been towed across in strings ferried waiting soldiers out to the larger ships standing off-shore. Tennant and his men had organized the ever-swelling crowd of soldiers into groups of 50, each with an officer or seaman in charge. They were led to the sea's edge as the rescue boats put in for them. The very fact that the navy was there seemed to fill the troops with confidence. To the sailors approaching the beaches it seemed as if a myriad fireflies were hovering in the darkness ahead; thousands of the silent soldiers were drawing on cigarettes.

The troops stood stolidly in their slow-moving queues which, hour by hour, took them out into the sea ankle-deep, knee-deep, waist-high, then breast-high before the little boats picked them up. In the ebb and flow of tides, they were nudged by their own dead who had been killed by enemy fire or drowned in the sinking of rescue ships.

All the time, the destroyers were not only taking off troops but were fighting off E-boats, submarines and bombers. Sometimes they swept in close to bombard the German guns at Calais, Gravelines and Nieuport. As the tense and often desperate day of May 28 neared its close, hope had revived for the trapped army. The troops were holding the vital defence perimeter, and as men entered the bridgehead behind these defences, they were pounced upon by officers and senior N.C.O.s who either directed them to take up positions in the perimeter, or handed them identification numbers to join queues for

evacuation. By the end of the day, 17,804 men had been taken off, 11,874 from the harbour and 5,930 from the beaches.

On May 29, with some 200,000 of the best British fighting troops still around, but not within, the perimeter, the Luftwaffe went for the kill. It was to prove a desperate day for the British. Three destroyers and 21 other vessels were sunk, and many more badly damaged. More and more improvisations were gradually speeding up the still naggingly slow embarkation. At the East Mole, where a 15-foot rise and fall of tide added to the difficulties, planks, baulks of timber, and even water-polo goal posts were used for extra gangplanks. Bewildered newcomers on the rescue vessels felt their task was impossible when they first saw the immense black masses of men covering the beaches. What appeared to be solid piers thrusting into the sea at intervals of little more than a few yards were in fact columns of men patiently awaiting rescue boats, the foremost of them up to their chins in the water. All the time, the orderly three-abreast line down the long mole was moving forward at the rate of 1,000 men per hour.

That afternoon, the Stukas attacked again. At that time there were no R.A.F. patrols over Dunkirk and the Stukas had only to contend with ground fire and flak from the warships. They, and the low-flying Heinkels that followed, wrought such terrible execution that in the night Admiral Ramsay was compelled to pull his eight most modern destroyers out of the battle; for he would not risk warships vital to the forthcoming fight against the German invasion. Only 15 destroyers remained to continue the evacuation.

Yet by the end of the day, 47,310 men had been rescued, 33,558 from the harbour and 13,752 from the beaches. That day Winston Churchill stressed that as many as possible of the French soldiers at Dunkirk should be snatched from the Germans' grasp – even if it meant replacing them in the firing line with fresh divisions sent out from England. He sent a message to Reynaud in Paris, 'We wish French troops to share in evacuation to the fullest possible extent and Admiralty have been instructed to aid the French Marine as required. We do not know how many will be forced to capitulate, but we must share this loss together, as best we can.'

The French poured into the perimeter with huge numbers of vehicles. For two days the road

*Top* Some of the immortal 'little ships' that helped perform the miracle of Dunkirk being towed down the River Thames to the sea

*Middle* A bombed destroyer sinking off Dunkirk, with soldiers just picked up from the beaches beginning to jump overboard

*Bottom* Soldiers evacuated from France look back at the blazing port as they head for home

from La Panne to Dunkirk was blocked solid. Lord Gort had the beach at Malo-les-Bains reserved for their sole use, and two ships were allocated to transport them. Now, the enemy were shelling the beaches and Dunkirk channel not only from behind Nieuport, but also from Mardyck, to the west, where they had captured the fort. And the vital East Mole, from which the greatest number of troops were being embarked, was constantly under fire from artillery and machine-guns, besides the screaming dive-bombers.

Somehow, despite it all, the long black lines of men remained unbroken and the rescue vessels, both large and small, plied back and forth through the hail of death as though unaware of it. On the beaches the soldiers had found that the soft sand cushioned most of the blast, so that a bomb could explode almost beside a spread-eagled man without doing more than shake him. And between air raids jaunty British tommies played football and cricket on the sands, went bathing in the oily surf, or even made sand castles.

In face of attacks on the eastern sector, Lord Gort reported on May 30 that an enemy break-through must be anticipated by dawn on June 1. To meet the eventuality he proposed to shorten the line. Still greater efforts and sacrifices would have to be made if the estimated 200,000 soldiers still in the bridgehead, of whom only 80,000 were now British, were to be saved. Later, Gort postponed his deadline until midnight on June 1, but he decided that the line would then have to be contracted drastically for the last stand.

By now the harbour and approaches to Dunkirk were such a forest of wrecks, and the sea so turgid with oil and debris, half-sunk small boats, tentacles of drifting ropes, sodden clothing and wallowing bodies, that rescue ships had to edge their way in. The East Mole, miraculously standing after thousands of hits and near misses from bombs and shells, was only usable on parts of the seaward side when the tides allowed, for the inner side was completely blocked by sunken ships. Evacuation by daylight was now well-nigh suicidal; it had to be done only by night, and very few berths still remained along the narrow five-foot gangway of the mole.

It was indeed fortunate that at this time the sea fell calm, the wind died and low cloud descended over Dunkirk, merging with the black pall from the burning oil tanks. As though in answer to prayers of intercession in Westminster Abbey, a thick, woolly fog swelled up out of the sea to blanket Dunkirk, its beaches, and its sea approaches. The target area of the Germans was completely hidden from view. Meanwhile the most fantastic fleet that had ever put out from the shores of England began to rock and bob its way across the Channel – an incredible armada of little boats, manned mostly by civilian volunteers. On May 30, 29,512 men were brought off from the beaches by the little boats, and 24,311 men were taken from the harbour by destroyers and other larger vessels – French and British soldiers in equal numbers.

On May 31 Churchill flew to Paris to try to discover what was happening in France. He found Marshal Pétain, now at Reynaud's right hand, taking an extremely pessimistic view. To Churchill's amazement the French government seemed to have no clear idea about the fate of their armies, except that they were everywhere being defeated. When Churchill told them that the B.E.F. was being evacuated through Dunkirk, and that 150,000 British and 15,000 French had already been saved, the French leaders professed astonishment. As a result of Churchill's visit, Admiral Darlan sent a telegram to Admiral Abrial at Dunkirk, ordering that when no more troops outside the perimeter could possibly get in to be evacuated, the divisions holding the perimeter should withdraw and embark. Furthermore, Darlan stated the British forces should embark first; but Churchill immediately intervened – the evacuation *must* be on equal terms.

On the same day Lord Gort handed over command of the British forces to Major-General Alexander, who had recently arrived on a bicycle, having abandoned and burned his staff car beside the blocked road outside Dunkirk. He had led his magnificent 1st Division in the fight back from Lille. Gort was ordered home, to pass on his valuable experience, despite his protestations that he should stay and fight to the death.

The weather took a turn for the worse. A fresh northerly breeze whipped the sea into an angry chop. In the vital hour immediately after high water, an alarmingly high proportion of the motor-boats which were needed to tow the small boats were stranded on the shore. The breakers also rendered unusable piers of lorries laboriously put together by the tired troops. Soon after mid-day the Germans took advantage of the perimeter withdrawal. They surged forward, accompanied by a violent bombardment of the beaches. About a mile out in the Dunkirk Roads the destroyers and other larger ships waited for the boat-loads of troops who did not come. Fortunately the wind lessened during the afternoon and the shuttling began in earnest. At this time a fleet of tugs played a vital role pulling stranded ships off sandbanks and towing ones that had gone astray. French vessels – destroyers, trawlers and ferryboats – were at last ordered in by their government. But perhaps the most spectacular vessel to join the day's vast armada was a Thames fire-float, complete with its crew of London firemen.

The message which Winston Churchill sent General Weygand at this moment succinctly summed up the situation. It stated: 'Crisis in evacuation now reached. Five fighter squadrons, acting almost continuously, is the most we can do, but six ships, several filled with troops, sunk

*Above* An assortment of vessels in mid Channel, each one crowded with British soldiers

*Right* Journey's end – two boat-loads of troops arrive safely at a Channel port

by bombing this morning. Artillery fire menacing any practicable channel. Enemy closing in on reduced bridgehead. By trying to hold on 'till tomorrow we may lose all. By going tonight much may certainly be saved, though much will be lost. Nothing like numbers of effective French troops you mention believed in bridgehead now, and we doubt whether such large numbers remain in area. Situation cannot be fully judged by Admiral Abrial in the fortress, nor by you, nor by us here. We have therefore ordered General Alexander, commanding British sector of bridgehead, to judge, in consultation with Admiral Abrial whether to try to stay over tomorrow or not. Trust you will agree.'

Six thousand men of the 4th Division, holding the eastern perimeter at Nieuport, were ordered to march back ten miles along the fire-swept beaches to embark on vessels sent specially for them. They set off for La Panne on the night of May 31. On another section of the drastically shortened canal line now held by 39,000 British (50,000 French soldiers still stood fast along the western approach) the fighting became increasingly desperate. The only Victoria Cross (Britain's highest award for valour) gained at

Dunkirk was won on this day by Captain Harold Ervine-Andrews of the East Lancashire Regiment. Under nerve-shattering bombardment for ten hours on end, Ervine-Andrews and his company held their vital sector against massive enemy attacks. When a gap was forced on his flank he charged out at the head of 36 men and drove off a swarm of at least 500 enemy. Later, when the building which he was defending was ruined and set afire, and when all ammunition had been expended, he led back eight survivors swimming or wading over one mile in chin-deep water. Then he turned with his men and again defied the advancing enemy. It was valour like this, multiplied a thousand times and more, that still held the enemy at bay so that, on this day, 68,014 British and French soldiers were rescued – 45,072 from the mole and 22,942 from the beaches. There still remained 20,000 of the best and bravest of the B.E.F. to fight the ultimate battle, protecting from now on a predominantly French evacuation.

The all-out assault by the Luftwaffe on June 1 was synchronized with a surge forward by German infantry, curtained by a formidable artillery barrage, and strongly supported by tanks. The huge force of German bombers was predominantly Stukas, but powerful formations of Ju 88s, Heinkels and Dorniers, escorted by fighters, attacked from a higher level. The Germans made their major attacks when the R.A.F. fighter patrols were away refuelling. All through the day, however, air crews of Fighter and Coastal Commands and the Fleet Air Arm fought with the utmost bravery, though always outnumbered. Everything that could be put in the air against the Luftwaffe took off from England, including Spitfires, Hurricanes, two-seater gun-turreted Defiants and even Hudson bombers, biplane Swordfish torpedo-bombers, and lumbering reconnaissance Ansons. No less than 31 ships were sunk and 11 badly damaged on June 1 – the heaviest toll exacted during the whole nine days of the evacuation, almost equalling the total of the previous seven days. Despite these catastrophes, however, it was now possible to plan the next moves instead of improvising them for the first time since Operation Dynamo started. This was largely because the front-line troops were gradually dropping back to the ultimate line of defence. They still held fast, while the evacuation of the battle-weary troops

continued apace. Soon there were only 4,000 British soldiers fighting in the final rearguard. They had just 12 anti-tank guns and seven light anti-aircraft guns as their artillery. The remainder of the shrunken perimeter was held by French soldiers who all along had fought beside their fast-disappearing allies with the utmost bravery.

That day, wave after wave of enemy warplanes blackened the sky. The beaches, the mole and the harbour were a hell of bursting bombs and shells. Yet there was a matter-of-factness bordering on insolence among the troops. General Alexander, dapper and imperturbable, set an example of easy nonchalance, observing with interest the surrounding turmoil from a deck-chair, strolling the erupting beaches while chewing an apple, or cheerfully passing the time of day with the waiting men. Among the sand dunes a Guards colonel stood erect amidst a howling Stuka attack, calmly shaving before a mirror held by his equally unruffled batman. On the stern of one off-shore rescue ship a sailor fished.

Retreating towards the beaches, the battle-stained rearguard fought back until the moment of embarkation. Among them were some 26 officers and 450 men of the Loyal Regiment who maintained their defiance from the ancient ramparts of Bergues beneath a thunderous artillery bombardment. To the west of them, where von

All is over, and German soldiers stride along the beach past a bombed destroyer and a wrecked British army truck

Kleist's Panzers were cautiously nosing out into flooded fields, thousands of gallons of industrial alcohol were released across the fields and set ablaze by shell-fire. Several German tanks were caught in the flames, and the advance came to a full stop. But fire, too, finally drove the Loyals from Bergues where the heat and smoke from burning buildings became too much to bear. That afternoon they took up another position, along the exposed canal bank to the north of the town – but they still held the enemy back. Then the wind changed and blew the choking smoke blanket over the Germans, so that more tanks were lost, toppling into the canal in the blackness. It was not until night had fallen that the Loyals pulled out and marched back to the beaches behind them. That night General Alexander and Admiral Abrial decided that the moment had come to withdraw the last of the British troops from the front line and leave the defence of the shrunken perimeter to the last rearguard – 30,000 resolute French soldiers under General Barthélemy who knew they had scant hope of escape.

The bitter experiences of June 1 had shown all too clearly that daylight evacuation was suicide. Admiral Ramsay ordered embarkation by night only, and marshalled every available vessel from destroyers to rowing boats that could possibly play a part. As dusk fell upon the Channel, the indomitable armada put out to sea again. Between them they took off thousands more soldiers, by now mostly French, from the battered mole and from the stretch of two and a half miles of beach east of it. Between midnight and 3 a.m. they rescued the bulk of the survivors of the British rearguard, along with the French. That night 26,256 men were saved, 19,561 by the bigger ships from the harbour and 6,695 by the small craft from the beaches.

The main transporting fleet – the destroyers and the Channel personnel ships – had suffered terribly. Seven destroyers had been sunk, 20 were badly damaged, while eight personnel vessels had been lost and eight more put out of action. Loss of life was heavy among the crews and soldiers aboard. If the rescued troops were exhausted, the predicament of their rescuers was even worse. Some of the crews who had sailed their ships back and forth across the Channel since the beginning, under constant attack, now fell unconscious at their posts. Typical was the S.S. *Tynwald*. Its crew just could not continue any longer after a week's continuous effort in saving 4,500 men. The captain had only slept four hours during that perilous week. Wherever possible under such circumstances navy crews were put in, but there was hardly a sailor who had not already exerted himself to the limits of human endurance.

During the terrible day of June 2, in which no vessel could risk a rescue attempt in daylight, the Germans deliberately bombed a hospital ship whose presence had been announced to them by a British broadcast. General Alexander asked for every available vessel again that night. By midnight the last 3,000 of his heroic rearguard had been safely lifted from the mole. They marched down amidst a great stream of escaping French soldiers. Whenever there was a lull in the flow of troops, small parties of sailors from the British destroyers went into the inferno of Dunkirk searching for scattered survivors. The navigator of H.M.S. *Malcolm* actually strode through the burning streets playing bagpipes to rally stragglers from the ruins.

On June 3 a total of 26,746 soldiers, nearly all French, were taken off, 24,876 in ships from the harbour and 1,870 by the small boats from the shores. That morning, having toured the beaches with Captain Tennant, General Alexander was satisfied that all the B.E.F. men were away. Together they boarded a destroyer under machine-gun fire and were bombed most of the way home.

Finally, on June 4, a total of 26,175 French soldiers were landed at Dover, nearly all from British vessels. At 2.23 p.m. the British and French commanders agreed that Operation Dynamo should be ended. H.M.S. *Shikari*, laden with French soldiers, was the last vessel to churn out of the hideous harbour. Even as the battered British destroyer cleft the open seas, German tanks cautiously crawled into the ruined port, and the remaining French defenders fired the last rounds of their ammunition.

In the House of Commons later that day Winston Churchill, reporting on the miracle of Dunkirk, solemnly told the members: 'We must be very careful not to assign to this deliverance the attributes of a victory. Wars are not won by evacuation. But there was a victory inside this deliverance, which should be noted. It was gained by the Air Force. . . This was a great trial of strength between the British and German Air Forces. Can you conceive a greater objective for the Germans in the air than to make evacuation from these beaches impossible, and to sink all these ships which were displayed, almost to the extent of thousands? Could there have been an objective of greater military importance and significance for the whole purpose of the war than this? They tried hard, and they were beaten back; they were frustrated in their task. We got the army away; and they have paid fourfold for any losses which they have inflicted...'

The British casualties in the land fighting from May 10, culminating in the defence of Dunkirk, amounted to some 28,000 killed and wounded, and 40,000 prisoners. About 600 tanks, over 1,000 field and medium guns, 500 anti-tank and 850 anti-aircraft guns, and all the vehicles and equipment of the 10 divisions of the B.E.F. were lost. The Germans suffered some 61,000 casualties.

At sea the casualties suffered by the destroyers were the most serious, as destroyers were so vital now to combat invasion. Of the 200 destroyers which the Royal Navy still possessed, only 74 remained undamaged and ready for immediate action.

During the same period in May and June the R.A.F. had lost 959 aircraft, of which 477 were fighters, while 1,284 planes of the Luftwaffe had been destroyed, most by the fighters of the R.A.F. As events were soon to prove, these Luftwaffe losses were significant. Impossible though it seemed at the time, the defeat of Germany had been begun at Dunkirk.

Defiant resistance was predicted by Winston Churchill on June 4. 'We shall not flag or fail. We shall go on to the end. . . . We shall fight on the seas and oceans, we shall fight with growing confidence and growing strength in the air; we shall defend our island whatever the cost may be. We shall fight on the beaches, we shall fight on the landing grounds, we shall fight in the fields and in the streets, we shall fight in the hills; we shall never surrender...'

Two soldiers arrive back in Britain – one is wearing only pyjamas

# 2. Battle of Britain

# 2. Battle of Britain

At the very beginning of the evacuation from Dunkirk, when there seemed little hope for the trapped British army, Winston Churchill, in sombre yet defiant mood, declared in the House of Commons: 'The House should prepare itself for hard and heavy tidings. I have only to add that nothing which may happen in the battle [of France] can in any way relieve us of our duty to defend the world cause to which we have vowed ourselves, nor should it destroy our confidence in our power to make our way, as on former occasions in our history, through disaster and through grief to the ultimate defeat of our enemies.'

On June 17, when Marshal Pétain asked for an armistice, Britain finally stood alone against the overwhelming might of triumphant Germany. For all Churchill's defiance and the will of the British people to fight on against any odds, the rest of the world gave Britain little chance. Hitler and his victory-flushed generals gave Britain no chance at all. In Paris, General von Studnitz declared to American diplomat Robert Murphy: 'The British do not have a single division intact and they have been forced to abandon most of their heavy equipment. Therefore the only conclusion is that further resistance must be impossible and the war will be over by the end of July.' Meanwhile Mussolini, convinced Britain's position was hopeless, insisted on sending 10 Italian divisions and 30 squadrons of warplanes to join in the invasion.

On July 19 Hitler made his final 'appeal to reason' to the British people. He said that,

*Top left* Adolf Hitler made an 'appeal to reason' to Britain – promising a peace treaty in which Britain could keep her empire if she permitted Germany a free hand in Europe

*Above* Across the Channel, where the British had little more than rifles to fight off the threatened invasion, Winston Churchill inspects front-line troops

*Above* Clearly demonstrating that the Luftwaffe dominated the English Channel as the hour for the Battle of Britain neared, Messerschmitt 109 fighters fly low along the white cliffs of England

*Below* Hermann Goering (sixth from the right) stands with a group of Luftwaffe and staff officers gazing towards England. Goering boasted that his bombers would soon beat Britain to her knees

*Above* Hurricane fighters of the R.A.F. which outnumbered Spitfires in the Battle of Britain

*Opposite* Field-Marshal Goering and staff officers plan the next strike of the German bombers and fighters

'speaking as the victor', he could see no reason why the war should go on. He was grieved to think of the sacrifices it must claim if it did. The speech was immediately followed by German diplomatic representations through the United States, the Vatican and Sweden, suggesting it was only reasonable for Britain to accept what Germany had already achieved because she was not really in a position to do anything about it. Any hopes that America would come to Britain's rescue were dashed by Senator Key Pittman, chairman of the Senate Foreign Relations Committee, who advised the British government to surrender: 'It is no secret that Great Britain is totally unprepared and that nothing the United States has to give can more than delay the result', he insisted. There were hints through diplomatic channels that if Britain accepted Hitler as the master of Europe she could keep her empire and her place in the world beyond Europe. Hitler remarked on the folly of inflicting a savage defeat on Britain in order to benefit Japan and the United States, and he was anxious to avoid the danger of a two-front war against Russia.

Britain's defiance was not mere bravado. Churchill knew that, so long as the R.A.F. could outfight the Luftwaffe, the Royal Navy could guarantee command of the narrow waters of the English Channel. Although vulnerability to bombing meant that the huge battleships and cruisers had to operate from harbours in the Firth of Forth and northwards, or west of Plymouth, there were some 800 fast, light warships, including destroyers and motor torpedo boats, to fall upon any German armada trying to cross. The Royal Navy could be relied upon to dominate the Channel unless obliterated by massive airpower. While it could not prevent small enemy forces of a few thousand men slipping through under cover of night or fog, it could certainly destroy full-scale invasion. And the one or two battle-proven divisions back from Dunkirk, already formed into a mobile striking force by General Brooke, would surely take care of a few thousand Germans.

The air fighting over France had shown the Luftwaffe's limitations. In the Battle of France,

at odds of two or three to one, the R.A.F. had inflicted losses of nearly three to one. Over Dunkirk, at odds of four or five to one, the ratio of losses inflicted on the Germans had been even higher. Now, with the prospect of fighting over Britain itself, even though the concentrated strength of the Luftwaffe might give the Germans an eight-to-one superiority, the R.A.F. was likely to take an even more severe toll. And Germans shot down over Britain would be out of the war even if they survived, unlike the 400 Luftwaffe pilots already shot down in France and later released.

The Luftwaffe, meanwhile, was no more ready to launch an immediate all-out attack on Britain than the small German Navy was prepared to take on the Royal Navy. The German Navy had been savagely mauled a few weeks earlier in the sea fighting of the Norwegian campaign, where it had lost 11 destroyers. In addition, a pocket-battleship, a battle-cruiser, two other cruisers and several more destroyers had been damaged. During the latter part of June and the first fortnight of July, the depleted Luftwaffe squadrons had to be built up to full strength and deployed over 400 airfields from the western corner of France to Norway. Mostly they were massed in northern France and Belgium, with the strategic advantage of flying from numerous widely distributed airfields, permitting feints to draw the British fighters in one direction while the main attack came from another.

However invincible Germany might be as a military power, the crossing of the English Channel posed problems beyond her experience. In the face of the fury with which the Royal Navy would certainly attack, regardless of cost, the project could swiftly become a disaster for the German Army. Only with complete mastery of the skies and seas could an invasion force embark with any hope of success. One Nazi leader who had no doubts at all was the flamboyant Hermann Goering. Despite the failure of his Luftwaffe to destroy the B.E.F. at Dunkirk, he now boasted that his fighters would swiftly decimate the R.A.F. and his bombers would so devastate Britain and terrify her people that they would soon plead for peace at any price.

The all-conquering German Army now massed a first wave of 13 crack divisions along the Channel coast. Beginning on July 17, they carried out embarkation and invasion exercises with vigour and eagerness. On fine evenings, when the heat shimmer waned with the sun's setting, the German soldiers could see the white cliffs of Dover glimmering tantalizingly across the Channel. The swift campaign with which the commander-in-chief, Field-Marshal Walter von Brauchitsch, planned to storm Britain was given the code name Operation Sealion.

Along the northern coast of France and Belgium Goering had innumerable airfields, captured intact. And so prodigious were the available supplies of high-octane aviation spirit, bombs, cannon shells and bullets that the anticipated four-weeks air warfare would hardly affect them. All the Luftwaffe had to do in fact was destroy the 50 squadrons of Hurricanes and Spitfires which R.A.F. Fighter Command could send up against them. As he had the initiative, choice of targets and direction of attack, Goering knew he could always vastly outnumber any intercepting fighters, as Air-Chief-Marshal Dowding's force had to cover the whole of England.

In addition to Goering's underestimation of the R.A.F. there was another factor he had not taken into account – for the very good reason that he did not know much about it. This was the existence of a radar network (or R.D.F. – Radio Direction Finding, as it was guardedly called). It could give such good warning of approaching warplanes that intercepting fighters could be sent up to exactly the right sector to engage them. This meant that the R.A.F. fighters would not have to fly exhausting patrols all the hours of daylight over vast airspace. But thanks to the secret network of linked early-warning stations along the south coast of England and up the east coast as far as Scotland, no

such patrols were required. Although the Germans could not have failed to notice the towering pylon-like masts of the R.D.F. stations, and did in fact partly guess their purpose, they did not imagine radar would be able to differentiate between main air assaults and small decoy raids.

For the impending battle upon which the fate of Britain depended, the country was split among four fighter groups, each group area subdivided into sectors. The immediate frontline of southeast England, with London as its centre, was defended by No. 11 Group under Air-Vice-Marshal Park. West of this was No. 10 Group under Air-Vice-Marshal Brand, and immediately north and stretching up into Yorkshire was No. 12 Group under Air-Vice-Marshal Leigh-Mallory. No. 13 Group, commanded by Air-Vice-Marshal Saul, covered the area northwards from there to the lowlands of Scotland. Dowding had his Fighter Command H.Q. at Bentley Priory, an old mansion and former girls' school at Stanmore, Middlesex. He was prepared to delegate control of each air battle to the group immediately involved, and groups would in turn decide which of their sector formations should challenge the enemy. Once airborne, the fighters would be directed towards the approaching enemy by sector controllers. The heavy and light anti-aircraft guns defending towns and factories throughout the country (under 2,000 – less than a quarter of the minimum necessary for an adequate defence), were integrated into the system, gun operations rooms being linked directly to each R.A.F. Group

*Top* A doomed Heinkel 111 with a Spitfire closing in for the kill

*Above* Spitfires fly over the fields of Kent, heading towards another wave of German bombers and fighters

*Opposite* Radar stations have given warning that German warplanes are approaching and fighter pilots of the R.A.F. 'scramble' for their Hurricanes

H.Q. Searchlights and balloon barrages were similarly linked up in the defence system.

Goering's Luftwaffe was divided into *Luftflotten*, or air fleets. Two of these fleets, under Field-Marshal Kesselring and Field-Marshal Sperrle, deployed along the coast from Brest in the west of France to the north of Holland. On a curving 500-mile front they menaced England from Land's End to the Wash. Kesselring had

43

played the dominant role in the aerial blitz on Poland; Sperrle had commanded the German air force aiding Franco in the Spanish Civil War. Both were battle-experienced commanders who could be reckoned to conduct the blitz on Britain with the utmost determination.

From headquarters near Brussels, Kesselring was to attack a sector east of a line drawn from Selsey Bill through Oxford and Birmingham to just east of Manchester, and thence northwards to the Yorkshire–Lancashire border. Sperrle's formations were to assault England and Wales west of this line. General Stumpff's third Luft-flotte was to extend the menace still farther north in England and Scotland, and although it had barely half the strength of the other fleets, and a far greater distance to fly across the North Sea, it could strike grievous blows. Stumpff too had made a name for himself by the devastating role his air corps had played in the Scandinavian campaign.

The Germans massed a total of 2,669 war-planes, including 1,015 bombers, 346 Stuka dive-bombers, 933 single-engined Messer-schmitt Me 109 fighters and 375 Me 110 twin-engined long-range fighters.

To challenge this formidable array, R.A.F. Fighter Command had rather less than 700 fighters of which just on 600 were Hurricanes and Spitfires. But, whereas at the beginning of June there had only been 36 Hurricanes and Spitfires in reserve, the aircraft industry had so responded to Churchill's call that on the eve of the Battle of Britain there were around 280. Meanwhile, 50 fighter pilots from the Fleet Air Arm had been loaned to the R.A.F., and additional reinforcements had come – one squadron from Canada, and four squadrons made up of the heroic survivors of the air forces of Poland and Czechoslovakia. Nevertheless, there was not

*Top* A German Me 109 fighter shot down in the South of England and virtually undamaged. Soldiers from a nearby army unit stand guard

*Middle* A Junkers Ju88 – the fastest and best bomber in service with the Luftwaffe at the time – which was shot down in Southern England during the Battle of Britain

*Bottom* Captured German airmen being marched off after their aircraft had been shot down by a Hurricane of the R.A.F.

a hope of providing for the imminent battle anything remotely approaching the 120 fighter squadrons which the Air Staff deemed necessary as a consequence of the fall of France.

Indeed, that Great Britain had any fighter aircraft at all capable of challenging the Me 109s was entirely due to the persistence of a few far-seeing R.A.F. officers and patriotic civilians. In the 1930s, the R.A.F. and the British aircraft industry had both been run down to the verge of obsolescence. With no orders or encouragement from the government, the Supermarine and Hawker aircraft companies had separately conceived and developed the Spitfire and Hurricane low-wing monoplanes powered by a Rolls-Royce Merlin engine. The prototype from which R. J. Mitchell developed the Spitfire was the Supermarine seaplane which won the Schneider Trophy for Britain against American and Italian competition in 1931. Even then, but for a patriotic gift of £50,000 by Lady Houston, its development would not have been possible.

The comparative performances of the British and German fighters was described by Sir Winston Churchill. 'There was little to choose – the Germans were faster, with a better rate of climb; ours more manoeuvrable, better armed.' In fact, the Hurricane – of which there were 27 operational squadrons against only 19 squadrons of Spitfires – was no match for the Me 109; with its top speed of 305 mph it was nearly 50 mph slower and had nothing like its manoeuvrability above 20,000 feet. The Spitfire, however, not only had a top speed at 19,000 feet of 355 mph, but it was blissfully manoeuvrable and at least equal to the Me 109. Britain started rearming so late that both these fighters were under development while the Messerschmitts, like other German warplanes, had been secretly produced – and improved – since 1925. The first Spitfires were not delivered for squadron service until September 1938. The first Hurricane had gone into R.A.F. service only nine months earlier. But even the Spitfires as delivered to the R.A.F. on the eve of battle might not have been war-winning fighters had not an unauthorized improvement been made to each one during May, June and July, 1940. This was the fitting of variable-pitch propellors to replace constant-pitch ones. Ex-fighter-pilot Geoffrey de Havil-land, of the famous aircraft firm, was so convinced that propellor change would be vital in the great air battle to come that, on his own initiative, he privately arranged with individual stations to fit them. This conversion, which produced performance improvement described by pilots as 'miraculous', was completed in the very nick of time.

Rather than wait for Raeder to mass his invasion fleet, Kesselring and Sperrle set their warplanes to work on British shipping and ports early in July. Colonel-General Alfred Jodl, chief of operational staff of the German Supreme Command and Hitler's personal military adviser, had impressed upon his Führer that everything should be done to interrupt supplies to the beleaguered island, to accelerate surrender. Goering therefore ordered his warplanes, in addition to probing the British defences and troop dispositions, to attack ports and shipping. While sinking ships and destroying docks, the Luftwaffe would also get a chance to shoot down intercepting enemy fighters, thus weakening the R.A.F. before the all-out assault. The dramatic air battle, soon named the Battle of Britain, then commenced with attacks on British shipping and ports.

The first engagement took place in the afternoon of July 10, when the Germans attacked a coastal convoy of small ships, carrying coal and coke urgently required by war factories. Because of the massing of heavy German guns and aircraft along the near French coastline, the decision had already been made to reroute convoys to west-coast ports. But this convoy, one of the last, had been risked. As it passed Dover, the radar picked up a large number of enemy aircraft beyond Calais, and six Hurricanes were sent up from Manston airfield near Ramsgate. Accurately directed towards the approaching enemy, the pilots were astounded to see, towering up in three tiers before them, 20 Dornier bombers, with a layer of close-support Me 110 fighters above, and a still higher layer of Me 109 fighters. Three Hurricanes hurtled straight at the Dorniers, three at the Me 110s. Suddenly the sky above the convoy was strident with the howl of engines and whirling, twisting, dogfighting warplanes. Shaken, the bombers hastily unloaded. Only one vessel was hit, and three German planes, trailing lurid smoke, plummeted into the sea. All six Hurricane pilots returned, amazed and exhilarated by their victory.

Engagements on two succeeding days underlined this promising start. Again, handfuls of fighters took on swarming Luftwaffe formations to inflict disproportionate casualties. On July 13, the Germans bombed a coastal convoy off Harwich and on July 14 another convoy off Dover, while strong formations of escorted bombers attacked warships and the dockyards at Portsmouth and Portland. Met by furious anti-aircraft fire from land batteries, warships and R.A.F. fighters, the enemy bombed inaccurately and did little damage. Such attacks on shipping continued for nine days altogether, by which time 61 German aircraft had been shot down for a loss of 28 British.

The R.A.F. had a bad day on July 19, when a squadron of Defiants, whose revolving gun turrets had exacted great execution over Dunkirk against enemies who mistook them for Hurricanes, proved too slow now that their true character was revealed. Six out of nine were lost off Dover, and that day cost the R.A.F. eight planes altogether for only two German ones destroyed. For the next two days exchanges were fairly even. Then two days of cloudy weather caused a lull, by which time 85 enemy planes had been destroyed for the loss of 45 R.A.F. fighters. With clearer skies on July 24, Kesselring sent in simultaneous strong attacks on convoys in the Straits of Dover and in the Thames estuary, and again greatly outnumbered R.A.F. fighters gave much better than they received. On July 25, determined attacks were made on a convoy off Deal by a flock of 30 Stukas with an escort of Me 109s. A handful of Spitfires and Hurricanes shot down many of the highly vulnerable dive-bombers, but a following wave of escorted long-range bombers badly damaged the convoy and compelled the Admiralty to suspend Channel convoys completely.

The disappearance of merchant ships from the narrow waters robbed the Luftwaffe of convenient targets. But there were still warships, and on July 27 strong forces of Kesselring's bombers sank two Dover-based destroyers. The Admiralty decided to risk losing no more in the Straits and moved the Dover destroyers to Portsmouth. It was an admission that by daylight the Germans commanded the Straits. Two days later yet another destroyer was sunk by a swarm of Sperrle's escorted dive-bombers, and only the tough little mine-sweepers continued to defy the bombers in the narrow seas. But the

*Above* Air-Chief-Marshal 'Stuffy' Dowding, who master-minded the R.A.F. victory in the Battle of Britain, talks to fighter pilots, including Douglas ('Tinlegs') Bader (with hands together)

*Right* The Luftwaffe's ace of aces – Adolf Galland, who had started shooting down enemy aircraft in the days of the Spanish Civil War. In the Battle of Britain he was aware of the waning morale of the German fighter pilots

preliminary sparring between Luftwaffe and R.A.F., overture to the Luftwaffe's all-out assault, was drawing to a close. It had achieved little towards destroying the British warships that would attack the invasion fleet, nor had it exhausted the R.A.F. fighter-pilots, because deliberately few had been committed. On July 30, Adolf Hitler announced that he expected 'the great air battle of the German Air Force against England' to commence almost immediately.

For all his bombast, Goering still had not completed his plan. Under pressure from the Führer, he indicated his intention to preserve the Me 109 fighters for the big showdown against the Hurricanes and Spitfires, ordering Kesselring and Sperrle meanwhile to escort their bombers with the long-range Me 110s. Consequently, bombing attacks diminished for some days. When Goering did issue his Battle of Britain directive on August 2, it was for Sperrle and Kesselring to make devastating attacks on specified objectives in the south of England, with Stumpff joining in on the second day to assail objectives in the Midlands and north. Goering assured them that the air defences in

the south would collapse within four days and the R.A.F. would have been shot out of the skies all over Britain inside four weeks. On August 6 he ordered his commanders to begin the all-out assault on August 10, which would be known as Eagle Day (*Adler-Tag*).

The first unmistakable evidence of the intended invasion now began to come in. High-flying photographic reconnaissance Spitfires and low-flying Hudsons, ranging widely over enemy ports from western France to Scandinavia, brought back pictures of increasing concentrations of barges. The R.A.F. bombers, which since the fall of France had unremittingly attacked German aircraft factories by night and airfields by day, now largely switched their attentions to enemy harbours and shipping. At the same time the Luftwaffe stepped up attacks on Channel objectives. On August 8 their raids on shipping off Dover and the Isle of Wight were so heavy that at first this was supposed to mark the beginning of the all-out onslaught. In desperate air battles against fearsome odds the R.A.F. lost 20 fighters for a toll of 28 enemies.

The fighting between July 10 and Eagle Day cost the Luftwaffe 227 planes and the R.A.F. 96.

*Above* A Dornier 17 bomber (nicknamed the 'Flying Pencil' because it was so long and thin) which was shot down by an army Lewis-gunner while machine-gunning the streets of a South Coast town

*Left* Field-Marshal Goering, looking rather less confident than at the beginning, inspects German air crew just returned from a flight

*Opposite page* Hurricane fighters roar away above the clouds to meet another German attack. As the Battle of Britain developed, Hurricanes were used to attack the bombers while the Spitfires fought it out with the German fighter escort

*Left* Heinkel 111 bomber flies over London during the first daylight attack. The winding River Thames with its unmistakable landmarks guided the enemy to important dockland and other targets

*Right* London's dockland burns after the first daylight attacks

Thanks to their aircraft industry, however, the Germans had more available now than when the fighting started, while the R.A.F. had received no less than 500 new fighters. The British output for July exceeded its target by 51 per cent.

The British aircraft factories were to be one of the main objectives in the great bombing assault to begin on Eagle Day. Fighter airfields, ground organizations, supply installations and the R.D.F. early-warning stations were also scheduled for destruction. Meanwhile, the mass of the Luftwaffe fighters would destroy the R.A.F. fighters in furious air battles. But Goering also directed Kesselring, Sperrle and Stumpff to attack ports, shipping and naval installations. He was convinced that if he bombed widespread targets it would terrorize the British people to the point of surrender, even without invasion.

When Eagle Day did dawn, the weather was deemed unfavourable and it was postponed until August 13. Nevertheless, there was intense German activity two days previously when the R.A.F. lost 32 fighters to the Luftwaffe's 35 in fierce engagements over Dover and Portland. And on August 12 six such massive attacks were made by forces of hundreds of warplanes, and the Battle of Britain can be said to have started

then, even if the Germans regarded August 13 as Eagle Day. Determined attacks were made on the forward fighter stations at Manston, Hawkinge and Lympne, and six radar stations on the south coast were dive-bombed, all being damaged. The one at Ventnor, in the Isle of Wight, was put out of action for two weeks. All the major raids were detected early on and hotly challenged; the R.A.F. lost 22 planes and destroyed 36 of the enemy's.

The weather on Eagle Day was even more unsuitable, but Goering could delay no longer. There was thick cloud often as low as 4,000 feet over Sussex and Kent, rendering impossible the planned combination of heavy bombing and high-level fighter sweeps. It meant the Hurricanes and Spitfires would be able to ignore the Me 109s supposed to destroy them, and concentrate upon the bombers. There was a confused start when powerful German bomber formations took off before a cancelling order could reach them. But the order stopped their escorts, so that the bombers set out without a fighter cover. A formidable formation of 80 Dorniers flew to bomb Eastchurch airfield and Sheerness harbour where anti-invasion warships were massed. A similar number of Ju 88s roared over

the coast, bound for Odiham and Farnborough. A swarm of Stukas ranged along the Hampshire coastline with a fearsome escort of fighters. The choice of targets for the much-vaunted Eagle Day was indeed peculiar, for none was a British fighter base.

Fighter Command had ample warning, thanks to radar. Park sent up one squadron of Spitfires and two of Hurricanes to cover a convoy in the Thames estuary and the forward airfields of Hawkinge and Manston. Meanwhile, he despatched smaller formations to patrol airfields in Suffolk and Sussex (particularly Tangmere) and over Canterbury. He held back two thirds of his Spitfires and half his Hurricanes to challenge the enemy's main attack once it had become apparent. To the west, Brand sent up two and a half squadrons of Hurricanes over Dorset. Almost an hour elapsed before the air over southern England began to reverberate to the thunder of Goering's bombers. Many German airmen, exhilarated at the very idea of this war-winning Eagle Day, had painted maps of the British Isles on their planes with the confident caption 'London. 15 August. Finish'.

The Dorniers bound for Eastchurch loomed suddenly out of the thick cloud cover almost on top of their targets. The Spitfires patrolling there had no chance to sweep in with a concerted attack. They engaged individually, and soon Dorniers were going down in flames. However, many bombed with accuracy. The bombers heading for Sheerness were less lucky, being caught by a Hurricane squadron. More Hurricanes then pounced upon the Eastchurch Dorniers and shot a number of them down. Two massive formations of Sperrle's bombers with strong fighter escort were attacked by the Hurricanes over Canterbury.

A second massive armada of dive-bombers, heavily screened by fighters, flew along the coast hoping to decoy British fighters, but they failed, for the R.A.F. ignored them completely. The R.A.F. did, however, assail a group of Me 110s that had arrived too late to escort bombers, and shot five of them into the sea. As the day progressed the cloud thickened, making the great fighter battle intended for Eagle Day even less likely. Nevertheless, strong formations of bombers, powerfully escorted, next attacked airfields around the Thames Estuary and on Salisbury Plain, and blitzed Southampton docks in the teeth of furious anti-aircraft fire. Although prevented from bombing accurately, they did much damage to the towns and docks.

Yet another bomber wave was intercepted by Spitfires from Middle Wallop just after crossing the coast, and many dropped their bombs off target. In the eastern sector, meanwhile, Spitfires tore into the fighter escort of a strong bomber formation that came in over Dover but were unable to prevent the bombers attacking Detling Coastal Command station near Maidstone. Yet another bomber force failed to locate targets north of the Thames and turned back, jettisoning bombs over countryside and sea when Hurricanes roared upon them.

By the end of Eagle Day the Luftwaffe had lost 47 aircraft with their trained crews; scores more had been damaged. In achieving this the R.A.F. had lost only 13 planes, from which eight pilots parachuted to safety.

The next day, August 14, could not be the second of Goering's boasted 'four great days', because the weather forecast was unfavourable. Nevertheless, in a series of small, widely scattered raids – in which the vulnerability of the once-dreaded Stuka was admitted by the substitution of Me 110s as dive-bombers – 19 German planes were shot down while the British lost 8. But August 15 dawned favourably enough. Stumpff

sent strong bomber formations across the North Sea to reinforce the general assault from the south. A main object of Eagle Day had been to destroy so many R.A.F. fighters in the south that squadrons from the north would have to be sent to replace them, opening up the north and the Midlands to Stumpff's long-range bombers. But Air-Marshal Saul's No. 13 Group was still there at full strength to meet Stumpff's 65 Heinkels and 50 Ju 88s, escorted by 35 Me 110s, heading for airfields in the north-east. Because the twin-engined Me 110s were flying at extreme range they had been fitted with additional fuel tanks, and rear gunners were left behind. They were to escort the Heinkels to Newcastle while the faster, more modern Ju 88s flew unescorted over Yorkshire. The enemy formations were still far out over the North Sea when radar began to record their approach.

*Below* Dornier bombers of the Luftwaffe press home the attack on London. Railway stations and communication centres were among their primary targets

*Opposite page* A sight that became common during the blitz on London. A high-explosive bomb has blown a crater in the path of a bus, which has toppled in

Saul ordered five squadrons into the air. First contact was made 30 miles out where 12 Spitfires engaged no less than 100 aircraft. The German bombers and fighters loomed up in two tiers, a flock of bombers leading, with the Me 110s stepped up in two black waves behind. From 3,000 feet above them the Spitfires screamed down out of the sun, two-thirds going for the bombers and the others for the fighters. This ferocious onslaught, at odds of over eight to one, achieved instant and spectacular results. The Me 110s jettisoned their extra fuel tanks, and while some formed a defensive circle the rest dived to sea level and headed home. The air was filled with the cacophony of machine-guns and cannons – and bombers plummeted seawards trailing smoke and flames.

The bombers split into two formations, one group of Heinkels heading for Tyneside, the other wheeling south-east to attack airfields at Dishforth and Linton-upon-Ouse. The first, beset by fighters and bombarded by the Tyneside guns, unloaded mostly into the sea. The second was forced to scatter bombs hurriedly around Sunderland and Seaham harbour. Between them, fighters and guns destroyed eight Heinkels and seven Me 110s, without a single R.A.F. casualty.

The 50 unescorted Ju 88s, meanwhile, went flat out to obliterate the bomber station at Great Driffield in Leigh-Mallory's No. 12 sector. Radar had long been tracking them, and they were challenged off Flamborough Head by a squadron of Spitfires, then by one flight of Hurricanes as they crossed the coast. Eight Ju 88s plunged in flames and a number scattered and turned away, but 30 pressed on to attack the airfield. Others dropped bombs on and around Bridlington.

By this time powerful German bomber forces were also flying in near Felixstowe, Harwich and Orfordness. Long-range bombers so badly smashed the Short factory at Rochester that production of Britain's first four-engined heavy bomber, the Stirling, was held up. Other formidable bomber fleets of 100 and 150 planes crossed the coast near Deal and Folkestone and made attacks on Eastchurch, Hawkinge, Worthy Down, Middle Wallop, West Malling and Croydon.

All over the south of England the skies were filled with the thunder of bombers, the howl of zooming, weaving, diving fighters, the furious chatter of machine-guns and the thumping of cannons. Particularly ferocious battles were fought off Portsmouth and Portland where 150 Spitfires and Hurricanes, the largest force yet put up by Fighter Command, arose to challenge long before the radar-spotted enemy formations had crossed the Channel. Many bombers were driven back before they reached the coast, jettisoning their bombs in the sea. By the end of the day five major air attacks had been launched upon Britain from Portland to the Tyne, yet considering the magnitude of the assault the damage was insignificant.

No less than 1,790 sorties, 520 by bombers and 1,270 by fighters, were flown by Goering's warplanes that day, while Dowding's fighters flew 1,000. Practically the whole might of the Luftwaffe was being flung against Britain. Certainly the intent to bring the R.A.F. fighters to full battle had met with a measure of success – but not the expected result. Instead of the R.A.F. suffering a crippling blow, the Luftwaffe had lost 74 aircraft to the R.A.F.'s 34.

Because German intelligence had wildly exaggerated the R.A.F. losses, put at 770 since the beginning of July instead of an actual 205, the Luftwaffe embarked upon the third of Goering's all-out 'four great days' on a false premise. Goering believed the R.A.F. now had no more than 430 fighters, with only 300 immediately serviceable. But the true position was that Dowding, if challenged to pitched battle by all Goering's Me 109s, could have matched their numbers. As it was, strategy required that he only maintain some 300 fighters to confront the enemy in the main aerial battlefield over south and south-east England. He not only had to distribute his force across the whole country against the possibility of widespread raids, but he intended to keep a reserve of trained pilots to relieve those who must finally succumb to battle exhaustion.

Already, Goering was worried by his bomber losses. When the attack was resumed on August 16, he instructed more Me 109s to stay in close escort to the Heinkels, Dorniers and Junkers instead of free-ranging high above, waiting to pounce upon British fighters, and he ordered that no bombers operating over Britain should carry more than one officer. Goering indicated his failure to grasp the essentials of defeating the R.A.F. by discouraging attacks on coastal radar

installations as a waste of time.

While the shaken Germans were realizing they were not the unchallengeable masters of the skies, the British fighter pilots were plunging into the fray with what almost amounted to light-hearted abandon. The growing German uneasiness at the dash and daring of the British fighter pilots was already evident on August 16, Goering's third 'great day'. Kesselring sent 70 long-range bombers with close fighter escort against the fighter station at West Malling. A Hurricane squadron from Hawkinge went straight for them, hurtling down head-on, but although they shot down a number of bombers and fighters, they failed to break up the attack. West Malling was heavily bombed. In Sperrle's sector, heavily escorted bombers badly battered Tangmere, where 14 aircraft caught on the ground were destroyed or badly damaged, although Spitfires continued to take off and land there. Other strong formations also bombed the Fleet Air Arm base at Gosport and a Coastal Command airfield at Lee-on-Solent. And, despite Goering's order, the radar station at Ventnor was bombed again.

It was during the Gosport attack that Flight Lieutenant J. B. Nicholson, of 249 Squadron from Middle Wallop, won the first Victoria

Some of the precautions taken in London during the blitz

Cross to be awarded to Fighter Command. In the midst of a whirling dogfight, his Hurricane was struck by four cannon shells, two hitting him and another setting fire to the reserve petrol tank. In flames, Nicholson was just about to bale out when he saw a Me 110 below him. He attacked it and sent it plunging to destruction. Only then did he struggle clear – to be shot in the buttocks, as he neared the ground, by a Home Guard who mistook him for a German parachutist. Miraculously Nicholson survived.

Sperrle's bombers ranged as far as Brize Norton in Oxfordshire, where they destroyed 46 training aircraft in hangers. Although this, the third of the Luftwaffe's three great assaults, had penetrated farther inland, it had petered out into small attacks on relatively unimportant targets. The R.A.F. lost only 21 fighters in combat, and a number on the ground, while the Luftwaffe lost 45 planes. However, in a day of major effort the Germans had done damage to fighter airfields.

On August 17, instead of another all-out assault, the Germans showed they were feeling the pace. Despite reasonable weather, no major

Perhaps the most famous of all London blitz pictures – St Paul's Cathedral, miraculously spared from the holocaust around it, stands illuminated by flames

attacks were made. But the Luftwaffe returned to the attack on August 18, with determined raids on Biggin Hill, Kenley, West Malling and Croydon. The massive raid on Biggin Hill was begun by two big groups of high-level, long-range bombers, successively attacking at five-minute intervals. While all was confusion, a single squadron of Ju 88s was to streak in at low level to complete the devastation. That the Luftwaffe was aiming a knockout blow at Biggin Hill was soon realized, and the station's two squadrons of Hurricanes and one of Spitfires took off.

Kesselring's high-level bombers were 20 minutes late making rendezvous with their fighters;

consequently, the intended knock-out blow by the fast low-level bombers was delivered first. The Ju 88s ran into the devastating fire of heavy and light anti-aircraft guns, machine-guns and rifles of the ground defences. In addition, batteries of rockets streaked up to release a curtain of thin steel cables hanging from parachutes. The bombers unloaded without much pretence at aiming and almost immediately were swooped upon by the British fighters. Only two Ju 88s returned to base.

Another powerful force attacked the vital Kenley sector station. It caught six Hurricanes on the ground, wrecked many buildings and knocked out the operations room. One Kenley squadron had to be switched to another airfield, although it was still possible to operate two; the operations room was in the meantime reopened in a local butcher's shop. Considerable damage was also done to West Malling and Croydon. Along the south coast Sperrle later sent in a series of raids against the airfields at Thorney Island, Gosport and Ford, and he severely damaged the radar station at Poling – the last attack made on a radar installation.

Just before dusk, Kesselring delivered the final powerful blow meant to send the R.A.F. reeling from the skies. A large bomber force with strong Me 110 escort, loomed over the Thames estuary heading for Park's sector station at North Weald. But two squadrons of Hurricanes from North Weald and Spitfires from Hornchurch tore into them near Harwich. They shot the formations to pieces, and the enemy bombers achieved nothing more than the machine-gunning of Manston as they fled. By the day's end no less than 71 German planes lay in smouldering ashes across the English countryside, while only 27 R.A.F. fighters had been lost.

Although it was not realized at the time, Goering's plan had failed. Instead of clearing the skies of R.A.F. fighters, it was the Luftwaffe which was weakening. Dowding still had 161 Hurricanes and Spitfires in reserve. The Luftwaffe pilots were increasingly cynical of Goering's bombastic claims. Despite its awesome numerical disadvantage, the R.A.F. was shooting down two German planes for every one lost. From August 8 to August 18 the R.A.F. destroyed 367 for a loss of 183.

The R.A.F. was well supplied with machines, but not with pilots. In the same ten days 154 pilots had been killed, were missing or severely wounded and only 63 new ones had taken their places. However brave, these new young men had nothing like the same skill. Of Fighter Command's immediate reinforcements, 20 came from Bomber Command's Fairey Battles and 33 from Army Co-operation Lysanders. They were declared to be fighter pilots after only six days instruction. Volunteers from Bomber and Coastal Command training schools, and from Allied air forces whose remnants were in Britain, were also enrolled for special shortened fighter courses. An additional worry was that the pilots who had been fighting from the beginning had been subjected to incessant strain and lack of sleep.

Goering's 'great' days had now gone without the forecast result, but he still had ten days to fulfill his boast. He might insist the Luftwaffe had victory in their grasp, but he was compelled to take a step that indicated how the R.A.F. had shaken them. All Stuka dive-bombers were withdrawn; they just could not stand such heavy losses any longer.

On August 19 Goering collected his commanders together and demanded the immediate destruction of Fighter Command. Every available single-engine fighter would be thrown in and pressure would be ceaselessly maintained. For 24 hours every day, small groups of bombers and even single raiders must streak in to attack aircraft factories and fighter fields. Even if the weather precluded large-scale raids, small ones would keep the defenders in a state of constant, exhausting alertness. Nearly all the Me 109s were massed under Kesselring's command, and all the Me 110s from Stumpff's command were brought down to provide escorts for Sperrle's bombers. After the disaster to Stumpff's long-range bombers in the north, they were restricted to a night attack on Glasgow. Sperrle meanwhile was to bomb Liverpool by night. Goering's decision to concentrate on south-east England was intended to devastate the defending fighters and airfields and destroy communications, so that the invasion coast and the hinterland right back to London would be laid wide open to attack.

Hitler did have cause to blame the weather from August 19 to 23. Continuous heavy cloud restricted the Luftwaffe to sporadic raids, although another raid on Manston was quite heavy. Night attacks on Bristol and Castle Bromwich did some industrial damage, though many bombs were dropped on open countryside. But August 24 dawned to the Luftwaffe's full advantage, and Goering now opened his second all-out attack to destroy Fighter Command. Kesselring's formations were the spearhead, aiming to compel the R.A.F. to challenge a fighter force superior in numbers. At the same time Sperrle's bombers were to attack aircraft factories from cloud cover or by night.

On the crucial sector of south-east England, some 200 Spitfires and Hurricanes now confronted a total of 1,000 long-range bombers and Me 109 fighters. Goering's orders were that no more than 300 bombers, always with heavy fighter escort, should raid at a time. Even though radar could warn the British when the enemy planes were airborne over France, it naturally could not predict which was the major attack; neither could it differentiate between bombers and fighters. Thus Kesselring was able to begin with a swift and successful raid on Manston by one of five formations put up, catching some Defiants refuelling.

Another big formation of closely escorted bombers attacked Hornchurch three hours later, again catching Defiants on the ground. Somehow they took off amidst the bursting bombs to give battle, and the anti-aircraft defences at Hornchurch were so accurate that the bombing was wild. North Weald, and Manston again, were also heavily attacked; at the former seven Hurricanes rose in the nick of time to engage the heavily escorted bombers. In the ensuing fight, joined by Hurricanes from Rochford, five German bombers and four fighters were shot down for the loss of eight Hurricanes, five of whose pilots parachuted to safety.

The next attack was by over 50 bombers from Sperrle's sector, escorted by a cloud of Me 109s, which thundered in over Portsmouth. Although three and a half squadrons of British fighters were airborne over the Isle of Wight, only one squadron managed to engage, but the guns around Portsmouth put up such a devastating barrage that the bombers wavered. They missed the dockyards but caused heavy civilian casualties. By the day's end the Luftwaffe had lost 38 planes and the R.A.F. 22, a ratio definitely to the R.A.F.'s disadvantage. During the night 170 German bombers attacked targets in south and south-east England, some as far as Cardiff, Swansea and South Shields. It was indicative of their general inaccuracy that for the first time bombs fell on London – although definitely not a target for the night.

This fateful mistake goaded Winston Churchill to order a retaliatory raid upon Berlin, whose people had been promised by Goering that the British could never get through. The raid – by 81 bombers, the biggest number yet sent out by the R.A.F. – on the night of August 25, so enraged Hitler in his turn that he demanded non-stop massive raids on London. By doing so he switched from the vital target that had to be destroyed if the Luftwaffe was to win the war – the sector stations which controlled Britain's fighter defences, the airfields and the fighters themselves. Meanwhile, the destruction of the British fighters was clearly the intention

of the first massive raid on August 25, by 45 bombers, surrounded by 200 fighters. Their objective was Warmwell airfield in Dorset, in the Middle Wallop sector. Brand and Park had nearly every Hurricane and Spitfire in the Middle Wallop, Tangmere and Filton sectors airborne. In the ensuing desperate battle, 11 British fighters were shot down for a loss of 11 German fighters and only one bomber. It had been impossible to get at the bombers for the mass of milling fighters.

On August 26 heavy attacks were made on the three sector stations of Hornchurch, North Weald and Debden. Park's fighters prevented accurate bombing of North Weald and Hornchurch, but Debden was heavily hit because the two R.A.F. squadrons engaged there could not penetrate the fighter screen. Westwards, on Sperrle's front, a big bomber force with a strong escort was so shaken by three squadrons of Park's fighters and Portsmouth's anti-aircraft guns that it unloaded nearly all its bombs, intended for the dockyard, into the sea. Despite their massive escorts, 19 German bombers were shot down that day, along with 26 fighters. The R.A.F. lost 31 fighters. If Hitler had kept to his original plan for invading Britain, this should have been the day for his first wave of shock-troops to set sail. But the R.A.F. seemed as strong as ever; he was compelled to defer his invasion.

The Luftwaffe resumed its raids on August 28, with strongly escorted bombers raiding Eastchurch, although another equally powerful force was prevented by R.A.F. fighters from bombing Rochford effectively. Then, during the afternoon, the Luftwaffe at last had a really significant success; they tempted seven of Park's squadrons to engage in a dogfight at 25,000 feet with successive waves of Me 109s. Had it been possible to ascertain that there were no bombers with this force, no R.A.F. fighters and pilots (particularly pilots) would have been risked. As a result the day's toll of Fighter Command was 20 aircraft against 30 German.

During the night, Sperrle's bombers attacked Liverpool, the first of four successive raids in which 600 German bombers flew over England. Only seven were shot down, because radar available to the R.A.F. night fighters and anti-aircraft gunners was as yet elementary. But if the British defences were problematical, the navigation of the raiders was even more so. So

King George VI inspects bomb damage in the East End of London, so soon after an attack that debris is still burning. The King himself narrowly escaped death when a bomb dropped over Buckingham Palace blew in a window of a room which he had just vacated

widely were the bombs scattered over the Midlands, West Country and Wales that it was difficult to discover the Luftwaffe's intended target. On the first night of the supposed blitz on Liverpool 160 long-range bombers set out at two-minute intervals so that defences should get as little rest as possible. On the second night, 176 bombers were despatched, 119 on the third, and 145 on the fourth night – yet it was not until the final raid that Merseyside was badly hit. Even then, nearly all the damage was residential. The docks were hardly touched.

More high-flying fighter sweeps were made on August 29, and in the ensuing dogfights the Luftwaffe lost 17 planes to the R.A.F.'s 9. This did little to persuade the Luftwaffe that there was any truth in that day's assertion by General von Doring, in command of Kessel-

ring's fighter groups that 'unlimited fighter superiority has now been attained'. But it prompted Hitler to name invasion day. Operation Sealion would begin at dawn on September 21. He gave his army commanders ten days to mass their troops on the coast and gather together the invasion vessels.

The Luftwaffe's reconnaissance of targets in Britain was increasingly unreliable owing to the fact that accurate anti-aircraft fire forced them to fly at great heights. The highly trained reconnaissance pilots, most of whom had flown with the Condor Legion in the Spanish Civil War, were so disconcerted by the accuracy of the ground fire that they were switched from Dornier 17 aircraft to the faster Me 110s. Nevertheless, they were invariably forced to dodge and dive so that their missions were ruined.

Although the R.A.F. was still strong, the pressure was beginning to tell. Fighter pilots closely engaged since Dunkirk were not only desperately tired but were experiencing the additional strain of having to nurse inexperienced new pilots. The bigger and tighter formations which the German fighters were now adopting made it increasingly difficult to get at the bombers. Yet despite this strain upon his front-line pilots, Dowding still kept his reserves farther north uncommitted, in readiness for a deeper German onslaught.

But Dowding's carefully reasoned strategy did not always succeed, and sometimes Leigh-Mallory did not strictly obey. Neither he nor some of his senior squadron commanders were content to wait to be called in by Park. They were eager for glory, straining at the leash to launch themselves at the enemy, and Leigh-Mallory considered he knew better than Dowding or Park how to deal with the Luftwaffe. This was by putting his squadrons up in 'Big Wings', comprising such a formidable force of fighters that enemy planes could be shot down in large numbers and their pilots intimidated.

If in theory Leigh-Mallory's method seemed right, in practice it did not work satisfactorily during this phase of the battle. Above all, Dowding required No. 12 Group to come to the aid of Park's No. 11 Group whenever they were desperately pressed. This meant that, however much Leigh-Mallory's supremely brave young pilots itched to get into the fray, they just had to be patient. The result of impatience was that they were too far away to come to Park's aid when his vital sector stations were under attack, or they took so long assembling that the enemy had gone before they could engage.

A bitter row developed in which Park accused Leigh-Mallory of leaving him in the lurch while his fighters were at full stretch protecting southeast England and London. Later he was to decry what he called a 'dirty little intrigue' which resulted in his posting to Training Command after the Battle of Britain, and in Dowding being sacked.

Royal Artillery 3·7 anti-aircraft guns hit back at the night bombers as the blitz on London carries on during the nights as well as by day

Meanwhile the Germans were also tiring. Goering's pilots were being driven even harder than Dowding's. At the same time, the R.A.F. losses were greatly overestimated because Luftwaffe claims were not checked as exactingly as the R.A.F.'s. As early as August 12, Stumpff had reported eight major R.A.F. airfields utterly destroyed, and for every German fighter lost he claimed five R.A.F. fighters had been shot down.

British pilots' reports too were optimistic. For instance the 76 enemy aircraft shot down on August 15 were announced as 182 certainly and 53 probably destroyed. The figure of 185 officially announced for September 15 should have been 60. (The true figures were found in German archives after the war.) But it was very easy to make mistakes in the heat of battle; inevitably, more than one fighter pilot, amidst the whirling, roaring maelstrom, sometimes claimed the same plane. In addition, many sorely pressed German pilots dived steeply, issuing smoke, to hedge-hop towards the sea. British pilots were neither permitted, nor had the time, to follow their victims down to see them crash.

On August 30, Goering's H.Q. was gloating that the R.A.F. pilots were losing heart, even as Kesselring's bombers, making strong and damaging attacks on Biggin Hill, Detling and the Vauxhall factory at Luton, were being assailed by Spitfires and Hurricanes in even greater numbers. By the day's end no less than 1,000 sorties had been flown by R.A.F. fighters with 37 Luftwaffe planes shot down for the loss of 26 R.A.F. Though German pilots were disconcerted by the continued strength of the R.A.F., they could claim August 30 as an unusually successful day. Detling airfield was put out of action for 15 hours, the bombing of Luton was destructive, and Biggin Hill was devastatingly bombed. Hangars, workshops and stores were wrecked, power and water supplies were cut off, and some 65 station staff killed. On this black day for Fighter Command, Hitler officially announced that he would give his final invasion decision on September 10.

The all-out attacks on airfields continued next day. Biggin Hill, Hornchurch, Debden, Croydon and Eastchurch were subjected to massive bombing. Again the German bombers were so effectively escorted that the Hurricanes and Spitfires had the greatest difficulty penetrating to the bombers. After its sixth raid in three days Biggin Hill was so badly damaged that Park had to withdraw two squadrons, leaving only one, operated from a somewhat unconventional control room in a local estate office. At Hornchurch and Debden, buildings and communications were also very badly damaged. Of the heavily attacked stations only Duxford really escaped, as Hurricanes intercepted the bombers and forced them to jettison their bombs. The day's bitter fighting cost the R.A.F. 39 fighters shot down and 10 destroyed on the ground, while the Luftwaffe lost 41.

At last, after his false start, Goering seemed to be getting somewhere. The R.A.F. fighter stations of Manston, Hawkinge, West Malling and Lympne had virtually been knocked out and Biggin Hill grievously damaged. If he could have similarly struck Tangmere, Kenley, Croydon, Gravesend and Westhampnett he would have wiped away London's main defence line to the south. It seemed that complete air superiority over south-east England, required before invasion, had almost been achieved.

But in the eight days that ensued, days of real crisis for Fighter Command, Goering again failed to confine his attacks to the essentials. Although German bombers continued to attack

fighter stations, raids on the Vickers-Armstrong and Hawker factories had no direct bearing on the battle.

In the crescendo of battle, the pilots of Fighter Command fought at full stretch with desperate heroism for over a week. Many had been rising to challenge the enemy two or three times a day, or even more, since early July. Some had been shot down three or four times. From dawn to dusk, the skies over south-east England were filled with Me 109s and Me 110s. Each night, half a dozen pilots slept at every dispersal hut, ready to roar off at first light to challenge the first wave of raiders. From then until about eight o'clock at night, the R.A.F. pilots were almost constantly in the air, only coming down for hurried refuelling and rearming, usually landing at about two-minute intervals.

On August 30 the Luftwaffe flew over 1,300 sorties over Britain and over 1,400 on the day after, but such pressure could not be sustained and it soon became apparent that the Luftwaffe's efforts were waning. The morale of the German airmen had been shaken by the loss of over 800 aircraft in less than two months. Now, if caught at a disadvantage with R.A.F. fighters diving down upon them, the Luftwaffe pilots would rarely stay to fight.

The losses were heavy on both sides during the period of fighter warfare, between August 31 and September 6. In shooting down 189 German planes, the R.A.F. lost 161 fighters. But, significantly, the R.A.F. were now flying more sorties each day than the enemy fighters, who never reached 1,000 per day during the first six days of September. The truth was that Kesselring had only 530 short-range fighters and 450 long-range bombers left and that Sperrle had barely 70 fighters to reinforce him. On September 6, the R.A.F. actually flew more fighter sorties than the Luftwaffe's fighters and bombers combined.

For some days, aerial reconnaissance had revealed increasing evidence of invasion's imminence, and the main attention of R.A.F. Bomber Command was switched to the gathering invasion fleets. So far, their main day targets had been enemy airfields in occupied territory, as well as factories and communications centres in Germany. On the night of August 12 a particularly memorable raid was made on an aqueduct carrying a section of the Dortmund–Ems Canal. Five obsolescent Hampden bombers

During the blitz tens of thousands of Londoners sought safety in the underground stations, where the current was cut off by night so that they could sleep both on platforms and between the tracks. Here an ENSA concert party is entertaining below ground while the bombs explode above

went in at low level amidst an inferno of anti-aircraft fire and the blaze of searchlights. Two were shot down, two forced away crippled, but the fifth dived to 150 feet and achieved such near misses that the canal was blocked for ten days. The direct result of this determined bombing was that a vital fleet of barges and motorboats, en route from the Rhine to the invasion ports, was held up, causing a six-day postponement of Operation Sealion.

By the order which he now gave for a day and night blitz on London, Hitler hoped to break the spirit of the British people even without an invasion, while Dowding would be compelled to throw in any reserves he might still have in the Midlands and north. Kesselring was instructed to raid London by day, to be followed by Sperrle's bombers by night. Chief objectives were the docks and public-utility installations over the rest of London. Although Hitler ordered that the residential districts should not be deliberately bombed, General Hans Jeschonnek, chief of staff of the Luftwaffe, was eager it should be done 'to produce mass panic'. To render Hitler's spoken threats more vivid, German bombers dropped flares over London on the night of September 4. On the next two nights a

few bombs were scattered in dockland districts.

On the eve of the great blitz on London Kesselring had over 450 long-range bombers concentrated for the daylight attacks, while Sperrle had rather more than 300 for night raids. To escort the daylight raiders, there were some 600 Me 109s available and 100 twin-engined Me 110s. To challenge them, Park could put up 21 squadrons of Spitfires and Hurricanes, with available reserves in neighbouring sectors of a further nine squadrons – in all around 350 fighters. The R.A.F. had the advantage that the Me 109s would be fighting at extreme range and be capable of short periods of combat only.

The blitz began about tea-time on Saturday, September 7. Goering had propaganda photographs taken of himself standing on a French clifftop with the white cliffs of Dover glimmering in the distance and waves of his bombers streaming across. Over 300, escorted by 600 fighters, set out in the new aerial armada that was to bring Britain to her knees. On airfields behind them the Stukas clustered, ready to blitz ahead of the invasion that would follow.

By the time it became apparent that the huge mass of enemy aircraft was heading too far east to threaten the vital fighter stations south of London, for which the defences were prepared, more than half the fighters which rose to intercept could not do so before the bombers were over their targets. The first wave dropped high explosives on Thameshaven, the East End, the docks and Woolwich arsenal fairly accurately, even though some escorting Me 109s had already withdrawn with diminishing fuel. Although 21 of 23 squadrons roared into the vast aerial combat which developed over London, they could not prevent the bombers unloading nearly 300 tons of high explosive on the capital. The tremendous sprawl of London with its distinctive landmarks, in particular along the winding Thames, made it inevitable that any bombs dropped must do damage.

While the scattered formation of the first attack fought its way back, three more waves of heavily escorted bombers loomed up over London. For an hour and a half they successively converged upon the huge burning target they could not miss, increasing the inferno of Thameshaven's blazing oil and the towering pall of black smoke and dust that arose from the East End and the docks. Residential districts miles away from the docks, even as far as Kensington, Croydon and Tottenham, suffered heavily, and a great swathe of burning desolation, one and a half miles long and half a mile wide, was blasted out of the Thames-side East End along the north bank. Devastated Silvertown was engulfed in flames, which trapped many people so that a little fleet of tugs, barges and boats had to go in through the smoke and heat to rescue men, women and children from the blistering banks.

In that day's furious fighting above and around London, 41 German planes, mostly bombers, were shot down for a loss of 29 R.A.F. fighters. The fires were still glowing that night, when 250 bombers from Sperrle's forces came in to add to the destruction. Hour after hour, from 8 p.m. until 2 a.m., the black bombers growled in sinister procession over the capital.

Meanwhile, invasion appeared imminent. Reconnaissance photographs revealed that not only were hundreds of barges massed in the Channel ports, but the Stuka dive-bombers were being concentrated just across the Straits. At the same time, the landing of German agents, swiftly captured and interrogated, on British shores, convinced the chiefs of staff that the invasion force was about to set out. The tides and moon would be at their most favourable on September 8–10. Everything seemed to indicate that the hour of Britain's greatest trial was upon her.

That night the code-word 'Cromwell', meaning 'invasion imminent', was sent out to Southern and Eastern Commands, to the two Corps held in readiness as G.H.Q. reserve, and formations immediately around London. In some parts, church bells were rung – the signal that the hour of invasion was nigh. That night, for the first time, the heavy bombers of the R.A.F. joined in the non-stop raids on the invasion ports and their ominous barge fleets.

When the sun rose again on London, its beam could barely penetrate the black smoke pall enshrouding many districts, particularly the East End. Amidst the welter of devastation three railway termini had been knocked out, seriously dislocating rail traffic between London and the south. Although the Luftwaffe had been savagely mauled by day, the night bombers, while dropping a bigger load than the day raiders, had lost only one. They had not been troubled by the few R.A.F. night fighters. And although the 264 anti-aircraft guns defending London had here and there spattered the sky with bursting salvoes, the gunners had been forbidden to fire at any target not clearly illuminated by searchlights and identified as hostile. Despite the heroism and fortitude already demonstrated by the people of London, especially the East Enders, great indignation at the apparent lack of defence against the night bombers was voiced. Among the most vociferous were some who, little more than a year earlier, had demanded that Britain should disarm as an example to the world.

Next day Dowding ordered No. 11 Group to be strengthened by the best pilots from less heavily engaged sectors. At the same time heavy anti-aircraft batteries were withdrawn from the defences of other towns in the south, the west and the Midlands to be rushed to London. Within a few days, a thunderous barrage was being put up over the capital, deterring the raiders though not shooting many down. Many south coast gunners had now been constantly in action day and night for nearly two months. Practically out on their feet from exhaustion, they nevertheless kept up a ferocious fire.

Fortunately, the Luftwaffe did not return to attack London heavily on September 8, but next day over 200 massively escorted bombers attacked between five and six p.m. – because then the shifts in the war factories and at the docks would be changing over. But this time the R.A.F. was ready. Even as radar gave warning of the enemy massing across the Channel, squadrons of Spitfires and Hurricanes took off to guard anticipated targets. As the first bombers, almost completely surrounded by fighters, came in over Dover, two of Park's squadrons tore into them. Orders now were that the Hurricanes should go for the bombers while the Spitfires took on the fighters. The soft blue skies were soon streaked and swirling with the white vapour trails of British and German fighters in desperate individual combats, vivid warning to the German bomber pilots that there was no hope of reaching London unassailed.

Three more of Park's squadrons tore into them over Sussex. Fighters were also waiting for the second enemy wave, which next came in near Beachy Head. Their vicious assaults drove the bombers west into another of Park's squadrons and a whole wing from Duxford. There was little pretence at aiming the bombs that were now scattered across south-west London and its outskirts between Chelsea and Richmond. In all, less than half the German bomber force even reached residential London. Hardly any military or industrial targets were hit. The cost to the Luftwaffe was 28 planes and to the R.A.F. 19 fighters. If the success of the first London raid had persuaded some Germans that the R.A.F. had almost shot its bolt, the pulverizing power of the fighter punch which hit their follow-up attack horrified them. It made complete nonsense of all Goering's boasts (he believed the R.A.F. were down to their last hundred fighters). At the same time it gave the German naval war staff cause to stress that the undisputed air supremacy required for invasion had most certainly not been achieved. Hitler further postponed his decision until September 14.

The Luftwaffe tried again with a heavy attack on London next day. A force of 100 bombers, surrounded by clouds of Messerschmitts, succeeded in penetrating to the docks and the City, doing extensive damage and causing heavy loss of life. That same afternoon a compact force flew, fast and unerringly, to bomb a new aircraft factory near Southampton. It was definitely not a good day for Fighter Command which lost 25 in shooting down 29. As if to underline Hitler's assertion that Fighter Command had shot its bolt, a fourth daylight raid on London on September 14 met ineffective opposition. For the loss of 14 planes the Luftwaffe destroyed 14 R.A.F. fighters. Hitler warned his service chiefs to be prepared to invade on September 27, when the tides and moon would again be favourable.

Bomber Command had, meanwhile, played an important part in causing the further postponement of invasion. The day before Hitler announced the new date, R.A.F. bombers had sunk 80 barges, and Admiral Raeder pleaded that the risk was still too great. There were more than 1,000 invasion barges in the French ports by now, with an additional 600 waiting up river at Antwerp, and they made a magnificent target for the Bleinheims, Wellingtons, Whitleys and Hampdens which nightly made the short haul across the Channel with maximum bomb loads. In two weeks' sustained bombing they not only destroyed 12 per cent of the invasion fleet, but disrupted embarkation facilities and communications behind the ports and hampered minesweeping along the chosen invasion route. To the British bomber crews the whole French coast from Boulogne to Ostend nightly appeared lurid with fires that devoured barges and dock installations, with a myriad vivid bomb bursts erupting amidst the general inferno. This, and the showers of multicoloured tracers that interminably swarmed up at them, caused them to call it 'the Blackpool Front'.

At this fateful hour, a significant change was made in the tactics of Fighter Command. Until now, although the formidably larger Luftwaffe had been stretched to its full attacking capacity, the R.A.F. had deliberately fought at much greater odds than necessary. Sure of the prowess and unshakeable courage of his front-line fighter pilots, Dowding had retained a considerable

Other cities besides London were heavily blitzed by night bombers and Coventry was one of the first victims. The city's beautiful medieval cathedral was almost completely destroyed

reserve behind London and still farther north. Even if all the sector-control airfields in the crescent of defences before London had been crippled, there were still plenty more well-equipped airfields beyond and flanking London that could have carried on the fight. This is the vital factor overlooked today by those who claim that if Hitler had not switched the attack to London, Fighter Command would have been knocked out and invasion would soon have followed. No longer were the Spitfires and Hurricanes to be hurled into the fray in scattered squadrons; they were to confront the Luftwaffe in fleet formation that would vie with those of the enemy. The day of the Big Wing had come! The Spitfires would go for the Me 109s, and the Hurricanes for the bombers. 'The object is to ensure that we meet the enemy in maximum strength, employing our fighter squadrons in pairs of the same type where possible', wrote Park in an instruction issued on September 11.

Goering had to wait no more than a few hours for his next fine day. Sunday, September 15, awoke softly to one of those golden autumn dawns which give promise of warm sunshine and sparkling visibility. The young fighter pilots of the R.A.F., many in action now for weeks on end, gathered early in dispersal huts all over south-east England and around London.

The Luftwaffe was certainly not what it had been at the opening of the battle. Kesselring's bomber force had been halved. His fighters had suffered so heavily that he had to organize bomber raids so that one force of fighters would switch its cover from one raid to the next. Inevitably, this was to the advantage of the defenders, because it meant that German raids were not likely to catch R.A.F. formations on the ground refuelling and rearming. The best Kesselring could do for diversions, on this fateful day of September 15, was to get Sperrle to send a small bomber force to Portland and a formation of Me 110 fighter-bombers to attack the Spitfire factory near Southampton.

It was almost 10.30 in the morning, with clouds just beginning to smudge the soft beauty of the day, when the first concentration of German aircraft over France was spotted by British radar. Winston Churchill was in Park's operations room to watch. Coolly observing the radar's recording of the massing of the enemy forces, Park's controllers paired up the No. 11 Group

squadrons and ordered them into perfect intercepting positions. With even more time to dispose of his squadrons, Leigh-Mallory, to Park's north, prepared a veritable hornet's nest from No. 12. Smoothly, the organization of defence went into action; fighter pilots leaped to their cockpits and anti-aircraft gunners manned their guns. When the first wave reached the English coast an hour later 11 of Park's 21 fighter squadrons were riding high to challenge them. At the same time fighters from Middle Wallop and more from Duxford were converging from west and east. Into this swarm of Hurricanes and Spitfires around London, 100 long-range German bombers and 400 fighters now thundered.

Two crack Spitfire squadrons, Nos. 72 and 92, who respectively had won their spurs against Stumpff's ill-fated raid on the north and against the awful odds over Dunkirk, were the first to hurtle into action. Fighting against huge odds seemed always to have been their lot, so they sped straight into the nearest bomber formations, guns blazing. Glowering black smoke streamed from bomber after bomber, plunging to destruction, before a furious swarm of Me 109s could swoop upon the Spitfires. As they zoomed clear from this breathless battle, they were riddled by bullets and raked by cannon shells, but remained miraculously intact. Then Spitfires of No. 603 (City of Edinburgh) squadron plunged into the fray and more blazing bombers dived earthwards.

Even while the ferocious Spitfire onslaught was shaking the German force, squadrons of Hurricanes tore in above Maidstone. The shock of the fighter attacks was already causing the bombers to lose formation, increasing the difficulties of the protecting Messerschmitts. The comparatively short range of the Me 109 meant the German pilots were faced with running out of fuel over England or the Channel if diverted too far from their escort routes. And still more British fighters dived into the great air battle, six squadrons, sweeping in from north of the Thames.

As dogfights between Hurricanes and Spitfires and the Me 109s developed all round the disintegrating air fleet, German bombers were increasingly left without escort. They were compelled to unload their bombs indiscriminately over the south-eastern suburbs and make for home fast. But before many could even attempt

Seaham

Great Driffield

*North Sea*

**E N G L A N D**

• Ford

Birmingham

Orford

Duxford
Felixstowe
Luton
Harwich

Brize Norton

**HOLLAND**

Filton
Oxford
London
Hornchurch
Eastchurch

Farnborough
Hawkinge
Canterbury
Odiham
Folkestone
Dover
Ostend

Middle Wallop
Gosport
Dunkirk

**B E L G I U M**

Southampton
Portsmouth
Calais

*Isle of Wight*
*Beachy*
*Head*
Boulogne

Portland
Ventnor

*English Channel*

**F R A N C E**

Rochester
Sheerness
Gravesend
Croydon
Biggin Hill
Canterbury
Deal
Farnborough
Maidstone
West Malling
Lympne
Hawkinge

**Battle of Britain**

this they were ferociously attacked by yet more Hurricane squadrons speeding in from the northern sectors. The high azure September sky was everywhere laced with the white vapour trails of milling fighters.

At this moment in the vast confused battle, Douglas Bader's formidable Duxford wing of five fighter squadrons arrived. This formation was the most powerful single force of fighters the Luftwaffe had ever encountered. Soon the Duxford fighters were furiously engaged with a swarm of Me 109s, still bravely but desperately striving to save the bombers. And as the scattered, defeated German air armada streamed back towards the coast, Park sent up his last four squadrons to complete the execution.

Kesselring sent in his second attack soon after 2 p.m. Again radar gave ample warning and Park had six squadrons, in pairs, up to meet the enemy armada while still over the sea. As again the seemingly unending waves of German aircraft crossed the coast, two more pairs of squadrons and three and a half individual squadrons raced towards them. Bader's wing loomed from the north-east and squadrons of Brand's fighters sped in from the west.

This time, however, it was not a compact mass of fighter-surrounded bombers with which the R.A.F. gave battle. So many Me 109s had been shot down or badly damaged in the morning's dogfights that there were now insufficient to give adequate cover for the bombers. In addition, clouds were beginning to bank over south-east England up towards London. The oncoming bombers roared London-wards in two separate formations, each with a small close escort of Me 109s. A large high-flying fighter force meanwhile surged on with orders to clear the skies of British fighters over the capital.

Fighters from Hornchurch made contact over Kent. Two squadrons from Tangmere pounced on the left flank of the enemy bombers, causing a number to jettison their loads and flee. The spearheading cloud of German fighters was challenged over Dartford and the surrounding Kent countryside by some 15 R.A.F. fighter squadrons. The German pilots were astounded to meet more Spitfires and Hurricanes than ever before. Even if disillusioned, the Luftwaffe pilots were brave enough, and the ensuing battle was sufficiently even to permit a number of the German bombers to attack their targets. Extensive

Rescue parties worked without cease to save people from the devastation in London

damage was done along both banks of the River Thames.

Bader's Duxford wing did not join the battle until the climax was past and the bombers already fleeing. Most ruthless in the ensuing execution were the Polish and Czech pilots, each with so much to avenge. Although the diversionary attack on Portland that afternoon managed to reach its objective and elude intercepting fighters, little damage was done. Meanwhile the tight formations which raced in to bomb the

68

Spitfire factory near Southampton, though they too evaded interception, completely missed their target from only 2,000 feet.

By the day's end, the morale of the Luftwaffe bomber crews was shaken as never before. Although the actual number of German aircraft shot down in the two attacks on London on September 15 was not above 60 (the R.A.F. lost 26) dozens of returning bombers staggered home riddled with bullets and shell splinters, many with one or more crew members dead or desperately wounded. As for the German fighter pilots, although they had acquitted themselves well, they too were becoming increasingly disheartened at the appearance in apparently ever-growing strength of Spitfires and Hurricanes supposed to have been cleared from the skies days before. Twice in that one day Fighter Command had put over 300 fighters over southern England.

Never again, after that significant day, did the Luftwaffe seek an all-out fighter battle with the R.A.F. On September 16, Kesselring's fighters and bombers nearly all stayed at home, licking their wounds both physical and mental. 'Our pursuit, Stuka and fighter forces had naturally suffered grievous losses in material, personnel and morale. The uncertainty about the continuation of the air offensive reflected itself down to the last pilot', wrote Adolf Galland, Germany's greatest fighter pilot who in this very September recorded his fortieth 'kill'. He told his brother that things could not go on much longer as they were. 'You could count on your fingers when your turn would come', wrote Galland. 'The logic of the theory of probabilities showed us incontestably that one's number was up after so many sorties. For some it was sooner, for some later. . . We saw one comrade after the other, old and tested brothers in combat, vanish from our ranks. . .'

Adolf Galland did not hesitate to tell Reichsmarschall Goering exactly what he thought, even before the catastrophes suffered by the Luftwaffe in the bombing of London. 'Goering refused to understand that his Luftwaffe, this shining and so far successful sword, threatened to turn blunt in his hand', Galland recorded. 'He believed there was not enough fighting spirit and a lack of confidence in ultimate victory. . . I tried to point out that the Me 109 was superior in the attack and not so suitable for purely defensive purposes as the Spitfire, which, although a little slower [about 10 to 15 mph] was more manoeuvrable. He rejected my objection. We [the German fighter pilots] received many more harsh words. Finally, as his time ran short, he grew more amiable and asked what were the requirements for our squadrons. . . I did not hesitate long. "I should like an outfit of Spitfires for my group", I said. . . Such brazenfaced impudence made even Goering speechless. He stamped off, growling as he went.'

On September 17 Hitler himself admitted that the Royal Air Force was 'still by no means defeated'. He decided to postpone invasion 'until further notice'. And on the next day, with the relentless bombing of his invasion barges being pressed home by aircrews of Bomber Command, the Führer ordered that the barges should be dispersed. From that moment he was committed to doing something he had promised the German people he would never ask them to do – fight on two fronts. It meant attacking Russia now before Germany was fully ready, to try to destroy the enemy in the East before the one in the West could gather strength to hit back.

What ensued after September 15 was sheer anticlimax. Nevertheless, it was terrible and terrifying, as London and other great cities like Birmingham, Liverpool, Coventry, Bristol, Southampton and Cardiff were heavily bombed,

night after night, for eight months. But the morale of the British people did not crack.

Kesselring attempted another escorted daylight raid on London, on September 18, but sent only 70 bombers, which were so roughly handled that their bombing was erratic. A week later, 60 of Sperrle's bombers made a damaging attack on the Bristol aircraft factory and a nearby fighter station but, when they tried a repeat on September 27, they were intercepted and unloaded their bombs across the countryside. On the same day three attempts were also made to raid London, but only a few bombers managed to penetrate. The day's fighting cost the Luftwaffe 45 planes and the R.A.F. 28. Three days later, a strong force of R.A.F. fighters scattered a major attack intended for the Westland factory at Yeovil, and again the bombs burst across open country. The Luftwaffe's final big daylight attack on London was on September 30 when it lost 47 aircraft to the R.A.F.'s 20.

The Battle of Britain had virtually petered out when, at last, Mussolini's pilots were permitted to strike their glorious blow for Italy. Some 15 bombers ineffectually attacked Harwich by night on October 25, and on October 29 there was an attempted daylight raid by 15 bombers escorted by over 70 C.R.42 biplane fighters.

The sight of the first anti-aircraft bursts discouraged them from getting close enough even to be recognized as Italians, and the British did not realize that the Italians were engaged until November 11, when three bombers and three fighters of a 50-strong Italian force were shot down. The flight of 88 Italian warplanes from a salvo of anti-aircraft fire on October 31 is officially reckoned to be the end of the Battle of Britain.

The battle had cost the Germans 1,733 planes and more than 6,000 airmen, and the R.A.F. 915 planes and 414 fighter pilots. Hitler himself acknowledged defeat on October 12 by postponing Operation Sealion 'until the Spring of 1941'. The war against Britain was now to be one of blockade by U-boats and night bombing. Victory had been achieved by a mere thousand brave young men, of whom Winston Churchill declared: 'Never in the field of human conflict was so much owed by so many to so few'.

A successful attempt by the Luftwaffe to disrupt Britain's communications

# 3. Keren

# 3. Keren

By September 13, 1940, Benito Mussolini, certain that Britain was about to be overwhelmed, determined to seize all her African possessions. Obsessed with his desire to create a new Roman empire, he envisaged the swift conquest of territories that would make him absolute ruler from Libya to the Indian Ocean. He made no secret of his grand strategy. It was to combine an advance along the Mediterranean coast from Libya into Egypt with a push westwards from Eritrea and Ethiopia and eastwards to British Somaliland, to fulfil the Italian dream of an all-green line from Tripoli to the Horn of Africa. Mussolini had openly prepared for this ever since his proclamation of June 1, 1936, that the Italian East African empire would stretch 1,500 miles from north to south, between the Tropic of Cancer and the Equator, and over 1,000 miles at its greatest width.

To achieve his dream, of which the seizure of Ethiopia in 1935 was the beginning, Mussolini had two huge armies strategically massed on the African continent. Some 300,000 men in Libya were poised to invade Egypt. The other army, of 250,000, was in Eritrea and Ethiopia, ready to invade British Somaliland, the Sudan, and thence Kenya, Uganda, Rhodesia, and perhaps eventually South Africa itself.

To challenge these formidable armies there were some 50,000 British and Indian troops under General Sir Archibald Wavell in Egypt; to the south, under the command of General Sir William Platt, were three infantry battalions plus the 4,500-strong British-officered Sudan Defence Force. Kenya was defended by six African battalions led by British officers, while British Somaliland had a Camel Corps of 600 men plus one African battalion. For tanks they had a few home-made armoured cars and, with the exception of two ancient howitzers used for official salutes in Khartoum, there was not one piece of artillery in any of the British East African territories.

The R.A.F. meanwhile faced the might of the Regia Aeronautica in the Sudan–East Africa theatre with six ancient 'stringbag' Vincent biplanes of 1928 vintage and a few borrowed civil DH Dragon Rapides. For many weeks after fighting began there was a standing order to 'fire at anything more than one' because there could never be more than one Vincent airborne – there was only one serviceable carburettor to share between them. The 200 warplanes of the Italians were formidably modern by comparison.

The Italian army between Eritrea and Ethiopia was well organized with artillery, tanks and copious transport. It contained the cream of

*Above* Benito Mussolini, seen here haranguing a frenzied crowd from the balcony of the Palazzo Venezia. His plan of conquest envisaged an Italian empire from Tripoli to the Horn of Africa

*Opposite page* Marshal Graziani, Governor General of the Italian East African possessions, inspecting crack Blackshirt troops, many of whom manned the mountain fortress of Keren

Italy's fighting men. Mussolini had planned the conquest of British Africa from his highly developed and well-stocked bases in Eritrea, and as the British knew, Italian engineers had lately built great modern autostradas in Eritrea and Ethiopia.

Mussolini's forces had made the first move on July 4, 1940. A column of two brigades of infantry with artillery and tanks supported by aircraft bore down in a storm of dust from Eritrea upon the ancient Sudanese frontier town of Kassala. 400 Sudanese and their British officers faced 8,000 Italians and Eritrean levies. Deliberately, no attempt was made to fight within the town, but out on the flanks and at the tails of each Italian column lorry-borne machine-guns repeatedly opened up, maintained fire as they closed quickly, then disappeared as quickly.

When Kassala had been captured British losses were a dozen men and seven vehicles to 500 Italian dead. On the same day, 200 miles farther south, the Italians struck another hammer blow against the little fortress and frontier village of Gallabat. There 100 men of the Sudan Defence Force fought with skill and gallantry against 2,000 before withdrawing.

Kassala and Gallabat were the two strategic points the Italians required to open the way for the invasion of Egypt from the south but, alarmed by the reserves which General Platt now brought into this ominously threatened area, the Italian invasion forces ground to a halt, dug defences and surrounded themselves with festoons of barbed wire. Platt's reserves actually amounted to 120 tough soldiers of the 2nd West Yorkshires with two bren-gun carriers, but they so terrorized the Italians by hit-and-run attacks from the thorny wilderness that they were reported by enemy intelligence as '5,000 heavily armed regular British troops with many tanks'.

On August 4 the Italians attacked and soon overran British Somaliland with its Red Sea coastline. A force of 25,000 picked troops with armour, many guns and massive air cover compelled the 2,500 British, Indian and African defenders to evacuate.

After this memorable victory Mussolini immediately urged Marshal 'Butcher' Graziani in Libya to conquer Egypt forthwith. But the Italian commander-in-chief was worried about water supplies in the desert and asked for more

Some of the 25,000-strong invasion force which seized British Somaliland. In Rome the end of British power in Africa was grandiloquently proclaimed

time. Mussolini allowed him a month, but when Graziani asked for a further month the furious Duce threatened, 'Attack next Monday or you will be replaced!'

So on September 13 an 80,000-strong spearhead of the huge Italian Libyan army rolled ponderously across the Egyptian frontier. British regular soldiers, already tough veterans of many desert raids, began a planned withdrawal which continued until the huge Italian force halted at Sidi Barrani, some 60 miles into Egypt. By September 17 they had lost 500 men and 150 vehicles to 40 British casualties. At Sidi Baranni Graziani decided to consolidate while he built up an overwhelming force to complete the invasion. The Italians began to construct a chain of massive fortified positions stretching southwards across the desert.

This lull allowed the British a chance to strengthen, although their reinforcements were laughable by comparison. Some 10,000 men of the understrength 5th Indian Division* arrived in the East African theatre. And in Egypt Wavell, with 10,000 reinforcements, was able to build up a striking force of 30,000. Their offensive power was considerably strengthened by the arrival of a brigade of tanks.

On December 9 Wavell's little army, after a long and stealthy approach across the desert, fell upon the Italian desert fortresses. The Italians were soon surrendering in droves, Sidi Barrani was captured swiftly and the routed enemy rushed westwards in headlong flight, hotly pursued. About 130,000 men, 400 tanks and 1,290 guns were captured. The 4th Indian Division, largely responsible for the initial devastating attack, Wavell now plucked from the midst of their triumph and sent 700 miles down the Nile to join General Platt's forces.

On January 17, with Bardia in the Libyan desert fallen to the Australians and British troops surrounding Tobruk, General Platt ordered his men to attack in the Sudan. Only the advance guard of the 4th Indian had as yet reached him, but his troops were eager. First he unleashed the

* It is not generally realized that an Indian Division was a blend of Indian and British troops, all commanded by British officers, at a ratio of five Indian soldiers to three British.

Gazelle Force, a hard-hitting mobile formation comprising Sudan Defence Force machine-gunners, Indian infantry and British artillery. The Kassala garrison fled and Gazelle Force pursued the Italians until finally they stood and fought on the rocky hills above the Keru Gorge. Gazelle was spearheading the still-arriving 4th Indian Division with orders to attack towards Keren through Keru and Agordat. The 5th Indian Division meanwhile was to drive for Keren on a more southerly route through Sabderat, Tessenei and Barentu.

Five of the Italians' best battalions manned the long-prepared positions at Keru, but while their full strength was concentrated to stop Gazelle Force, they were taken in the rear by 5th Indian troops led by Brigadier William Slim, of whom more was to be heard later in the war. They fled that night towards the towering moun-tains of Eritrea, where lay their most impreg-nable fortress – the peak-girdled town of Keren.

The unexpectedly easy victory at Keru had a significant impact on the whole course of the campaign. It caused a panic among officers of the Italian High Command from which they never recovered. On hearing the astounding news of the fall of 'impregnable' Keru, they made a dramatic reorientation of their entire forces to concentrate the bulk of their best troops in the natural fortress of Keren, 4,300 feet above sea level, with mountains forming a terrifying stronghold of jagged peaks, dizzying precipices, and rocks and crags blistered to untouchable heat by the blazing sun. The main urgency which now obsessed the Italian forces between the British and Keren was whether they could get there before Dongolaas Gorge was blown in and the fortress gates thundered shut.

Before Gazelle Force reached Keren there was one more formidable nut to crack at Agordat, where an élite Italian colonial division fought determinedly from rocky mountain positions. After some bitter fighting, they were overcome by February 1, with the capture of a great spoil of guns, vehicles and stores. Once more Gazelle Force raced ahead, its destination the Dongolaas Gorge and Keren high above.

Hearing a distant explosion amidst the mountain mass, the little band of onrushing British and Indian soldiers knew they were too late. The thunder that echoed and re-echoed from peak to peak around the heights of Keren could only mean one thing – Dongolaas Gorge was blown in and the only way through blocked. But if the vital sea route between South Africa and the Suez Canal was to be protected, Keren would have to be stormed. Already there were signs that the Germans were coming to Italy's aid in Africa and General Erwin Rommel was preparing his armoured Afrika Korps to intervene.

Gazelle Force arrived at the threshold of Keren on the evening of February 2. For as far as the eye could see, the mountain walls reared up in vast black cliffs, dominated by ranks of brooding peaks which seemed to impale the sky. Into that threatening mass the one roadway to Keren disappeared. And, with the blowing up of the gorge, the entrance was barred.

The Dongolaas Gorge was in fact the only way through a mountain wall hundreds of miles long that stretched from the far Red Sea hills almost to the shores of Lake Rudolph. It seemed that the only way to defeat the enemy now was by clambering up the sides of the awful mountains and grappling hand to hand with the waiting defenders at the top.

The ultimate objective, the town of Keren, invisible behind the savage skyline, sprawled across a pleasant plateau some 4,300 feet above sea level. Through binoculars a scar along the mountain face could be seen where a railway line clung before diving into a tunnel. It emerged round the shoulder of the mountain, back beyond the devastation in the Dongolaas Gorge, and ran on to Keren. Near the tunnel entrance and half-way up the mountain a spur stood out abruptly. It was over 2,500 feet up, flattened into a platform, itself overshadowed by two jagged peaks above. This platform – it was to be named Cameron Ridge – dropped away in a

sheer, terrifying precipice to yawning blackness. The dominant peak on the right was named Sanchil, that on the left the British called 'Brig's Peak'. Two other soaring peaks called 'Flat Top' and 'Hog's Back' stood out farther to the left. The Italians had manned a continuous line between these four sentinel peaks.

To the right of Sanchil the mountainside dropped down in a series of precipices to the blocked Dongalaas Gorge at the bottom. The gorge was flanked by a mountain barrier on the left and on the right. Here the dominant features were first Dologorodoc, and then peaks called 'Sphinx' and Zelale. Between these embattled peaks the Italians manned another defensive rampart of crests overlooking the valley along which any attacking force must advance. This obvious death-trap the British chose to call 'Happy Valley'.

Dologorodoc, like Sanchil, looked down directly upon the Dongolaas Gorge and also back behind the Italian lines into the town of Keren itself. The Italians had constructed a fort on this vital position, with concrete emplacements and entrenchments cut into the rock and shale of the face. Dologorodoc was in turn overlooked by Sanchil and Brig's Peak across the gorge, and by two more Italian fortified positions behind the Dologorodoc-Sphinx line which were the peaks of Falestoh and Zeban. These four peaks were all over 200 feet higher than Dologorodoc.

Defensive trenches had been dug into the rocky shale wherever possible, and pillboxes had been constructed at natural strongpoints. The jagged skyline which the attackers would have to storm was solid rock, providing natural ramparts. The enemy positions were along knife-edged ridges of such steepness that any normal artillery barrage would merely lob over and burst harmlessly hundreds of feet away down the far mountainside. To make matters even worse for the attackers, whole stretches of the acute slopes were of loose shale, and the boulders and patches of scabrous thorn which somehow

*Opposite, top* A German picture showing the victory march through Addis Ababa of a jubilant native brigade after the conquest of British Somaliland

*Opposite, bottom* Italian infantry advancing through arid scrubland as they close in for the kill in the Sudan

78

Field-Marshal Sir Archibald Wavell, Commander-in-Chief, Middle East, talks tactics with General R. N. O'Connor, commander of the British force in the North African desert. O'Connor's brilliant handling of armour contributed largely to the Italian debacle there

clung to the mountain faces were festooned with barbed-wire.

The battle had to be fought on the summit. On February 3 the Camerons were sent in on the left of the Dongolaas Gorge while the Rajputanas went in on the right. A devastating fire halted the Indians as they entered Happy Valley, but the Scots thought they could capture the ridge over the railway tunnel as an intermediate stage towards Brig's Peak and the key objective of Sanchil. Next day, under sporadic fire, they made the killing climb, but when finally they arrived breathless at the tunnel they were pinned down by a machine-gun post. A fierce attack by the Highlanders proved too much for the Italians manning it and they surrendered. It was discovered then that the railway tunnel had been blocked by a train blown up deep inside.

Another company of Camerons had tougher fighting before they overcame numerous machine-gun posts dug into the side of the mountain. They also had to overcome bombing squads of Italians who issued from caves to hurl down upon them the little red grenades which the Italians found so useful in mountain warfare. Making skilful use of the scant cover provided by ledges and boulders the Scots fought on and up until both companies arrived at the ridge destined to be called Cameron Ridge. At the end of four hours' climbing and fighting they fanned out into battle positions along the ridge determined to hold at all costs this perilous foothold high up the mountain.

During the night Punjabi infantry stealthily crept through the ranks of the Scots and clambered on up the rocky sides of Brig's Peak. They surprised and overwhelmed the defending Italians who had imagined the climb was impossible, and when day dawned the Punjabis proudly gazed down from their mist-wreathed pinnacle on the wide sweep to the Keren plateau. It was a moment in which the whole way ahead seemed suddenly possible. But it quickly became obvious that the Italians realized the danger. A terrific bombardment fell upon Brig's Peak;

before the crack Italian Alpini soldiers waiting to counter-attack, the silhouetted skyline suddenly erupted boulders, rock fragments and bodies of Indian soldiers. Behind this barrage the Savoia Grenadiers went in headlong attack, the ferocity and weight of their assault hurling the surviving Indians from their rocky vantage points and down towards Cameron Ridge.

The Italians pressed their attack down to the very ridge itself, but in the nick of time reinforcements of Rajputanas clambered up. Although almost breathless, they turned the tide and Cameron Ridge was held. The power of the Italian counter-attack showed they were in great strength around Sanchil and indeed, so much importance did they place on it that they had even laid a fresh-water pipeline up to that peak.

As if to emphasize the hopelessness of trying to storm Sanchil or Brig's Peak, the Italians made life a hell for the Highlanders and Indians clinging precariously to the ridge below. By day and night daring bombing squads dodged down the mountainside among the huge boulders and, at twice the range of the British Mills grenade, flung their deadly little bombs with devastating accuracy.

Even more damaging were the Italian heavy-calibre mortars. Far away beyond the shimmering skyline the attackers would hear faint 'pops', rapidly followed by a noise like an express train culminating in a shattering explosion. There was nothing the men could do but hug the hot, gritty ground and hope that the scything shower of steel and rock splinters would sweep over them.

The Scots and Indians endured, but not without exacting retribution. Little bands of stalkers wriggled out intent on giving the enemy a taste of cold steel, and bloody man-to-man engagements ensued.

Across Happy Valley the whole divisional artillery of 120 guns now opened up on Mount Dologorodoc. When 5th Indian Brigade, comprising the Royal Fusiliers, Punjabis and Rajputanas, moved into the valley at dusk there was no challenge from the fort. The Fusiliers and Punjabis deployed among the scant cover of thorn thickets and boulders on the valley's far side while the Rajputanas moved warily towards the low curve in the darkening skyline that marked Acqua Col, at the far end of Happy

Valley and on the Italians' extreme right.

The brooding peaks above were eerily still. Then, shatteringly, as the Rajputanas neared the first crest, the heavy mortars, machine-guns and light automatics of the waiting Italians poured in a devastating fire. Men fell dead and wounded everywhere, among them the company commander. As his C.O. fell, Subedar Richpal Ram charged to the front shouting the Rajputana war cry and stormed on with the leading platoons. Some 30 reached the crest and in furious hand-to-hand fighting established themselves there. The Italians answered fury with fury in successive violent counter-attacks, but the Indians bitterly repulsed them. Shortly before dawn, however, having fired their last rounds, the gallant Subedar and nine surviving riflemen fought back to their comrades dug in just below the crest of the ridge. At daylight the enemy opened up with artillery and mortars on the precariously exposed Rajputanas, and intermittent dive-bombing inflicted further casual-

*Above* British machine-gunners pour fire into Italian positions in the North African desert

*Opposite page* Some of the thousands of Italian prisoners taken by Wavell's 30,000. The 4th Indian Division alone captured 20,000

ties. The Italians flung down grenades in thousands and, although they did not always kill, many of the Indians were wounded again and again. Seared by a sun more savage than their native land's, their wounds suppurated (untreated wounds festered within the hour) and hoards of whining flies fell upon them. Yet, unflinchingly, they held on until ultimately ordered back.

Despite the desperate ordeal of the Rajputanas, it was decided to attack Acqua Col again, as the main Keren position was so frightful that General Platt wanted to avoid a direct assault. This time an attempt would first be made to knock out the enemy's hidden artillery covering

Acqua Col, for which task an observation post was urgently needed to range the British guns.

Brig's Peak was chosen, and to capture it, Punjabis were sent up from Cameron Ridge on the afternoon of February 10. The whole divisional artillery obliterated the peak with smoke and dust ahead of them. Although the Italians had hidden behind the razor ridge and were manning the peak in strength, somehow the gasping Punjabis managed to establish themselves. All through the bitter night they lay out there, and in the grey dawn they rose and swept up and out along the easy saddle connecting Brig's Peak to the near slopes of Sanchil. With bayonet and grenade they destroyed the defenders. For a moment it seemed as though their magnificent feat of arms had fulfilled its purpose.

But the Punjabis had suffered grievously in their skyline assault; hardly one of their British officers had survived. A deluge of shells and bombs still descended on them, and soon barely two platoons survived. Some of the men had to

act as porters up and down the dizzying mountainside, precariously carrying ammunition, water, food and wounded.

The Punjabis now concentrated their dwindling strength on Brig's Peak, and a little group of artillery officers and men ran the gauntlet of fire to establish the vital O.P. They trailed out behind them the wires through which the data would be passed to the massed artillery waiting to silence the Italian guns. Meanwhile, reinforcements were moved up for the coming assault.

Darkness fell, and the mountains merged in one vast brooding bulk, blacker than the night itself. Soon, distant thunder rumbled and a storm of fire burst on the rocky spires of Brig's Peak and Sanchil, outlining them in flame against the darkness. Savage hand-to-hand fighting next ensued. It was too much for the gallant, battered Punjabis. The survivors were driven down to the refuge of Cameron Ridge. They had sustained crippling casualties, including two commanding officers, three company commanders and 280 other ranks. The Gunners' observation group was completely liquidated.

Nevertheless, it was decided the attack on Acqua Col would proceed. At 5.30 a.m., behind a heavy barrage, the Rajputanas charged up the slope. They were to find that the British shells had had little effect on the waiting Italians, who rose in hundreds from behind the rocky ridges and showered grenades upon the attackers. By desperate fighting the Indians forced them from one defended ridge, only to be confronted immediately by another. Yet, small groups fought through and seized the col itself. The stark heroism of Subedar Richpal Ram shone again like a living flame until he lost his life (and earned the Victoria Cross) high up on the slopes.

While the Rajputanas gained Acqua Col, the Sikhs swarmed up the stony, frowning heights of Sphinx. A fierce bayonet rush took the lower slope, but then they were pinned down by a torrent of grenades. Neither they nor the Rajputanas could advance farther; the Indians had reached the limits of human endurance. The waiting reinforcements were not committed, and under cover of night the survivors stole silently past the ominous, black bulk of Dologorodoc, leaving Happy Valley to a haunted peace.

There could be no dramatic breakthrough anywhere along the terrible mountain wall. General Platt and his divisional commanders were certain they could not take Keren by any method of frontal assault yet attempted, and by all the rules of warfare, Platt knew, the Keren mountain stronghold was completely impregnable. Yet it had to be taken.

Fearing imminent German intervention, General Platt realized the need for victory here. The first convoys of Western Desert troops had barely sailed to the aid of Greece when there were alarming signs that the newly arrived General Rommel, with his crack German troops, was preparing an offensive. Meanwhile, in Iraq, Raschid Ali had seized power and invoked German assistance, and in Vichy Syria airfields were being prepared for the Luftwaffe. Not only had General Platt to conquer Keren quickly, but he must see that the 4th and 5th Indian Divisions remained strong enough afterwards to meet the looming perils in the north.

Platt gave his force one month to prepare for the assault which *must* take Keren. Divisional

sappers and miners worked non-stop boring water holes, clearing deep wells, repairing captured vehicles, machinery and weapons, going out under fire to build defilade walls on the mountainside to protect the infantry so grimly hanging on there, and making paths for carrying ammunition and food up to front-line troops. Secretly, the sappers worked to clear the blocked tunnel below Cameron Ridge. And all the time, high up on the torrid Cameron Ridge, beneath the muzzles of the enemy's guns, the two battalions of infantry held on unflinchingly.

The enemy continued to make frequent attacks on Cameron Ridge, mostly night bombing raids. A desperate bitterness had entered the fighting, for in one raid an Italian officer held his hands aloft in surrender only to fling down grenades at the feet of the Highlander who stepped forward to receive him. On this particular sector the enraged Scots took no more prisoners. The spine-chilling screams of more than one Italian soldier pushed over the precipice echoed from the black abyss below Cameron Ridge. During those four weeks life continued to be perilous for the officers and men of the Royal Artillery who continued to man the death-trap O.P.s high up on the mountain slopes. There was a high casualty rate among signallers too, chiefly because destruction of field-telephone wires by shell bursts and the inadequacy of available radios among the towering mountains meant that heliographs had to be used. The helio beams stood out like searchlights, and the signallers presented all too easily identified targets.

While the 4th and 5th Indian Divisions planned a headlong frontal attack Brigadier Harold Briggs was leading a small force up to the 'back door' of Keren, compelling General Frusci to detach strong formations to protect his rear. Briggs's force comprised one battalion of the Royal Sussex and one of the Punjabis, and also a little band of Free French. In a dramatic advance they had crossed the Sudan–Eritrea frontier on the Red Sea coast, struck inland into the mountains to defeat an outpost at Cub Cub, and on March 1 had broken into the Mescelit Pass only 15 miles north-east of Keren.

The main road into Keren behind its frontal mountain barrier, however, still remained open for the enemy to draw in reserves. They came from Addis Ababa, Gondar and Metemma,

British artillerymen bombard Italian positions from a thicket on the Sudan-Eritrea border as General Platt's force goes over to the attack

from Um Hagar and other garrisons in the mountains of Eritrea and Ethiopia. The whole of the 6th Colonial Brigade marched into the fortress as did the Italians' best Blackshirt Legion, the 11th.

While the main battle for Keren loomed, spectacular advances were made elsewhere: by Orde Wingate's 300, who routed the Italians at Debra Markos; and by General Cunningham from Kenya, who covered over 1,000 miles in 30 days. Indian troops, who had landed in British Somaliland, raced inland to join Cunningham's men, and Somaliland was British once more. Later, on April 6, Addis Ababa was

to fall, and Wingate, astride a white horse, was to ride at the head of Haile Selassie's procession into his capital. But all this could not have happened had not the wasps been drawn in their thousands to the Keren honey-pot as the battle developed there.

The new assault had to be made at some place within the range of the massed British guns. This could only be somewhere along the most formidable part of the whole mountain fortress, either immediately to the left or right of the Dongolaas Gorge. General Heath, commanding 5th Indian Division, suggested that the mountain fortress of Dologorodoc itself should be stormed and from there an attack be mounted to Falestoh and Zeban. Not only would Dologorodoc provide the vital O.P., but the ground beyond, past the flanks of rising Falestoh and

*Right* As Platt's two divisions strike deep into Eritrea, the Emperor of Ethiopia, who sought refuge in Britain when the Italians seized his country, heads back to his homeland. The small force that accompanied him through mountains and jungle was commanded by Brigadier Orde Wingate

*Below* Mahratta infantry of the 5th Indian Division charge enemy defences near Agordat

Zeban, was not quite so formidable. Heath had no hesitation in naming the man to lead this desperate assault – Brigadier Messervy, commander of the successful Gazelle Force.

The new plan was this. The 4th Indian Division of General Beresford-Peirse would first attack on the left from Sanchil to Samanna, then the 5th Indian would engage on the right from Dologorodoc to Sphinx and suddenly punch hard for Dologorodoc. Once the fort had been taken the enemy domination of the gorge could be broken, and under cover of the British guns the sappers would blast away the roadblock for the tanks to head a powerful thrust through into the upland plain. To ensure maximum bombardment from the massed guns the attacks were to be consecutive, each in turn supported by the entire available artillery. Although the plan sounded simple, it entailed grave risks for so small an army. There were too few men, too few guns, too few planes, too little ammunition; above all – with the threat of German intervention looming closer each day – too little time.

The date selected, March 15, was itself significant – the Ides of March. During the four weeks of build-up all available transport was pressed into service to ferry supplies into the Ascidera Valley; even camels brought in petrol cans on their swaying backs. The 5th Indian Division was moved back from Barentu to the railhead near Kassala and underwent intensive mountain training on features almost identical to the real thing. Around a large-scale model of the Keren stronghold Messervy familiarized his brigade with every feature of the Dologorodoc heights. One heartening factor was the growing ascendancy of the R.A.F. A few newly arrived Hurricanes had, in three devastating days, burned up Italian squadrons caught on the ground at Asmara, Gura and Makalle. General Platt now also had three bomber squadrons, a fighter flight specially for close support, and one squadron and a flight of Army Co-operation aircraft based on the captured airfield at Agordat. On the eve of the battle R.A.F. Wellesleys destroyed an ammunition train bound from Asmara to Keren.

During this four weeks' lull the Italians were not idle. All the way from Acqua Col on the right to Samanna on the left still more barbed wire had been run out, much of it hidden by jutting crags and swelling outcrops, which the attackers would first have to surmount.

The full plan for the assault on the soaring mountain wall of Keren, behind which 42 battalions now awaited the attack of 19 was this: 4th Indian Division were to send in 5 Brigade and 11 Brigade against the series of dominating peaks on the left of the Dongolaas Gorge, with 11 Brigade deploying on the yawning edge of Cameron Ridge while 5 Brigade mustered on a start line 4,000 yards to their left around Mount Samanna. Because of the desperate nature of 11 Brigade's task, the Royal Fusiliers and the Rajputanas were to be held in reserve. The 5 Brigade striking force consisted of Sikhs, Punjabis, a motor machine-gun unit, and 51 Palestine Commando, a tough band of Jews and Arabs lately arrived. The Camerons were to assault the deadly crests of Brig's Peak and Sanchil while the Rajputanas were to storm Hog's Back, the high ground adjoining Brig's Peak to the west. Meanwhile, objectives for the Mahrattas were Flat Top and Mole Hill, the buttress of the main massif on the left of the Rajputanas' front. The Sikhs and the Palestine commandos were to attack Mount Samanna to hold any possible Italian outflanking move.

On the night of March 14, the 5th Indian Division moved swiftly and silently forward to mass for the assault. Messervy's 9 Brigade assembled in Happy Valley behind the foothills below Cameron Ridge. In the cold, dappled night, under the looming black mass of the mountain they had to assault, his men were well aware that theirs was the key role in the whole desperate battle.

But the crucial factor was to be the early capture of Sanchil and Brig's Peak by 4th Indian on the left. Unless these were captured 5th Indian Division were not to move, for enemy shelling from those dominating heights would devastate Messervy's men as they attacked. Zero hour for 4th Indian to open the battle was 7 a.m. At 6.30 a.m. the sun would rise over the mountains and blind the attacking troops and their artillery O.P.s, so they had to wait another half-hour for the sun to climb higher. Also, the Italians always stood-to on the crests at dawn for half an hour, after which they went back several hundred yards to breakfast. The British guns would put down a barrage between the breakfasting troops and their vacated positions. It was hoped the vital peaks would be captured by 9 a.m.

Nature set the scene in dramatic fashion. The

The awe-inspiring mountains that the British troops had to assault to capture Keren (on the plateau, top left corner). This picture shows how precarious a foothold was Cameron ridge, above its precipice, and how Fort Dologorodoc lay under the guns of Sanchil, Zeban and Falestoh.

dawn of March 15 was like no other dawn the British or Italian soldiers had experienced, glowering from ominous skies in waves of sulphurous light. Thunderstorms rumbled among the peaks, and lightning struck from the sultry air. Suddenly, as if forewarned of doom, packs of yelping baboons scampered frantically away from the topmost heights.

With a shattering roar that stunned the senses and drowned the thunder, the massed guns opened up on the 4th Indian Division objectives. From Sanchil on the right to Samanna on the left the whole crestline of mountain dissolved into fire and disappeared in billowing dust. High up on Cameron Ridge once more the order was rapped, 'Camerons, Go!', and the Scots began to clamber towards Brig's Peak and Sanchil.

As the sweating, cursing Camerons struggled up the almost sheer mountainside, ensnared and torn by wire and thorns, the Savoia Grenadiers jumped from behind huge boulders and from sangars and caves to pour murderous fire into the toiling troops. To the defending Italians it seemed impossible that anyone could survive below them, yet, as menacingly as death itself, the Scots came on; came on until, impossibly, terrifyingly, the up-reaching swathe of khaki that was dead and dying Camerons resolved itself into little groups of desperate Highlanders plying cold steel with demoniacal fury. They burst through the last wire barriers, and as they raged among the defenders they slew every man within reach.

Brig's Peak was theirs. Sanchil was theirs. At a cost of eight officers and 280 men they had gained those awful summits. But again, it was the story of too few surviving. The Italians soon recovered, and a deluge of heavy mortar and grenades and shell-fire rendered the positions untenable.

The Royal Fusiliers too set off resolutely, grimly, into the teeth of the enemy fire. But their fate was to be the same as the Camerons'. The higher they climbed the fewer survived until, in the shadows of the ultimate peaks, the leading company had only eight men left. Yet even then the remnants never gave up and all through that whole campaign, handfuls of Fusiliers and Camerons fought on from their precarious footholds on the highest slopes.

Farther to the left the Rajputanas amazingly captured Hog's Back, but lost over half the

Viewed across Happy Valley, the formidable heights that had to be stormed to reach Fort Dologorodoc

battalion. Two more companies climbed up to reinforce, so that by nightfall Hog's Back was strongly held. Still farther left, the Mahrattas carried Flat Top at bayonet point, but most were left scattered dead and wounded up the cruel slopes.

When night fell Flat Top was still held, although thinly, and a number of counter-attacks had been blasted back. Some 3,000 yards farther to the left, across a hollow which the troops had named Bloody Hell, Sikhs stormed up towards the triple peaks of Mount Samanna. They carried one crest, but the middle one proved to be a fortress of huge boulders linked with festoons of barbed wire. A deluge of fire pinned them down at perfect range for the light Italian bombs which exploded among them in the hundreds. After the bloody lesson of Acqua Col, the Sikhs had come prepared. Some had fashioned bucklers from sheets of corrugated iron which they donned as armour. One giant Sikh had six grenades explode against his armour, causing nothing worse than bruises and a headache. Yet still they could not surmount the final obstacles.

As night fell, with the surviving attackers clinging precariously to their bitterly won gains, the Italian commander brought up a fresh colonial brigade. He was well satisfied with the day's fighting. Shortly before dawn fierce counter-

89

Nowhere in the valley that they had to cross in order to reach the foot of the enemy's mountain fastness could the attackers escape coming under heavy fire. Here British infantry are under bombardment

attacks were launched all along the mountain parapet from Sanchil to Mole Hill. Below Brig's Peak the enemy clashed headlong with two companies of Rajputanas who had just arrived on Cameron Ridge. Both sides were pinned to the ground unable to advance either up or down.

On Hog's Back and Flat Top two fresh battalions of Italians surged furiously into the Mahrattas' positions but were thrown back.

But at the end of a day and night of incredible valour, the British and Indian soldiers still alive on the terrible mountain were in a precarious position indeed. To General Beresford-Peirse, as he surveyed the desperate picture and counted his division's awful losses, it suggested the fortress of Keren was going to prove impregnable after all.

Meanwhile, over on the 5th Indian Division front that thunderous day had also begun disastrously. Although the enemy was fully alerted along the whole length of the embattled mountain line, and any attack on the right must now leave a dangerously exposed left flank, General Platt decided to carry on the assault of Dologorodoc. The terrain was rugged and difficult. No sooner did the Highland Light Infantry emerge into the entrance of Dongolaas Gorge than devastating artillery fire burst among them, laced with vicious machine-gun and mortar fire from Sanchil, from the slopes above the gorge and from Dologorodoc itself. They were pinned in the open, seared by the fierce sun, and suffering the torments of thirst and heat exhaustion. As hour followed stifling hour, and the heroic attacks on the distant heights by 4th Indian Division were successively broken, the Italians were able to bring still more fire against the unfortunate Scots. They could only suffer and pray for the night.

While the H.L.I. were undergoing their ordeal by fire, Heath and Messervy crept out to where the end of Cameron Ridge overlooked the Dongolaas Gorge. Calmly they worked out a fresh plan to slip a battalion of Mahrattas across Happy Valley at last light. A sudden artillery barrage would be dropped on the 1,000 foot peak of Pinnacle, the first hill of Dologoro-

doc, and on Dologorodoc above. The barrage was to be exactly the same as for the H.L.I.'s unsuccessful daylight attack on the right. The Indian infantry, however, were to storm the mountain frontally in the darkness.

This subterfuge was to meet with considerable success, for the night barrage led the Italians again to rush their reserves to reinforce the crests on their right. Surprise, the most important factor in any attack, was the main feature. The new attack was aimed at the most precipitous part of Pinnacle, least likely to be stormed. The Mahrattas were set to capture Pinnacle and Pimple, successive peaks on the way up to Dologorodoc.

By 5 p.m. the artillery was ready. Colonel

Denys Reid, the Mahrattas' C.O., deliberately led his battalion away from the scene to deceive the enemy and give his men a good view of Pinnacle. They saw a formidable rocky mass rising abruptly from the plain, strewn with great boulders and pock-marked with black caves and thorny scrub. One small shoulder alone seemed to offer a footing. In the brief dusk the Mahrattas, tough, wiry little men, rose to their feet and crept swiftly and silently towards the sheer walls of rock. Instantly the Italian guns thundered from the mountains and hidden machine-guns opened up a destructive flanking fire.

Men fell fast, but the advance did not flag. And the Mahrattas were at the foot of the moun-tain and somehow catching at rocks and gnarled tree stumps to haul themselves upwards. As they did so, the enemy hurled down such a volume of grenades and petrol bombs that it seemed the whole face of Pinnacle had burst into flames. But the Mahrattas would not be denied even if they died to the last man. Their fearful war cry 'Shivaji ki jai!' (Victory to Shivaji) pierced the uproar and rang across the now moonlit valley. Three times the Italians blasted back the Mahrattas, but at the fourth attempt the watchers realized that the frightening war cries were com-ing from much higher – until they mingled with the screams of terror-stricken men. The Mahrattas were in among the defenders with the bayonet! Pinnacle was theirs.

Now, maintaining the impetus, Pathan and Dogra companies passed through the gallant Mahrattas and clambered on and up towards Pimple, while down in the valley, where the West Yorkshires were moving up to launch the final phase of the attack on Dologorodoc fort itself, a chunky Yorkshireman listened to the Indian war cries and muttered, 'I only hope that scares the Eyeties like it scares me!'

The Pathans and Dogras were met by a less intense fire. As they crawled closer and closer, the defenders, aware of the fate of their comrades on the lower peak, began to falter. Bayonets flashed and were still. A success signal soared. The peak was taken. Although the enemy launched a furious counter-attack down from the fort, it was held, and the Italians regrouped on the hillside to attack again at dawn.

The West Yorkshires now prepared for the final and most perilous assault – along a precarious sheer-sided rocky spine which soared from Pimple up to Dologorodoc. As stealthily as they could they crept out on to the dizzy Razor Ridge, which the Italians had considered impassable. It was nearly 5 a.m. At dawn the massed British guns were to send a pulverizing barrage on to the fort if the success signal had not been fired. As the West Yorkshires laboriously drew closer, Fort Dologorodoc stood out starkly in the bright moonlight, like a castle in one of Grimm's Fairy Tales. And then suddenly it was dawn and, in the grey light, two British platoons were revealed less than 300 feet below the fort! Almost at once the fort came to life and bullets whistled among the scattering West Yorkshires. Out on their left flank, barely 200 yards away, an enemy machine-gun nest could be seen frenziedly preparing for action. In a mad race against time a 2-inch mortar was somehow scrambled into action and fired so quickly that a second bomb was already looping up as the first burst short. The second bomb burst among the machine-gunners.

If the climb had so far been perilous, it was nothing to what the West Yorkshires experienced during the last 300 feet. The welcome crump of the British artillery below and across the valley was followed not by the expected whine of a shell passing over, but by a blinding flash among the toiling attackers, blowing some off their feet. Then another shell exploded back among the reserve platoon, and another erupted farther up the hill. Evidently the broad yellow patches, fixed to the men's backs to identify them, could not be seen from the valley. Fortunately, an artillery observation officer spotted what was happening, and the main barrage was halted in the nick of time. Even as the gunners below relaxed, men of A Company of the heroic West Yorkshires emerged from the rubble and dust around the fort and swarmed over its ramparts.

The defenders appeared dazed by the unexpected daring of this attack. The survivors fled across the jagged ground towards Falestoh and Zeban. Many fell beneath the fire of the victorious West Yorkshires, who were so delighted that some now danced on the ramparts and hurled abuse after the enemy.

Down below the Italians lying out in the open tried another attack on Pimple and Pinnacle, but being repulsed they turned and made for the sanctuary of the fort. Not until the West Yorkshires opened up on them did they realize what had happened. In their desperate plight many fought to the death until all had been either killed or captured.

In the light of the new day, the West Yorkshires took stock of their prize, on which the success or failure of the battle of Keren now depended. As a fort it was a sorry wreck indeed, little more than a concrete trench encircling a rocky, splintered hill-top. The few foxholes and dug-outs which the Italians had constructed naturally faced the wrong way for the British, and their one hope of surviving the inevitable counter-attack was to lie up behind the steep crest and man the trench only at the last minute when the attackers were nearly upon them.

Then the storm fell upon Dologorodoc like a volcano erupting. From three sides the Italians poured in a deluge of shells and mortar bombs, filling the air with sulphurous dust and a myriad splinters of hot metal and jagged fragments of rock. As two Italian battalions charged down the rugged slopes from their strongholds on Falestoh and Zeban, the British artillery struck back. Now, at last, they could fire to accurate observation from an O.P. in the fort.

Their shells exploded shatteringly 200 yards beyond the British position; then machine-guns and rifles took up the furious battle song. Bredas and brens and grenades by the hundred

*Above* While General Platt prepared his final, all-out assault on Keren, Royal Engineers successfully bored for vital water. On Dologorodoc British soldiers' tongues became black and swollen when water could not be got up to them. Here Sikhs draw water from a collapsible tank

*Left* A war artist's impression of Indian infantry on the fire-swept slopes of Keren

All available reinforcements were hurried into the Italian mountain-top fortress during the lull in the battle. Here men of a crack infantry battalion march past General Frusci, Italian Commander-in-Chief, who boasted that he would scatter the absurd English like chaff

joined in the ear-splitting cacophony, which was to continue not for one hour, nor one day, but almost constantly for ten terrible days.

To maintain troops holding this perilous place was a feat both of physical courage and endurance. Dominated by Sanchil and other peaks, Dologorodoc could only be supplied by way of the almost sheer mountainside behind the fort invisible to the enemy. Even so, anyone venturing up or down ran a gauntlet of shells and mortar bombs, and until two Cypriot mule companies arrived some days later, the West Yorkshires had to manhandle their own supplies up the mountainside. Their fighting strength was inevitably reduced.

During the first twelve most hazardous hours

Messervy ordered that ammunition should take priority even over water, while some of the thirsty men fought with their tongues hanging out black and swollen. When the mules arrived, invaluable though they were, they constituted a danger to the wounded being manhandled down. Sometimes a mule would bolt when a shell exploded, knocking wounded from stretchers often carried by six men on the arduous descent. Sometimes a mule would lose its footing and bounce down the mountain face, a pathetic bundle of flailing legs and flapping panniers, the precious water, food or ammunition scattered and lost.

All through the first day the enemy flung in counter-attack after counter-attack, but the West Yorkshires fought back unwaveringly. Sometimes a wave of Italians and Eritreans would surge to the very ramparts, but always the Yorkshiremen fought them off. The Italian Air Force reappeared, but the R.A.F. kept control of the skies.

At the end of that first desperate day on

Dologorodoc Generals Platt, Heath and Beresford-Peirse agreed that the time had come to deliver powerful and simultaneous punches on the left and the right of Dongolaas Gorge. It was to be an all-out attack to break through.

So on the 4th Indians' front 10 Brigade of 5th Indian Division was brought forward, and the Baluchis and Garhwalis set off up the fated mountain. It was the same dreadful story again as the laboriously climbing troops were met by a hail of fire. The Garhwalis suffered particularly heavily, losing all but one of their British Officers.

That night and throughout the next day furious fighting continued around Sanchil and Brig's Peak, but gradually the Garhwalis, as they became fewer and fewer, were pushed back to the lines held by the Fusiliers. On their left the Baluchis, also terribly thinned by casualties, could hold a line no nearer than 200 yards

Before the assault on Keren that *had* to succeed, British and Indian (seen here) soldiers were given intensive training in attacking up mountain slopes. Loose shale sliding away under foot was only one of the hazards

below Brig's Peak. While the Indians and their British officers fought to the death on the uppermost spires of the Keren fortress, the H.L.I. went up to strengthen the remnants of the Camerons and Fusiliers still holding the steep slopes of the col below the two peaks.

At last, with the attackers facing extermination, it was decided that they should be withdrawn. This, the third withdrawal, was to be the last. Understandably, Beresford-Peirse was depressed and pessimistic. Again he advised that without a far larger and better equipped army there could be no hope of reducing Keren. The

95

*Above* Indian Sappers and Miners plodding up a rocky height on the British side of Happy Valley to prepare gun positions. Their apparently untroubled ascent was possible because they were just out of range of the Italian artillery. The valley below them, however, was a death trap

*Opposite, top* Men of the West Yorkshire Regiment, who dramatically stormed Fort Dologorodoc, the key to the battle, face up to yet another counter-attack from amongst huge boulders

*Opposite, bottom* Behind the crest of Dologorodoc, Brigadier Messervy poses with Col. Denys Reid and an Indian jemadar during a brief lull in the incessant bombardment

Rajputanas remained on Hog's Back and the Mahrattas on Flat Top, while the surviving Camerons and Fusiliers returned to hold on in the filth and peril of Cameron Ridge. The surviving Garhwalis and Baluchis and the H.L.I. were ordered to rejoin 5th Indian Division on the other side of the gorge. The bitter end had been reached on the 4th Indian front.

While the British and Indians had been making their epic but unavailing sacrifices on the crests of Brig's Peak and Sanchil, 29 Brigade had climbed to Dologorodoc and deployed through the West Yorkshires to attack across the scarred uplands towards Falestoh and Zeban. The Worcestershires went first. By dawn they were established on a little peak about 100

Indian soldiers move across rocky uplands in the final advance on Keren

yards short of the Falestoh ridges. On their left the Punjabis attacked strongly, until pinned down by fire from Sanchil, and an hour after dawn the Frontier Force Rifles charged on the Punjabis' left flank across ground swept by fire.

As they lay out before Falestoh and Zeban through the torrid day, the pinned-down attackers were subjected to a terrible ordeal by fire and sun. Obviously this position was as untenable as Brig's Peak and Sanchil. That night the forward troops were pulled back and men of the Frontier Force Regiment came up from Pimple to hold the fire-swept ground on the West Yorkshires' right front. The ordeal on Dologorodoc was to continue for another ten days and nights. Men who survived this battle and lived through later desperate ones in North Africa, Italy and Burma, declared they never again experienced anything like the hellfire of Keren.

The Italians brought up all available reserves to liquidate the British salient. By day and night they flung in attack after attack, pulling in reinforcements from Gondar and elsewhere.

They even brought in medium tanks, to send them clattering across the rugged no-man's-land before Fort Dologorodoc. The defenders did not have to be reminded of their leader's order that 'Every man must understand that there is only one degree of resistance – to the end'.

Once a heavy Italian night attack penetrated the lines of the Frontier Force Regiment, but the Indians counter-attacked ferociously and the position was restored. Some nights later a completely fresh Italian battalion, with four medium tanks, thrust in from the rear of the Frontier Force positions after a hazardous approach along a remote track, but next morning, only Italian corpses remained in the Indian positions.

With this mountain vantage-point for their vital O.P.s the massed guns of the two divisions wrought dreadful execution. Each time the Italians gathered to attack, huge concentrations of fire fell upon them. In one such crash of gun

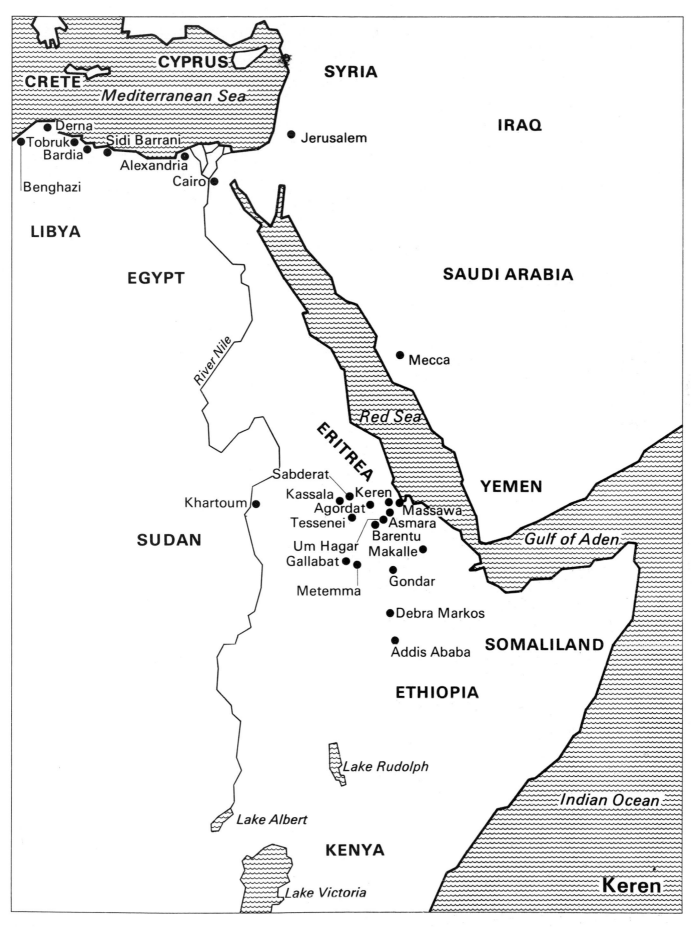

CRETE

CYPRUS

SYRIA

IRAQ

*Mediterranean Sea*

Derna
Tobruk
Bardia
Sidi Barrani
Alexandria
Cairo

Benghazi

Jerusalem

LIBYA

EGYPT

SAUDI ARABIA

*River Nile*

Mecca

ERITREA

*Red Sea*

Sabderat
Kassala
Keren
Agordat
Massawa
Khartoum
Tessenei
Asmara
Barentu
Um Hagar
Makalle
Gallabat
Metemma
Gondar

YEMEN

*Gulf of Aden*

SUDAN

Debra Markos

Addis Ababa

SOMALILAND

ETHIOPIA

*Lake Rudolph*

*Indian Ocean*

*Lake Albert*

KENYA

*Lake Victoria*

Keren

fire, the head of the brave young General Lorenzini, fiery conqueror of British Somaliland, was blown from his shoulders.

While the heroes of Dologorodoc continued to hold the key to the pass, the British commanders set about forcing it. Once the Dongolaas Gorge was opened, the tanks and bren carriers would be able to thrust into the very heart of the enemy defences. Heath was the driving force in the planning now. After he had received reports of a daring exploratory penetration of the gorge by Royal Engineers and Frontier Force Rifles he was suddenly certain that the way to victory had been discovered, through the tunnel below Cameron Ridge and out on to the foothills known as Railway Bumps, round the shoulder of Sanchil and under observation from Dologorodoc. With Dologorodoc on one side already held, the clearing of the roadblock below became feasible, if the enemy could be cleared from the bumps on the other side. But before this plan could be put into force, Heath had to wait until 10 Brigade, so savagely mauled on Sanchil, was reorganized. It was the very last reserve. Until it was ready Messervy's forces would have to stand alone on the heights against everything the enemy could hurl at them. The sappers of the 4th Indian Division now set about clearing the tunnel, which they said would take two days.

As part of 10 Brigade's reorganization a stocky little Welsh Colonel named Pete Rees was put in command. Bernard Fletcher, of the H.L.I., was given a mobile column called Fletcher Force to deliver a knock-out punch through the gorge. It was to hide under the mountain wall, awaiting the moment when the gorge should be opened. When the enemy became aware that the British were attacking Railway Bumps, the heroes of the ravaged 4th Indian Division were once more to assault those dreadful heights already littered with their dead. Meanwhile, across the gorge, Messervy's men would rise from the ruins of their fort to capture the line of hillocks half-way to Zeban and deny the enemy command of the gorge from that side. Others would then pass through them to storm Zeban itself and thrust farther east to Mount Cannabai, which dominated not only the town of Kercn, but the enemy's escape road to Asmara.

First light on March 25 was zero hour, nine days and ten nights since the West Yorkshires had captured Dologorodoc. Just before midnight on March 24, patrols of the West Yorkshires stole out to occupy one of the hillocks and Reid's Mahrattas moved silently through them to seize two hillocks to their left directly overlooking the gorge. It was past 3 a.m. when the enemy reacted. The battle flared up to fill the rocky amphitheatre once more with a fury of noise. The Italians had in fact been massing men for another powerful attack on Dologorodoc and were behind the hillocks in considerable strength. The Mahrattas found themselves embroiled in a desperate struggle, the British right swing having landed flush on the enemy's guard. Meanwhile, the surprise left swing was being delivered by Pete Rees and his men through the tunnel below Cameron Ridge.

Rees's force comprised two battalions of the H.L.I. and Baluchis. They entered the tunnel as night fell, their attack from the far end timed for 3 a.m. It was a black eerie night, relieved only by the firefly glow of drawn cigarettes and the occasional vacillating passage of a hooded torch as hot tea and rum circulated. In this macabre cavern the Indians whispered among themselves, but the Scots were in ribald good humour and burst into a raucous rendering of 'Annie Laurie'. Not wanting to subdue their good humour unless absolutely necessary, Rees tiptoed to the Italian end of the tunnel to see if they could be heard, but found the curves suppressed the sound.

Exactly what troops the enemy had on Railway Bumps was not known, but the tunnel's mouth was certain to be covered by machine-guns firing on fixed lines. When zero hour arrived, the leading company of H.L.I. emerged and swarmed up the steep embankment of the railway cutting before the enemy awoke to their danger. The other two companies followed in a bold charge along the line and simultaneously erupted along the upper ridge where the Italians were likely to be in force.

*Opposite, top* Indian soldiers take a breather on the 'safe' side of Dologorodoc as they go up to join the West Yorkshires in the mountain fort's defence

*Opposite, bottom* Achieving the apparently impossible, armoured cars are manhandled along the blasted Dongolaas gorge

Awakening to find the British apparently in their midst on the left of the gorge, the Italians at last lost their nerve. After little more than two hours' fighting, the H.L.I. and Baluchis had captured all their objectives. For the first time since the bitter battle of Keren was joined, many Italians came down from their mountain stronghold with hands raised in surrender.

With so much of the menace on the left now removed, and Messervy's men still inflexible on the opposite heights, the pay-off – the armoured punch through the gorge – became feasible. On the Dologorodoc heights at this time the Mahrattas fought onwards in the teeth of the most furious opposition and secured their objective, the hills on the right flank of the Dongolaas Gorge.

The slopes each side of the gorge were in British hands. It remained to capture the high ground known as Railway Ridge which, coming down to the gorge where it turned right towards Keren town, faced almost directly on to the roadblock. A massive artillery barrage was now directed on to this ridge, and under its cover Punjabis stormed it. The 5th Indian Division was through the gorge. At last it could be cleared!

Over on the 4th Indian Division's front the exhausted, bloodied soldiers somehow found one last reserve of strength to send out gaunt-eyed fighting patrols which compelled the enemy to face them and not Dongolaas Gorge. In the gorge entrance the sappers worked unflaggingly under frequent shell-fire to tear away the formidable barrier. Next day 4th Indian Division observers, hardly believing it themselves, reported that they thought some Italian artillery had moved back. Then 10 Brigade vantage points reported movements of troops and equipment back towards the Keren plain. Next, the dour West Yorkshires beyond Dologorodoc reported with surprise that hardly anyone seemed to be shooting at them. There could be little doubt that Heath's plan had achieved success. The impregnable fortress of Keren was about to fall.

The Italians made their last effort to save the day on the afternoon of March 26. Supported by tanks and heavy artillery, they charged the

Soldiers of an Italian native brigade march through Addis Ababa again – this time as some of the 40,000 prisoners taken

Punjabi lines on Railway Ridge but were driven back. Across the gorge three strong attacks fell upon the Mahrattas. They too held fast. The battle was nearly over.

At 4.30 a.m. on March 27, in pitch blackness, the granite peaks of Zeban and Falestoh once more erupted in smoke and flame as the British guns thundered. It was the signal for the Worcestershires and Garhwalis to go in for the final assault. For the first time since the battle began 53 days earlier, the Italians did not fight back. At 6 a.m., while the towering black mountain fortress brooded in an eerie silence, the first golden rays of the sun shone on something the attackers had feared they would never see – the white flag of surrender.

It was a moment of deep emotion both for the British and for the courageous Italian troops who had stood and fought so staunchly on those awful peaks.

Down in the Dongolaas Gorge the sappers had that night completed a 12-foot-wide roadway through, and Fletcher Force now rumbled out to deliver the *coup de grâce*. At 10 a.m. they reached the Keren plain to find the enemy gone. Fletcher Force was ordered to pursue at top speed.

The West Yorkshires left their positions to join in the general advance and were ordered to assemble in a wadi full of the bloated corpses of Italian and Eritrean soldiers, dead horses and mules, and shattered light tanks and armoured cars. All bore testimony to the ferocity of the fighting around Dologorodoc. In that ravine of death the West Yorkshires were now permitted to rest.

Keren was a glorious victory against tremendous odds and over as formidable a natural fortress as man had ever been called upon to conquer. It was a victory brought about by heroic fighting against bitter opposition. An experienced commander, General Donald Bateman, a brigade major at Keren and later brigade commander at Cassino, said at the war's end: 'No German paratrooper on Cassino ever fought more determinedly than the Italian soldiers on Keren. There is no doubt in my mind, from experience of both, that Keren was the tougher battle'. Yet, because in those days Britain was facing invasion and attention was soon diverted by Rommel's war in the North African Desert, this battle, one of the most

significant victories of the Second World War, has remained almost unknown. When special campaign stars were awarded there were none for those who had taken part in this battle.

As a direct result of the Battle of Keren, Asmara fell on April 1. A week later Massawa surrendered. The whole of Eritrea was in British hands and Wavell was able to move the 4th Indian Division at once to Egypt, where it played a decisive part in checking the German advance across Cyrenaica. Between January 19 and April 8 some 65 Italian battalions ceased to exist and over 40,000 prisoners and 300 guns were captured. In addition, tens of thousands

of African troops deserted the Italians. Cunningham's forces entered Addis Ababa from the south on April 6 so that, with the capture of Massawa on April 8, Italian power ceased to exist in East Africa. The threat to the British rear in the Middle East was removed. A new air route across Africa and the sea route by the Red Sea were assured as channels of reinforcements. Because the Red Sea now became officially a non-belligerent area, President Roosevelt was able to authorize United States vessels to sail through it with supplies vital to the British cause. With all of this now possible, ultimate victory in the Middle East was a real prospect.

*Above* A memorial service for British and Indian dead after the battle of Keren. The 4th and 5th Indian Divisions suffered nearly 5,000 casualties in dead and wounded

*Opposite* page Truck-borne troops of Gazelle Force hot on the heels of the retreating Italians

# 4. Operation Crusader

# 4. Operation Crusader

The complete destruction of the Italian forces in Cyrenaica and the British advance across North Africa between December 9, 1940, and February 9, 1941, raised British hopes that resistance to Axis encroachment in the Balkans would harden. To this desirable development, the 'desert flank' in North Africa, as Churchill called it, was vital. The importance of securing the desert was impressed upon General Wavell.

After reports that German troops had landed in Italian Tripolitania Wavell advised the chiefs of staff, on February 27, that there was no evidence of more than one German armoured brigade in Tripoli, and in view of the vast and arid Libyan desert he did not expect any appreciable German intervention 'in the near future'. It was 646 miles from Tripoli to Benghazi (the main British forward base) and 471 miles to El Agheila on the Tripolitania–Libyan frontier, the western gateway to the vast Libyan desert. Wavell expected no German–Italian offensive before the end of the summer, and he considered three or four divisions to be the maximum force which could be maintained from Tripoli over such vast desert distances.

At the end of February, therefore, the main British forces were withdrawn to rest and re-equip, to be replaced by new formations not fully trained and short of heavy equipment.

On March 1 German Panzer columns rumbled into Bulgaria and on to the Greek frontier. British, Australian and New Zealand divisions began to move into Greece on March 5. Seven R.A.F. squadrons, comprising 80 warplanes, had already joined battle with the enemy over Greece and Albania. The bulk of the Greek army was fighting the Italians in Albania, having beaten back their attempted invasion of Greece.

But from the moment the Germans hurled in the full weight of 15 divisions, the British army of 53,000 stood little chance, and they were forced to evacuate by the end of April. About 80 per cent of the troops were taken off in a minor Dunkirk operation, but most of their tanks, guns and transport were lost.

While this battle was joined in Greece, the German armour in Tripolitania under the command of General Erwin Rommel made a daring foray into Libya on April 1. Simultaneously, large numbers of German aircraft from Tripoli, Sicily and the Dodecanese islands began to attack the scattered British formations in the desert. Wavell was compelled to order a withdrawal to Benghazi. But the disorganized and scattered British armour was soon defeated in detail by Rommel's powerfully concentrated

*Above* General Sir Claude Auchinleck confers with General Sir Archibald Wavell, whom he superseded as Commander-in-Chief, Middle East. Wavell, who became Commander-in-Chief, India, had at one time conducted five major campaigns simultaneously in the Middle East with a minimum of troops, tanks and guns

*Opposite page* An aerial view of Tobruk, which became a symbol of British resistance and whose capture obsessed Rommel

*Above* Trucks of the Long-Range Desert Group in the great sand sea which bounded the desert battlefield on its southern flank

*Opposite page* Men of the Long-Range Desert Group, which came to dominate the North African desert

force. Benghazi became untenable. Soon the British were in headlong retreat and, by April 11, back on the Egyptian frontier. General O'Connor, commanding British troops in Egypt, and General Neame, commanding in Libya, were both captured.

'There'll be consternation amongst our masters in Tripoli and Rome and perhaps in Berlin too,' Rommel wrote. 'I took the risk against all orders because the opportunity seemed favourable. . .'

But Rommel could not get farther than the Egyptian frontier until he had removed the thorn in his flank that was Tobruk. There for many months his increasingly powerful investing force was to be defied and beaten back by an Anglo–Australian garrison of 23,000, reinforced by sea, in a siege that became an epic of the war.

Meanwhile more troops, including the 4th Indian Division from Keren, barred his path to the Nile delta, and British tank reinforcements arrived in the nick of time in a daring convoy direct through the Mediterranean. Strengthened by this armour Wavell mounted a limited offensive by 7th Armoured Division and 4th Indian in mid-June. But Rommel, well briefed by his Intelligence, was expecting them. The attack was beaten back with the loss of much of the precious armour. There was one good thing

about this Operation Battleaxe, as it was called. It increased Rommel's urge to take Tobruk and distracted him from more important developments, such as the reinforcement of the British Desert Army and Air Force.

The failure of Battleaxe proved fatal to Wavell. Churchill had anticipated a resounding triumph, not a dismal defeat. He spent hours wandering disconsolately in the valley at Chartwell and made up his mind that Wavell must go.

This decision came after Wavell had conducted six major campaigns between February 7 and July 14, 1941, with resources so slender that he was frequently compelled to juggle with single battle-scarred divisions between one theatre and another.

As the mauled Western Desert Force licked its wounds on Egypt's burning plains there came news that electrified British and Germans – the massive German invasion of Soviet Russia had begun. Britain no longer defied the full might

of the Axis alone! In the desert, it was now a question of who would recover first. The British built fortifications at Baqqush in case Rommel attacked first. Sixty miles back, where nature had provided a natural bottleneck between the sea and the impassable Qattara Depression, they constructed a final fight-to-the-finish line. It was a remote spot where a little railway station bore the name El Alamein.

Rommel obtained permission to launch an all-out onslaught on November 23 to overwhelm the obstinate fortress of Tobruk, but while he was completing his plan of attack the British Desert Force, now designated the 8th Army, struck the first blow. The operation was code-named Crusader.

The 8th Army's commander was General Alan Cunningham, chosen by Auchinleck (Wavell's successor) because of his spectacular advance from Kenya and his conduct of the ultimate, victorious battles in Ethiopia. Winston Churchill and his chiefs of staff had wanted General Maitland ('Jumbo') Wilson, who had commanded the British forces in Greece and led the victorious Syrian campaign against the Vichy French. 'We were all very sorry that we could not persuade Auchinleck to entrust the battle, when it should come, to General Maitland Wilson', Churchill afterwards wrote. Auchinleck had apparently been so dazzled by the rapidity of Cunningham's advance in East Africa that he had not appreciated what alone had made it possible – the epic contest at Keren. Cunningham had only had to contend with Italians either already on the run or shaken in their morale by the events at Keren.

Operation Crusader started shortly before first light on November 18, 1941. To a sulphurous overture of thunder, vivid lightning and pouring rain the British 8th Army surged westwards across the North African desert in a vast wheeled and tracked armada of 10,000 vehicles

and 100,000 men. Its main object was to seek out and destroy the crack German Afrika Korps. Unfortunately at this time few senior British officers had experience of handling armour in battle or fully understood the administrative problems. But the troops were heartened by Churchill's assurance: 'For the first time British and Empire troops will meet the German with an ample equipment in modern weapons of all kinds. Now is the time to strike the hardest blow yet struck for final victory, home and freedom'.

The 8th Army needed such an assurance from the top. Although their morale was high, they had no illusions about the superiority of the tanks and anti tank guns of the Afrika Korps hitherto. The slow British Matilda and Valentine infantry tanks were just no match for their German counterparts, the fast, powerfully gunned Mark III and Mark IV Panzers. Apart from the disparity in speed, the British tanks could fire nothing more lethal than a 2-pound shell, while the lightest projectile fired by a German tank was a $4\frac{1}{2}$-pounder, and the heaviest

*Above* Field-Marshal Erwin Rommel, whose brilliant leadership of the German Afrika Korps in the desert earned him the name of 'the Desert Fox'

*Opposite, top* British Matilda infantry tanks in line astern. Although heavily armoured they were slow-moving and under-gunned

*Opposite, bottom* A British Matilda tank moves towards the enemy as shell-fire erupts all around in the confused desert fighting. An 8th Army officer, meanwhile, observes from the cover of his truck. The flat, gravelly Libyan plateau provided good going for wheeled and tracked vehicles alike

a terrifying 14-pounder. In addition, the panzers had formidable screens of mobile long-range anti-tank guns, behind which they could withdraw when hard pressed.

Despite the sinking of half his reinforcements by the British navy and air force, Rommel had

built up his force to 11 divisions. The full strategic potential of North Africa was now apparent to Hitler, who was determined to retrieve the dangerous situation created by Wavell's crushing defeat of the Italians. Hitler not only approved the return to the Mediterranean of all Italian submarines helping the German navy in the Atlantic, but he ordered 27 U-boats from the Atlantic to the Mediterranean, with flotillas of motor torpedo boats and minesweepers. He also ordered the headquarters of Luftflotte 2 and Fliegerkorps 11 with its defences and long-range night fighters to be transferred from Russia.

The Afrika Korps comprised 15 and 21 Panzer Divisions and 90 Light Divisions, backed by two complete corps of Italians. Four divisions were besieging Tobruk, while six were massed for the decisive onslaught on this fortress and the ensuing all-out attack on Egypt. This powerful army was established in strongly fortified encampments, girt about with minefields stretching in huge crescents from Tobruk to a point 30 miles deep in the desert, then curving back to Halfaya. On the outer arc of the crescent Rommel's fortresses were deeply dug, flush with the ground and barely discernible. They bristled with machine-guns and artillery, including the dreaded high velocity 88-mm anti-aircraft guns in an anti-tank role. These fortresses were at El Gubi deep in the desert, at El Adem on the threshold of Tobruk, and above all at the Omars south-west of Capuzzo, three formidable positions called Libyan Omar, Omar Nuovo and Cova.

These desert strongholds were intended, if attacked, to wreak maximum execution and hold fast until the tank fleets swept up. As the ultimate weapon of destruction Rommel's massed Panzers roamed the 3,000 square miles of his defended area, ready to descend on whoever dared enter. Meanwhile, the fortresses must first be overcome should the British seek to drive the Afrika Korps out. Rommel's army was, in fact, in a very strong position. Behind lay the sea, on the eastern flank a towering escarpment, and on the western flank Tripolitania and Vichy France's vast territories of Tunisia and Algeria. An attack could come only from the south, deep in the desert. To win the battle the British armour would have to defeat the Afrika Korps' massed armour which, as

Rommel knew, could shatter any number of outgunned British armoured columns engaged separately.

The 8th Army tanks now numbered 756. They were 336 cruisers (mostly Crusaders), 195 Honeys and 225 'I' tanks (Matildas and Valentines). Rommel's German tank force, although totalling only 320, had a formidable, hard core of 174 heavy 'battleship' Mark IIIs and Mark IVs.

Of the British total, 90 were sealed off within Tobruk, serving as mobile pillboxes. The Honeys were powered by a radial aircraft engine which required high-octane aviation spirit. They were light and very fast American tanks with heavier frontal armour but small-calibre cannon. The new British Crusader tank, although it had quite a good turn of speed, was as seriously underarmoured and undergunned as its predecessors. Meanwhile, since the last tank clash in the abortive Battleaxe operation, the Panzers' frontal armour had been greatly increased. A one-sided fight between destroyers and battleships again seemed inevitable.

The Germans' most significant advantage was the greatly increased number of long-barrelled Pak 38 50-mm anti-tank guns with far greater penetration than the British 2-pounders. Coupled with the terrifying 88s, they formed a formidable artillery group – in itself a potent weapon capable of deciding a pitched battle.

The 8th Army moved out divided into two corps – the 13th under Lieutenant-General A. R. Godwin-Austen, and the 30th under Lieutenant-General Willoughby Norrie. The former comprised the 4th Indian and 2nd New Zealand Divisions together with the 1st Army Tank Brigade; 30 Corps comprised 7th Armoured Division, and 1st South African Division and 22 Guards Brigade. Lieutenant-General W. H. W. ('Strafer') Gott was in command of 7th Armoured, and 4th Indian were commanded by Major-General Frank Messervy, promoted since his heroic stand on Keren's Dologorodoc.

The more powerful 30 Corps, containing the bulk of the armour, was to sweep across the desert, seek out and defeat Rommel's armour, and relieve Tobruk. At the crucial moment the defenders of Tobruk would burst out and join the attackers.

Italian anti-tank gunners go into action as British armour is reported to be approaching

As the great British army thundered westwards across the desert the enemy was astonishingly unready to meet the attackers. In fact Rommel, that forceful commander whose cunning earned him the name of 'Desert Fox', nearly missed being there to receive them, having just returned from the headquarters of the High Command in Rome.

The terrain into which the armoured 30 Corps thrust out ahead of the 8th Army was the wide and desolate Libyan plateau. This scorched plateau was barren and gently rolling, almost everywhere suitable for mobile war, and for that reason it was to become the most fought-over battleground of the Second World War. To reach it from the Egyptian desert, a towering escarpment had first to be penetrated. There

were only three ways for vehicles to pass it – at the Mediterranean's edge at Sollum, at Halfaya farther inland (the 'Hellfire Pass'), and much farther south at a place called Halfway House. The Germans held the main passes in strength, particularly Halfaya. The German armour was massed in the vicinity of Tobruk in readiness for Rommel's all-out onslaught on the beleaguered fortress.

As the British armour surged onwards some 80 miles south of the Mediterranean, only the roar and clangour of their passing disturbed the eternal desert silence. Not even the groan of a German reconnaissance aircraft, nor the throb of an enemy scout car, added to the omnipotent mutter of the advancing armoured host. At 10.15 a.m. South African armoured cars had the first brush with the enemy, a powerfully gunned small formation of Rommel's farthest-flung roving reconnaissance unit. The foremost armoured cars of the King's Dragoon Guards and the 11th Hussars also came under fleeting fire from enemy mobile outposts.

Around mid-day the tanks of 7th Armoured Brigade advanced towards Sidi Rezegh, a natural arena on an escarpment above Tobruk. Behind its screen of armoured cars the brigade crossed the Trig el Abd, an old slave-caravan trail across the desert, and reached its objective for the day, a few miles north-west of Gabr Saleh. To the east the 4th Armoured Brigade also attained its objective with only slight skirmishing. But away on the left 22nd Armoured Brigade was still ten miles from its objective when it halted at the day's end. Meanwhile the South African Division crossed the frontier 30 miles south-west of Maddalena to cover the west flank of 30 Corps.

While this formidable British force was going through the first moves of encircling them against the sea, the German–Italian forces appeared ignorant of the impending danger. It was not until half an hour before sunset that an alarming message was received from the reconnaissance unit that '200 British tanks' were advancing. But beyond strengthening the outer scouting troops, Rommel dismissed the approaching 8th Army as a reconnaissance in force and pressed on with his preparations to attack Tobruk.

Early the following morning, while 22 Armoured Brigade was converging on the objective it had failed to reach before nightfall, it was ordered by Gott to attack Bir el Gubi, where the Italian Ariete Armoured Division was believed to be. As the full noonday heat began to conjure up shimmering mirages of fantastic palaces and oases the Gloucestershire Hussars, followed by two regiments of the County of London Yeomanry, charged full tilt into a force of Italian tanks. A ferocious pitched battle erupted between this one brigade of the 7th Armoured Division and the whole of the Italian Ariete Division, which was certainly *not* according to plan. The hell-for-leather, cavalry-style charge of the gallant but over-eager yeomanry regiments of 22 Armoured Brigade cost the 8th Army dear, not for the only time. With the Italian anti-tank artillery well camouflaged and dug in, and their tanks hull down behind rolling dunes, the British armour suffered heavily. It had, indeed, been squandered on

*Above* A swarm of Stuka dive-bombers on the look-out for shipping supplying the British garrison in Tobruk

*Opposite page* Italian tanks in a depression in the desert. Note the sandbags heaped on the front of each tank, placed there to make them less vulnerable to anti-tank shells

Italian tanks and guns when it should have been reserved for the full-scale armoured onslaught on the powerful Afrika Korps. The Brigade lost 50 per cent of their tanks, a total of 82. At least 30 of these were out of action through mechanical failure (the Crusader cruisers were particularly unreliable). Many Italians who had surrendered as the British tanks burst into their positions returned to the battle when no supporting infantry came to take them away.

Meanwhile 30 Corps boldly sought to incite Rommel's armour to battle by drawing a horseshoe-shaped cordon around it from Maddalena to beyond the outskirts of Tobruk. The

4th Indian Division contained the enemy desert fortresses of the Omars, and the New Zealand Division began its sweep along the coast road through Gambut to link up with the out-bursting Tobruk garrison. Far away to the south, from Jarabub oasis, a diversionary force composed largely of Indian troops attacked the Italian-held fortress oasis of Jalo.

As the second day of the Crusader offensive drew to a close with the main battle still not joined, Cunningham ordered 7th Armoured Brigade alone to advance on Sidi Rezegh, instructing 4th Armoured Brigade to maintain its limited operations east of Gabr Saleh. The remarkable surprise achieved by the 8th Army militated against the British: faced by no German reaction at all, General Cunningham was at a loss. While Rommel seemed unaware of his danger, Cunningham did not know what to do.

On the third day the Afrika Korps reacted at last to the challenge at Sidi Rezegh, and bitter tank fighting ensued. Finally convinced he had

a full-scale British attack to cope with, Rommel sent a powerful tank force to Gabr Saleh with orders to destroy the enemy there. Thus Rommel, too, was splitting up his armoured force. This battle group was about equal in numbers to the armoured brigade commanded by Brigadier Alec Gatehouse which it was challenging. It was, however, vastly superior in gun power and in mobile heavy-calibre anti-tank artillery. In the last glowering light of November 19, against a murky backcloth of looming rain clouds, the two forces clashed head-on.

As artillery roared out its challenge, the desert arena boiled up into a furious forest of mushrooming shell-bursts. Then, the British tanks charged. The light American-built Honeys hurtled towards the enemy at 40 mph, weaving, zigzagging and cascading out great wakes of sand. Aware that the German guns outranged him by a full half-mile, Gatehouse risked all with this charge, hoping sheer speed and

manoeuvrability would carry him through. At killing distance the gunners in the Honeys did kill, but when they got back to their starting point, they were less some 30 of their original number.

That same afternoon Brigadier Jock Campbell's Support Group had spearheaded 7th Armoured Brigade's advance on Sidi Rezegh, deliberately provoking the whole of the Afrika Korps to attack. They had surprised the enemy there and had seized the airfield, armoured cars and tanks of the 6th Royal Tanks plunging down from the escarpment so swiftly that they shot up and burned enemy planes caught on the ground. The orders for the Support Group were to hold the area as a pivot of manoeuvre for the main force of tanks when the enemy came up. At the same time they had to threaten the enemy's communications between Tobruk and the frontier.

This bold action certainly did provoke Rommel's Afrika Korps. Rommel at last called off the Tobruk attack and began to concentrate his scattered armour. He determined to make a massive armoured onslaught to destroy any British tanks that might confront him, then

*Above* German 'soft-skinned' vehicles on the move in the wake of the Panzers as they raced towards Egypt in the surprise move which became known as 'Rommel's Swan'

*Opposite, top* A British artillery shell bursts among infantry of the Afrika Korps on the stony desert, where there was no place to hide

*Opposite, bottom* Junkers Ju 88s head for Tobruk in the early days of the Crusader battle

punch out westwards to give himself room to manoeuvre in the desert.

Rommel had not realized his peril until the evening of November 20, when he was visibly shocked to hear a B.B.C. news bulletin that 'the 8th Army, with about 75,000 men excellently armed and equipped, has started a general offensive with the aim of destroying the German–Italian forces in Cyrenaica'. Straightway, he ordered 15 Panzer Division to cease fighting Gatehouse's 4th Armoured Brigade and, with 21 Panzer Division, 'to attack and destroy the enemy force which has advanced on Tobruk'.

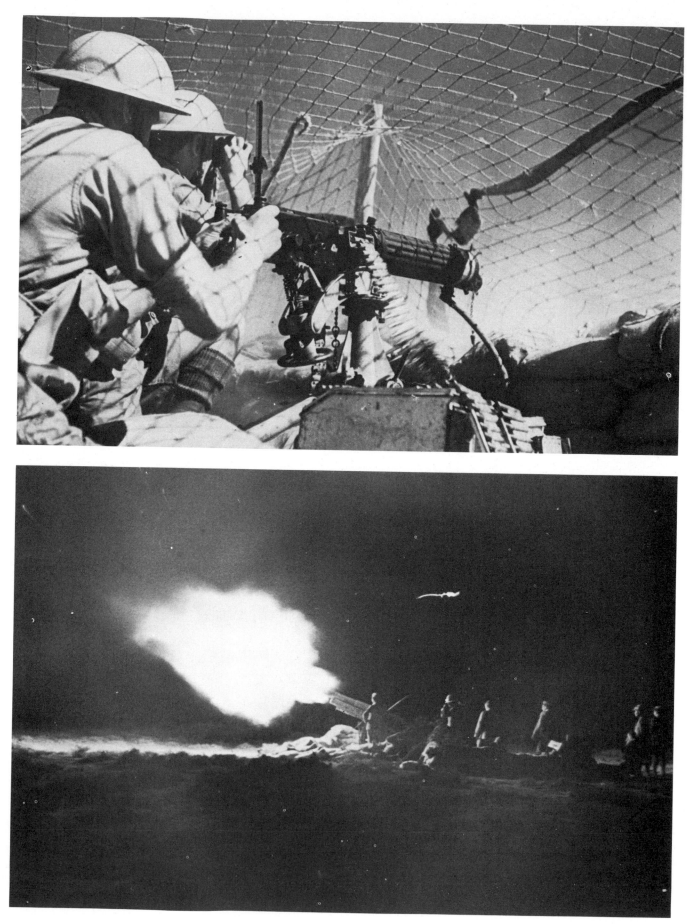

For the 4th Indian Division and the New Zealanders in 13 Corps the Crusader operation had started uneventfully. Unaware of increasing calamities in the west – communications between 30 Corps and 13 Corps were spasmodic in the ensuing confusion – Messervy pressed Cunningham to let his brigade attack the Omars. It was irksome to have to sit down outside the Omars when their capture would give the 8th Army an island fortress in the vast wilderness over which the armoured fleets were to decide the issue. If the worst happened, the 8th Army would have a rallying point in the midst of the battle. Messervy also had a strong (and correct) hunch that Rommel intended to use the obviously well-stocked Omars to replenish his Panzers on the field of battle. Had Messervy not convinced Cunningham that the Omars should be captured, the ultimate outcome of Operation Crusader could well have been disaster for Britain.

The three positions known as the Omars were roughly two miles apart, each on slightly rising ground. They had been prepared with great skill and ingenuity, and each position was encircled with minefields. They were garrisoned by the complete Savona Division, stiffened with crack German units including batteries of the terrible 88s.

The Royal Sussex were to open the battle by attacking the keystone position, Omar Nuovo's two by one and a half miles of fortifications. Next, Punjabis would fall upon Libyan Omar while Sikhs would mask Cova and New Zealanders would watch over things in the north.

The first fury fell upon Omar Nuovo at dawn on November 22, with an artillery barrage synchronized with bombing by the R.A.F. bombers. Meanwhile, a smoke-screen was laid to blind the Italian artillery spotters in Libyan Omar.

As the men of the Sussex moved up in lorries, they saw against the horizon the uprising ladders of enemy artillery spotters. Suddenly, they felt exposed and helpless, careering in towards the hidden guns. In a matter of moments three carriers and four tanks were blown up. Although it took more than a mine to knock out a Matilda, tracks were blown off within point-blank range of the hidden 88s, which now did dreadful execution among them. As the crippled tanks carried no H.E. (high-explosive) shell, they could only machine-gun the gun-positions unavailingly. The second echelon of tanks ran on to the mines to suffer a similar fate. Only two got through.

Despite this calamity the surviving carriers managed to charge through with the surviving tanks, followed by infantry. Men surged in with the bayonet and ferocious hand-to-hand fighting followed. Then Italians began to emerge from their almost invisible slit-trenches with hands raised. All resistance had been overcome by 5 p.m., at the cost of 200 casualties (50 per cent).

While the Sussex were still mopping up, the Punjabis headed by tanks and covered by an artillery bombardment, attacked Libyan Omar. An apparent gap in the minefield was a trap, which was covered by a dug-in battery of 88s. At 800-yard range they could not miss. The leading tanks erupted into horrible, flaming wrecks. As the second squadron of tanks swung away from this intolerable fire, they fouled the minefield and were blown to bits by the fire of the German guns. There were only five tanks still in action when the Punjabis hurled themselves at the fire-breathing fortress. By nightfall they had penetrated several hundred yards on the eastern side.

Next day a company of Sikhs came to help the Punjabis, and at the end of two days, one third of Libyan Omar was in their hands. But for a whole week enemy positions were to hold out, so that Libyan Omar remained a place of danger. Meanwhile the New Zealanders, intent on raising the siege of Tobruk, had pushed on northwards without opposition, leaving the flank of 7 Brigade uncovered, and Messervy called in 5 Brigade, which was in reserve near Sidi Barrani.

Elsewhere, disaster had overtaken 8th Army at Sidi Rezegh on November 23. The desert amphitheatre was contained by a sun-scorched rocky ridge, with a gradually sloping valley to the north which at its far side rose again to a

plateau on which the ancient tomb of Sidi Rezegh gauntly stood. On this plateau the airfield was situated. The ground was flat to south and west.

The infantry and artillery of 7 Support Group which had seized the airfield at Sidi Rezegh watched the rolling dust cloud that was the advancing armour of the Afrika Korps, too thick at first for individual tanks to be picked out. As it drew closer and silhouettes appeared, the guns steadily took toll, but firing as it came, the terrific mass of armour thundered on. The gunners ran out of solid shot and anything that could be fired was fired into the advancing tanks. When the end seemed near, the Panzers broke, and left the field strewn with blazing wrecks. But attacks by German armour increased in intensity as the day wore on. Shelled, battered from the air and machine-gunned by infantry, the gunners steadily fought back. Infantry positions were heavily attacked and overrun by tanks. A troop of field guns, moved up to the airfield to deal with these tanks, was overrun and destroyed. Then, at last, through

As seen through German eyes – clouds of smoke and sand billow up from the battlefield under bombardment. Note the boundary wire which Mussolini had caused to be erected, stretching from the sea deep into the desert on the Libya–Egypt border

the gun positions came British tanks, and the exhausted gunners relaxed. But the relief was short, for the British tanks were hopelessly outgunned, and one after the other went up in flames. As their remnants limped from the battlefield it was left once more to the gunners.

The extent of the devastation, which spread as far as the eye could see was appalling. Captain Cyril Joly, commanding a squadron of Honeys in 4th Armoured Brigade, described how dead and dying were strewn all over the battlefield, in trucks and bren carriers, in trenches or toppled over the trails of their guns, some silent and grey in death, others groaning with pain. The desert was stained dark with blood, and in shattered bodies white stumps of bone showed brightly against the dark brown of dried blood. Trucks, ammunition, odd bits of clothing smouldered

Armoured troop-carriers, motorcyclists and other German vehicles sweep across the desert. The smoke comes from burning tanks and trucks beyond them

or burned; here and there ammunition exploded with spurts of flame and black smoke. Tanks of all kinds – Italian, German and British – littered the whole area, facing all ways, intermingled, blackened by fire or distorted by explosion.

The first, most savage phase of Operation Crusader had ended by nightfall on November 23. At Sidi Rezegh 'Strafer' Gott had barely a dozen tanks left of the hundred he had committed to the battle. From El Adem in the north and from the jagged Tobruk escarpment the Germans were heavily attacking. As night fell, approaching Verey lights from the west revealed them closing in from that direction too. Yet at this moment a British military spokesman in Cairo told the world: 'We have the beast's head in the bag and he is still lashing with his tail'!

Rommel gathered together the main force of his armour for the most fantastic thrust of his career. Deserting the field of victory he stormed eastwards on what was to become known variously as 'Rommel's Dash to the Wire' and 'Rommel's Swan'. His exact orders were,

'Afrika Korps' task is to co-operate with the Italian Motorized Corps, bottle-up and destroy the enemy east of the Sollum front, west of the Sollum front, and at Bardia'. He was set on the utter destruction of the 8th Army's other corps. What Rommel did not know, however, was that 4th Indian Division had already broken into the Omars and was ready for the Panzers.

But Cunningham was thinking of breaking off. In conference with 'the Auk' he made it clear that he thought the battle lost; the 8th Army should retreat to preserve Egypt. Auchinleck was unperturbed. He dismissed Rommel's dash as of no strategic importance and re-emphasized the original purpose of Crusader, to 'destroy the enemy and drive him out of Cyrenaica'. He returned to Cairo, sacked Cunningham and replaced him 'temporarily' with his own deputy chief of staff, General Neil Ritchie.

The 4th Indian Division first learned of the disaster in the west by radio. Soon they observed shoals of soft-skinned transport fleeing for the gaps in the frontier wire. Rommel's massed Panzers were rumbling eastwards along the Trigh El Abd. The worst was confirmed when 30 Corps H.Q. arrived seeking sanctuary, and telling how Rommel's armour in terrible strength was loose on the battlefield.

The British vehicles streaming eastwards were intent only on escape. Bewildered drivers drove in undisciplined swarms of vehicles. Confusion heaped on confusion, tragedy on tragedy. The dust stirred up by the panic flight, ironically named the 'November Handicap', rolled in great clouds that hid the sun. The R.A.F. turned up on the battlefield in full strength in an effort to halt Rommel's Panzers, but – with pursuers and pursued so impossibly mixed up – they had difficulty in telling friend from foe.

Messervy's insistence on capturing the Omar fortresses now proved the salvation of the 8th Army. He pulled his troops in close about him and stood to face the holocaust. Apart from Tobruk, reinforced by some New Zealanders, the determined concentration of his 4th Indian

*Opposite, top* Just how vulnerable the infantry soldiers were if caught by tanks in the desert is shown by these British soldiers awaiting an enemy attack in the only cover available to them – a shallow depression in the sand

*Opposite, bottom* General Sir Frank Messervy, whose decision to capture the enemy desert fortresses at the Omars played such a decisive part in the battle

*Top* German tanks ablaze in a corner of the battlefield of Sidi Rezegh, scene of some of the bloodiest fighting of the desert war

*Above* A German photograph showing a recovery team inspecting a hopelessly damaged tank on the battlefield by night

Division seemed to be the only major British bastion in a far-flung battlefield of utter confusion. Curiously enough the coming of night helped Messervy establish the whereabouts of his enemies, if not his friends. The various German Panzer groups fired brilliant, coloured signals to tell each other where they were. They told Messervy quite clearly that he was right in the middle of them all!

At first light the main mass of enemy armour moved again. One powerful Panzer force rumbled on to the gap in the frontier wire at Sheferzen but was held off by seven hastily repaired Matildas, which only withdrew much later, when Panzers forced through farther south to outflank them. Their dogged fight against such heavy odds gave 4th Indian Division invaluable extra time. Some units that had still been outside the Omar fortifications just managed to slip inside.

At 7 a.m., an armoured car raced up reporting a strong enemy tank force approaching. The gunners out on the wide stony desert coolly prepared to stand in the path of the invincible Panzers. Silently the officers and men deployed their 25-pounders in batteries in echelon. Then, as there was no time to dig slit-trenches, they calmly lay down to wait. Soon the sinister squat shapes of the Panzers – the heavy Mark IIIs and Mark IVs – loomed over the horizon. They made no armoured bull-rush upon the exposed artillery. Instead, 28 tanks spread out in fleet formation of lines, five abreast, 30 yards between each tank and 70 yards between each rank, so that all could fire at the same time.

It seemed an age before the unusually cautious Panzers had crept to within 2,000 yards, then they halted and opened fire. The gunners did not move. After the first blaze of shell-fire the Panzers ground forward again, halted, relaid and fired with cannon and long-range machine-guns. Still the gunners did not move. Then the Panzers rumbled forward once more. It became apparent that they were converging

*Top* A British 2-inch anti-tank gun in action. They proved hopelessly inadequate to deal with the powerfully gunned and armoured Afrika Korps Panzers

*Bottom* Armoured warfare in the Libyan desert was likened to naval engagements, and these German tanks could well be warships at sea

on 52 Battery on the extreme left; obviously, they were going to liquidate the batteries one by one. The Panzers crept closer and closer. One gun was hit, then another. Casualties mounted. Only when the Panzers had closed to 800 yards and were poised for the final crushing charge did the order 'Fire!' ring out from the guns. Those prone men who were still alive leaped to their feet and the 25-pounders crashed back their defiance.

For ten minutes all was sound and fury, the sharp crack of the tanks' 75-mm cannons and the deeper note of the British guns building up to a crescendo. One by one the Panzers broke formation, seeking cover behind a low ridge 400 yards away. Hull down, ten tanks in line, the Panzers continued the battle. With no vestige of cover, the gunners fired back defiantly, and when the Panzers roared over the ridge down upon the guns of 52 Battery the gunners, loading and firing, loading and firing, drove them off. Seven shattered tanks remained to prove the efficiency of the British 25-pounders.

A Sikh water-carrier, one Rattan Singh, veteran of Keren, added an incongruous touch to the scene. He had been preparing breakfast in a slit-trench for his comrades before the Sikhs withdrew on the Panzers' approach. He had been 'too busy', so had remained out between guns and tanks with the fury of their fire raging above him. Now, in the silence, the head of Rattan Singh stuck up from the desert, and he called in a loud voice, 'Tea is ready!'

Although the Panzers had been rudely shaken, during the afternoon a further 28 heavy tanks cautiously moved towards Omar Nuovo from the south and opened fire from 4,000 yards. On Messervy's orders, again no guns replied. 'We will let them get in to 600 yards', Brigadier Ray Mirrlees ordered. As the Panzers crept in, the watching troops hardly dared breathe. Some forgot the danger and stood up in their slit-trenches, or even climbed up to use lorries as grandstands.

When the range had closed to 1,000 yards, a Bofors gunner could stand the suspense no longer and loosed off. Immediately Mirrlees gave the order, 'Fire!' and the 25-pounders roared. Every gun on that side of the fortress, from the deep-throated mediums to the whip-crack Bofors, erupted with fury. The Panzers flinched before the storm and pulled away.

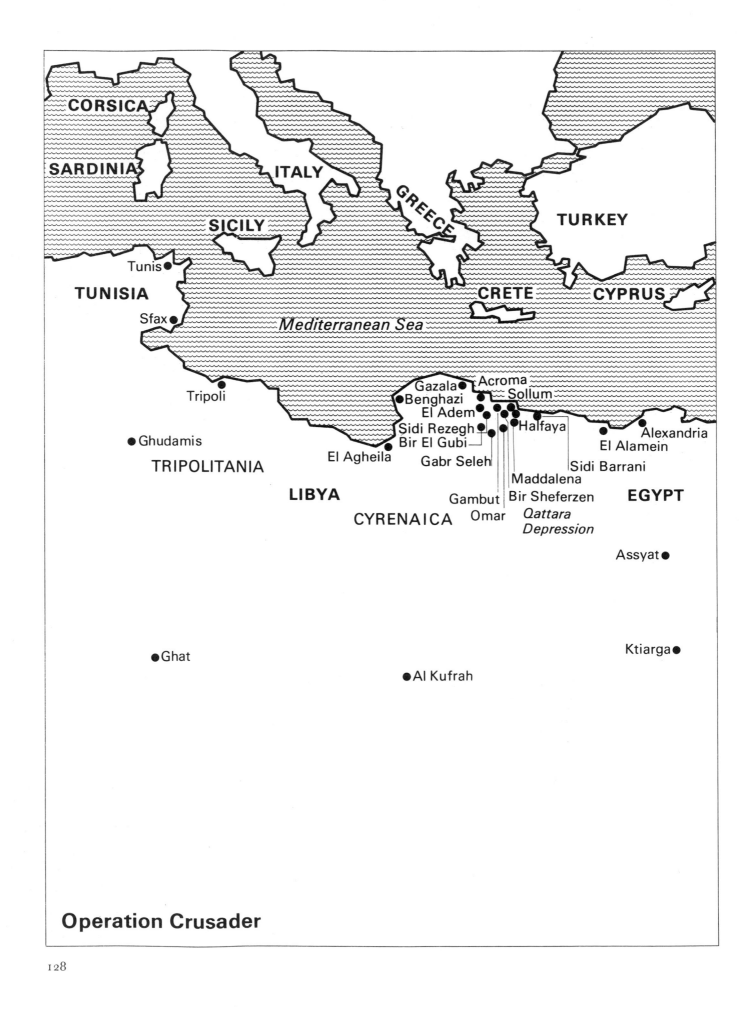

**Operation Crusader**

Spitfires of 303 (Polish) Squadron R.A.F. on patrol.
This squadron, based at Northolt, fought in the
Battle of Britain

*The Battle of Britain*, painted by Paul Nash

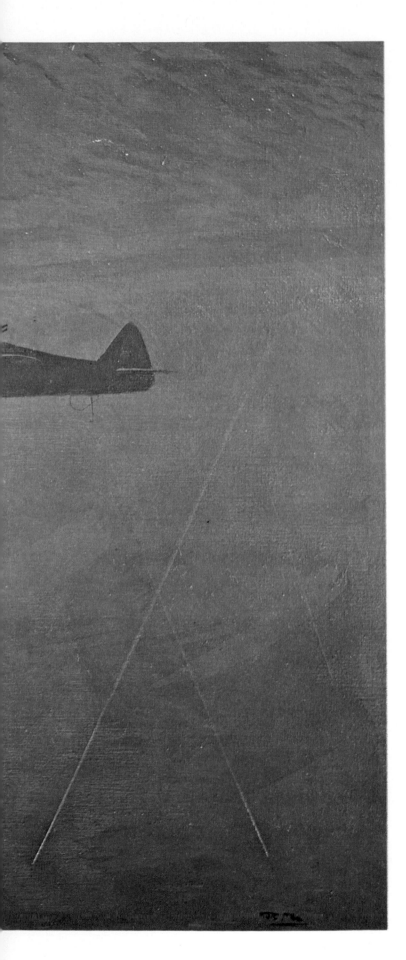

*Stalking the Night Raider*, a painting by Roy Nockolds

The withdrawal from Dunkirk, painted by
Charles Cundall

An American airman dozes in the shade of his plane
during a lull in the Battle of Midway

British tank crews race to get their light American 'Honey' tanks into action against the approaching enemy

In this second encounter the gunners' casualties were miraculously light. The 5th German Panzer Regiment, however, had not only lost 19 heavy tanks, with many more badly damaged, but also had nothing to show for it. It was a proud day for the Royal Artillery, and a significant day for the 8th Army. From then onwards the Panzers were chary of plunging in with their formidable bull-rushes, henceforth requiring the massive support of self-propelled guns and other artillery before they would try conclusions with the British 25-pounders. Of more immediate significance, 5th Panzer Regiment had been completely paralysed by Messervy's gunners – Rommel did not hear of it again for two days and nights.

Things were going awry for Rommel. He had to abandon his spectacular plans and hurry back to retrieve the situation at Tobruk, where the garrison and the New Zealanders were fighting towards each other in a bloody infantry battle. The stubborn defiance of 4th Indian Division in the Omars, standing as the only considerable centre of British resistance in a furious sea of enemy armour, had been the turning point. General Auchinleck could maintain his original objective. The New Zealanders fought on, along the coast road, towards Tobruk, while Messervy's division began to clear the frontier area.

The fighting was confused. A British storeman, looking after a remote dump in an ancient Roman cistern, emerged one morning to discover a troop of enemy armoured cars replenishing. Unobserved, he sent out an urgent call for help, and a detached South African force hurried in to surprise the Germans. Elsewhere a British corporal of military police on traffic control duty suddenly found himself in the midst of a German armoured rush. Without batting an eyelid he continued to control traffic, and the enemy drivers obeyed his signals without hesitation – one group of Panzers even turning off in an entirely wrong direction at the wave of his hand. A dressing station at Bir Sheferzen was captured by German armour and the doctors and orderlies were told they would now work under an Italian officer. In the middle of the night a British artillery officer, lost in the desert, came in, fortunately entering behind a guard's back. Major Aird, a British surgeon operating at the time, was able to utter a whispered warning to go quickly. 'How very embarrassing! I will do so at once', answered the officer, tip-toeing out.

Rallied by an inspiring Auchinleck, the 8th Army was beginning to shape victory from defeat. On November 27 the New Zealanders and the Tobruk garrison fought through, to link up. Rommel had to recall all his Panzers. As they had been denied access to the stores at the Omars, their supplies of ammunition and fuel were dangerously low. Rommel now formed a defence line from the perimeter of Tobruk to the strongholds of El Adem and El Gubi.

When 5th Indian Brigade rejoined the division, the attack on the desperate defenders in Libyan Omar was stepped up and at last the subjection of the Omars completed.

While he reorganized for a major attack, General Auchinleck fell back upon that most British of all desert expedients; he split sections of his armour, guns and lorried infantry into roving Jock Columns, invented by Brigadier Jock Campbell, hero of Sidi Rezegh. The columns were usually a troop of armoured cars with two or three troops of guns and a company of lorried infantry, carrying supplies for a week or more. 'Get out into the desert behind them and attack anything and everything!' were their orders. As these daring, piratical bands ravaged Rommel's rear areas, he slowly relaxed his grip around Tobruk.

The vast confused battle, which began when Operation Crusader was set in motion on November 18, had ebbed and flowed across the Libyan desert unceasingly for 19 days. Despite Rommel's onslaught at Sidi Rezegh, the 8th Army's armour had now regained some of its strength thanks to repairs and new tanks rushed up from the rear areas. And while the Afrika Korps' triumphant Panzers had been spreading confusion behind the British lines during Rommel's 'dash', the by-passed fighting formations had got on with the desert battle. 'Strafer' Gott

fought on in the coastal area, and at Sidi Rezegh tanks of the 4th Armoured Brigade were locked in a hundred thunderous duels with the Panzers. Gatehouse, almost incessantly in action for two weeks, was in the forefront of his brigade's battle, conducting the fighting from an old armchair secured to the top of his shell-torn tank.

No complete picture has ever been built up from this sprawling confusion of battles. Deeds of magnificent valour were to leave neither memory nor trace other than smoke-blackened tank wrecks and scattered, bleached bones upon the desert. Around Sidi Rezegh especially, charred and blackened aircraft, shattered lorries and guns, and scores of blasted and burned-out tanks created a scene of indescribable desolation.

The Western Desert was no place for men without protection of armour and guns. For the next stage of the fighting Messervy organized 4th Indian Division into brigade groups of combined infantry, tanks and guns. They advanced on El Adem and Acroma, and the Germans seemed to vanish before them. By the afternoon of December 9 they had pushed through to the escarpment edge and contacted 23 Infantry Brigade from Tobruk itself. Rommel had had enough. He was getting out while he still had a force which he could usefully reorganize.

The Afrika Korps was pursued by 7th Armoured and 4th Indian, the two magnificent divisions that had for so long dominated the desert warfare. Messervy ordered his division on and established his battle H.Q. with the hardest-hitting group. They set off on December 11. The bare desert soon gave place to harsh, ridged terrain, scarred by dried-up water-courses and shadowed with patches of brittle scrub and parched grass.

At this time the front-line troops heard the news that Japan had treacherously attacked Pearl Harbor, and that the United States, with its immense resources, was in the war on Britain's side.

*Top* With the first of a column of close-support Matilda tanks rumbling up behind, British infantry board a lorry that will drive them into the midst of the battle

*Bottom* A British 2-pounder gun firing at enemy motor transport. Choking clouds of dust were raised every time a gun was fired

There could be no doubt that the Germans were in full retreat. At Gambut where Rommel had had his desert headquarters, the advancing 8th Army found evidence of a hasty departure. The area was strewn with the wreckage of many German warplanes, including Me 109s, Stukas, Dorniers and Ju 88s. Beyond Gambut, where the Afrika Korps' main workshops were situated beside the sea, the Germans had relinquished most of their personal belongings. The elaborate concrete-floored tank-repair workshops still housed undamaged machinery. Sheets of armour plate, coils of new tank tracks, and boxes full of new 50-mm tank guns had been abandoned by the Germans in their sudden flight.

The 4th Indian Division ran up against a strongly defended line from Gazala to the Trigh El Abd, 40 miles to the west. A patrolling bren carrier rattled in to report the approach of German tanks with mobile artillery and lorried

*Above* A Crusader cruiser tank of the 7th Armoured Division approaches a burning German tank knocked out in the clash of armour. Out-ranged by the heavier guns of the Panzers, British tanks had to go in suicidally close to stand any chance of destroying them

*Opposite page* Cruiser tanks of the 8th Army reforming beyond Sidi Rezegh after their terrible clash with the Afrika Corps Panzers

infantry. Infantry took up positions covering the 16 guns of the 25th Field Regiment in echelon with ten Valentine tanks on their left and anti-tank guns both sides. A mile west 31 Field Regiment swung their guns round to give support from long range. Soon a huge and ominous dust cloud billowed up beyond a ridge to herald the approaching Panzers. Black shapes topped the ridge at high speed and fanned out. They halted and opened fire, the heavy tanks putting down a barrage while the mediums

rumbled forward. At 1,200 yards, the British gunners retaliated. The leading tanks were shattered and burst into flames, but the rest of the force came on. The Panzers flooded over one battery and then over another, gun fighting tank at point-blank range. In the end the Panzers gave ground before the sustained firing of 25-pounders, anti-tank guns and some Valentine tanks which came up and joined in. Suddenly the German lorried infantry wheeled and drove away to the north. The tanks slowly followed, leaving a dozen wrecks.

While 4th Indian fought off these blows, the New Zealanders captured Gazala airfield. The Polish Carpathian Brigade, who had issued forth from Tobruk with a great eagerness, closed up on the right. As reports came in that the enemy were massing heavily, Messervy sent forward 31 Field Regiment with a squadron of tanks and detachments of anti-tank and Bofors guns.

The Germans now put new tactics into practice. Three battalions of lorried infantry swung out to the flanks with self-propelled guns to support the tanks from each side. When all the British gunners lay dead or wounded around their smoking guns, the Germans pressed forward.

The tanks next roared upon Point 204, the key position of the battlefield, and the British defenders were completely overwhelmed, although somehow enough gunners crawled back for 13 Field Regiment to man one battery. But the German 115 Lorried Infantry Regiment had suffered such casualties that it could not press on with its task of breaking through and rolling up the 4th Indian Division front.

Early next day the Poles breached the enemy's front and thrust on along the winding coastal escarpment road, while the 4th Armoured Brigade swung out through Tmimi south-east to menace the enemy's rear. Rommel decided

*Above* British infantry being driven along the coastal road. Whoever dominated this vital highway usually dictated the flow of the fighting

*Opposite, top* British bren-carriers, used for rushing troops with light automatic arms into action, pass shattered buildings in Fort Capuzzo, scene of some of the bitterest fighting

*Opposite, bottom* A German bomber pilot's view of burning vehicles on the desert

on disengagement. After 27 days of the bitterest fighting, upon which he had embarked as commander of an army of 119,000 men, he led from the field a battered remnant of 35,000 infantry, 3,000 vehicles and only 30 tanks.

At long last the 8th Army could think in terms of full pursuit. At 10 a.m. on December 17, they surged forward, but the weather aided Rommel. Swept by slashing, icy rainstorms the pursuers were slowed down in marshy ground. Nevertheless, aircraft were still standing on Derna airfield when it came into the view of Sikhs upon the escarpment. A great elation overcame them. They roared down and spread out across the

runways, swiftly overcoming the ground crews. The Sikhs could hardly believe their luck when 12 three-engined Junkers-52 troop-carriers lumbered across the sky and nosed down. Fingers itching on triggers, they waited for all to put down and then blazed away at point-blank range. Only two aircraft escaped. The Sikhs' final haul was 183 aircraft, including a huge six-engined transport, a dozen gliders and vast stores of ammunition, petrol and food. When they entered Derna on the morning of December 19 no enemy remained.

And now all resistance ceased. Rommel withdrew his battered Afrika Korps behind the treacherous salt marshes south of El Agheila, whence he had first emerged as a new force in the desert to undo all that Wavell's brilliant victory had achieved. Now 7th Armoured Division sent a force to Benghazi, headed by the experienced King's Dragoon Guards. On Christmas morning, 1941, Messervy received the message, 'C.I.H. patrols Benghazi 18.00 hours. Dancing girls arrived three hours previously.' The said dancing girls were, in fact, the King's Dragoon Guards. Their greetings to the C.I.H., as the latter entered Benghazi believing themselves first in, had been frankly fruity.

This first desert victory of the 8th Army was won by sheer courage and fortitude. Victory had been achieved, not by a force vastly superior in numbers, tanks and guns, but by an army of about equal numbers armed with weapons that were inferior. The 8th Army had gone into battle 118,000 strong against the 119,000 Axis troops in prepared positions. And this army of British and Dominion soldiers was not a long-established, rigidly disciplined professional army. It contained a large percentage of Territorial Army volunteers who had, in their own spare time, prepared to fight the Nazi menace when they saw war was inevitable.

The 8th Army had sustained 17,704 casualties and lost 278 tanks. Though 13,000 Germans and 20,000 Italians had been killed or captured, and 300 enemy tanks destroyed, complete victory slipped from their grasp. They lacked the huge resources of Montgomery's later days. But the actual achievement of this campaign, which is still misunderstood, should never be underestimated. It brought about the first defeat of a German army in the Second World War.

# 5. Moscow

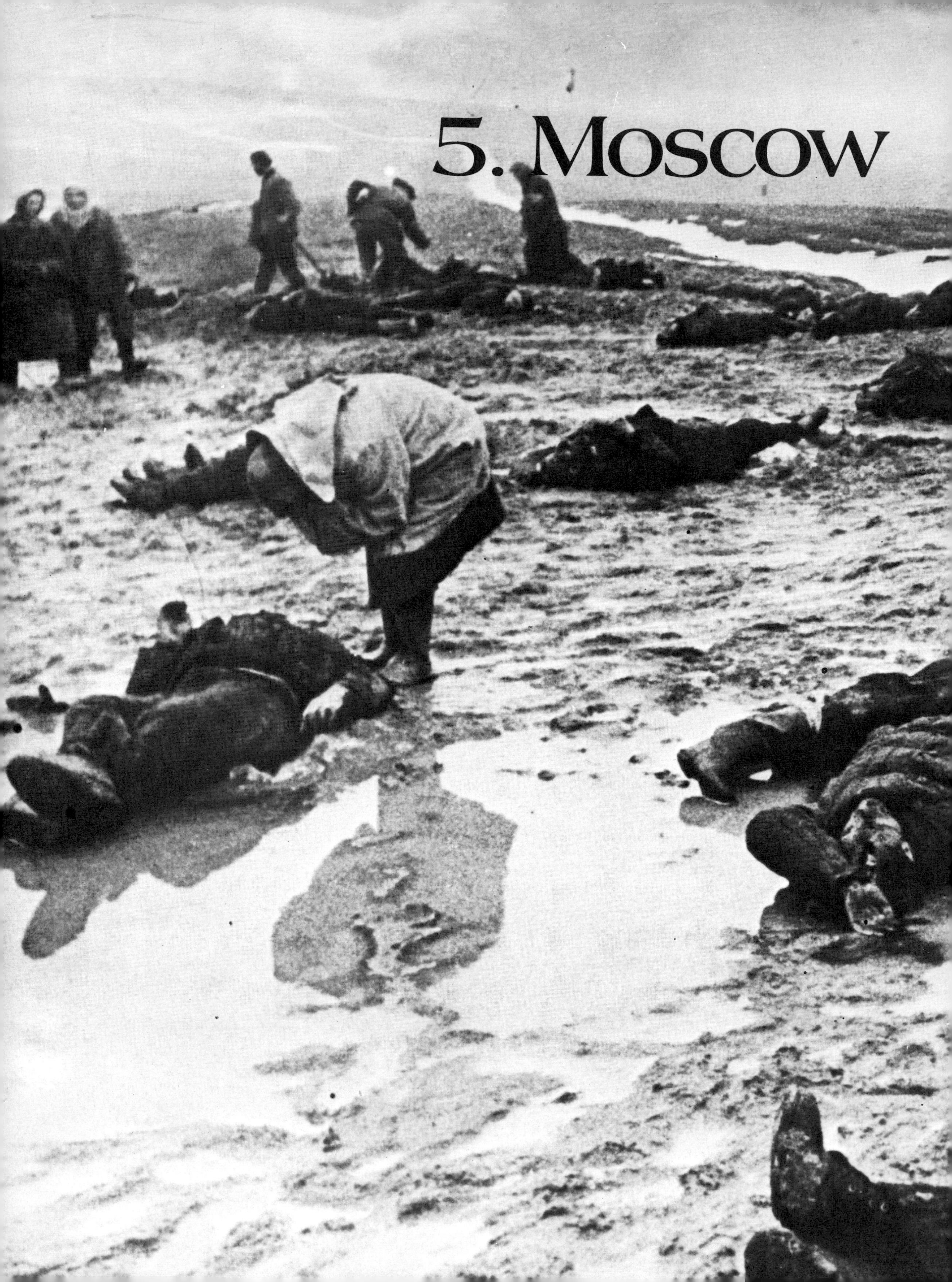

# 5. MOSCOW

In June, 1941, 146 German divisions were poised on the Russian frontier. They comprised seven armies, four Panzer groups and three air fleets, with 3,580 armoured fighting vehicles, 600,000 transport vehicles, 7,184 guns, 1,830 warplanes and 750,000 horses. In addition, the Rumanian 3rd and 4th Armies were ready to attack with them in the far south.

Most of the 3,000,000 German soldiers silently taking up positions near the 1,000-mile frontier during the night of June 19, believed that, after the victory over France, they only had to defeat one more enemy – Great Britain. Rumour explained their surprising move eastwards as an elaborate subterfuge: the British would think an attack on Russia imminent, but instead, the Germans would race through Russia to storm the Persian back-door to the Middle East and overwhelm Britain's desert army from the rear. Because of the German–Soviet treaty, signed in Moscow on August 23, 1939, most Germans really did believe war with Russia was impossible. But Hitler had planned to conquer first in the west, while Stalin complimented himself on gaining valuable time to build up Soviet strength. They both knew war was inevitable.

'Directive No. 21 – Case Barbarossa' (the attack on Russia) was precipitated by Britain's defiance and its likely consequences, among which was America's possible entry into the war. But resistance in the Balkans, another of the consequences, compelled the Germans to invade Greece, Crete and Yugoslavia, which had distracted armoured and infantry divisions,

guns and warplanes vital to the planned Barbarossa operation. As a result the invasion had to be postponed for four weeks – four weeks of good campaigning weather which might have made all the difference to the outcome.

Operation Barbarossa envisaged the quick defeat of the Russian army in the west by deeply penetrating Panzer wedges, pushing the Russians back far enough to prevent air attack on Germany. Asian Russia would be screened off, and the last industrial region, in the Urals, destroyed by the Luftwaffe. A two-pronged attack from the Warsaw area and East Prussia was aimed at the Baltic region and Leningrad. Following the occupation of Leningrad, the Germans would turn on Moscow. Hitler noted two major objectives: seizure of the Donetz basin, important for the war economy; and the capture of Moscow, the chief communications centre, which would be politically and economically decisive.

The ultimate plan of the German High Command divided the vast front into three sectors – North, Centre and South. The objective of Army Group North – comprising two armies, one

*Above* General Guderian, whose tanks played a decisive role in the battle

*Opposite, top* German troops in inflatable boats crossing a river virtually unopposed as the surprise attack on their 'ally' Russia is launched

*Opposite, bottom* A German armoured column rolls along a leafy lane with no sign of Russian opposition

Just as in France, the German columns race on almost nose to tail, untroubled by air attack because the Luftwaffe already controls the skies over Russia

Panzer group and an air fleet under the command of Field-Marshal Ritter von Leeb – was the destruction of the Soviet forces in the Baltic in a swift advance from East Prussia across the River Memel. Army Group Centre under Field-Marshal von Bock – it consisted of two armies, two Panzer groups and Kesselring's 2nd Air Fleet – was to surge forward on a 250-mile front from Romintener Heide to south of Brest-Litovsk. With its immense armoured force and the bombing power of Kesselring's air fleet, increased by many Stuka wings, Army Group Centre was by far the most formidable. It was to annihilate the considerable Soviet army that stood in its path, and to rush on to take Smolensk

before wheeling northwards to seize Moscow. Army Group South under the direction of Field-Marshal von Rundstedt – it included three armies, one Panzer group and an air fleet – was to advance between the Pripet Marshes and the Carpathian mountains into Galicia and western Ukraine. After having forced a crossing of the great River Dnieper it was to make Kiev its main objective. When these assaults were under way, the Finnish Army in the north and the Rumanian Army in the south, with German reinforcements, would be drawn in.

By smashing home their most powerful attack in the centre, the Germans aimed to repeat the tactics which had secured such success on the western front. Soviet Intelligence had missed the ominous gathering of the tanks in the forests and thickets and the high waving corn beyond the Pripet Marshes and the fortress of Brest-

Litovsk. Stalin and his marshals expected that any German attack would be mounted in the south, where the vast flat steppes and warmer climate would be much more suitable for the German blitzkrieg. In consequence, 64 Russian divisions with 14 armoured brigades stood ready opposite the German Army Group South, while there were only 45 divisions and 15 armoured brigades in the centre, and only 30 divisions and eight armoured brigades in the north. In all, the Russians had deployed ten armies, a total of some 4,500,000 men, in the immediate frontier area or as mobile reserves within striking distance.

The illusions of the German soldiers about the solemn pact of friendship between Hitler and Stalin came to an end at 10 p.m. on June 21. A message from the Führer dispelled any remaining doubts:

'Weighed down for many months by grave anxieties. . . I can at last speak openly to you, my soldiers. About 160 Russian divisions are lined up along our frontier. For weeks this frontier has been violated continually. . . Many Russian patrols have penetrated into Reich territory and have been driven back only after prolonged exchanges of fire. At this moment, soldiers of the Eastern Front, a build-up is in progress which has no equal in world history, either in extent or in numbers. Allied with Finnish divisions, our comrades are standing side by side with the victors of Narvik on the Arctic sea in the north. You are standing on the Eastern Front in Rumania, on the banks of the Prut, on the Danube down to the shores of the Black Sea; German and Rumanian troops are standing side by side. If this greatest front in world history is now going into action, then it does so not only in order to create the necessary conditions for the final conclusion of this great war, or to protect the countries threatened at this moment, but in order to save the whole of European civilization and culture. German soldiers! You are about to join battle, a hard and crucial battle. The destiny of Europe, the future of the German Reich, the existence of our nation, now lie in your hands alone. May the Almighty help us all in this struggle.'

Zero hour was 3.15 a.m. next morning. Over 7,000 German guns of all calibres hurtled high explosive upon targets already precisely pin-pointed. Over 1,000 bombers cascaded bombs upon airfields, military headquarters and communication centres deep in Russia. 'Barbarossa' had begun.

Where rivers such as the Bug formed the frontier, some bridges were seized by surprise minutes before zero hour. Sleepy Russian guards were machine-gunned as they stumbled to their weapons. Where there were no bridges, shock-troops paddled silently over in rubber dinghies, or surged across in powered assault boats, before the Russians could open fire. In some places amphibious tanks, watertight and fitted with 'snorkel' breathing pipes, originally intended for the invasion of Britain, crawled over the river bed and plunged through the Russian defences.

The iron spearhead of Army Group Centre soon burst through the lightly defended frontier positions, and the Panzers raced out on the road to Minsk and Smolensk, almost contemptuously blasting aside Russian armoured cars and anti-tank guns. Meanwhile, von Rundstedt's army group made good though less easy progress; on their southern flank the Germans suffered heavy casualties at the hands of Russian infantry-men. On the far distant front of Army Group North, the soldiers of the Wehrmacht who surged into Soviet-occupied Lithuania were confronted by furiously fighting Mongolian troops and halted for a time.

On this northern front the German spearhead thrust 40 miles deep into Soviet territory within 34 hours. General von Manstein, commanding the powerful Panzer corps delivering this first devastating punch, was one of those realists among Hitler's generals who believed Barbarossa could only succeed if the main military strength of the Russians was utterly destroyed in the first few weeks, Moscow seized, and the ruling regime overthrown. Otherwise, he thought, the invasion of Russia could become a terrible disaster for Germany. It was with this in mind that Manstein, more than any other German commander, urged his Panzer troops on without respite. The immediate target he set them was to seize the towns of Daugavpils and the bridge across the River Daugava, 230 miles across the plains.

But in the north, there was also a revelation even more significant than the desperate valour

*Above* Another Russian town goes up in flames as the advancing Germans subject it to a preliminary artillery bombardment

*Opposite page* German soldiers pause to look upon the Dnieper at Kiev. None of the Russian rivers, however wide, stemmed the onrush of the German armour

of Russian infantrymen. As the massed Panzers roared towards the distant Daugava, their left flank was suddenly menaced by enemy armour formidable beyond all imagining. Gigantic Russian tanks, monsters far larger than the German soldiers had expected, loomed upon the formations behind Manstein's racing spearheads. They overran an infantry battalion, then ground down upon the supporting artillery. The lighter anti-tank projectiles of the infantry and even the armour-piercing shells of the Panzerjäger (specialized anti-tank artillery), bounced off the huge Russian Klim Voroshilov KV 1 and KV 2 tanks, which weighed 43 and 52 tons respectively. There ensued a desperate two days' battle between the whole German 41 Panzer Corps and the Crack Soviet III Armoured Corps, involving no less than 400 Russian tanks the majority of which were the super-heavy KVs with armour plating from 88 mm to 120 mm thick.

By bringing in their high-velocity 88-mm heavy anti-aircraft guns and by massive artillery support, the Germans ultimately triumphed.

At the climax of the battle German guns were firing point-blank at the huge enemy tanks, while the faster and better-led Panzers swarmed around from all sides to halt them by blowing off their tracks. Then incredibly brave infantry soldiers rushed in to blow them up with sticky bombs. At the end of the battle the two German Panzer divisions, with one motorized and one infantry division, had destroyed 200 Soviet tanks, 29 of them the KV monsters. The bulk of the Russian armoured force on the northern front had, in fact, been smashed.

The thrust for the River Daugava could resume. At dawn on June 26, a German armoured spearhead roaring along the great highroad from Kaunas to Leningrad was barely five miles

144

from Daugavpils, the vital railway centre between Vilna and Leningrad. It had come 190 miles through rolling hills, sandy plains, marshes and forests, scattering hastily assembled opposition. By sheer speed and daring it had blasted its way through two whole confused Russian armies. Thus close to its objective, four captured lorries were sent on ahead; in them, hidden beneath tarpaulins, were specialized troops with orders to seize Daugavpils' vital river bridge. The Russian-speaking German drivers, in Russian uniforms, assured the Soviet outposts that the Germans were miles away. Then the lorries mingled with the town's regular traffic until they reached the great road and railway bridges. Shooting down the guards, the Germans seized the bridges almost intact – only one short stretch of the rail bridge was damaged by an explosive charge. Soon Manstein's armour came surging through the town, and crossed the great wide river.

As German armoured spearheads thrust deep into Russia, the increasingly confused Soviet High Command were completely ignorant of the true position in the north. Manstein was eager to exploit his boldly seized bridgehead and race on towards Leningrad, but Hitler suddenly lost his nerve and had Manstein's Panzers halted for six days at Daugavpils while the army's left wing moved up. This break gave the panicking Russians time to reorganize sufficiently to man the old Stalin Line defences along the Russian–Estonian frontier.

While the onslaughts towards Leningrad and Moscow were progressing so spectacularly, the advance on the southern front was meeting with stiffer opposition. There, four Russian armies were deployed in depth, manning cunningly camouflaged positions which included innumerable disguised pillboxes and hidden artillery. The attackers were compelled to fight bitterly all the way, and the stubbornly defended Russian positions were overcome at heavy cost.

When, after several days' furious fighting, the way at last seemed clear for von Kleist's Panzer group to break out towards Lvov, formations of super-heavy Soviet tanks launched an awe-inspiring counter-attack.

In addition to the huge KV 1s and KV 2s there was an even more alarming surprise in the shape of an almost impregnable iron-clad mammoth with five revolving turrets. And, for the first time, there was also the Russian T 34 tank – not so big (a mere 26 tons), but even more formidable because of its speed and its almost impenetrable, steeply sloped armour. Again the high-velocity 88-mm anti-aircraft guns had to be brought up to deal with them. After a few days' fighting the German forces on the southern front were no more than 60 miles into Soviet territory. The planned encirclement and destruction of the opposing Russian force was not even a wild hope.

But dramatic success now attended the main assault on the central front where the decisive blow, the capture of Moscow, had been intended from the beginning. The armoured divisions under Guderian and Hoth, with their closely attendant motorized infantry divisions and artillery, broke through devastatingly on each flank of Army Group Centre. The German High Command, exploiting this success, ordered Colonel-General Hoepner's 4th Panzer Group to switch from Army Group North to join in the great rush to capture Moscow and encircle and destroy the Russian armies, which were disintegrating in confusion. More than 1,600 German tanks swept forward in triumphant blitzkrieg. The attackers were held only at the ancient fortified citadel of Brest-Litovsk, in Russian-occupied Poland. By-passed by the racing Panzers, the Russian garrison fought desperately against the besieging troops until June 30, when the shattered, burning fortress finally fell.

The Russian central front now was in utter chaos. Every attempt to stand and fight was swiftly encircled and cut to ribbons by Panzers, mobile artillery, Stukas and the merciless machine-gun fire of motorized infantry. Churchill had repeatedly warned Stalin of Hitler's intentions. So had his own secret service. But the warnings had been disregarded. Stalin was also culpable for the Red Army's desperate dearth of suitable senior commanders, which

was having grievous consequences. In 1937–38 he had liquidated nearly 35,000 serving officers, including 90 per cent of all generals. Years later, when the ruthless dictator was dead and gone, this slaughtering of the Red Army's officer corps was put forward as the main reason for the tragic debacle of the summer of 1941.

Stalin now looked for a military leader to save the day. He chose General Andrey Yeremenko, commander of the 1st Far Eastern Army. Yeremenko was a Red Army veteran with a reputation for being tough, brave, and an outstanding tactician. His record as a fighting commander during the Soviet Revolution convinced Stalin that he had the flair for improvisation which alone could rescue the Red Army from its desperate calamity. When he arrived in Moscow to receive his orders things were desperate indeed on the central front. Three Soviet infantry divisions had just laid down their arms after shooting their political commissars who had urged them to fight. The onrushing Panzers were wheeling towards Minsk

*Above* On the threshold of a Russian town, a German artillery observer assesses the damage done by their guns

*Opposite page* These Russian soldiers fought to the death in their bunker in the Stalin line. Despite the bravery of many Russian soldiers their sacrifice did little to halt the German advance

and Smolensk, closing a steel trap round masses of fleeing, disorganized Russian soldiers. Colonel-General Heinz Guderian – perhaps Germany's most brilliant exponent of blitzkrieg – was already issuing orders for the next onslaught from his command vehicle barely 50 miles from Minsk.

The 17th Panzer Division swiftly closed in from the south on Minsk, whilst in the north Colonel-General Hoth's 3rd Panzer Group raced round to complete the pincers. On June 26 spearheads of these two forces met. Four Soviet armies, some 500,000 men, were trapped. The encircled Russians tried desper-

ately to claw an escape gap through the southern perimeter of the merciless iron ring. Near the small town of Zelba, a thick forest permitted them to mass with their remaining tanks and guns for a do-or-die charge through the surrounding enemy. The Russians charged out, spearheaded by furiously galloping cavalry, with sabres and carbines flourished on high and shouting choruses of 'Urra! Urra!' They charged in waves of infantry, packed close together, a myriad menacing bayonets thrust out before them. They charged in waves, arms linked, shouting always with monotonous, hopeless defiance, 'Urra! Urra!' They were mown down by the waiting German machine guns and infantry until the wide fields were heaped brown with their bodies.

Just before nightfall, they tried again, this time in an armoured train. But German engineers had blown up the track, and German guns blew the train to pieces. The encircling iron ring remained unbroken. The Soviet soldiers within were doomed.

When General Yeremenko, on June 28, learned the facts of the awful catastrophe which he was expected to remedy he was horrified. Faced by such an apparently hopeless position, he asked, 'What is the task on this front then?' Marshal Timoshenko, the Soviet Defence Minister, told him tersely, 'Stop the enemy advance!' Otherwise Moscow was indeed doomed. Stalin himself seemed to be absent from Moscow. He had not even put in an appearance to welcome the British military mission, which arrived there on June 27 with a pledge of all the armed help which a beleaguered Britain, Russia's only ally, could give.

On the central front, the spearheading tanks of the victorious Germans were already roaring up the only two roads that existed in the vast sun-baked stretch of Russia that lay between them and Moscow. Their support followed – 27,000 lorries and trucks bumping along, almost nose to tail, to maintain the great impetus of armoured attack. In their wake another 60,000 vehicles brought the infantry

and communication troops. The vulnerable supply columns passed virtually unhindered because the Luftwaffe had dealt a shattering blow to the Russian Air Force at the outset, and because the well-armed Russian forces still in the area were hopelessly unco-ordinated.

The city of Minsk, 420 miles west of Moscow, was stormed by the 20th Panzer Division on June 28. The city was in flames when the Panzers entered, in accordance with Stalin's desperate scorched-earth policy. It was the latest reported calamity as General Yeremenko arrived at the headquarters of General Pavlov at Mogilev, just over 300 miles from Moscow. Without comment Yeremenko handed a letter of dismissal to Pavlov who complained that the debacle on the central sector had been caused because he had been given no warning from the Kremlin that the Germans were intending attack. The frontier units had not been alerted and the enemy just drove straight through them. Bitterly, he obeyed the recall to Moscow and accepted an implied invitation to commit suicide.

The new commander-in-chief issued his first

*Above* In the wake of the Panzers a Russian workers' settlement – like the majority of them built of wood – has been reduced to ashes

*Opposite page* General 'Fast Heinz' Guderian, master of the armoured blitzkrieg, confers with staff officers as he plans another deep-thrust into Russia

order without delay. It was a tough backs-to-the-wall call; the Germans were to be halted on the banks of the River Beresina. But Yeremenko was issuing orders to divisions non-existent as fighting units.

The 18th Panzer Division roared eastwards, 50 miles ahead of the main German force. Moving off on June 30 its advanced elements reached Borisov on the Beresina in less than 30 hours of almost non-stop driving. There they were confronted by officer cadets and N.C.O.s of a training establishment for armoured warfare. These Russians were prepared to fight to the death in strongly fortified positions defending the river bridge. The attackers were halted and suffered heavy casualties in the ensuing fighting.

There was a desperate race against time by both sides to reinforce at this crucial crossing. Yeremenko, hourly more disillusioned at the lack of available fighting formations, threw in every unit he could locate in the immediate area. But the main force of the 18th Panzer Division arrived before any formidable Russian defence could be massed there. During the afternoon of July 1 a determined onslaught by German tanks and infantry penetrated the positions of the Russians on the western bank who were still defending the bridge. Then a daring charge across its wide span overwhelmed the demolition squad even as the plunger was about to be pushed down. Tanks and motorcycle troops immediately roared across, closely followed by artillery which included the formidable 88-mm guns. Some 50 miles farther south, General Model's 3rd Panzer Division also forced a crossing at Bobruysk, swiftly followed by the 4th Panzers swarming across still farther south.

Marshal Timoshenko took over supreme command, with Yeremenko as his second-in-command. The German thrust for Moscow was hourly developing into a massive drive. More

and more armour and guns and lorried infantry rolled eastwards. On July 3, 1941, only 12 days after the thunder of that first great barrage had swelled along the 1,000-mile front, the German High Command was already recording a magnificent victory. The considerable Russian force in the Bialystok Bend had been virtually destroyed by the German Army Group Centre. Army Group North had obliterated some 15 enemy divisions. Although less progress had been made in the south, the German Army Group South had almost destroyed the Soviet armies before the Dnieper and Western Dvina rivers.

On July 8 Field-Marshal von Bock addressed a special and triumphant Order of the Day to Army Group Centre. He told them, 'The double battle of Minsk is over'. He enumerated the staggering losses sustained by the four Russian armies which had been shattered by Army Group Centre – 32 infantry and eight armoured divisions, six motorized or mechanized brigades and three cavalry divisions. Tens of thousands of Russian soldiers were dead and 287,704 were prisoners. A total of 2,585 tanks,

*Above* Marshal Timoshenko, one of the Russian commanders who unavailingly tried to stem the advance of the immense German army

*Opposite, top* As it became evident that Moscow was in peril, thousands of women were rushed out to help dig deep anti-tank trenches in the city's outer defences

*Opposite, bottom* With the German armoured columns hourly drawing nearer, Russian women in armament factories worked strenuously to provide more munitions for the defenders

over 1,500 guns and 250 aircraft had been captured or destroyed. Incalculable quantities of small arms ammunition, fuel, provisions and thousands of motor vehicles had also been taken.

This was intoxicating news for the victorious Germans, but it was by no means the end of the

world for Stalin and his High Command. The Soviet Union had 190,000,000 inhabitants, including 16,000,000 men of military age. The huge and efficient armaments industry was still safe behind the Ural mountains. What was needed above all was time in which to reorganize far away to the east. Timoshenko gave a brutally simple directive to Yeremenko. It amounted to, 'Stop the German tanks. Hold them while we reorganize.' They had to be held on the Dnieper and Western Dvina, if they were to be prevented from reaching Smolensk, which lay only 230 miles from Moscow. If Moscow fell, that could be the end of the war. The immense federation of disparate peoples that made up the Soviet Union might fall apart if the traditional seat of government were lost.

The first effects of Timoshenko's grim resolve were felt by Army Group Centre on July 3. Air reconnaissance discovered a strong Russian armoured force rolling towards them on both sides of the highway from Smolensk to Borisov. It was the crack 1st Moscow Motorized Rifle Division, formidably equipped with over 100 tanks including the fast, massively armoured T 34s and a single, massive KV 2.

The predominating smaller and more vulnerable Russian T 26s and BT tanks were soon boiling up into flaming pyres all along the line, but the huge, apparently impenetrable Russian KV giant advanced, scattering the German Mark III and Mark IV tanks before it. But the Russian tank men were unsure of themselves, their rate of fire was too slow, and German Mark IVs ultimately closed in from each side. The KV 2 met its end when its engine broke down and it was hastily abandoned by its crew. The German tanks meanwhile swarmed around the T 34s and blew off their tracks. Three T 34s were captured intact west of Borisov, having run into a swamp.

The defeat of their Goliaths, and the destruction of most of the smaller tanks brought the counter-attack of the 1st Moscow Division to an end. Their tactics had been faulty. They

Like Londoners, the people of Moscow learn what it is like to be blitzed by night, and seek the shelter of the underground railway stations. The imperial splendour of the Mayakovskaya metro station, seen here, is a reminder of the Tsarist days

should have sent in their heavy tanks together to deal sledgehammer blows while covering each other with crossfire. Although the individual Russian soldiers continued to fight bravely, they had delayed the German advance but briefly.

Part of the Soviet 19th Army was ordered up from the south to Vitebsk. Men were flung into battle as they arrived. Yeremenko was fully aware that this was no way to fight a vital battle, but he had no option. He could not wait to mass his six divisions to fight the battle as he would have wished.

But luck was also with the other side. The Germans had captured a Russian artillery officer carrying the complete counter-attack plan. Immediate counter-measures were taken. German armoured and motorized formations which had crossed the Western Dvina at Ulla raced along the river towards Vitebsk. They fell upon the Russian rear where arriving troops were detraining, while Yeremenko's counter-attack force was assailed frontally by two Panzer divisions. On July 10 the 20th Panzer Division thundered through Vitebsk, leaving the town to be devoured by the flames of Stalin's scorched-earth policy. The next, and most significant, objective of the racing Panzers was Smolensk.

By this time, only the 19th day of the blitzkrieg, the Germans could claim further great triumphs. Army Group Centre had penetrated almost to Smolensk. Army Group North had taken Pskov, south of Lake Peipus, and Ostrov, and was about to swing north-east towards Leningrad. Guderian was over the Berezina and thrusting towards the Dnieper, eager to force a crossing before the Russians could bar his way. Aerial reconnaissance showed considerable reinforcements being hurried there. When Field-Marshal von Kluge personally visited his advanced headquarters, Guderian (affectionately called 'Fast Heinz' by his troops) implored him, 'I am convinced of the success of this operation. If we strike quickly at Moscow, this campaign can be decided before the end of the year.' Kluge did not always approve of the hell-for-leather manner in which Guderian led his Panzers far into the enemy's rear, but in this case he gave way.

Guderian's spearheads made three thrusts at the main Dnieper crossings at Rogochev, Mogilev and Orsha but were repulsed. The

Russians had strongly fortified the crossing, and were rushing division after division up to hold the vital line of the river.

By July 11 the newly reorganized Soviet Army Group, western sector, comprised 31 infantry, seven armoured and four motorized divisions, plus surviving remnants of the 4th Army which had been shattered at Minsk, and components of the 16th Army from the south. A total of 42 Soviet divisions was lining up along the Dnieper to face Guderian's tanks.

Guderian was not deterred. His tanks had swept through Poland to Warsaw in eight days, had burst right through the French Army to the Channel coast in ten days, and 42 Russian divisions strung along the Dnieper were not going to keep him from Moscow! His probing forward units found weakly held crossing places at Staryy Bykhov, Kopys, and Shklov. At Staryy Bykhov motorcycle shock-troops crossed

*Above* The first rains of late Autumn have begun to turn hard ground into mud, seen on the boots of these German soldiers riding on a tank as the great advance slows down

*Opposite, top* As the rains continue, roads, tracks and fields become quagmires impassable to wheeled vehicles of any sort

*Opposite, bottom* Even horse-drawn vehicles could not get through the deep, clinging mud which halted the German onrush. Here German soldiers are seen trying to extricate a horse which has sunk into the mud

in assault boats to seize a bridgehead. Following engineers built a pontoon bridge with amazing speed and within hours two Panzer divisions rumbled over. At Kopys motorized infantry in assault boats stormed across despite heavy artillery fire and air attacks. At Shklov a

machine-gun regiment forced a crossing after a short fight and engineers built a bridge even faster than at Staryy Bykhov for the 10th Panzer Division.

Ignoring the considerable garrisons of Orsha, Mogilev and Rogochev, Guderian sent his Panzer divisions towards Smolensk. In a desperate effort to stop them, Timoshenko ordered a powerful force of 20 divisions around Gomel to attack from the southern flank. Amazingly, a German cavalry division – the only major German cavalry force engaged in the assault on Russia – played a vital role in this instance of fast-moving mechanized warfare. As the Russian force moved in to strike at Guderian's exposed flank, its flank in turn was furiously assailed by the cavalry, for whom the wild scrubby terrain of the fringes of the Pripet Marshes was favourable. The 10th Motorized Infantry Division backed up the cavalry assault and, where the going was better, formations of the 4th Panzer Division joined in. The counter-attack was smashed. Guderian's armour raced on unimpeded towards Smolensk.

Stukas swarmed down to blast Russian artillery and defences. The Luftwaffe made a huge effort to synchronize with the rampaging tanks; their bombers shattered both the motor highway and the railway line linking Smolensk with Moscow, and the 15 Soviet divisions within the tightening iron ring were virtually trapped. Smolensk was the key to Moscow now as it had been nearly 130 years earlier when Napoleon's all-conquering Grande Armée marched upon Moscow.

The Smolensk garrison was ordered to carry out 'total defence' – fighting to the last man. They were to be reinforced by state police and militia drawn from every able-bodied man in every factory and office. If the regular troops could not hold the Germans at the outer defences, then every man able to bear arms was to fight them in the streets. Nevertheless, Smolensk fell within 24 hours.

Before the main attack went in, the vital Dnieper bridge east of the city was seized by a dare-devil surprise attack, and heroically held despite the bitterest Russian attempts to win it back. Then, early on July 15, the 71st Infantry Regiment made a brilliantly executed and unexpected approach along a farm track from the south-west. The German soldiers overran the

*Above* As the German war machine ground to a halt the Russians threw in a number of desperate counter-attacks. Here infantry of the Red Army are seen launching an assault from across a river

*Opposite, top* After the rains – the frost. At first, before it became cripplingly severe, the Russian winter facilitated the continued German advance by putting a hard crust on the mud, as can be seen in this picture

*Opposite, bottom* German tanks could once more go into action across the hard ground, and this picture shows a section of Panzer-borne infantry assaulting a Russian defence post

defenders' vital heavy batteries almost before their presence was suspected. Learning from prisoners taken that the main southern approach was heavily fortified, they swung round to attack from the south-east. Heavy artillery, 88-mm guns, self-propelled guns, and flame-throwing tanks blasted and burned a way for them. Russian soldiers, police and militia fought with furious heroism, but could only briefly delay the inevitable. Although house after house had to be cleared by grenade and bayonet, the Germans had swept right across Smolensk by nightfall on July 16.

Within 25 days the German armies had smashed their way 440 miles into Russia and were 220 miles from Moscow. The remaining distance was not likely to present much of a

*Above* Russian soldiers, trained and equipped for fighting in the cruel winter of their homeland, almost invisible as they lie in wait for advancing German patrols

*Opposite, top* German infantry, some of the comparatively few provided with overcoats and warmer winter clothing, attack across the snow towards Moscow

*Opposite, bottom* As the winter intensified and the snow deepened, the Panzer columns were finally immobilized. In desperation the Germans used horses to try to drag guns, ammunition and supplies up to the front-line soldiers

problem, for the great natural river barriers and main garrison towns had all been overcome.

The all-out assault on Moscow was to be launched from Roslavl, Krichev and Gomel. After the necessary pause for refitting and reorganizing, Guderian attacked Roslavl on August 1. The Russians fought bitterly, particularly in a thick stretch of swampy forest where they were more at home than the Germans. In the gloom amidst crowding trees they lurked in cunningly camouflaged foxholes, and did not fire until presented with the target of a German back as the unsuspecting enemy passed them by. The encircling Germans also ran into trouble at a place called Kazaki, where Guderian himself drove up to take charge. With a hastily organized combat force of tanks, self propelled and 88-mm guns, he closed the gap torn by

Russian armour and left it littered with the blazing hulks of Russian tanks.

It took just over a week to bring the battle of encirclement to a victorious close. The ferocious battle for Roslavl had achieved the destruction of the Soviet 28th Army and torn a yawning gap in the Russian defence line before Moscow. There was not a solitary Soviet fighting formation left for 25 miles in the direction of Bryansk. Guderian decided to secure his flank by taking Krichev, an operation completed by August 14. These two swift victories left only the strong Russian force at Gomel to deal with. On August 21, Guderian was ready to accomplish this final preliminary before the onslaught on the Russian capital began.

At this point the incredible happened. Orders came from Hitler on August 22 that the attack on Moscow was postponed. Instead, all available forces, including the major part of Army Group Centre, were to plunge southwards deep into the Ukraine and Crimea.

Hitler stated a number of reasons for making the Crimean peninsula the prime objective. It was to secure Germany's oil supply from Rumania, and to bring within reach of the Wehrmacht the Russian oil in the Caucasus, the great industrial and coal-mining region of the Donets, and all the vast grain-growing lands of the Ukraine.

Hitler also named another objective as more important than Moscow. This was Leningrad, where Army Group North was to link up with the Finns to annihilate the Russian 5th Army.

Hitler's reasoning did not convince many of his generals in the field. Field-Marshal von Bock and his commanders of Army Group Centre held angry discussions. Halder and Guderian flew to the Führer's forest headquarters at Rastenburg in East Prussia, where Guderian made an impassioned plea that Moscow be reinstated as the prime objective. But Hitler was adamant. Furious almost to the point of resignation Guderian returned to his battle front.

Apart from nine Panzer divisions left to defend his most forward position at Yelna, Guderian wheeled his Panzer groups through 90 degrees and drove determinedly due south. Swiftly they bore down upon Marshal Budennyy's unwieldly mass of 1,000,000 men, already in dire trouble from the armoured onslaughts of Kleist and Reichenau. Guderian's powerful force, on their right, surged past the Russian 5th Army and remnants of other shattered formations grouped around Gomel. On their left, they by-passed the Russian forces of Kuznetsov and Yeremenko.

The dramatic, complete change of direction by Guderian's armour took the Russians by surprise. On August 10, Stalin had received a report from his so-far infallible top agent in Switzerland that Army Group Centre was going to attack Moscow by way of Bryansk. At that time this was, in fact, the intention of the German High Command; even they did not know that Hitler had other plans. Stalin therefore ordered Yeremenko to cover the vital sector south-west of Moscow with the most powerful force he could muster. But Guderian's Panzers were thundering down towards the Desna, to take Budennyy's huge Russian army around Kiev in the rear. Through a desolate region of scrubland, marsh and deep black forests, they were plunging 80 miles behind the Russian 5th Army, their objective some 120 miles farther to the south. Meanwhile a totally deceived Stalin ordered up two armies protecting northern Ukraine to defend Moscow.

Field-Marshal von Rundstedt's Army Group South now moved forward to join the massive all-out offensive. Intending another masterly battle of encirclement, Kleist's Panzer group was to force a crossing of the lower Dnieper then swing north to meet Guderian's Panzers driving down towards them. When they met, a ring of steel and guns would have been drawn round a vast Russian army whose destruction would give Germany all the rich Ukraine and Donets basin, just as Hitler had planned.

Kleist had only 600 Panzers, yet they reached the Dnieper near Kremenchug by September 10. In the blinding rain of a thunderstorm they bridged the river next day. Spearheading tank formations, wheeling northwards, roared over 40 miles onwards within 12 hours. By September 12 Kleist's Panzers had broken through the exhausted Russian 38th Army, and Guderian's 3rd Panzer Division was racing south, almost unimpeded, over dry, flat steppes. On September 14 they met, closing the trap 130 miles east of Kiev.

Budennyy's immense army was encircled. Stalin had refused to let him withdraw and without fuel, without ammunition, the Russian

In the thick forests around the Russian capital, Russian guerrilla fighters go into action against a German night patrol

soldiers were blasted to death in their thousands, as whole battalions made mass bayonet charges against tanks, guns and machine-guns. Many died with Stalin's voice dinning in their ears, as loudspeakers blared his exhortations over the battlefield. Though without hope, the Russians fought ferociously, even with fists and boots and teeth if they could get to close quarters. There were five days and nights of horrific slaughter. By September 26 it was all over. Kiev had fallen in the greatest battle of annihilation the world had ever known.

As the Germans exulted over their victory, Hitler at last gave the order for the assault on Moscow. The code name for the operation was Typhoon. D-Day was October 2. Hitler and his High Command were convinced that the loss of Moscow would finish Russia for, accord-

ing to the German estimate, probably quite accurate, total Russian losses amounted to about 2,500,000 men killed, wounded, or prisoners, 22,000 guns, 18,000 tanks and 14,000 aircraft. Surely even the huge Red Army could not long survive that? The Germans had already practically achieved the objectives of Operation Barbarossa. They had seized the grain fields of the Ukraine and the industrial Donets basin, Leningrad was cut off and Moscow about to be assaulted.

All three army groups, three quarters of the whole German force on the Eastern Front, were to join in the assault on Moscow. All the Panzer groups, with the exception of Kleist's which was to complete the subjection of the Ukraine, were to make the onslaught on a 150-mile front. General Hoepner, from the north, was to attack in the centre, the 9th and 4th Armies on one side of him and the 2nd Army on the other. As in the previous immense encirclement battles, the massed Panzer armies of Hoth and Guderian were on the extreme flanks.

When Hoepner broke through the Russian centre, Hoth's armour would swing round Vyazma, and Guderian's round Bryansk. The Russian armies would then be encircled and overwhelmed, and the German armies would be able to winter in the Russian capital.

The Russian mood was one of grim determination, although the commanders had to deploy their defences amidst defeat and chaos. Marshal Ivan Koniev was newly appointed commander of the 'Western Front', as it was now called, and Yeremenko commanded the 'Bryansk Front'. Many gaps between the two main forces had to be hurriedly plugged with troops from the so-called 'Reserve Front'. Arriving directly through Moscow, these formations manned a defence arc on the line Yeltsi–Dorogobush and were astride the Yukhna approach to the capital. In addition, Yeremenko also planned a counter-attack towards Glukhov.

The Russians had a total of 15 armies of infantry to defend Moscow, in all half a million men, but though well supplied with small arms, they were woefully short of artillery. These were second-line troops moreover, mostly reservists who had been trained in pre-blitzkrieg days. But far away on the other side of the U.S.S.R., facing the Japanese, were 25 infantry divisions and nine armoured brigades of splendidly trained and equipped troops. Now, at this crucial moment, Stalin's spies in Tokyo told him that Japan's armed forces would only be directed against Britain and America. Thus the Siberian troops, trained for fighting in the most bitter climate, became available to defend Moscow.

The people of Moscow were not prepared for the German onslaught. The Germans were apparently solidly held at the Yelna Bend 200 miles westward, and censorship had not allowed them to know the truth about the heavy fighting that had taken place around Kiev and Leningrad.

The German Panzer groups, which moved out on September 30, were spearheading a truly formidable force. Field-Marshal von Bock was in command of three infantry armies, the two Panzer groups (Hoth's and Guderian's) of Army Group Centre, and Hoepner's 4th Panzer Group, sent down from the Leningrad sector, which totalled 14 armoured divisions, eight motorized divisions, two motorized brigades and 46 infantry divisions, with massive supporting artillery including hundreds of 88-mm guns. For air support he had two air fleets to spy out and blast the way ahead. The planning of this terrible onslaught was as good as it could possibly be, with all the intense German knowledge and experience of armoured warfare behind it. The only conceivable flaw was that it should really have been begun at least one month earlier. The awful Russian winter was the factor that could halt the attack before Moscow was stormed.

The double battle of Vyazma and Bryansk opened with the explosive fury of all-out German blitzkrieg. Guderian drove his terrible spearhead straight at Bryansk, which was both Yeremenko's headquarters and the key point in Moscow's outer defences. With frightening ease the armoured columns cleft through the defences until, within three days, they had seized Orel, 125 miles behind the Bryansk front. German tanks rumbling into the town were greeted by waving tram passengers who thought they were welcoming Russian armour!

In swift succession the Panzers cut the Bryansk–Orel road, entered Karachev and rumbled round towards Bryansk. Yeremenko feared encirclement but was ordered to stand and fight to the death. By October 6, Bryansk had been stormed and the bridge over the Desna captured intact. Guderian's 2nd Panzer Group linked up with the 2nd Army fighting in from the west. Three Russian armies were caught. On the same day, the 10th Panzer Division thrust to within 11 miles of Vyazma and soon that encirclement was also completed. By the end of the double battle of Vyazma and Bryansk, the first phase of Operation Typhoon was completed. An awesome breach had been smashed through Moscow's main defence line.

On October 13 Kaluga, 100 miles south-west of Moscow, was entered. Then Kalinin, 93 miles north-west of the capital, was taken. The charging Panzers not only cut the Moscow–Leningrad railway, but captured intact a bridge across the wide Volga. The next main onslaught

*Top* Behind a white-painted tank, Russian tommy-gunners counter-attack enemy troops lurking among fir and larch trees

*Bottom* A Russian tank in winter camouflage – note how the gun is painted white – advances on a German Panzer it has surprised and destroyed

was upon the central fortifications around Borodino, only 62 miles from the capital and barring the way along the great motor road.

It was at Borodino, in 1812, that Napoleon had been dealt a crippling blow. Stalin desperately hoped that his troops would do the same to Hitler's invaders in 1941. He rushed over a crack rifle division from Vladivostok, which included two armoured brigades equipped with T 34 and KV 2 tanks. These powerfully armed, splendidly disciplined Siberians, fur-capped and with high fur boots and long coats, fought with unflinching valour for the high ground of Borodino. The T 34 tanks charged in massed formations for the first time, and Russian Stormovik dive-bombers plunged down upon the battlefield to vie with the howling Stukas. Increasing numbers of German tanks were drawn into the fearful clash of iron monsters and the entire army artillery on the sector was bombarding before the battle ended. The Germans suffered awful casualties, and one regiment was completely annihilated, but the victory was theirs.

Panic swept Moscow. Secret papers were burned by the hundredweight in the Kremlin. Lenin, in his glass coffin, was removed from Red Square to safety. The firing squads were detailed to deal with any sign of subversion, looting or cowardice. More than 200,000 Muscovites were conscripted, given four days training, and sent out to man the defences. Every man and woman in Moscow was in some way made part of the military machine. Women and boys dug earthworks all through the day and the increasingly cold nights.

And then the rain began – the rain that, as both sides knew, precedes the snow and the frost. Overnight the fields became too sodden for the tanks. Only the roads could be used now, and many of them were mere rutted dirt tracks which rain turned to quagmires.

The tearaway onslaught with which Operation Typhoon had begun had suddenly slowed to a deadly crawl. With the loss of its heady impetus, the verve to attack and attack had gone. And while the German Panzers stuck in the mud of the fields the broad-tracked Russian T 34s were able to cruise across the treacherous surface. They descended from the hills to make dangerous hit-and-run attacks. Nevertheless, the German infantry fought forward. They slew

and were slain amidst a forest of half-hidden pillboxes and entrenchments manned by Mongolians and Siberians, who neither expected to be taken prisoner nor took prisoners.

The icy rain lashed down. The Germans shivered in their summer uniforms and picked at the lice that infested them. But Moscow was so near now, so very near – the ultimate objective, whose winning must end the war on the cursed Eastern Front.

Key defence posts still to be overcome along the vital avenues of highway and railroad into Moscow were Naro–Fominsk and Krimskoye, Istra and Tula, Dmitrov and Zvenigorod – each a fortress of pillboxes and entrenchments. Every yard was paid for in blood. And when the Germans fought their way up on to the great Moscow highway, the road surface was hopelessly pitted with shell craters, brimming with mud and icy water.

Nevertheless, the armour had no option but to press on, exerting the main pressure along the Moscow motor road. The 10th Panzers, determined to be first there, soon floundered to a halt: tank and gun and vehicle stuck fast in the mud. Neither provisions nor ammunition could be brought up. And as they stuck there, bands of the broad-tracked Russian T 34s swirled across the soggy ground, killing and crippling with hit-and-run raids. Some 30 miles south, the 78th Infantry Division also fought to within 40 miles of Moscow before its attack too petered out in the mud. Naro-Fominsk, west of the capital, was taken by motorized troops, but they, too, were soon halted. They had forced a bridgehead across the Nara, but the tanks that should have used it were stuck in the mud. Von Bock had no alternative but to order a general halt until the ground should freeze solid.

In the south the blitz expert Guderian, with his Panzer army of $12\frac{1}{2}$ divisions, had been straining every nerve to take Tula and turn the southern flank. After his brilliant beginning with the capture of Orel, Guderian's battle-hardened Panzers had run into the mud barrier, but by fighting forward with great determination, and calling down the Stukas to blast strongpoints, the spearheads were only three miles from Tula by October 29. If they could overcome Tula, it should be possible to plunge on to take Moscow in the rear. Then the encirclement would be complete.

SWEDEN

FINLAND

White Sea

Archangel

Baltic Sea

Leningrad

RUSSIA

ESTONIA

Lake Peipus

LATVIA

LITHUANIA

Pskov

Daugava

Kalinin

Moscow-Volga Canal

Daugavpils

Dvina

Klin

Dmitrov

Volga

Kaunas

Vilna

Vitebsk

Vyazma

Borodino

Moscow

Konigsberg

Orsha

EAST

Bialystok

Borisov

Smolensk

Tula

PRUSSIA

Minsk

Shklov

Mogilev

Kaluga

Bobrysk

Roslavl

Gorki

Warsaw

Bug

Brest Litovsk

Bryansk

POLAND

Pripet

Rogachev

Gomel

Orel

Marshes

Glukhov

Ostrov

Desna

Don

Lvov

Kiev

Donets

Stalingrad

Carpathian Mountains

U K R A I N E

Dnieper

Rostov-on-Don

RUMANIA

CRIMEA

Caspian Sea

BULGARIA

Black Sea

TURKEY

Moscow

The leather masks worn by some Germans in the biting cold presented a fearsome aspect

Tula was formidably defended and, despite the most ferocious attack upon the city's outer defences, Guderian's advance was halted. Everywhere around mud squelched and sucked; transport was bogged down, supplies could not get through, and the men and the guns went hungry.

Along the entire 600-mile front of Army Group Centre the advance had petered out by November. Increasingly now, the seasoned Siberians were arriving to stiffen the Russian resistance, while the Germans' strength was sapped by the wilderness of mud, as they waited desperately for the frost. During the night of November 6 it came at last. Suddenly the ground was hard enough for the tanks and guns to roll forward. But the frost that freed the armour from the mud cruelly ravaged the men who had to fight and drive.

The first onslaught was on Klin, a town north-west of Moscow on the Kalinin road. In a desperate, hopeless attempt to stem the German advance, two regiments of Mongolian cavalry made a wild, suicidal charge out of the dark forest. Some 2,000 were slaughtered and not one German wounded. Panzers swiftly by-passed Klin to the south-west, while the town itself was stormed by another Panzer force. Even as the Germans rejoiced in this easy victory, the thermometer fell still lower. Snowflakes fluttered across the brittle land, and a freezing fog closed in upon them to snatch their breath away.

The German advance rolled forward to storm Solnechnogorsk on November 23, despite the town's determined defences. Some two dozen Russian tanks, including British Mark IIIs, were knocked out in this battle. German and Russian tank design was far in advance of the Western Allies – so far in advance that few of the huge contributions to Russia (5,250 tanks from America, 4,260 from Britain, and 1,220 from Canada) were ever used in combat on the Eastern Front. The only Allied tank which could have been any use in the East, the American Sherman, did not start production until summer 1942, when by Russian standards it was already obsolete. At that date, the superior T 34 had been in full production for 18 months, and the T 34/85 and the awesome German Tiger were already laid down.

Two days after Solnechnogorsk, the Germans also took the town of Peshki, to the south-east. The 2nd Panzer Division was now only 37 miles from Moscow and heading down a really good road at last. The Moscow–Volga Canal was outflanked from the north, where three infantry divisions were pressing forward on the heels of the armour. The German advance seemed to have regained its ferocity.

Amidst the growing Russian apprehension motorcycle patrols of Panzer engineers roared into Khimki, Moscow's small port on the Volga only five miles from the outskirts of the great capital. They met no opposition, and although they returned from this foray with equal speed, they left behind a panicking populace.

Soon, the news was even blacker. Elements of an infantry division with artillery support, attacking on the right of the 2nd Panzers, penetrated to Lunevo. Everything pointed to a full-scale German breakthrough to Moscow from the north, where a strong bridgehead had been established on the eastern bank of the Moscow–Volga Canal. A Russian armoured

Almost reminiscent of a scene from Napoleon's retreat from Moscow, German soldiers trudge wearily away from the great Russian capital that defeated them, too, in the end

train that attempted to intervene was knocked out by Panzers which had crossed the canal. The great power station near the canal, upon which Moscow relied for most of its electricity, was captured intact.

The fall of Moscow seemed only a matter of a few more days, when on November 27 the thermometer suddenly fell 20 degrees in two hours, to 40 below zero. Thousands of German soldiers were crippled by frostbite and gripped by a blood-chilling, paralysing ague. The few consignments of winter clothing that had reached them since November 19 had been ridiculously inadequate. Hitler and his generals later complained that the attack on Moscow was thwarted only because of the unusually early onset of the Russian winter, but the truth was not that winter was early, the German Command had not planned for it.

The terrible cold seized upon machines and weapons as well as upon men. Tank engines went dead, machine-guns and automatic weapons froze solid, rifle bolts were jammed by frozen oil. And at this moment the Soviet 1st Striking Army burst upon the scene, their machine-guns cloaked against the crushing cold, their weapons smoothly lubricated with winter oil, and each man warmly clad against the climate. They were massively supported by T 34 tanks, designed and built to operate under just such frigid conditions. They launched themselves upon the torpid, agonized Germans and swept them back from the canal bridgehead that was so vital to their last great surge forward upon Moscow.

Farther south, below Rogachevo, the Germans still made progress towards the capital. A Panzer corps hammered its way forward through driving snow to force another canal crossing at Lobnya on December 1. A combat group detached from the 2nd Panzer Division stormed the village of Ozeretskoye, 20 miles from the Kremlin itself. Krasnaya Polyana, Pushki and Katyushki were taken in quick succession. By now literally tens of thousands of workers – the Opolchentsy (Home Guard) – had been crowded into breaches in the defences, with hurried instruction on how to fire the old rifles thrust into their hands. Inevitably they were slaughtered in their thousands by the tanks and infinitely better armed and trained infantry soldiers of the Wehrmacht, but in many places they held up the Germans until the Russian tanks could intervene.

The workers in the armament factories on the far eastern outskirts of Moscow worked at a frantic tempo, to turn out T 34 tanks which rumbled from the production lines straight into the streets and across the city to charge, guns blazing, into the enemy. Through Moscow's grim, deserted thoroughfares rattled lorry after lorry laden with workers' militia on their way to the railway stations where trains were waiting to rush them out against the enemy salients at Gorki and Katyushki. Every available motor vehicle, including requisitioned cars, taxis and even the black limousines of senior party officials, went speeding east to west across the city, hurrying Siberian troops, as they arrived, into action against the foe on Moscow's threshold.

A furious German attack to achieve a final breakthrough from the north-west was mounted along the axis of the road from Staritsa, through Volokolamsk, to Moscow. At the same time, with a howling blizzard blowing around them, the Germans battled on to take Polevo and Vyoskovo, and were within 20 miles of Moscow from that direction too.

But too many German soldiers had reached the absolute extreme of their endurance. The awful, endless cold was more than the human body could stand. The continual appearance of more Russians and yet more Russians before them, when the very last reserves of the Russians were supposed to have been destroyed, was more than human mind could accept. Everywhere the German attack had spent its strength, ground to a halt, gripped by the agony of the cold. The hotchpotch of Russian troops and armed workers who now held them back almost in artillery range of Moscow would undoubtedly have been scattered by the Panzers two months before. But not now. An increasing number of German soldiers were flinging themselves down, frostbitten, in the snow, sobbing hysterically, 'I can't go on any more! I just can't go on!'

On the night of December 5 it finally became apparent to the German commanders that their troops could do no more. With the 2nd Panzer Division only ten miles from Moscow to the north, and to the south Guderian's iron columns poised to sweep around Tula, orders were given to break off the attack. For the first time since his imnipotent Panzers had overrun Poland, Guderian had to pull back to form a line for defence. And even as the Germans, in their misery, attempted to dig in to the iron-hard ground beneath the frozen snow, the Russians began to counter-attack. In haunting night forays from out of the snow, white-clad Siberian soldiers with white-painted automatics dealt sudden death and as suddenly slipped away. Overwhelmed by deep depression, in Tolstoy's old home at Yasnaya Polyana, Guderian noted, 'The attack against Moscow has failed. We have suffered defeat.'

The crack divisions of Army Group Centre were never to be the same again. They had been bled and frozen to death amidst the deep snows at the very threshold of Moscow, ultimately unable to fight in temperatures that plummeted as low as $-52°C$. And Hitler and his general staff had arrogantly underestimated both the numbers of the Russian troops available and their fighting power and morale.

The total German casualties on the Eastern Front at this time were 750,000 men. Although the Russian casualties were far greater, they had so many reserves that, at the height of Moscow's peril, it had been possible to switch to the capital's defence 30 fresh rifle divisions, 6 armoured and three cavalry divisions, and 33 rifle brigades. The German Army Group Centre, meanwhile, was not reinforced by so much as one division.

Had Hitler not committed Germany to fighting on two fronts, had not the British fought on despite the impossible odds after the fall of France, the outcome might have been very different. If, in the final hour of faltering before Moscow, the Wehrmacht could have been reinforced by the German troops then committed against Britain in Africa, or compelled warily to stand guard in Western Europe and on the Mediterranean, if they could have thrown in the crack airborne battalions decimated in the bloody battle for Crete, if all the warplanes and their crews shot down in the Battle of Britain had been available, then Moscow must have fallen. Above all, had the start of Operation Barbarossa not been delayed four weeks by Wavell's victory in North Africa, and by Germany's engagement in the Balkans, total victory would probably have been achieved in Russia before the onset of winter.

Thousands of German soldiers were overcome by the bitter cold on the threshold of Moscow, and this Russian picture shows just two who succumbed

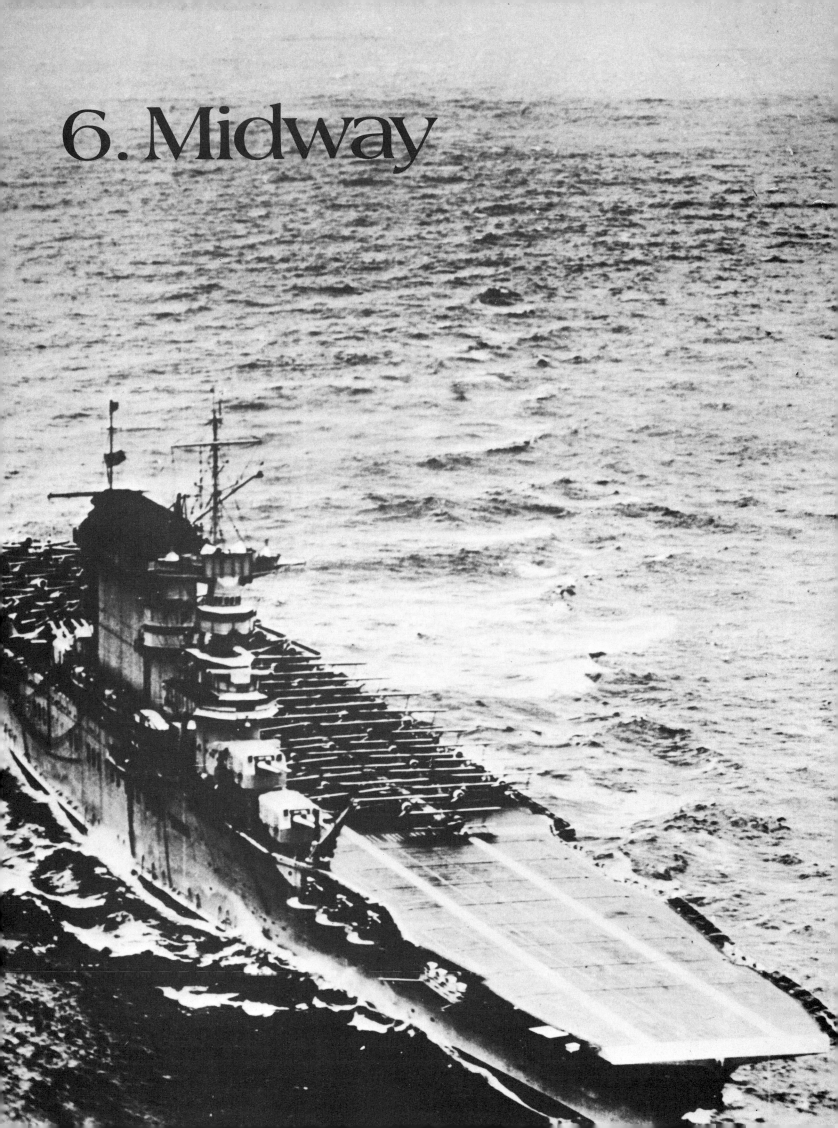

# 6. Midway

# 6. Midway

At 7.55 a.m. on Sunday, December 7, 1941, 354 Japanese warplanes attacked Pearl Harbor, the great American naval base in Hawaii, without any warning. In less than two hours they crippled the American Pacific Fleet, killed 2,403 Americans and wounded another 1,176. Suddenly, the United States was in the war.

Emerging as a world power from victorious wars against Russia, the aggressively militant Japanese had attacked China in 1937. That gave them an opportunity to train men under the tough conditions of a shooting war, and provided them with strategic jumping-off places on the Asian continent for taking British colonial strongholds in the rear. The nation's war industries were put on a full-scale war footing which gave them, in some cases, superior armaments to those of the Western Allies.

The most significant of Japan's new weapons were their aircraft carriers, and the dive-bombers, torpedo-bombers and fighters, the most advanced of their type in the world, to fly from them. The Japanese were first to appreciate that aircraft carriers and not battleships would dictate the tempo of war in the Pacific.

Japan's warlords believed that the Pacific would be at their mercy if they could knock out the American Fleet with one violent unexpected blow. The instigator of the attack on Pearl Harbor was Admiral Isoroku Yamamoto, the Japanese commander-in-chief. He had secretly massed a formidable armada of six huge aircraft carriers, with a strong protecting force of battleships, cruisers, destroyers and submarines, in a remote mist-shrouded anchorage in the Kurile Islands to the north of Japan. On November 26 they set sail under the command of Vice-Admiral Chuichi Nagumo, to steal upon the unsuspecting American Pacific Fleet.

There were 94 warships, including eight battleships, lying at anchor in Pearl Harbor. It was only by chance that the three aircraft carriers and the strong cruiser force which usually anchored there were out on missions at the time. Aided by fogs and storms, the Japanese force remained undetected and unsuspected. When little more than 270 miles north of Pearl Harbor, the bombers and torpedo-bombers took off to attack. When they returned they had left the shattered American fleet shrouded in towering smoke amidst which the battleship *Arizona* had been blown to pieces. Every other battleship, except the *Pennsylvania*, had been grievously damaged. The *Oklahoma* had capsized. The *West Virginia* and *California* had foundered at their moorings. Meanwhile the bomb-pitted

*Above* Admiral Yamamoto, who commanded the massive Japanese fleet that set out to destroy American naval power in the Pacific

*Opposite, top* The great U.S. Navy warship *California*, stricken and sinking, in the foreground, with two other victims of the Japanese attack on Pearl Harbor behind her already doomed and enveloped in black smoke

*Opposite, bottom* The U.S.S. *Shaw* exploding after a direct hit by a Japanese bomb during the attack on Pearl Harbor

airfields were strewn with the smoking wreckage of over 100 American aircraft. The Japanese had lost only 29 planes.

The Japanese were so satisfied with the havoc they had wrought that they made no attempt to seek out the three great American aircraft carriers, *Enterprise*, *Lexington* and *Saratoga*, which were within range. The survival of these three carriers was to cost the Japanese Navy dear in the months to come. At the time of the attack 11 cruisers and 11 destroyers were also out to sea, while 5 cruisers and 29 destroyers had somehow survived amidst the holocaust in the harbour.

The destruction of Pearl Harbor itself was not as serious as it looked. The Japanese dive-bombers had ignored the dockyards, with their immense repair facilities, and the vast array of brimming oil tanks were still intact. Vice Admiral Nagumo, commander-in-chief of the 1st Air Fleet which had made the attack, was uneasy about the whole operation, and turned

for home with the task unfinished.

As Churchill had promised, Britain declared war on Japan immediately after Pearl Harbor. Within hours Japanese bombers raided British Hong Kong and a powerful Japanese invasion armada loomed in the Gulf of Siam. Soon troops began to swarm ashore on the long, undefended coast of Malaya. Three days after Pearl Harbor the great British battleships *Prince of Wales* and *Repulse*, rushed east to aid the Americans, were sunk by squadrons of Japanese bombers and torpedo-bombers. A heavy air and sea bombardment was opened on the American bases in the Philippines, as a prelude to invasion. The whole of South-East Asia lay open to Japan. The American Pacific strongholds of Wake Island and Guam were stormed. Hong Kong fell. The Dutch East Indies – Sumatra, Java, Borneo and neighbouring islands – were invaded. Singapore, Britain's great Far Eastern naval base on which all defence in the Pacific was founded, was taken on February 15, 1942.

*Above* An American B25 Mitchell medium bomber, of the type used to bomb Tokyo, seen making an attack on Japanese shipping in the Pacific

*Opposite page* Another view of the devastation at Pearl Harbor seen across the wreckage-strewn naval air station

Tough and resourceful Japanese soldiers swarmed through Thailand, Malaya and onwards through Burma toward the threshold of India. In the Philippines the Americans under General Douglas MacArthur made a heroic but hopeless stand at Corregidor. By March, 1942, the Japanese had gained a vast empire of untold wealth and natural resources, including the rich oil fields of South-East Asia, so necessary to them for a far-ranging war at sea.

At least one of the Japanese leaders was not blinded by illusion of complete supremacy. This was Admiral Yamamoto, commander-in-chief of the combined fleets of the Imperial Japanese Navy. He did not let the exhilaration of the moment overwhelm him because he knew America and the Americans better perhaps than all the rest. Yamamoto had studied at Harvard and had been Japan's naval attaché in Washington for some years. During that time he had travelled the country extensively and studied the Americans' war potential in great depth. One fact had impressed itself upon his mind above everything else – America's production capacities were so immense that once the nation was fully geared to war Japan would stand little chance. The war, he knew, would have to be finished off quickly, before this could happen.

To achieve this goal, Yamamoto knew that he would have to destroy the already badly crippled American Pacific Fleet. The American commander, Admiral Chester Nimitz, was understandably reluctant to join battle. In the five months immediately after Pearl Harbor he risked only such hit and run raids as would

provide propaganda material likely to bring a glimmer of hope to the badly shaken Allied morale in the Far East. On January 23 American marines landed on Samoa, covered by the U.S. carriers *Yorktown* and *Enterprise*, with cruisers and destroyers in support. On February 20, the *Lexington*, with a group of warships, was sent to attack Rabaul in New Britain where the Japanese were establishing a strong land and sea base. Although the raid was abandoned after shore-based enemy bombers came out to attack the American carriers, Wildcat fighters from the *Lexington* gave heartening promises of things to come. They shot down nearly all the bombers before any damage could be done. But even as the Americans were scoring this small success, Nagumo's carrier force made a devastating raid on the Australian port of Darwin.

The Americans hit back again. A combined force of warplanes from the *Lexington* and *Yorktown* raided and sank Japanese vessels which were extending their conquests towards Australia through Papua and New Guinea. But Nagumo's carriers were not in the vicinity. The *Akagi*, *Soryu*, *Hiryu*, *Shokaku* and *Zuikaku* and their massive escort of battleships, cruisers and destroyers

*Above* A Catalina (PBY) amphibious long-range reconnaissance plane such as the United States navy used to shadow the Japanese fleet before the Battle of Midway

*Opposite, top* Emperor Hirohito inspecting bomb damage in Tokyo. The Japanese naval commanders were determined to avenge this insult to their Emperor when they set out to attack Midway Island

*Opposite, bottom* Admiral Chester Nimitz, Commander-in-Chief of the U.S. Pacific fleet

had surged into the Indian Ocean to destroy the British Far Eastern Fleet. Their aircraft massively raided the naval bases of Colombo and Trincomalee, but the forewarned British had dispersed their fleet, and Nagumo only sank the small carrier *Hermes*, the cruisers *Cornwall* and *Dorsetshire*, a destroyer and a corvette.

Early in May occurred the so-called Battle of the Coral Sea, south of New Guinea. An American carrier force intercepted and turned back an invasion force headed for Port Moresby. At the end of the battle, the Americans had lost the carrier *Lexington*, and the *Yorktown* had been damaged. On the other hand, the small Japanese carrier *Shoho*, and both the huge fleet carriers *Shokaku* and *Zuikaku* were badly dam-

aged, while many skilled aircrews who had played vital roles in Japan's dazzling successes so far were shot down. Strategically, the battle was an American victory, and it was the first reverse that the Japanese had sustained since they had set out upon their campaign of conquest.

Meanwhile, on April 18, Japan itself received a rude blow – a raid on Tokyo by a small number of Mitchell B 25 medium bombers, led by Colonel James Dolittle. They had been specially adapted for their long-range (700-mile) raid, and arrangements had been made for them to fly on to airfields in China instead of returning to their carriers. As a result Dolittle's force achieved complete surprise, and bombed Tokyo, Yokohama, Kawasaki, Yokosuka and other towns before anything could be done to stop them. The material damage was slight, but the hurt to Japan's pride was immense. The Emperor, whom the nation venerated as a god, had been assured by his commanders that no enemy bomb would ever be permitted to fall upon his sacred country. Admiral Yamamoto made his abject apologies to the Emperor and determined to destroy the American carrier force without delay.

First, he had to lure them into battle, and that was to be achieved by an attack on the American island base of Midway, 1,136 miles north-west of Pearl Harbor. The Americans had developed Midway – consisting of two islands, Sand and Eastern – as an advanced base for naval patrol planes vital to the protection of Pearl Harbor. Without Midway as a forward observation post, Pearl Harbor would become untenable, and the Pacific would be abandoned to the Japanese.

The crucial day for the Midway assault was designated N-Day. But the operation would actually commence three days earlier with a diversionary seaborne attack on the Aleutian Islands, strung out into the North Pacific in a ragged crescent from Alaska. The Americans were bound to send warships to investigate, whereupon the main force under Nagumo would attack Midway from the north-west. On N-Day itself the invasion force would swarm in from all sides, covered by the guns of the 2nd Fleet under Admiral Nobutake Kondo. Yamamoto's battlefleet, stationed 300 miles to the rear, would move in when the American fleet approached. Then the main object of the operation would be achieved by a few thunderous broadsides from those mighty battleships, of which Yamamoto's flagship, the 64,000-ton *Yamoto*, was not only the biggest but the mightiest battleship in the world.

Although the Japanese had no radar, they were confident that their submarine screens and scout planes would spot the Americans' approach. Two cordons of submarines were already in place between Hawaii and Midway, some of them carrying aviation spirit to refuel the far-ranging Japanese seaplanes at lonely atolls. Other long-range submarines set out, carrying midget submarines piggy-back, to further confuse the issue by raiding shipping and harbour installations from Sydney to Madagascar.

By May 20 the might of the Japanese Navy had concentrated in readiness in the inland sea anchorage of Hashirajima. There were 11 battleships, 22 cruisers, 8 aircraft carriers, 2 seaplane carriers, 65 destroyers and 21 submarines. With its service vessels, the fleet numbered in all over 200 ships. The U.S. Navy could only muster 3 aircraft carriers, 3 cruisers and 14 destroyers. So confident were the Japan-

*Above* The U.S.S. *Hornet*, the other aircraft carrier in Admiral Spruance's Task Force 16

*Opposite, top* The mighty U.S. Navy carrier *Enterprise* which played such a vital role in the American victory of Midway

*Opposite, bottom* A Japanese medium bomber of the type known to the Allies as the 'Betty'

ese that they arranged for their mail to be sent to Midway.

To confuse, as well as to envelop, the American fleet, the huge armada was split up into eight task forces. Two of them were detailed for the diversionary attack and landings on the eastern Aleutian Islands of Attu and Kiska, and a third was to obliterate the small American base at Dutch Harbor, farther along this island chain towards Alaska. When the Japanese aircraft started bombing Dutch Harbor, the American fleet would come hurrying north, and the great battleships and fleet carriers of the fourth and main task force in these northern waters would fall upon them. This fourth task force, designated the Aleutian Support Force, had a formidable hard core of four battleships.

Heading for Midway, meanwhile, would be the troops who would storm the island, their

transports screened by cruisers and destroyers, and by a farther-ranging and formidable force that included two battleships. Designated the Occupation Force, these three groups were commanded by Vice-Admiral Kondo.

But the force that would wreak the most devastating execution upon the Americans was Nagumo's force of four great fleet carriers with their warplanes and experienced aircrews. They were accompanied by the battleships *Kirishima* and *Haruna*, 3 cruisers and 11 destroyers. Yamamoto's main body, with the terrifying fire-power of the three leviathan battleships *Mutsu*, *Nagato* and *Yamoto*, completed this execution armada.

The Japanese Combined Fleet Headquarters selected June 7 as N-Day. The moonlight would at that time be most favourable for night actions and landings. The massive air assault to be launched from Nagumo's force while still 250 miles north-west of Midway on N-day minus 2 was not only to shatter the island's air force and defences, but also to sink all American warships in the vicinity. On N minus 1 a small Seaplane Tender Force under Admiral Fujita was to descend on the little atoll of Kure, 60 miles north-west of Midway, and establish a base to give support to the landings and provide far-ranging reconnaissance to spy out the approach of the American warships lured into the trap. At first light on June 7, Japanese marines would simultaneously storm ashore on both Sand and Eastern Islands behind a bombardment by Rear-Admiral Kurita's support group of heavy cruisers. While this invasion was being accomplished the southern and south-western approaches to Midway would be covered by Vice-Admiral Kondo's main invasion force. The Japanese Combined Fleet H.Q. expected the Americans to be too bewildered by the simultaneous attacks on Midway and the Aleutians to mount serious resistance before the landings had been completed.

Yamamoto's battleships were to wait 600 miles north-west of Midway, while Nagumo lurked 300 miles to the east. Vice-Admiral Shiro Takasu's force of 4 battleships, 2 light cruisers and 12 destroyers, would be 500 miles to the north, and 300 miles east of Takasu would be Rear-Admiral Kakuji Kakuto with the light carriers *Ryugo* and *Junyo*, two heavy cruisers and three destroyers. Three lines of submarines cordoned the whole area to give early warning of approaching enemy ships.

Despite the Japanese machinations designed to confuse them, the Americans had a good idea of what was afoot. At Pearl Harbor, Commander Joseph J. Rochefort Jr. had cracked the Japanese code. The most significant references in the stream of messages ·which crackled across the Pacific were the letters 'AF', which obviously signified some massive operation. Rochefort's group of decoders found an earlier reference to 'AF' in a Japanese message that concerned a seaplane attack on Pearl Harbor two months earlier. The planes had been ordered to refuel at a little atoll near 'AF' which, the Americans deduced, could only refer to Midway. To make doubly sure, the navy commander at Midway was instructed to pass a decoy radio message in plain English reporting the island's freshwater plant out of action. Soon afterwards a Japanese code message was intercepted stating that 'AF' was likely to be short of fresh water.

The force that Admiral Nimitz was able to muster to defend Midway was so small that even to contemplate challenging the huge Japanese fleet appeared suicidal. He had only three aircraft carriers: the *Enterprise* and the *Hornet*, which were far to the south around the Solomon Islands, and the *Yorktown*, damaged in the Battle of the Coral Sea. In addition, Nimitz could muster only 8 cruisers and 14 destroyers. To add to the American Navy's worries, Vice-Admiral William F. Halsey on the *Enterprise* was hospitalized with shingles on

*Above* Vice-Admiral Kondo, who commanded the
Japanese Second Fleet deputed to cover the invasion of
Midway island, seen here on his way to be received by
the Emperor in Tokyo

*Opposite page* The Japanese battleship *Nagato*, one of the
huge capital ships which gave the Japanese navy such
overwhelming firepower

May 26. He was replaced by Rear-Admiral
Raymond A. Spruance, who had been commanding the cruisers and destroyers of the
carrier's screening force. One day later the
badly damaged *Yorktown* limped into Pearl
Harbor. Day and night efforts made her battle-
worthy again by May 30.

Being aware of Japanese plans, the Americans
themselves could plan to lay a trap. Admirals
Spruance and Fletcher (on the *Yorktown*) were
to lie in wait 200 miles north-east of Midway.
Although Nimitz himself was certain that Midway was the Japanese objective, others were
not convinced, and the position north-east of
Midway was chosen so that the carriers could
also move to defend Hawaii or the American
west coast.

The reinforcement of Midway was meanwhile proceeding at furious pace. Two squadrons of long-range B 17 Flying Fortresses had
already landed there, along with four squadrons
of Mitchells adapted for torpedo attacks. A
whole shipload of fighters and dive-bombers
had been put ashore, and more and more anti-
aircraft guns were arriving. Hundreds of miles
of barbed wire, sandbags by tens of thousands
and huge quantities of ammunition, were unloaded and rushed out to the thickening defences.
Fast PT (torpedo) boats were hustled into the
lagoon. Squadrons of B 17s were also stationed
at Pearl Harbor.

By now the American decoders had discovered
not only how many Japanese warships and
troops were heading for Midway, but also the
actual units involved, the captains of all the
ships, and even the courses they would sail.
This was extremely fortunate, because immediately after they had set out for Midway the
Japanese switched to a different code.

By daybreak on June 2 the various Japanese
task forces were in position far out upon the
Pacific. About this time radio operators on the
great battleship *Yamoto* intercepted a long and
obviously urgent message from a far-ranging
American submarine which had spotted the
advancing troop transports and their escorts.
The Japanese could not decode the message,
but it had obviously been directed to Midway –
an indication the Americans must now be
expecting an attack.

Rather than disturb the Japanese commanders, this news delighted them. They felt
sure that the American reaction would be to
send up their fleet from Pearl Harbor to its
inevitable destruction, and this was of course
the main purpose of the attack upon Midway.

To the north of the island, Nagumo was unaware of the American submarine's warning to
Midway, and bad visibility prevented him
sending out spotter planes. While fog and murk
effectively masked his formation from any (unlikely) enemy warships that might approach,
he himself was blinded.

Dawn on June 3 brought thicker fog. Even
searchlights could barely penetrate the murk.

Because of the danger of collision, Nagumo was compelled to break radio silence to issue orders to his ships.

The Americans planned to give battle to the huge Japanese armada in two separate forces. Task Force 16, commanded by Admiral Spruance, comprised the carriers *Hornet* and *Enterprise*, screened by five heavy cruisers, one light cruiser and nine destroyers. Task Force 17, under Admiral Fletcher, consisted of the carrier *Yorktown* with two heavy cruisers and six destroyers. The first force sailed from Pearl Harbor on May 28; the second put out on May 30. They were under instructions to rendezvous with fleet tankers on June 3 to refuel, then take up position under Admiral Fletcher's command north-east of Midway. There they were to lie in wait for Nagumo's

*Top* The Japanese aircraft carrier *Kaga* with crew members lined up across the great flight deck

*Above* The Japanese battleship *Kagato*, one of the immensely powerful warships sent against Midway

*Opposite, top* Rear-Admiral Raymond A. Spruance of the United States Navy, whose Task Force 16 included the carriers *Hornet* and *Enterprise*

*Opposite, bottom* Rear-Admiral Frank Fletcher, commander of Task Force 17, which included the carrier *Yorktown*

carriers, whose orders were well-known. Meanwhile, Yamamoto was informed that the surviving enemy carriers were certainly far away in the Solomon Islands.

With rain still enshrouding them, the huge Japanese formations began to move into position on the morning of June 3. Takasu's guard force, heading northwards to cover the Aleutian landings, was scheduled to be within 500 miles of Kiska Island on June 6. By then Yamamoto's main body would be 500 miles south of him, so that the two forces could quickly join up should an enemy counter-attack develop in either area. However, Takasu's force had been steaming north for barely 30 minutes when Yamamoto had to make a change of plan. He received news that the Japanese transport force making full speed for Midway was being shadowed from the air. The Americans would now expect an invasion and an early attack by bombers from Midway had to be reckoned with.

Nine Flying Fortresses soon appeared, but their bombs spouted harmlessly in the ocean and the Japanese transports and their escorts forged ahead undamaged. Early next morning, a small formation of sea-skimming torpedo-bombers pressed home an attack, but achieved only one hit, on a tanker at the rear of the convoy. Nevertheless, Yamamoto was concerned. He had expected Nagumo's dive-bombers to blast Midway and its airfields before the Americans even suspected the approach of the invasion fleet.

Meanwhile, in the early hours of June 3, the orders had been given for the attack on Dutch Harbor. The air was bitter, with seven degrees of frost, and leaden clouds crowded upon the sea as the bombers and their escorts took off for their 180-mile flight to the American base in the Aleutians. When they returned, they reported that they had been unable to locate their targets, but they had discovered that the Americans did have an air base on the island. Four Japanese reconnaissance seaplanes had dared the filthiest weather to probe the enemy coast; they were fiercely assailed by Wildcat fighters which shot down two of them.

To the south, excitement among Nagumo's forces was mounting. They were clear of the fog by 10 a.m. on June 3, and the way ahead was sparkling and bright. They churned the smooth blue seas white as they ploughed on at

24 knots, a great circle of grey steel in which the gun-bristling battleships *Haruna* and *Kirishima* loomed large, and the four great carriers cruised majestically in the centre. At dawn the next day, it was suddenly zero hour.

The first faint suffusion of dawn was just easing the sky from the sea when the floodlights sprang out along the vast flight decks of the *Akagi*, *Kaga*, *Hiryu* and *Soryu*. Within 15 minutes, 108 planes – 36 each of dive-bombers, level-bombers and Zero fighters – arose from the carriers' decks, roared around in an impressive circle, and then swept away to the south-east. They were but a distant mutter in the reddening sky when the aircraft for the second attack wave began to come up on to the flight decks. The red orb of the rising sun – so like the triumphant flag of Japan – was up clear of the horizon by the time the flight decks were once more filled with planes. This time, it was hoped, there would be some enemy warships to hit as well as shore installations. The torpedo-plane pilots were the elite of the Japanese air arm, and although all the Japanese commanders were certain that there were no American carriers anywhere near, Nagumo had kept his most brilliant aircrews back for the second wave, just in case.

But the Americans on Midway were ready and waiting for Nagumo's first wave. A formation of 26 Wildcat fighters throbbed in the skies above the island as the leading Japanese squadrons closed in. Suddenly, while the enemy were still 30 miles distant, a brilliant flare burst out above and dead behind them, fired by the crew of a Catalina who had courageously shadowed the attackers. Minutes later the sky was full of diving, zooming, dog-fighting warplanes as the Japanese escort engaged the American fighters before they could get in among the bombers. The crack Zero pilots fulfilled their mission brilliantly, for they prevented the Wildcats shooting down even one bomber, but the bombers found only empty runways and empty hangars to bomb – all the planes were aloft.

A number of Wildcats were shot down, and nearly all the rest were damaged, while only six attackers failed to return. However, the Japanese had achieved little of their object – to destroy the bombers on Midway. They would have to launch a second attack. By the time the second wave, already warming up on the

carriers, roared in over Midway, the American bombers which had fled the approach of the first would have been compelled to land, to be utterly destroyed.

While the first wave was away, the Zero fighters patrolling the advancing carrier force had a frustrating time trying to catch the watching Catalinas. For all their comparative unwieldiness, the American flying-boats led them an infuriating dance, slipping in and out of the clouds and sending constant reports of their activities.

Suddenly American torpedo-bombers appeared in the sky. Flags were run up to mast-heads, alarm bugles rang out, and the Zeros went into action. In a few seconds they had shot down three bombers into the sea, while a fourth made its escape.

Minutes later the great guns of the capital ships bellowed, and the rapid fire of anti-aircraft guns cracked ear-splittingly, as ten American torpedo-bombers, Avengers and Marauders, loomed to starboard. In a single line they came on, through shell-bursts, through air seared by hot steel splinters, droning in towards the great *Akagi*. Zeros shot three down in flames, but the other seven pressed onwards, nearer and nearer, towards the Japanese carriers. One after the other, they dropped their torpedoes and bounded up into the sky. One bomber barely skimmed the *Akagi* before bursting into flames.

The death-or-glory mission of these six Avenger torpedo-bombers, and the four Marauder medium bombers specially adapted to carry torpedoes, had failed, despite the great bravery of their crews who had no fighter escort. Only one Avenger and two Marauders returned to Midway.

Nagumo fully appreciated how nearly the attack had succeeded. At all costs, Midway's bomber force would have to be wiped out! He ordered his second wave of attacking planes to be rearmed with high-explosive bombs. With a furious urgency the flying crews and armourers aboard the *Akagi* and *Kaga* began to unload the torpedoes from planes all set to attack enemy warships. Hurriedly they were lowered to the rearming deck below the flight deck to prepare them for their new mission. This work was still feverishly going on when the clarion call of the air-raid bugles once more rang over the fleet! Fourteen Flying Fortresses, at 20,000 feet like

Superfortress long-range bombers, which made high-level attacks on the advancing Japanese fleet

murmuring moths, were glittering in from the south-east. They dropped their bombs, but when the water subsided the carriers were still serenely sailing onwards. The Japanese fighters made no attempt to catch the great multigunned Fortresses, and all returned to Midway safely.

Nagumo saw that his 18 airborne Zeros should be reinforced. He ordered aloft all the 36 fighters that had been intended to give cover to the second-wave bombers. They had barely climbed to combat height, before another American formation was sighted. This time there were 16 Devastator dive-bombers, raggedly scattered across the sky at a height insufficient for dive bombing, yet not low enough for torpedo attack. These semi-obsolescent planes were manned by Marine pilots with no experience of dive-bombing, in a do-or-die attack which few could have expected to survive. As the Zeros hurtled down upon them, they exploded, one after the other. Somehow, a handful got close enough to the *Hiryu* to bomb, and eight of the attackers managed to get back to Midway, riddled with bullets and shell splinters. They had done no damage, and Nagumo felt reassured that his vessels were in little danger from the Midway bombers, which his second wave would destroy anyway. They presented nothing like the menace of carrier-borne warplanes with crews trained to attack ships.

While the first wave of Japanese planes was still winging back from Midway, the crew of a wide-ranging scout plane from the Japanese escort cruiser *Tone* discovered something startling. At the very moment they were about to turn back at the end of their 300-mile search arc, they spotted ten ships heading south-east. When Nagumo, after some delay, received their report, he was immediately seized with alarm A swift calculation in the chart room revealed

that the enemy force was barely 200 miles distant. If, despite all the careful calculations of the Navy High Command, there were enemy carriers among those reported ten vessels, then Nagumo's four great carriers were, at that very moment, in the most dire peril. Had the Americans been setting an ambush, the position of those reported ships could not have been more favourable for the purpose. Nearly all the second-wave torpedo-bombers on the great *Akagi* and *Kaga* were down below on the rearming deck, being reloaded with high explosive for the follow-up attack on Midway's ground targets. Nagumo ordered that this rearming of his strike aircraft should be halted at once. Instead preparation must be made with the utmost urgency to attack enemy shipping targets. Then, while the fitters and armourers and aircrews worked frantically to rearm with ship-striking torpedoes, came relief from the *Tone*'s scout-plane: 'The enemy ships are five cruisers and five destroyers', it reported. Such an American force presented little threat to Nagumo, and again the rearming deck was thrown into confusion as the order was given to prepare to attack land targets after all.

The relief on Nagumo's bridge lasted precisely 21 minutes. Another message from the *Tone*'s reconnaissance plane revived all his foreboding: 'Enemy force accompanied by what appears to be aircraft carrier bringing up rear'. While the optimists on Nagumo's staff were pointing out the *Tone*'s plane had only reported there 'appeared to be' a carrier, there came an additional report of two more vessels, this time apparently cruisers, in the enemy force. The Japanese admiral became convinced that there must be at least one aircraft carrier in a force of such a size, whatever his own Intelligence might say. He gave orders that these ships must be attacked immediately. In the face of such apparent danger Midway could wait.

Nagumo was, in fact, in the very dilemma that was the nightmare of all commanders of aircraft carriers. His first wave had carried out an attack and had to be swiftly taken aboard

Wildcat fighters of the U.S. Navy returning from an attack on Japanese dive- and torpedo-bombers hunting the American aircraft carriers. Below them surf surges around a coral reef just off Midway Island

for refuelling; his second wave had not yet been able to take off; his fighters immediately covering the carriers against surprise attack were also running out of fuel. Should he now send the handful of torpedo-bombers on the flight decks of his carriers, still awaiting rearming with torpedoes, out against the enemy ships to attack with the comparatively ineffectual bombs in their racks? If he did, it would have to be without fighter escort, and Nagumo had only recently seen, brutally demonstrated before his eyes by his own Zeros, what happened to bombers that went in unescorted against fully protected carriers.

At that moment, Nagumo only had 36 dive-bombers armed and ready for take-off on the decks of the *Hiryu* and *Soryu*. Pitted against the enemy carriers, these would be without escort and therefore liable to crippling losses, with no certainty of striking any fatal blows. His returning first-wave warplanes had to be taken on first. Then, he decided, he would retire northwards until all his planes were suitably armed and refuelled and able to launch a massive assault on the enemy ships.

Flight decks were cleared, the first wave landed, the deadly Long Lance, ship-striking torpedoes were loaded. There was no time to send the unloaded bombs down to the ammunition magazines below; instead they were hastily piled to one side. As the men bent their energies to fitting the torpedoes, they were sealing their own doom.

Nagumo signalled his new plan to all ships, and to Admirals Yamamoto and Kondo. Apparently, pride forbade him mentioning that before engaging, he would retire to complete preparations.

While all this urgent activity was going on aboard the Japanese warships, an air of tense expectancy pervaded the American force which had caused it. Admiral Spruance, kept accurately informed by the shadowing Catalinas, had coolly bided his time until the Japanese carriers would be at maximum disadvantage – clearing decks to take in returning planes and refuelling and rearming them. When that time came, he dispatched a powerful force of 131 dive-bombers and torpedo-bombers to attack the Japanese carriers. It was immaculate timing. Within a few minutes of the last Japanese plane back from Midway putting down on its parent carrier,

the outmost vessels of Nagumo's scout screen reported American planes approaching.

The first to be sighted were 15 Devastator torpedo-bombers, skimming in low over the ocean to starboard. Unescorted, these obsolescent aircraft stood no chance at all when a crowd of nearly 50 Zeros swarmed upon them. The jubilant Japanese sailors had barely finished cheering the disappearance of the last of the 15 distant dots in a puff of smoke and flame before lookouts sent two more electrifying reports in quick succession: 'Enemy torpedo-bombers coming in low to starboard', 'Enemy torpedo-planes approaching to port'! But again the Americans had no fighter escorts. Each flying in a single column, there were 14 torpedo-bombers to starboard and 12 to port. The Zeros dived again and again until the labouring Devastators were one after the other ripped open by tearing swathes of bullets. Those that somehow struggled into range were shredded by the ships' guns. Just five bombers to starboard and two to port reached a range at which they could usefully

*Above* A squadron of Devastator torpedo-bombers on the flight deck of the *Enterprise* about to take off to attack the advancing Japanese fleet

*Opposite, top* The battle is joined – a furious barrage of shell-fire fills the sky around the *Yorktown* and its escorts as enemy torpedo bombers attack

*Opposite, bottom* The *Hornet* under simultaneous attack by Japanese torpedo and dive-bombers

launch their torpedoes at the *Hiryu*, but the great carrier swung away from the foaming tracks and all the torpedoes passed by harmlessly.

As the uproar of battle died, it could be seen that of the 41 attacking torpedo-bombers only 6 had survived. They somehow managed to limp back to the distant American carriers. The Japanese pilots who had wrought this execution were cheered as they dropped down to the carriers to refuel. Then, suddenly, a more serious threat appeared. A Japanese lookout,

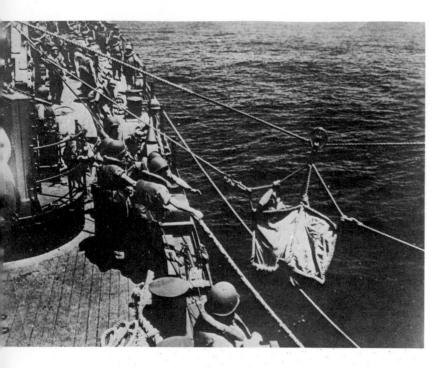

screamed, 'Hell-divers! Hell-divers!' He had spotted the vanguard of the Dauntless dive-bombers from the *Enterprise* and the *Yorktown*, flying high amongst the lofty clouds. Approaching unseen and unheard, they had arrived at precisely the right moment, when the Japanese carrier fleet could not fight back. What the American pilots saw below was a magnificent sight for any dive-bomber – a vast array of warships in a great circle and in the midst of this screening circle, four huge aircraft carriers! Best of all, the air above and around them was utterly clear of Japanese planes, which were lined up on the carrier's decks as though in ignorance of their peril. Moments later 37 dive-bombers were screaming down out of the bright blue sky upon the *Akagi* and *Kaga*. Seventeen planes from the *Yorktown* descended upon the *Soryu*, with never a Japanese fighter to challenge them, with no more than a few last-minute anti-aircraft bursts that came nowhere near them.

On the proud *Akagi*, Nagumo's flagship, where the orders had just been given for the fighters to take off, a brilliant flash seared the eyes of the officers on the bridge. A column of water climbed toweringly to topple over them. Almost simultaneously a second bomb plunged through the flight deck beyond the bridge and erupted with a thunderous uprush of flame and smoke. The first inner explosion, engulfing

*Left* A wounded American sailor is brought aboard an American cruiser from a smaller vessel which has come under enemy fire

*Above* U.S. Navy fighters range across the waters of the Pacific while a burning Japanese vessel can be seen below

planes and fuel and the carelessly unloaded bombs, triggered a second explosion that tore a vast section of the great ship asunder. Bomb after bomb tore through the deck to explode deep inside. Within seconds the terrifying internal inferno had boiled up and over to devour planes on the flight decks. The stern was shattered and the rudder out of action. As the great carrier lurched drunkenly it spewed flaming aircraft along its deck into the boiling sea. Nagumo himself seemed to be paralysed. His staff officers had to plead with him to leave the doomed, blazing hulk.

While the *Akagi* was blasted in just six tearaway minutes, another squadron from the *Enterprise* hurtled down upon the *Kaga*. This great vessel was crippled almost as swiftly, billowing oily smoke and livid with flame, shaken by repeated internal explosions and her warplanes consumed in the conflagration. Meanwhile the *Yorktown*'s dive-bombers fell upon the *Soryu*, and in minutes made her an exploding inferno.

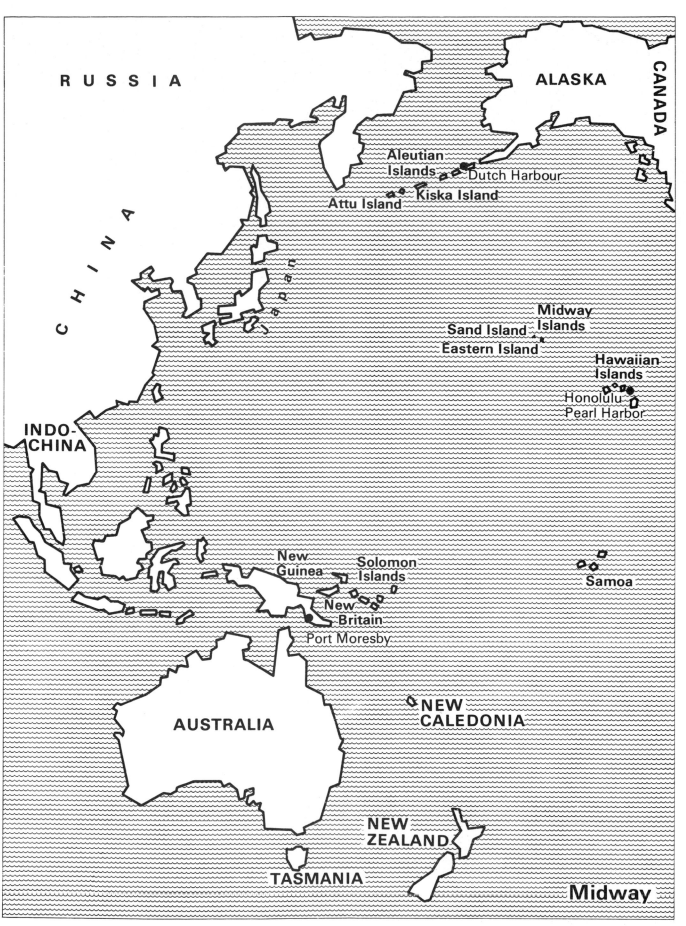

RUSSIA

ALASKA

CANADA

CHINA

Japan

Aleutian
Islands
Dutch Harbour

Attu Island
Kiska Island

Midway
Islands
Sand Island
Eastern Island

Hawaiian
Islands

Honolulu
Pearl Harbor

INDO-
CHINA

New
Guinea
Solomon
Islands

Samoa

New
Britain
Port Moresby

AUSTRALIA

NEW
CALEDONIA

NEW
ZEALAND

TASMANIA

Midway

All three great carriers were doomed beyond any hope. Huge, riven and blazing wrecks that only minutes before had been majestic aircraft carriers settled into the glittering Pacific.

While catastrophe overwhelmed his carrier striking force, Admiral Yamamoto, quite unaware, was ploughing onwards with his main force, 450 miles behind. It was at 10.30 a.m. that Yamamoto's dream of glory was abruptly interrupted by the message, 'The *Akagi* on fire'. The commander-in-chief said nothing. There were no words for such an event in a Japanese admiral's vocabulary, nor for the following message, 20 minutes later, 'Fires raging aboard *Kaga*, *Soryu* and *Akagi*, resulting from attacks by land-based and carrier-based planes. We are retiring north and assembling our forces'. The message intimated that the surviving *Hiryu* would counter-attack.

There was only one thing left for Yamamoto to do – sail on, with all the power at his command, and bring his great guns to bear on Midway and any American warships that dared intervene. Somehow he must exact a terrible retribution. Although his main force was now beset by fog, Yamamoto led it forward at 20 knots, plunging precariously through a murk so thick that each great ship was in a dim, dangerous shroud of its own. He ordered all his task forces to join up with his battleships, to prepare to fall upon the enemy. The transport group was to stand by, 500 miles west of Midway, ready to invade. The cruiser force, already detailed to deliver the pre-invasion bombardment, was to go in and do so that night. Meanwhile the surviving carrier *Hiryu* was to speed its warplanes away to exact immediate vengeance upon the American carriers.

The *Hiryu* swung into the battle. The aircrews of bombers and fighters were amazed to be told that they were all that was left, that on their heroism and skill alone depended the honour and glory of Japan. Within minutes their role had changed from carefree participators in the destruction of the surviving American

*Top* The *Yorktown* under heavy attack by Japanese carrier-borne bombers

*Bottom* The crippled *Yorktown* listing and beginning to sink after the Battle of Midway

fleet to one of a desperate fight against odds to avenge the loss of their three sister carriers. At noon the first attack-force of 18 Val dive-bombers, escorted by 6 Zeros, closed on the *Yorktown*. 12 American Wildcat fighters, orbiting high above, plunged down among them and shot down 6, but the remainder dipped into their bombing dives and, although more were ripped apart by anti-aircraft fire, three bombs struck the *Yorktown*. The explosions within the great ship spread death and destruction below and crippled her engines. Then a great silence settled as the surviving attackers vanished, leaving the wreckage and turgid oil slicks of 13 Vals and 3 Zeros patterning the ocean around. The smoking *Yorktown* was wallowing helplessly in the Pacific.

But Captain Elliot Buckmaster and his crew did not give up. Circled by watchful destroyers, the great carrier got under way, slowly, painfully, but nevertheless under way at five knots As the damage crews and the engineers worked desperately to save her, the *Yorktown*'s speed gradually increased until it reached a good 15 knots. Captain Buckmaster ran up a huge new Stars and Stripes as a sign of defiance, but it had barely streamed out its bold challenge before ten Japanese torpedo-bombers, escorted by six Zeros, roared in low over the sea – the second wave from the *Hiryu*. Somehow, Buckmaster managed to avoid the first salvo, but subsequently torpedoes struck the great carrier right and midships, and another put out all power, lights and communications. The *Yorktown* listed heavily to port and sluggishly swung at the mercy of wind and tide, a helpless target for the next Japanese attack. Buckmaster delayed as long as he dared, but at last gave the order to abandon ship.

Already the *Yorktown* was being avenged. A scout-plane that had taken off from the stricken carrier before the last deadly blows struck her had sighted to the west two Japanese battleships, three cruisers, four destroyers and, most important of all, the charge they were so carefully guarding – the aircraft carrier *Hiryu*. When this news crackled out over the *Enterprise*'s radio Admiral Spruance called together all the aircraft he could muster. The survivors of three ravaged squadrons of dive-bombers numbered exactly 24 planes. They roared off from the *Enterprise*, joined by dive-bombers from the

Crew members and airmen pick their way across the steeply sloping decks of the *Yorktown*

*Hornet*. Howling down out of the afternoon sun, they plumed the water around the Japanese carrier with near-misses, until a stick of three bombs burst in shattering succession right through the flight deck. As the *Hiryu*'s crew feverishly fought the consuming flames, Flying Fortresses from Midway muttered their menace high in the lazy sky. More and more waterspouts climbed up around the *Hiryu* as the great bombers near-missed, and then still more Fortresses from far-away Hawaii added to the bombing. There were no Zeros surviving to fight them off. When next the *Hornet*'s dive-bombers found the *Hiryu*, the carrier, torn by more bombs, afire from stem to stern, was doomed.

Although Yamamoto with his great battleships and their stupendous fire-power now loomed towards the scene he had to admit to himself the battle was over. With four carriers lost and two American carriers still opposing him, and with Midway still fully in the fight, Yamamoto, a highly competent professional, secretly knew he must admit defeat. For a time he contemplated bringing the two small carriers from the Kakuta Force down to join in the Midway battle. But thick fog still persisted around the Aleutians, and he knew it would take at least

four days before these warships could reach Midway – much too late to retrieve the disaster that had befallen the Imperial Japanese Navy.

The vulnerability of battleships to dive-bombers and torpedo-bombers had been demonstrated at Pearl Harbor, and by the fate of Britain's *Prince of Wales* and *Repulse* off Malaya. What Japanese warplanes could do to enemy battleships, American warplanes could do to Japanese. Yamamoto now radioed to all his commanders an order, the utter falsity of which emphasised the bitterness of the defeat he would not openly admit. His message was 'The enemy fleet, which has practically been destroyed, is retiring to the east . . .'

The stunned Nagumo received this message just as the burning and abandoned carrier *Soryu* sank and minutes before the charred and crippled *Kaga* also rolled over and plunged beneath the ocean. A few hours later the *Akagi* had to be scuttled, the first warship of the Imperial Japanese Navy ever to be sunk by its crew. The *Hiryu*, last to be stricken by the American dive-bombers, finally had to be abandoned.

Everything continued to go wrong for Yamamoto and his still-powerful fleet when he made one last desperate attempt to bring the elusive Americans to battle by night, a type of sea warfare for which the Japanese had long undergone specialized training, and in which they excelled. The astute Spruance swiftly led his little force away to the east in the darkness, to lurk on the fringe of the battle area and await the dawn. Even the order by Yamamoto to bombard Midway during the night was not carried out, because the four heavy cruisers detailed for the task could not get there in time. And they dared not face the fury of Midway's land-based bombers by day. To crown Yamamoto's day and night of catastrophe, two of the cruisers collided in the darkness and were badly damaged.

Bitterly, at 2.55 a.m. on June 5, the Japanese commander-in-chief ordered, 'Occupation of Midway cancelled'. Some of his admirals, prepared to risk the entire fleet in an attack on Midway without air cover rather than lose face, asked, 'How can we apologize to His Majesty for this defeat?'. Yamamoto replied brokenly, 'Leave that to me. I am the only one who must apologize to His Majesty.'

Bombed and battered by aircraft from the American carriers and the island of Midway itself, this Japanese heavy cruiser of the Mogami class was the last Japanese warship remaining on the scene after the defeated fleet had withdrawn

Dawn was the signal for Spruance to return to the attack. His far-ranging scout-planes told him that the Japanese armada was heading for home, already so far away and cruising so fast that it would not be wise to pursue. But on the following day his planes located the two damaged Japanese cruisers, and these two warships were subjected to a non-stop bombing by planes from the carriers and from Midway. Towards the day's end one sank, but the other, battered almost beyond recognition, survived until nightfall to make good its escape.

The ravaged *Yorktown* had somehow remained afloat, and a minesweeper took her in tow, heading for Pearl Harbor. But soon after dawn on June 6 a Japanese submarine located her and stalked her until she could loose off a spray of torpedoes. Too sluggish to manoeuvre, the *Yorktown* shuddered under the blows. One guardian destroyer, the *Hamann*, was sunk, but the great carrier lingered on until the early hours of June 7, when suddenly she rolled over and plunged to the bottom in a great boil of water.

With the sinking of the *Yorktown* the fantastic battle of Midway claimed its last victim. For the loss of one aircraft carrier, one destroyer and 147 warplanes the Americans had exacted the terrible toll of four fleet aircraft carriers and one cruiser, with 280 planes sunk in the carriers, a further 52 shot down, and several hundred highly experienced pilots and aircrew dead. Even worse for the Japanese was the blow to their pride. From the Battle of Midway onwards, until the end of the war their judgement in battle was to be warped by that bitter memory.

# 7. Guadalcanal

# 7.
# Guadalcanal

The frightening onrush of the Japanese invasion in South-East Asia might have received its first check at the sea battles of Midway and the Coral Sea. But although the Japanese sailors and airmen were shaken, the army had still not been checked.

On May 3, a force put ashore unopposed at Tulagi, one of the smaller Solomon Islands, with the immediate intention of cutting off Australia and New Zealand from American supply. The overall Japanese plan was to seize New Guinea, all the long chain of the Solomons and beyond them the Fiji and Loyalty Islands, Samoa, the Ellice Islands, and islands of the Phoenix group. This would provide a protective screen for their rapidly expanding new naval base at Rabaul in New Britain.

Japan's naval defeat at Midway, the first in 350 years, called for an immediate American initiative. Admiral Ernest King, commander of the United States Navy, named the place for it, a sprawling, rugged, jungle-clad island some 2,500 square miles in extent with the strange Spanish name of Guadalcanal. It was the most southerly island of the Solomons group, and near Tulagi, which was the closest Japanese thrust yet towards the vital United States–Australia lifeline.

King had, in fact, reached the decision to land a force on Guadalcanal nearly two months earlier. It was to be both the battleground on which the Japanese southerly invasion would be checked, and the beginning of an American amphibious, island-hopping counter-attack that would end only in the islands of Japan itself.

As it happened, the Japanese had also chosen Guadalcanal as their next major objective; the scene was set for one of the most fateful battles of the whole war.

The force allocated to make Guadalcanal American seemed unlikely to stem the Japanese advance. It was a single below-strength division of American Marines – the 1st Marine Division commanded by a granite-jawed Virginian of 33 years service, Major-General Archer Vandegrift. In New Zealand on June 25, 1941, Vandegrift was told by Admiral Robert Ghormley, responsible for the Solomon Islands, that his division was to seize Guadalcanal and Tulagi in five weeks' time. Two thirds of Vandegrift's division were then either in Samoa or still at sea, and most of his Marines had only been in uniform since the beginning of the year.

Before the Marines had even begun to organize, the Japanese were on Guadalcanal. A force of 1,000 Japanese had landed at Lunga, on the north-west end of the island, on July 1, according to a report that reached General Douglas

*Above* Admiral Ernest King, Commander-in-Chief of the United States fleet, who planned the great American 'island-hopping' attack that started with Guadalcanal

*Opposite, top* A section of the pattern of Pacific islands flanking 'The Slot' which leads down to the big island of Guadalcanal, scene of the first significant American land victory in the Pacific theatre

*Opposite, bottom* As U.S. Marines went ashore on to the island they anticipated immediate and violent enemy reaction – but it did not come

MacArthur's H.Q. in Australia by way of a radio message from Martin Clemens, a young British district officer on Guadalcanal.

The Japanese soon began to clear flat terrain just in-shore from their beachhead at Lunga for an airfield. They had decided to land in force on August 7; by chance the Americans picked the same day.

The Americans were worried by reports from Clemens that the Japanese airfield was nearing completion. Once the Japanese had flown in their formidable Zero fighters and Kate attack-bombers any attempt at invasion with the American forces available must be suicidal.

How the Marines lived in the eerie depths of the island's thick and steamy jungle

Archer Vandegrift, his forebodings under-lined by his dubbing the hazardous project 'Operation Shoestring', prepared to invade as ordered. All he knew about Guadalcanal, other than that it was a jungle island, was what he could discern from an old marine chart, a cluster of old photographs taken by missionaries, and a short story by Jack London. To add to the gloomy picture, Martin Clemens's scouts now estimated there were between 2,000 and 10,000

Japanese on the island, with smaller forces readily available on Tulagi and the near-by twin isles of Gavutu-Tanambogo.

Shortly before D-Day some Australians who had lived in the Solomon Islands were flown in to advise Vandegrift, and he was able to draw a sketchy map of his chosen landing area. This was east of the River Ilu, apparently unmenaced by enemy guns as the beaches west of Lunga were. A complementary landing would be made by smaller forces on Tulagi and Gavutu-Tanambogo. An unfortunate feature of Vandegrift's invasion map was that the Australians had identified the River Tenaru as the Ilu. Furthermore, whereas the watercourse was normally dried up at this time of year, an out-of-season deluge had just transformed it into a flowing river. Those same soaking rains made miserable the hasty loading of the inadequate invasion transports which could only take enough ammunition for ten days fighting, and rations, fuel and lubricants for a maximum of 60 days.

General Vandegrift had reason for gloom. Although his 19,000 Marines were being transported amidst a great invasion fleet of 89 ships, they were not to have the protection of the navy's guns and warplanes for long after landing. Admiral Fletcher predicted the invasion would be a failure, and was extremely reluctant to hazard his three carriers amidst the crowding islands of the Solomons. Vandegrift was horrified to hear that they would depart on the third day of the operation.

When the Japanese Lieutenant-General Haruyoshi Hyakutake arrived in Rabaul, prepared to invade New Guinea and seize Port Moresby, he knew nothing about the airfield being constructed for the navy on Guadalcanal, nor had he been informed of the defeat at Midway. Believing the falsified claims of American warships sunk and planes destroyed, he discounted an American counter-attack. He was satisfied the army could concentrate on storming Port Moresby, while the all-powerful navy controlled the seas around.

The unsuspecting Japanese on Guadalcanal and Tulagi were still asleep at 6.13 a.m. on August 7 when the American bombardment bellowed out. Specific targets were already pinpointed, thanks to Clemens and his faithful scouts. Dauntless dive-bombers and Avengers

A bomb-aimer's view of Henderson Field, the most vital piece of land on the whole of the island

from the carriers 100 miles to the south joined in, and behind the bombardment the assault boats foamed shorewards. Marines came swarming up the sandy, palm-fringed beaches of Guadalcanal virtually unopposed. Despairing radio messages were soon picked up by Admiral Gunichi Mikawa, in charge of a Japanese naval task force 600 miles to the north-west. 'American landing forces encountered; we are retreating into the jungle'. And from Tulagi a last despairing, 'The enemy force is overwhelming. We will defend our positions to the death, praying for everlasting victory.' Then silence.

On Tulagi attacking Raiders (American commandos) and Marines overran much of the island before encountering bitter opposition in the north. Marines who stormed the neighbouring Florida and twin islets Gavutu-Tanambogo met vicious fire from the latter, and sustained many casualties. Tanambogo had to be bombarded by destroyers and dive-bombers before being taken next day. Before sunset on August 8, Tulagi and Tanambogo were both in American hands. Meanwhile the easy progress on Guadalcanal was misleading. Already 24 Betty torpedo bombers were on their way, escorted by 27 Zeros ordered to fly the almost

impossible return distance of 600 miles.

Admiral Mikawa obtained permission to make a night attack on the American fleet in the narrow waters of 'the Slot' – the 300-mile channel running from Bougainville to Guadalcanal. Admiral Osami Nagamo, chief of naval general staff, ordered the combined fleet to make the recapture of Guadalcanal their immediate objective. Admiral Yamamoto nominated a South-east Area Force and put Vice-Admiral Nishizo Tsukahara, commander of the 11th Air Fleet, in charge of it.

On August 7 the approaching bombers were spotted more than an hour's flight away. Six American Wildcat fighters, waiting for them at 20,000 feet, shot several down in flames and forced the remainder to bomb ineffectually. The Zero fighters were also shot into disarray. Of 51 warplanes that had set out to decimate the American invasion force 30 were shot down, and they achieved nothing.

The day went well for the Americans. By dusk some 17,000 Marines were ashore, still covered by Admiral Fletcher's warships. The main force of around 10,000 had gone in on the so-called Landing Beach Red, in the centre of Guadalcanal's northern coast. The Marines swarmed up 2,000 yards of sandy beach and into exotic tropic-island vegetation dominated by coconut palms. The 5th Marines struck out west for the coastal village of Kukum and the 1st Marines advanced cautiously south-west towards high ground dominating the air strip. This, which they came to call Grassy Knoll, was four miles inland over jungle-choked, switchback terrain. In the humid heat and green gloom it was like advancing into an oven.

Some 1,700 Japanese naval pioneers had been working on the airstrip, with a bodyguard of the naval landing force. They had retreated hurriedly westwards and were soon out of sight and sound of the cautiously advancing Marines. That night, sodden with rain and breasting through unexpectedly swollen rivers, the Marines dug in. It was a haunted night of

*Top* American Marines examining the bodies of Japanese soldiers killed in a charge across an open beach

*Bottom* An American patrol cautiously investigates an apparently abandoned Japanese position. Even if cut off and alone the Japanese would lurk to kill

unfamiliar noises, eerie bird calls, grunting wild pigs and the scraping scuttle of land crabs, with overall the endless whining of blood-sucking mosquitoes. But of the enemy there was not a sound. Next morning the first Marines seized the airfield virtually unopposed. It was a prize of incalculable worth comprising not only a fully operational airstrip but also deep dug-outs, power and oxygen plants, a radio station, a road to the shore and facilities for unloading supplies. This jungle airfield was to become immortalized as 'Henderson Field', named after Major Loften Henderson, a Marine flying hero killed over Midway.

At Kukum the Marines found every evidence of a Japanese panic flight, including abandoned uniforms, rifles, mosquito nets and a huge supply of mouldering rice. Inside two days Vandegrift's Marines also occupied nearly all the high ground and river lines needed to defend it. On the landing beach a formidable problem was mounting, as the shuttling small craft dumped supplies, water, fuel, arms and ammunition faster than the men there could cope with them. The ferrying vessels were sitting ducks for the 45 Betty bombers, escorted by Zeros, which soon approached. Once again the Bettys were met by devastating fire and only one managed to limp away, having done negligible damage.

Despite this catastrophe, Admiral Mikawa pressed on with his eight warships into the Slot, but Fletcher, convinced by the torpedo-bomber attack on the transports that the risk to his precious carriers was too great, was already heading away south with his three carriers, one battleship, six cruisers and 16 destroyers.

Although the Japanese Navy did not have radar, many Japanese sailors had phenomenal night vision, a natural aptitude developed by practice. Mikawa's plan was to race through in darkness and shatter the American transport fleet with torpedoes and gunfire. Fortune was with him because daylight reconnaissance planes somehow missed his force as it surged southwards, and when his fleet was at last sighted, the report did not reach Admiral Richmond Turner's Australian H.Q. for eight hours. Furious at Fletcher's withdrawal, Turner decided to pull out the vulnerable transports off Guadalcanal even though most were not fully unloaded. He then ordered Rear-Admiral Sir Victor

Crutchley, the British officer commanding the attached Australian naval squadron, to challenge the enemy in the western approaches to the Slot, and another naval force under Rear-Admiral Scott to bar the less likely eastern approach.

Crutchley had six heavy cruisers, two screening destroyers ahead, and a radar destroyer on each flank. However it was the Japanese who first spotted their opponents in the straits between Savo island and Guadalcanal. Within minutes the cruiser *Canberra* was a blazing hulk and the cruiser *Chicago*'s bows were blown off. The American cruisers *Astoria* and *Quincy* erupted into towering flames and became the first of many American warships to litter 'Iron Bottom Bay'. Though fighting back furiously, and hitting the enemy cruiser *Kinugasa*, the U.S. cruiser *Vincennes* soon followed. In half an hour four Allied cruisers were sunk with the loss of 1,270 men killed, drowned or devoured by sharks, and over 700 wounded. Another

*Above* Landing craft taking in the first wave of American marines head away from the transport ships towards the unknown dangers of Guadalcanal

*Opposite page* American marines push on deeper into the palm-fringed jungle of the island, pulling a small trailer containing automatic weapons and other, heavier equipment

cruiser was badly damaged.

Something like 12 hours later Admiral Turner ordered his transports and supply vessels to head fast for New Caledonia. And when Marines marched down from Henderson Field to the beach next day they were horrified to see a blue and placid sea devoid both of warships and supply vessels.

They were on their own now, for how long nobody knew. The enemy could pour in reinforcements and assail them from land, sea and air as he chose. Therefore they must bring in all supplies on the beaches, construct peri-

meter defences around the airfield, and complete the landing ground in the hope that fighter planes would be sent to help them. The perimeter they must hold was some 7,500 yards from east to west and 3,500 deep inland at its widest. Its natural strength lay in the River Tenaru, its east flank, the jungle-clad Kukum hills on the west; tortuous, jumbled hills forming the inland southern flank; and the seashore from the Tenaru to Kukum forming its northern front.

Now the fleet had gone, General Vandegrift expected the main enemy attacks from the sea; he therefore ordered that defences should be dug immediately and manned. Other Marine formations would defend lines inland from the Tenaru river and curving back from the sea at Kukum. Vandegrift massed his tanks and artillery centrally to bring down a pulverizing concentration on any given point around the perimeter. Meanwhile 90-mm anti-aircraft guns were to dig in north-west of the airfield, and 75-mm guns on half-tracks were to do so to its north, whence they could roll down quickly to prepared positions on the beaches if required.

On August 9 came the first air bombardment of the airstrip, with 500-pounders and wicked anti-personnel bombs which sent steel slivers

scything through the undergrowth. This was swiftly followed by two earth-shaking night bombardments by enemy cruisers and destroyers, racing down the Slot to Iron Bottom Bay and back. The Marines called this force the Tokyo Express.

On August 12 a patrol of 26 men was ambushed after landing by night near Matanikau. They were cut down by hidden machine-guns and the wounded were slashed to death with sabres, as the three survivors told. This butchery was to establish a hideous pattern on Guadalcanal, for the enraged Marines decided they could be every bit as brutal.

On August 13 Imperial General Headquarters in Tokyo ordered General Hyakutake to destroy the enemy on Guadalcanal without further delay. He detailed a tigerish colonel named Kiyono Ichiki with a crack force of 2,000 men who had been trained to seize Midway.

On August 16 Colonel Ichiki and 900 men

sailed for Guadalcanal in six swift destroyers to land by night at Taivu Point, 22 miles east of the River Tenaru. To divert the Americans' attention, 250 men of the naval landing force were to go ashore to the west. Ichiki's main assault force, if needed, was following in slower vessels. General Vandegrift received several warnings of the attack. First Martin Clemens, with ten of his faithful scouts, came in to put themselves at Vandegrift's service and told of signs of a Japanese build-up. Then a message meant for the Japanese west of Kukum was accidentally dropped in the Marine lines, stating ominously, 'Help on the way. Banzai.' American Naval Intelligence gave further confirmation. The tension mounted when the luminous washes of fast-moving ships heading east by night were reported by beach sentries.

On August 19 Vandegrift ordered three companies of Marines to attack a Japanese concentration along the Matanikau river and

*Opposite page* From a clearing near Henderson Field American artillery prepares to shell Japanese positions

*Right* The strategic high ground above the airfield which, after the marines had repulsed a series of fanatical enemy attacks, became known as 'Bloody Ridge'

a strong patrol to probe east. The Matanikau attack was soon successful, but an amphibious assault mounted further west at Kukumba was shelled by a Japanese submarine and two Tokyo Express destroyers. Nevertheless the Marines landed and drove the defending Japanese into the jungle. By now Colonel Ichiki had landed at Taivu, and he decided to attack that night. The first brush occurred when one of his patrols was surprised by the Marine patrol probing east. The Marines brought back marked Japanese maps which showed that the enemy knew all the weak places in the Tenaru defence line. General Vandegrift strengthened them immediately.

The Imperial High Command believed the battle would draw what remained of the American fleet into the area. Admiral Yamamoto massed a formidable force of three aircraft carriers, three battleships, five cruisers, eight destroyers and a seaplane carrier and sent them south to finish it off. These were reinforced by Admiral Mikawa's four cruisers and five destroyers based on Rabaul, and 100 aircraft already operating from there. Warned by aerial reconnaissance and coast watchers of this massing fleet, Ghormley ordered Fletcher to straddle the approaches to the Solomons with the three-carrier force he had hurried away from Guadalcanal, and sent the carrier *Hornet* with escorting cruisers and destroyers as reinforcement.

Sensing the approach of a portentous battle Admiral King ordered the two recently completed battleships, the *Washington* and the *South Dakota*, with the anti-aircraft cruiser *Juneau* and destroyer escort, to sail via the Panama Canal from the Atlantic into the Pacific. The comparatively simple act of the surprise seizure of a jungle airstrip on a remote South Sea island by a small force of American Marines was developing into a vast sea battle which could decide the future of the war in the Pacific.

On Guadalcanal soon after 1 a.m. on August 21 500 Japanese hurled themselves towards the Americans defending a sandspit at the mouth of the Tenaru. Amidst a cacophony of mortars, machine-guns and automatics, the Marines held their fire – then opened up with every weapon, and the charge that had started with a fury of 'Banzais' disintegrated into a tumbled mass of dead and dying Japanese. Nowhere had Colonel Ichiki's elite troops even dented the American line. At 5 a.m. he sent in his second wave of 400, this time around the seaward side of the sandspit. This time not even one man reached the American wire.

When General Vandegrift learned that Japanese wounded were attempting to kill American medical corps men going to their aid, he decided that every remaining, resisting Japanese must be killed or captured, and sent in light tanks to finish them off. Overwhelmed with horror at his utter failure, Colonel Ichiki burned the regimental colours and shot himself.

Admiral Yamamoto pushed on with 'Operation Ka' to recapture Guadalcanal airfield. In the wake of the 1,500 crack troops of Ichiki's follow-up force already heading thence, he sent a big fast transport with 1,000 men of the naval landing force. Meanwhile he was massing in the waters around Truk a formidable battlefleet.

On August 22, having already despatched a screen of a dozen submarines south-east of Guadalcanal, Yamamoto concentrated his force 200 miles north of the southern Solomons. The

*Right* Major-General Roy Geiger, who commanded the first Marine Aircraft Wing (which became known as 'The Cactus Air Force') during the desperate days when they wrested control of the air from the Japanese air force

*Opposite page* Rear-Admiral Robert L. Chormley of the United States Navy, who had to risk his warships in the narrow waters of 'The Slot'

*Below* Japanese bombers skim in low over the sea, endeavouring to avoid furious anti-aircraft fire, as they go in to attack American warships and transports

splinters, and the guns of the battleship *North Carolina* roofed her over with black bursts and stinging steel, but three of the Japanese dive-bombers found their target. Yet with fire-fighting teams working furiously the burning American carrier raced on at 27 knots. Within an hour she was able to swing around into the wind for homing aircraft.

The battle of the Eastern Solomons, as it was called, had cost the Japanese the *Ryujo* and scores of planes, but the American carrier *Enterprise* was to be out of action for two months.

The returning Japanese pilots put in such remarkable claims that Admiral Mikawa in Rabaul was satisfied two American aircraft carriers had been sunk. He gave the all clear for the diverted invasion convoy to continue to Guadalcanal. Admiral Tamaka, commanding this force, pressed on southwards with all speed, sending five destroyers ahead into the Slot to bombard Henderson Field during the night of August 24. When his convoy was little more than 100 miles from Guadalcanal, a strong formation of Dauntless dive-bombers from Guadalcanal fell upon it. The Japanese were taken by surprise, with guns unloaded, and the hurtling dive-bombers blasted a big transport and Tamaka's flagship, the cruiser *Jintsu*. High flying B 17 Flying Fortresses, called up by the dive-bombers, finished off the blazing troopship and a destroyer trying to rescue survivors. The Japanese ships turned back and ploughed northwards out of range.

Angrily Yamamoto changed his tactics, planning a gradual build-up of an attacking force on Guadalcanal by stealthy night landings. But the first units of the crack Kawaguchi Brigade were so eager to be off that their sailing from Borneo in four destroyers on the night of August 20 made it inevitable they entered the narrow waters of the Slot in broad daylight. The Marine Dauntless pilots howled down out of a blazing sun upon the doomed Japanese. One destroyer disintegrated with a breathtaking eruption, another wallowed drunkenly, palled with black smoke, and a third, torn by explosives, reeled out of the fray. This additional loss of men and ships infuriated Tamaka who had advised against risking a daylight landing. Soon, however, he had the main force of Kawaguchi's troops with him landing on Shortland, just south of Bougainville.

light carrier *Ryujo* was to advance as bait for the American carriers, and while their aircraft were attacking her the warplanes from the main Japanese carrier force would sink them. After this the massive escort force of battleships, heavy cruisers and destroyers would sail down the Slot to devastate the Marines and recapture the airfield.

The first stage of the plan went rather too well. The decoy carrier *Ryujo* was annihilated by American dive-bombers and torpedo-bombers.

The *Saratoga* and *Enterprise* then headed towards the Japanese force, while the *Wasp* went south to refuel. Admiral Nagumo, however, believed the Americans had concentrated all three carriers to attack the decoy *Ryujo*, and ordered the aerial knockout blow to obliterate the American carrier force. The *Enterprise* was ready: tiered among the woolly clouds were 53 Wildcats, kept back from the *Ryujo* raid for just such a moment. For miles around the sky was filled with the screaming uproar of air warfare, soon joined by the American dive-bombers and torpedo-bombers returning from the *Ryujo* mission.

Half an hour later 30 Val dive-bombers slanted in. The carrier's guns tore the sky with

Kawaguchi had refused transport by destroyers, which he detested, and insisted on 'proper landing barges'. An angry deadlock produced a compromise instruction that the bulk of Kawaguchi's force would be transported by destroyers and the rest by barges. Next morning Kawaguchi and most of his men headed south in eight destroyers to enter the dangerous Slot in darkness. They safely disembarked at Taivu on Guadalcanal at midnight. But when, several days later, 1,000 men in barges were prevented by heavy swell from landing, they were caught out to sea at daybreak and decimated by the Cactus Air Force (Cactus was the code name for Guadalcanal). Despite his repeated warnings of just such a calamity, Admiral Tamaka was relieved of his command.

The Imperial General Headquarters, becoming steadily more furious at the Americans' retention of Henderson Field, made Guadalcanal the number one objective in the South Seas. On August 31 General Hyakutake was ordered to go on the defensive in New Guinea and concentrate against Guadalcanal. He would be formidably backed by the powerful 8th Fleet and the whole of the resources of South-east Area Air Force.

All this time Henderson Field was being subjected to daily bombing raids. But the tireless Marine pilots led by Captain John Smith had already destroyed the legend of the invincible Zero. Their stubby, radial-engined Wildcats had shot down enemy fighters and bombers at a rate of six or eight for every Wildcat lost. The superior fire-power and formation fighting of the Americans outweighed the greater speed and manoeuvrability of the Zeros, and, thanks to the early warnings of the coast watchers, the Wildcats were invariably able to jump the enemy out of the sun. Although Cactus Air Force was reinforced by 19 more Wildcats and 12 Dauntlesses, giving it 86 pilots and 64 planes, the Japanese gained 58 new aircraft at the same time.

The Japanese had also considerably increased their ground forces. The Cactus Air Force could do nothing about the nightly Tokyo Express, and the American Navy was not equipped to intervene in these perilous waters. Shattering bombardments by night and nerve-racking surprise attacks by day made Guadalcanal hideous. In addition to lack of sleep, the Marines were wearying from increasing dysentery, malaria, jungle rot and the ill effects of an inadequate diet, mainly sludgy rice. The worried Vandegrift appealed for more warplanes, including the new long-range Lightnings, to catch the approaching Tokyo Express while still in daylight. But Lightnings were scarce; General MacArthur could not spare any, nor would Admiral Ghormley divert any of his four aircraft carriers to counteract the Tokyo Express.

But the men on Guadalcanal were not ignored. A battalion of Seabees, naval construction veterans specializing in airfields, arrived in September to improve the explosion-torn Henderson Field. Two days later Brigadier-General Roy Geiger, a fighter ace of the First World War, flew in to take over Cactus Air Force.

General Vandegrift now ordered the Raiders and parachutists who had taken Tulagi to cross to Guadalcanal. They did so in the light destroyers *Little* and *Gregory* which soon afterwards, mistakenly illuminated by American flares, were blown to pieces by lurking Japanese warships. Next day a number of Skytrain air transports arrived bringing in machine-guns, and taking out wounded. This was the beginning of a regular supply-and-evacuation air service which meant much to the Americans' morale. Two big, escorted transports arrived with reinforcements just before the Japanese attack.

The Japanese planned to deliver the ultimate assault on September 12, with massive sea and air bombardments covering Kawaguchi's land attack. Kawaguchi had 6,200 men massed on Guadalcanal poised for a three-pronged attack, one from the north, another across the Tenaru, and the third across the Lunga. But he underestimated the physical effort required to press home a decisive thrust through the slimy swamps and tangled, spiny undergrowth of the jungle. Beset by stinging insects and blood-sucking

*Top* With the marines holding out against everything the enemy could pit against them, more equipment was rushed in. Here new types of landing barges are shown landing jeeps on a sandy beach of Guadalcanal

*Bottom* While the main battle was fought around Henderson Field both sides attempted attacks behind their adversaries' lines. Here an American fighting patrol has made a landing to strike at the enemy's rear through the thick jungle

President Roosevelt Broadcasts to the Nation. He finally made it clear that what had been a small-scale landing on Guadalcanal was developing into a battle of tremendous significance

leeches, his 3,000 crack troops were soon strung out in a most unmilitary manner, and even as they stumbled on through the green gloom, the Americans were fortifying the steep ridge along which the Japanese were aiming to burst through. Vandegrift manned it with 700 Raiders Raiders and parachutists and established his command post and H.Q. immediately behind.

The Wildcats on the much-bombarded airfield had been reduced to 11 by September 10 and Admiral Nimitz, disregarding protests from Admiral Fletcher, ordered 24 fighters to be flown in from the *Saratoga*. But Admiral Ghormley believed there was no hope for the Marines on Guadalcanal and that to confront the approaching invasion armada would only waste American warships. He therefore ordered all his vessels away.

On the night of September 12, the Americans on the ridge tensed to receive the attack. Suddenly a rocket soared from the jungle below. A crackling of machine-guns and automatic fire swelled from the black depths. Screaming

'Banzai!' the first wave of Japanese came charging up.

In some places they burst through, in others they forced the defenders to give ground. 'Red Mike' Edson, the Raiders' C.O., was compelled to pull back his left flank and reform. But for all their fanatical bravery the Japanese onslaughts lacked cohesion. Kawaguchi had sent in his leading troops while the consolidating second wave were still gasping and clawing through the jungle.

The full fury of the American artillery now crashed among those Japanese soldiers who had broken through. Bewildered, unaware of the layout of the American defences, they were either cut to pieces or slipped away through the undergrowth. At first light the Marines counter-attacked and the ridge – Bloody Ridge they called it from now on – was restored. Edson ran out still more barbed-wire aprons. When next they charged the Japanese would have to cover a full hundred yards of open ground swept by machine-guns and automatics.

Temporarily the action switched to Henderson Field where three successive air raids were made. In the nick of time the Cactus Air Force was again dramatically reinforced by 60 planes, mostly Wildcat fighters from the *Hornet* and the *Wasp* but also including six Avenger torpedo-bombers. But the Japanese Air Force was also considerably strengthened, 140 warplanes arriving at Rabaul and Bougainville.

Admiral Taukahara and General Hyakutake, impatiently awaiting the success signal from Kawaguchi, were sure their men must have at least captured the vital ridge, and for that reason no bombers were sent against it that day. Instead they were despatched against American troops reported to have landed at Tasimboko, behind Kawaguchi's force, and a devastating raid was made on Kawaguchi's rear troops, whom they mistook for Americans. Meanwhile away in the steaming jungle below Bloody Ridge, Kawaguchi was attempting to weld his battered first-wave survivors and exhausted new arrivals into an ordered assault force. He was unaware that only 400 Americans were on that ridge defying his 2,500. That night a full 2,000 of his warriors swarmed in six successive waves from the black depths of the jungle, screaming their battle cries. The whole American line became a horror of hand-to-hand slaughter,

American marines prepare to move into the jungle. Although their daring landing gave them the advantage of surprise, many weeks of fierce fighting and heavy bombardment lay ahead

but although it bent back in the centre, it remained unbroken. Henderson Field was torn by a bombardment from seven destroyers; from the east, along the Tenaru, the thunder of yet another battle swelled, but only a few Japanese managed to plunge through the American line.

Up on the ridge the terrible fire of the massed guns was brought down closer and closer to the American defence as the Japanese made renewed charges upon them. The slaughter was hideous, but the line held, the defenders knifing to death the Japanese who jumped into their foxholes. To the detonation of shells was now added the screams of scores of stricken men in this bloody inferno of pitiless battle. The American artillery, firing with deadly accuracy, shredded the onrushing Japanese waves. As the sun suddenly soared and night was day, cannon-firing P 400s swooped to scatter assembling Japanese survivors and complete their

defeat. Down by the Tenaru five Marine tanks put the remaining Japanese there to flight and the day chosen for their great victory parade on Guadalcanal found them in almost total defeat.

'Red Mike' Edson and his heroic few had, that terrible night, won the most vital and bloody battle of the campaign. It was at tremendous cost, for the Raiders had suffered 224 casualties, the parachutists 212, and the Marines, fed in as reinforcements, 263. But while Kawaguchi began to march his dazed remnants, carrying 400 wounded on litters, to Matanikau, the Americans were being reinforced. Six transports carrying 4,000 Marines sailed in, under cover of a formidable carrier group formed around the *Wasp* and *Hornet* and including the battleship *North Carolina*. But the big ships dared not risk destruction in the narrow seas, and withdrew during the night of September 14.

Not soon enough however. Next day the *Wasp* was mortally hit by torpedoes, which also seriously damaged a battleship and a destroyer. But Yamamoto could not immediately send his massive battlefleet south to finish off the American convoy. His warships had required refuelling, and he had recalled them some 200 miles north of Guadalcanal. It was decided when this was completed to send even more troops to Guadalcanal, including the crack Sendai Division and the tough battle-proven Nagoya Division. To complete the devastation of the American Marines causing them so much trouble on Guadalcanal the Japanese High Command ordered three new carriers to sail south from home waters.

Unaware that the Japanese battlefleet had turned back to refuel, Admiral Kelly Turner grimly pressed on with his scantily protected convoy. Lowering skies fortuitously closed in around, and on September 18 the troopships landed the Marines. Vandegrift now had over 19,000 men, sufficient to hold a continuous defence perimeter around Henderson Field and also mount a strong counter-attack force within. His artillery was also powerfully reinforced by some 5-inch naval guns and 155-mm 'Long Toms'. Unknown on Guadalcanal as yet, Admiral King had successfully demanded that Army Air Force Lightning fighters should be diverted there from the planned Anglo-American invasion of North Africa.

The predicament of many of the Japanese troops on Guadalcanal, disease-ridden and starving, was now desperate. When Kawaguchi's pitiful survivors began staggering in among the Matanikau troops they were quickly shuffled out of sight to rear areas.

Vandegrift decided to strike first. He sent in a three-pronged attack on September 27 to drive the enemy from a strong position along the Matanikau. Raiders were to cross the river

When the rains came many of the American marines had to live in flooded jungle encampments. Meanwhile conditions for fighting in the thick forest became almost impossible

a little over a mile inland and wheel right towards the sea in the Japanese rear. Simultaneously a Marine battalion would attack across a sand bar at the river's mouth and another battalion land behind the enemy and strike from the rear. But the Raiders were pinned down by murderous fire, the Marines attacking at the mouth of the Matanikau were driven back; the force that landed farther west walked right into a trap, and a determined Japanese raid on Henderson Field temporarily put all communications out of action. Vandegrift decided to abandon the operation as a failure.

On September 30, through the first heavy rain of the imminent monsoon, Admiral Nimitz himself flew into Henderson Field in a Flying Fortress, and promised to give 'support to the maximum of our resources'. Such an assurance was needed, for the enemy were reinforcing fast to deliver the ultimate crushing blow. Yet the next two massive raids on Henderson Field cost 29 bombers and 6 fighters for no American losses at all. By September's end the Japanese had lost over 200 planes for the destruction of 32 American ones.

General Hyakutake, certain that no Americans could match his splendid Sendai warriors, underestimated the strength of Vandegrift's force at 10,000. To make sure there were no more failures, Hyakutake took personal command and ordered the 38th Division from Borneo to join the Sendai Division. He arranged to establish his 17th Army H.Q. on Guadalcanal on October 9. Lieutenant-General Masoa Maruyama, the proud Sendai commander, set the chill tone of the battle to come in this order of the day: 'The occupying of Guadalcanal island is under the observation of the whole world. Do not expect to return, not even one man, if the occupation is not successful'. He planned to attack from across the Matanikau river on October 17.

Vandegrift now decided to launch another attack at Matanikau, far more powerful than the earlier failure. He chose to attack on October 7, the very day the Sendai spearheads thrust forward to establish jumping-off positions for the main assault. The two forces met head-on in the jungle and on the beaches, and everywhere furious and bloody fighting broke out. At

*Above* Admiral Osami Nagumo, Commander of the Japanese naval forces in the Solomons, who had vowed to destroy every American aircraft carrier to avenge the Japanese humiliation at Midway

*Opposite page* There was so little room for manoeuvre in 'The Slot' that every time a naval force confronted another heavy casualties were inevitable. Here an American task force is seen ploughing through to challenge advancing Japanese warships

nightfall both sides were pinned down, though the Americans had the best of the exchanges, killing 60 Japanese who tried to break out with a 'Banzai' charge. Then the monsoon broke, transforming dust into mud.

At this point Vandegrift learned how formidable was the Japanese invasion force nearing Guadalcanal.

As the Marines plunged through the jungle they surprised a whole Japanese battalion resting in a ravine. They called down an artillery bombardment to add to their own deluge of fire that killed the Japanese almost to a man. When they withdrew they had killed nearly 1,000 of Maruyama's soldiers while losing 65

men. Soon afterwards they were heartened by the arrival of 20 more Wildcats and, at last, aid from the American army. After the Marines had held on so tenaciously for two months, 3,000 soldiers of the 164th Infantry Regiment landed from two transports which had sailed from New Caledonia on October 9. The Navy too was preparing to challenge the enemy in the hitherto Japanese dominated water of the Slot. Finally convinced that Guadalcanal was a significant battleground, Ghormley was sending all reinforcements and warships available.

When General Hyakutake landed on Guadalcanal from a destroyer he learned of the slaughter of his unbeatable Sendai warriors and how they had been forced to retreat. He was still determined to pursue his original plan, but first called for powerful reinforcements, explaining that the situation in Guadalcanal was worse than had been estimated. Already 1,000 more of the Sendai Division were heading into the Slot on board six destroyers, with a further battalion on two seaplane carriers. With them was the bulk of Hyakutake's artillery, 16 tanks, ample ammunition and medical supplies. They were

217

The stricken American carrier *Wasp*, fatally hit by torpedoes while on a mission to reinforce the American 'Cactus Air Force' on Guadalcanal

escorted by three heavy cruisers, two destroyers, and many aircraft. Orders were to put Henderson Field out of action with an obliterating naval bombardment, and October 11 was the day named.

The powerful Japanese bombardment force was sighted by a Flying Fortress on October 11, and Rear-Admiral Norman Scott led his warships to intercept. Scott had four cruisers and five destroyers, the forward screen protecting troopships bringing 3,000 soldiers to Guadal-

canal. Not only were these warships equipped with radar, but Scott had intensively trained his crews in night fighting. By nightfall the American warships were speeding towards Savo island from one direction, and the Japanese were 50 miles north rushing forward on a collision course.

Suddenly the oppressive night was seared by the conflagration of an American spotter plane fired by its own flares in a launching mishap. It was sighted by Japanese look-outs, but was believed to be a bonfire signal on the Sendai Division's landing beach. Admiral Aritomo Goto was convinced that American ships would not dare challenge him in the darkness. But already the Japanese force had been spotted, and Scott's force, in battle formation, was squarely broadside to the onrushing Japanese armada when they made radar contact. At a range of 5,000 yards the still unsuspected American warships opened fire, and a salvo burst in a spectacular ball of flame upon Goto's flagship *Aoba*. Moments later other broadsides struck her and the Japanese admiral was mortally wounded, believing himself hit by the mistaken fire of his own vessels.

In the confusion Admiral Scott made a similar mistake. He ordered cease fire, but not all crews received the order and shells continued to pound the *Aoba*, and the *Surutake* until both cruisers were roaring infernos. Minutes later the searchlight of Scott's flagship, the cruiser *San Francisco*, revealed the destroyer *Fuvuki* which was blown to pieces. The U.S. cruiser *Boise* was badly hit, and the destroyer *Duncan*, fired on by both sides in the thunderous confusion, rapidly sank. Abruptly the great guns fell silent: the Japanese warships had turned and fled. The Battle of Cape Esperance, as it was to be called, had ended, and it was an undoubted American victory which signalled the end of the unchallenged Japanese dominance of the Slot. The morale of the Marines on Guadalcanal soared for they no longer felt themselves trapped on an island entirely surrounded by enemy.

But although the sea battle had prevented crushing bombardment, it did not stop the Japanese putting ashore Hyakutake's reinforcements during the early hours of October 12. Soon afterwards the destroyers that had landed them were destroyed by Cactus Dauntless dive-bombers. Meanwhile, much farther north, the furious Admiral Yamamoto was preparing retribution. His combined fleet, five carriers, five battleships, 14 cruisers and 44 destroyers, was ready to sail. This formidable armada was to support the landing of 10,000 troops on Guadalcanal during the night of October 14, ready for Hyakutake's all-out offensive on October 20. It would deliver a massive bombardment upon Henderson Field to obliterate every plane and pilot before the troop transports came in range. It was too late to prevent the 3,000 American reinforcements landing, but as the first American soldiers set foot on Guadalcanal, a heavy Japanese air raid thundered in. This time there was no warning, for the courage-

ous coast watchers to the north had been located and dislodged by the Japanese. The Wildcats could not climb fast enough to intercept effectively; the airfield was badly damaged, precious fuel was set ablaze and parked aircraft were smashed.

A second, equally damaging surprise raid soon followed, and for the first time Henderson Field was put out of action. As the planes left artillery shells began to burst on the runways also for the first time. The ominous significance was that the Japanese now possessed much heavier artillery, guns that could outrange the massed American artillery, which had played such a dominant role hitherto.

Shortly before midnight flares burst out to bathe Henderson Field in green brilliance, keeping the target area glaringly illuminated while the devastating fire of the battleships was directed upon it. For an hour and a half while the bombardment continued, the helpless Marines and soldiers crouched stunned and stupefied, with the earth rocking around their trenches.

At dawn the dazed defenders emerged, many barely sane, most stunned into speechlessness. Although only 41 had been killed, an alarming proportion were pilots – not that it seemed likely that anyone would every fly from Henderson Field again. Both main runways had been churned into smouldering pits and smoking hillocks, and around them were scattered the shredded remains of 34 of the Dauntless bombers, 16 of the 40 Wildcats, and practically every Avenger torpedo-bomber. Their air cover had gone, and the big force of Japanese troop transports was fast closing upon the island.

By fantastic exertions and improvizations the mechanics made ten bombers and 24 Wildcats airworthy to challenge the Japanese air-raids. Nine bombers and three Zeros fell for the loss of one Army pilot and two Marine pilots. Fuel had run out but more was obtained by draining the tanks of two wrecked Flying Fortresses, and from a hidden store of Japanese petrol captured weeks before and since forgotten. In ones, twos and ragged handfuls the heroic pilots in patched-up Dauntlesses, Wildcats, P 400s and Aerocobras, kept going out to bomb and strafe the approaching troop transports. Towards the day's end a high-flying formation of Fortresses loomed up from Espiritu Santu, in the New

*Above* A Marine jungle defence post with an American fighter coming in to land on Henderson Field after a mission against enemy bombers

*Right* General Vandegrift of the U.S. Marines giving orders as his men fight off Japanese attack. Note his rifle with fixed bayonet, ready to deal with any enemy who may break through to his headquarters

Hebrides, to join the attack. And then fuel began to be flown in from that distant base. All the time the indefatigable Seabees were repairing Henderson Field.

Every American airman with a plane to fly joined in the assault on the formidable Japanese invasion force. Two Japanese troopships were wrecked; the three other troopships in the convoy turned back, and the soldiers on board were forced to complete the voyage by barge. Four recently arrived motor torpedo boats attacked them by night and survivors of the Cactus Air

Force by day. Only 4,500 of Hyakutake's reinforcements reached him in time for his all-out attack.

On the night of October 15 Henderson Field was subjected to a nerve-shattering bombardment for the third successive night. Japanese cruisers poured in hundreds of 8-inch shells until only 27 assorted warplanes remained, and all the fuel had gone up in flames. In a last-minute effort to restore at least some air power, Lieutenant-Colonel Harold Bauer with a squadron of Wildcats was ordered north from Espiritu Santu, a long flight only just within their range. Meanwhile the converted destroyer *McFarland* sped north with 40,000 gallons of aviation fuel. A slow convoy of towed supply barges was also on the way. The *McFarland* hove to off the landing beaches on October 16 and was still unloading when Bauer with his 19 Wildcats came dropping down out of the hot bright sky. At that instant 14 Japanese dive bombers attacked and damaged the destroyer, but Bauer, his tanks almost empty, shot down four in one snarling swoop. The *McFarland* went on to complete unloading.

At this desperate moment Admiral Halsey was ordered to take over in the South Pacific. Vandegrift now had 23,000 men. He manned a 7,000-yard line facing the beach with Marines, engineers, pioneers and base and specialized units; a 6,500-yard front along the Tenaru curving back to Bloody Ridge with infantry-men; a 2,500-yard line from the Ridge west to the Lunga with more Marines; and another 3,500 yards west and finally curving round to the sea again with Marines. Held back in a reserve to counter-attack any breakthrough was one infantry battalion and most of a tank bat-talion, while all regimental commanders held one third of their men in reserve.

To attack the American jungle fortress General Hyakutake was preparing a three-pronged assault by 22,000 men, mostly of the Sendai Division. General Maruyama was to attack with 7,000 along much the same route as the ill-fated Kawaguchi's thrust, but this time army engineers would cut an avenue through the thick jungle. Maruyama's objective was the airfield and its vital communications centre. While Maruyama's shock-troops were thus storming the American's citadel, fierce diver-sionary attacks would keep the defenders at full stretch all along their perimeter. Throughout the defenders would be subjected to air attacks from Rabaul, Buka, and a recently completed airfield at Buin on Bougainville. To complete the crushing of the Americans, the fleet Yama-moto was holding in readiness to the north would surge into the narrow waters and con-sume the enemy with its guns. Planes flown into the captured airfield from aircraft carriers would hunt down all fugitive Americans still showing fight. All would surely be over by October 22.

But by October 22 the battle had not even begun. General Maruyama's Sendai warriors had only covered 29 of the required 35 miles in five days' marching. Maruyama now realized the jungle was as terrible as the scorned Kawa-guchi had described it. He reported that he could not launch his attack until October 23.

When the Japanese bombers and their high glittering escorts came on October 23, they were met by the Wildcats. On one attack 20 Zeros

American soldiers trudge wearily back from the jungle, where they have been in action for 21 days and nights

were shot down for not one Wildcat lost. There was no crippling bombing of Henderson Field because no Japanese bombers got through! Worse still, Kawaguchi's force scheduled to attack on Maruyama's right had not even reached its assembly area. In a cold fury Maruyama relieved Kawaguchi of his command and postponed his attack yet another 24 hours.

The news of the latest postponement failed to reach Major-General Sumoyoshi, poised to attack across the Matanikau mouth. At sunset his men went in and, along with their support-ing tanks, were blown to smithereens by the massed American artillery. This premature assault convinced the Americans that the main Japanese attack would come in from the west, most fiercely around Bloody Ridge. Major-General Roy Geiger, in command during

Vandegrift's temporary absence, switched a battalion from the southern defences to strengthen opposite the Matanikau river. Vandegrift had flown out to a conference at Naumea called by Halsey, where he emphasized the desperate urgency at Guadalcanal. 'I'll promise you everything I've got', growled Halsey. The great aircraft carrier *Enterprise* was undoubtedly his most potent contribution and at dawn on October 24 she was a little over 800 miles to the south-east, surrounded by her screening warships and supply vessels. Admiral Thomas Kincaid, in command, knew from Intelligence reports that the all-out Japanese onslaught on Guadalcanal would almost certainly take place that night. As they rushed on towards the beleaguered island the *Enterprise* force sighted another powerful formation heading the same way, the carrier *Hornet* and her bristling screen. Halsey had directed these two carriers with all speed to the rescue. Two battleships, nine cruisers and 24 destroyers sailed with them.

As the heat began to wane from the afternoon the battleship *Washington*, with three cruisers and seven destroyers, turned north-west to patrol Guadalcanal's southern shores, while the two carriers set off with their escorts at full speed north-eastwards, aiming to challenge Yamamoto's fleet.

Shortly before Maruyama's assault was due to begin the skies suddenly blackened and monsoon rains descended. Within minutes tracks and trails were skidding mud-slicks, units lost touch and communications faltered in the blinding downpour. Attempting to restore order out of chaos, Maruyama had to order a two-hour postponement, until 7 p.m.

The rain had abated to a murmur by 7 o'clock, but even then all his attacking force was not up to the starting line, and on the right Kawaguchi's successor, Colonel Shoji, had failed to get his men through on time. Maruyama could wait no longer. Abruptly he launched his left wing and the Japanese infantrymen abandoned all pretence of stealth as they clawed forward through the humid green gloom. Warned by an outpost, the waiting Marines held their fire until the enemy charge reached the wire, where the first wave of Japanese died

*Opposite page* Sick and starving Japanese soldiers after the capture of an enemy stronghold. The fact that they surrendered rather than committing suicide or fighting to the death indicated a decline in morale

*Below* The concentrated accuracy of the American artillery proved a major factor in the defeat of the Japanese. Here a battery of howitzers is seen bombarding Japanese concentrations preparing to attack

bloodily. The second wave flung themselves onwards, scrambling over the bodies of their comrades. At last even the fanatical Sendai soldiers could take no more slaughter, and the survivors scrambled, wide-eyed with horror, back to the cover of the jungle.

Only one break had been made in the wire. Through this Colonel Furumiya, leading his men with sabres fourished high, charged towards the concentration of American machine-guns. But the line was swiftly restored behind him and the colonel and his men were trapped. Desperately they assailed some of the machine-gun posts, killing and wounding a number of Marines, but the overrun positions were soon remanned and in action again.

Two and a half hours after their first bloodily unsuccessful assault, the Sendai charged furiously again. The right-wing troops were in action now, seeking by their ferocity to atone for the disgrace of being late for a battle. But the defenders stood their ground and kept on firing with every weapon at their command. In several places the Sendai penetrated, and reserves had to be rushed up, bringing soldiers of the American Army into action for the first time. Prematurely General Maruyama sent out the 'Banzai' message, meaning the airfield had been seized, and General Hyakutake immediately advised Admiral Mikawa in Rabaul who despatched three big destroyers to Koli, to land the troops to finish off the Americans.

But although the American line had been penetrated, it had not been broken, and Marines grimly hunted down the Japanese amongst them. Two hours later the Sendai came in again in a third wave, only to meet unabated defensive fire. As the night grew black a haunted silence settled on the battlefield, and the surviving Japanese crept down into the rain-sodden jungle. Dawn revealed the awful slaughter around the American positions. In one place where hidden anti-tank guns had caught them pointblank, a whole Japanese column lay mangled in the exact formation of their advance. General Maruyama sent another message to Hyakutake: 'I am having difficulty capturing the airfield', he admitted.

His admission was too late to halt the Koli landing. The troop-carrying destroyers rushing on towards Koli Point came under the fire of Marine 5-inch guns. Shells crashed into them, compelling them to turn away. The cruiser and five destroyers, detailed to give the covering bombardment for the landing, were sighted by a reconnaissance plane, and as soon as the sun had dried out the rain-sodden Henderson Field sufficiently, dive-bombers took off to blast the Japanese cruiser into a blazing wreck, force one destroyer ashore and put the other four to flight. Meanwhile 26 Japanese planes were shot down over Henderson Field and to the north, alarmed by an American scout-plane, Admiral Nagumo was so determined not to fall into a Midway-like trap that he turned his three carriers about and fled northwards, accompanied by the carrier *Junyo* whose planes were to have landed on the captured airfield.

Later that day General Maruyama prepared to make a 'final death-defying attack'. At last both his wings were firmly in position and in close liaison. For breathless minutes, as swift night swallowed jungle, sea and sky, a great restless silence enveloped Guadalcanal. Then, as American Marines and soldiers stood tensely in their weapon pits, the massed Japanese charged out of the jungle. The air was shrill with their screams of 'Banzai!' and 'Marines you die tonight!' But it was the Japanese soldiers who died in scores and hundreds. As the battle here waned an attack swinging seawards around Hill 67 went in. The Japanese charged headlong into the deadly fire of Marine machine-gunners. Those who survived closed

with the Marines in ferocious hand-to-hand fighting with sabres, knives, rifle butts and fists. Briefly some machine-guns were overrun but the Marines counter-attacked and drove the survivors off, leaving some 2,500 Japanese dead on the ground. The battle for Henderson Field had been virtually decided, for Maruyama ordered the surviving Sendai to retreat for the first time in their history. But though the Americans had won the vital land victory, the great sea battle that must be its inevitable sequel had still not been fought.

It was the inevitability of the clash between the two carrier forces that made the fighting on Guadalcanal – a small battle by comparison with the titanic armoured collisions in Europe and Russia – among the most significant of the war. While the Sendai Division was being decimated in the jungle, the two American aircraft carriers were rushing north-westwards from the Santa Cruz islands, 300 miles south of Guadalcanal. About the same time the huge Japanese battlefleet with its four carriers turned southwards to seek them. Soon after dawn on October 26 scout planes from the carrier *Shokaku* reported a considerable enemy force 200 miles east. Admiral Nagumo ordered immediate attacks by bombers from all three of his carriers, and attack planes also took off from the carrier *Junyo*, more than 100 miles to Nagumo's rear. About the same time, the Americans located the immense Japanese battlefleet north-west of them.

Just before 7 a.m. roving Dauntless dive-bombers sighted Nagumo's carrier force and tore in to attack through an angry swarm of Zeroes. The Japanese carriers swerved away, masking themselves with thick smoke, but two bombs hit the carrier *Zuiho* fair and square, sending her lurching from the battle. Now it was three Japanese carriers and two Americans.

While the American carrier *Enterprise* was shrouded in a rainstorm the *Hornet* was caught in the open by Japanese dive-bombers and torpedo-bombers. A Japanese pilot plunged his plane in a kamikaze suicide dive right through the flight deck to set a great fire boiling skywards. Minutes later two torpedoes struck home, followed by three more bombs but, with the whole ship likely to blow up, the fires were brought under control. Meanwhile the *Hornet*'s absent warplanes were already avenging her.

General Montgomery consults a map during the
North African campaign

Wildcat and Seafire aircraft preparing to take off from
the decks of *H.M.S. Formidable* during the North African
landings

Australian troops overrun an enemy position at
Tel El Eisa, painted by Ivor Hele

A crashed Junkers JU52 troop transport in North Africa

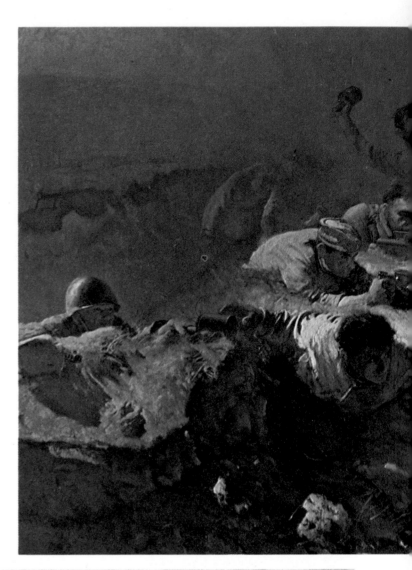

A 25-pounder gun and its crew in action on the
El Alamein front, painted by John Berry

Anti-tank riflemen at Stalingrad, painted by
I. E. Yevstigneyev

The battle for Krukovo Station on the outskirts of
Moscow, painted by A. A. Gorpenko

*After the Battle,* a painting by Nyeprintsev of a group of
Red Army soldiers

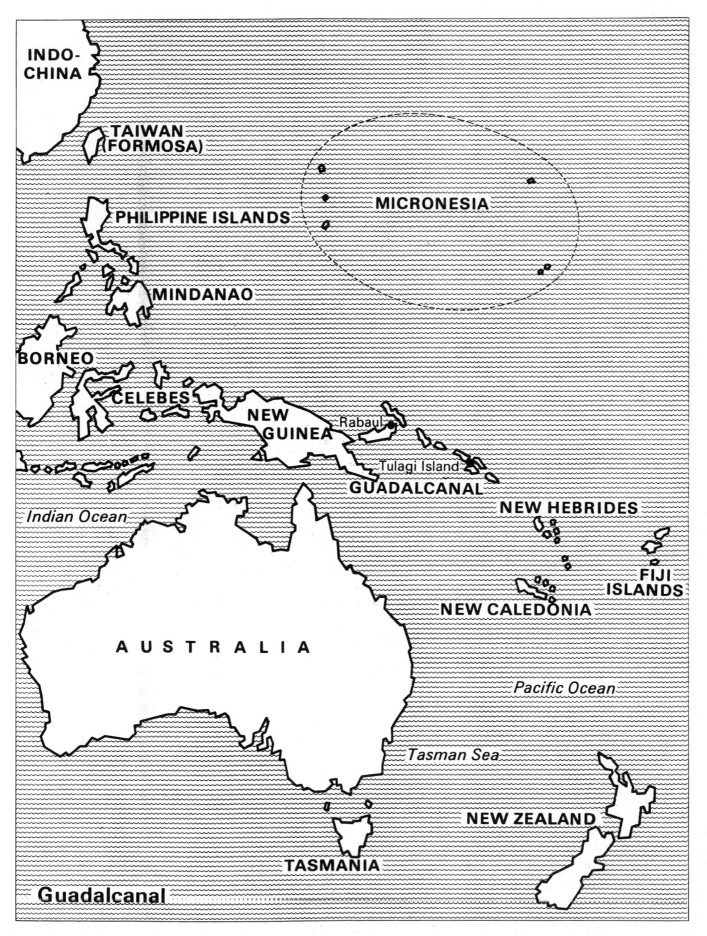

INDO-CHINA

TAIWAN (FORMOSA)

PHILIPPINE ISLANDS

MICRONESIA

MINDANAO

BORNEO

CELEBES

NEW GUINEA

Rabaul

Tulagi Island

GUADALCANAL

NEW HEBRIDES

Indian Ocean

FIJI ISLANDS

NEW CALEDONIA

AUSTRALIA

Pacific Ocean

Tasman Sea

NEW ZEALAND

TASMANIA

Guadalcanal

With sufficient American army reinforcements now on the island, the survivors of the first Marines landed pay their respects to their dead comrades before leaving Guadalcanal

They had located the Japanese carrier *Shokaku*, and Dauntless after Dauntless dived down through heavy flak to strike home with 1,000-pound bombs. Within minutes the *Shokaku* was ablaze from stem to stern, her guns silenced and her commander turning her away out of the fight. She was out of the war for a full nine months. Avenger torpedo-bombers which failed to find the *Shokaku* to finish her off put the cruiser *Chikuma* out of the battle badly damaged.

The *Enterprise* next fell victim to enemy dive-bombers. Assailed by a horde of Vals while narrowly avoiding torpedoes from a Japanese submarine, she took two bombs on the flight deck but evaded a succession of torpedoes

launched by waves of Kates. She was able to take on her aircraft and escape from danger. At the same time the great battleship *South Dakota* shot down 26 Vals which unavailingly attacked her. The unfortunate *Hornet* being towed at a mere three knots by the cruiser *Northampton* was caught by Japanese torpedo-bombers and had to be abandoned. The whole huge Japanese fleet was now speeding southwards, leaving Admiral Kincaid no choice but to withdraw his ships as swiftly as possible. Victory was announced in Tokyo, but the Japanese had paid too high a price. Not only had the carriers *Zuiho* and *Shokaku* been blasted out of the war, but the *Hiyo*, through attempting to do more than her inadequate engines could manage, was also out of action. In addition, over 100 aircraft with their irreplaceable, highly trained crews had been lost. Despite the 'victory', Admiral Nagumo was replaced.

226

On Guadalcanal the defenders would have no Japanese carrier-borne warplanes to contend with for some time. There was now stalemate on the island and as November, the fourth month of bitter struggle, came there were feverish attempts by both sides to reinforce. The Japanese Imperial General Headquarters planned an all-out onslaught from across the Matanikau accompanied by massive naval bombardment, and detailed immediate reinforcements of two divisions and a brigade. They believed the American fleet had been smashed and would not be able to reinforce.

The Americans were meanwhile organizing a speedy build-up of the Cactus Air Force, now reduced to 29 aircraft. President Roosevelt ordered all available weapons for land, sea and air to be rushed there. General Vandegrift commanded some 19,000 marines and 3,000 soldiers on Guadalcanal at this time. On November 1, he sent in 5,000 Marines to silence the Japanese long-range artillery and prevent the enemy from recovering and consolidating west of the Matanikau. In desperate fighting they drove the Japanese back, stormed Point Cruz and bridged the river.

On November 3 Nagumo's successor, Tameichi Hari, despatched three cruisers and eight destroyers in a renewed Tokyo Express through the Slot to bombard the Americans and land troops at Koli Point to reinforce the 2,500 starving, disillusioned Sendai survivors. During the following week, both sides gained more reinforcements including, for the Americans, two battalions of 155-mm 'Long Toms', which gave their artillery the ascendancy.

By November 10 the Japanese had 30,000 men to Vandegrift's 23,000. Two nights later Kondo planned to put ashore 14,000 more when the huge Japanese fleet of 2 aircraft carriers, 4 battleships, 11 cruisers and 49 destroyers, should arrive. Warning of the vast fleet approaching was duly given by the brave Australian coast watchers on Bougainville, and Halsey determined to put in everything he could to challenge the Japanese.

For days and nights hundreds of engineers, technicians, and Seabees had been working on the great carrier *Enterprise* in Naumea Harbour to get her back into the fight. Another 6,000 Marines and infantrymen were landed on Guadalcanal on November 11 and 12. It was

With five months of bitter fighting behind them the American Marines who defeated the first Japanese onslaughts embark for the waiting troop-ships that will take them away

a race against time! The Japanese armada was expected on the 12th. The *Enterprise* headed north on November 11 with repair teams still working on board; she was accompanied by the partly crippled battleship *South Dakota*, the battleship *Washington*, two cruisers and eight destroyers.

During the early hours of November 12, thickly masked by a rainstorm, the Japanese battleships and widespread destroyer escorts loomed into the Slot.

American reinforcements were still landing when 24 Betty bombers and 8 Zeros speeding ahead of the armada tore into the attack. Within minutes gunfire from American cruisers and destroyers and the Wildcats brought down 23 bombers and three fighters. The unloading was 90 per cent completed, with only one American cruiser and one destroyer damaged, when there came grim news that, in addition to the transports with the massive bombardment fleet, a convoy with 14,000 Japanese was being escorted over from Shortlands. Determined to prevent the bombardment of Henderson Field, whose warplanes would be vital in the hours ahead, Admiral Turner sent his immediately available warships – just five cruisers and eight destroyers – to challenge the Japanese fleet.

The terrible Japanese battlefleet loomed upon Savo island on November 13. The decks were stacked with high-explosive shells to bombard Henderson Field, and when a look-out sighted four warships 8,000 metres ahead there was utter consternation, for one shell on the ammunition deck could blow a ship to destruction. Admiral Hiroski Abe ordered all guns reloaded with armour-piercing shells, and the Japanese frenziedly sought to get the H.E. shells below and armour-piercing shells up.

In the blackness of the narrows, the battle was horrifying. Tackling the vast battleship *Hiei*, the American destroyer *Cushing* disintegrated beneath her guns, yet turned her away. The destroyer *Laffey* set the *Hiei* on fire by point-blank attack before herself shuddering beneath massive counter-blasts. The destroyer *O'Bannon* followed, and then the cruiser *San Francisco*, which poured fire into the Japanese battleship before a thunderous broadside shattered her and killed Admiral Callaghan. Also killed in the holocaust was Admiral Scott on the cruiser *Atlanta* which was caught in Japanese searchlights and savagely blasted. There was no semblance of order in the battle. Ship fired upon ship point-blank in a whirling maelstrom of warships. Inevitably, Japanese fired on Japanese and American on American, but the very confusion of the battle produced the result for which Admiral Turner had hoped. Rather than risk his capital ships in such a turmoil, Admiral Abe abandoned the bombardment of Henderson Field and led his huge force from the scene. He left behind the battleship *Hiei* crippled and helpless before the bombers when day dawned. In addition two big Japanese destroyers had been sunk, another was badly battered, and every Japanese warship had some damage.

The *Enterprise*, with her accompanying battleship force, was nearing Guadalcanal, not close enough to prevent Japanese cruisers and destroyers heavily bombarding Henderson Field the following night. Apprehension intensified when news came that the Tokyo Express, 12 destroyers and 11 fast transports, was again rushing southwards into the Slot, but American

bombers from the ravaged island airfield torpedoed and crippled the heavy cruiser *Kinugasa*, and warplanes from the *Enterprise* damaged three other cruisers.

Shortly after mid-day, still 150 miles from Guadalcanal, the troop convoy was discovered by roving American warplanes, which sank or turned back 7 out of 11 transports. That night yet another clash of giants occurred in the fatal waters of Iron Bottom Bay. Admiral Kondo, furious at his losses of the previous 48 hours, rushed down with the battleship *Kirishima*, four cruisers and eight destroyers. Near Savo island he encountered Rear-Admiral Willis Lee's battleships *Washington* and *South Dakota* and four destroyers. The night sky twitched and leaped with the flare and flame of great guns, and in quick succession three American destroyers were torn asunder. The battleship *South Dakota* shuddered beneath a terrible bombardment from the *Kirishima*, but was swiftly avenged by the *Washington* whose huge shells hit the Japanese battleship with a succession of lethal blows. Before her escort ships could flee they too were savagely mauled.

After that catastrophic night the Japanese dared not venture again into the waters around Guadalcanal with their big warships. The terrible sea battle that had gone on for three days within sight and sound of the shore had ended in a decisive American victory. Two huge Japanese battleships, one cruiser and three destroyers had been sunk for a loss of two American cruisers and five destroyers. But the Americans had also destroyed 11 troop transports carrying half of the Japanese 38th Division and 3,000 men of the naval landing force. The four transports that did survive were driven hard ashore at Tassafaronga, and subjected to merciless shelling and bombing while the troops were still struggling to disembark. There was little doubt now in the minds of the American fighting men who grimly enjoyed this spectacle that the tide had at last turned. After a hundred hellish days and nights, the battle of Guadalcanal had been won.

On this day, November 15, 1942, General Vandegrift felt sufficiently certain of victory to signal Admiral Halsey accordingly. The Japanese Imperial General Headquarters attempted in the ensuing weeks to mount a fifth and final invasion of Guadalcanal, but it never got started.

An American soldier comes across the remains of one of the thousands of Japanese dead whose bodies were left in the jungle

On January 4, 1943, Imperial General Headquarters finally had to accept the inevitable. The evacuation of those Japanese fighting men who still survived on Guadalcanal was completed by early February.

For Japan this was the beginning of the end in the South Pacific. It was the first American land victory in the South Sea Islands, one which set them off on their spectacular amphibious island-hopping campaign to the very threshold of Japan. Guadalcanal was a defeat that, against 1,592 American Marines and soldiers killed on land, had cost the Japanese 50,000 dead on land, sea and air. All this had been for what the Imperial High Command had called, at the time of the first American landing, 'this insignificant island in the South Seas'.

# 8. Alamein

# 8. Alamein

On July 1, 1942, the British 8th Army in the North African desert was on the very brink of total defeat at a place called El Alamein, barely two hours drive from Alexandria. Their plight was bewildering to the weary troops and to the stunned British public, for only 35 days earlier the 8th Army, the finest, most experienced British army, had been poised to deliver a crushing blow to Rommel's Afrika Korps from well-prepared positions in the Libyan desert some 750 miles to the west. Yet here it was, not just defeated but apparently disintegrating, with the triumphant German armour almost at the gates of Alexandria and Cairo.

The disaster that had forced the 8th Army to retreat thus far began in the Libyan Desert in January, 1942. At this time Rommel, after his defeat in the 'Crusader' battle, was holed up with the battered Afrika Korps behind the salt marshes of El Agheila, on the Libya–Tripolitania frontier. During the pause that followed, war came to the Far East, and tanks, guns and troops intended to reinforce the 8th Army were diverted there. Meanwhile Rommel was powerfully reinforced.

Hitler promoted the Afrika Korps' campaign to the status of a major strategic offensive to fit into his great plan for joining hands with the Japanese on the shores of the Indian Ocean. With 120 Panzers, many of them the powerful new Mark IVs, backed by 80 Italian tanks, the Afrika Korps burst through the British outposts and defeated the over-stretched 1st Armoured Division. Benghazi was evacuated on January 25 and the resurgent Afrika Korps swept on to the Gazala Line – a series of fortified positions in the desert that stretched 40 miles from Gazala on the coast down to Bir Hacheim, deemed to be the extreme range of Rommel's armour. In May, Rommel resumed his advance. His Panzers struck south of Bir Hacheim on May 27 and swiftly achieved a breakthrough.

When British tanks and infantry were sent in piecemeal to counter-attack, Rommel met them in an area of desert dominated by two German-held ridges with the aptly sinister name of the Cauldron. The ensuing battle was bloody and confused. The 8th Army's tank strength, with some 115 destroyed, dropped alarmingly so that once more they were outnumbered as well as outgunned. The support group of 22nd Armoured Brigade, four regiments of artillery, 10 Brigade, two battalions of 9 Brigade, and a battalion of 21st Indian Brigade were all massacred, and 50 out of 70 infantry support tanks were knocked out.

*Above* With total victory in North Africa in sight, Rommel exhorted his Afrika Korps to make a final all-out effort after they had beaten the 8th Army back to their ultimate defence line at El Alamein

*Opposite, top* German infantrymen clamber down from a tank to assault an outer defence position of the apparently defeated 8th Army

*Opposite, bottom* With the triumphant Afrika Korps just beyond the immediate horizon, British soldiers dig in, ready to bring their 3·7 anti-aircraft gun into action against advancing Panzers

232

By June 13, Rommel had driven the Free
French troops out of Bir Hacheim. El Adem
was overwhelmed on June 17. Three days later
Tobruk – the very name had come to mean an
unyielding fortress – fell to Rommel's victorious
Panzers, along with large stocks of fuel, food
and all manner of vital war equipment. Without pause Rommel urged on his formidable
100-tank spearhead. (The 8th Army had hardly
any armour remaining.) In rapid succession
Bardia, Sollum, and Halfaya were overrun and
not until Mersa Matruh did the 8th Army stand
and fight.

Knowing that if the 8th Army were finally
destroyed nothing could save the Nile delta and
the Middle East beyond, General Auchinleck
flew up to take over personal command. The
superb New Zealand Division momentarily
delayed the Afrika Korps long enough for him
to redirect the scattered army to stand on the

*Above* British tanks and infantry counter-attack after
General Auchinleck had beaten the enemy back in the
first battle of Alamein

*Opposite page* Afrika Korps vehicles burning on the
battlefield after their failure to break through the
8th Army line

Alamein line, which foremost tanks of the
German spearhead reached on June 30.

The route of the 8th Army and the fall of
Tobruk came as a greater shock to Winston
Churchill, who was in Washington conferring
with Roosevelt, than any of the calamities
British arms had so far suffered. The Germans
were poised to break through into Egypt with
all its vast military stores, to the Suez Canal,
and beyond to Palestine, Syria and Persia. The
southern flank of the hard-pressed Russians was
suddenly threatened. The Red Sea might be
opened for the Italian Fleet and German U

boats to dominate the South African shipping routes and penetrate the Indian Ocean. There was nothing to stop the Germans and the Japanese joining hands in India.

But the Afrika Korps, battle-weary although triumphant, was stopped on the Alamein line. They were halted by the New Zealanders, by the Australians who had been the original 'desert rats' of Tobruk, by British and Indian and South African soldiers who had come back from the holocaust deep in the desert, and by the R.A.F. Suddenly, Rommel's army was not sweeping through to the Middle East, but was stuck in the desert at the end of a long and precarious supply line.

The Germans began to lay extensive mine-fields, a clear indication that for the present they were more concerned with defence than offence, though Rommel had heartening news that infantry reinforcements and 260 tanks were

on their way. From July onwards Auchinleck mounted a series of increasingly strong counter-attacks which tested the enemy's defences. Then a strengthened Afrika Korps hit back with successive powerful attacks, all of which were repulsed. Each was in turn counter-attacked by the 8th Army. It was bitter, close-quarters combat with neither side showing signs of weakening.

Meanwhile, Auchinleck prepared an even more powerful offensive. It began with a massive bombardment, followed by a charge by the 9th Australian Division, newly arrived from Syria, who seized the high sandy ridge of Tel el Eisa. Rommel was compelled to fall back. Extremely worried, he noted that night: 'The enemy is in hot pursuit. . . There is serious danger they will break through and destroy our supplies'. On July 13 he countered in force, hurling in the armoured strength of the swiftly re-equipping Afrika Korps. This opened what was truly the first battle of Alamein, a fiercely fought battle that helped to make possible Montgomery's famous victory four months later.

At the day's end the German attack had achieved nothing, the Panzers everywhere being halted. Before Rommel could renew the attack Auchinleck struck a telling counter-blow by night with the New Zealanders and Indians, who overwhelmed two Italian divisions and resisted, though with heavy casualties, the savage counter-attacks of 21st and 15th Panzers.

Some of the most bitter of all the desert fighting took place on Ruweisat Ridge, captured by the 2nd West Yorkshires and 9th Indian Brigade who held on against ferocious attempts to regain it. But the 8th Army was badly supplied. If Auchinleck had been able to call on even a small part of the immense reinforcements of armour, men and guns that were to become available to his successor, the battle of El Alamein, and the war in Africa, might have been won there and then.

The news that Rostov was on the point of falling to the Panzer armies rolling across the Russian steppes increased the danger of German armoured columns bursting out through the Caucasus to complete the long-feared pincer movement upon the Middle East. The vital oil wells of the Middle East, the Indian sub-continent, and the main Allied supply route to hard-pressed Russia through Persia demanded maximum British forces to guard against so disastrous a conjunction. With this heavy responsibility in his rear, General Auchinleck was unable to draw on troops in Iraq and Persia for the reserves he needed to defeat Rommel. Despite his limited resources, he sent the 8th Army into the attack again on July 21. Although his two-pronged assault gained some ground with its first thrust, it did not achieve its main purpose, which was to split the Axis army in half, and the second thrust, having lost the element of surprise, met strongly prepared opposition when it went in on the night of July 26. The infantry suffered heavy casualties when caught by enemy tanks; the battle became increasingly confused, and was getting the 8th Army nowhere, so that Auchinleck decided to call off the attack.

However, Auchinleck had, it seemed, checked

236

EIGHTH ARMY

# PERSONAL MESSAGE
## from the
# ARMY COMMANDER

#### TO BE READ OUT TO ALL TROOPS.

1. When I assumed command of the Eighth Army I said that the mandate was to destroy ROMMEL and his Army, and that it would be done as soon as we were ready.

2. We are ready NOW.

The battle which is now about to begin will be one of the decisive battles of history. It will be the turning point of the war. The eyes of the whole world will be on us, watching anxiously which way the battle will swing.

We can give them their answer at once, «It will swing our way».

3. We have first-class equipment; good tanks; good anti-tank guns; plenty of artillery and plenty of ammunition; and we are backed up by the finest air striking force in the world.

All that is necessary is that each one of us, every officer and man, should enter this battle with the determination to see it through — to fight and to kill — and finally, to win.

If we all do this there can be only one result — together we will hit the enemy for «six», right out of North Africa.

4. The sooner we win this battle, which will be the turning point of the war, the sooner we shall all get back home to our families.

5. Therefore, let every officer and man enter the battle with a stout heart, and the determination to do his duty so long as he has breath in his body.

AND LET NO MAN SURRENDER SO LONG AS HE IS UNWOUNDED AND CAN FIGHT.

Let us all pray that «the Lord mighty in battle» will give us the victory.

*B. L. Montgomery.*

23-10-42.
Middle East Forces.                    Lieutenant-General, G.O.C.-in-C., Eighth Army.

*Above* General Montgomery's message to all soldiers of the 8th Army, which was read out to them on the eve of the Battle of El Alamein

*Opposite page* General Montgomery, complete with Tank Corps beret and two cap badges, whose arrival in North Africa coincided with the significant reinforcement of the 8th Army

the imminent threat to the Middle East from North Africa. He also foresaw Rommel's next moves with almost complete accuracy and was able to plan to defeat Rommel's next attack which, he estimated, would be an attempt to turn the Alamein line from the south with an armoured assault on Alam Halfa ridge. Meanwhile, General Bayerlein, Rommel's chief of staff, noted, 'When Rommel lost Tel el Eisa and Ruweisat, he and all of us knew we were lost.'

The bloody July battles which were fought,

for the first time in the desert war, along a short fortified line, cost a total of some 10,000 8th Army and Axis dead, and Rommel used up nearly all the war materials captured in Tobruk. Although he was being reinforced with tanks, guns and troops across the Mediterranean, the R.A.F. and Royal Navy were exacting a cruel toll of his supplies and the 8th Army was now being strengthened by convoys round the Cape. With United States war production getting into gear, an influx of American tanks in particular brought a welcome strengthening to the 8th Army's armour. A whole division was equipped with the new Sherman tank, armed with a 75-mm gun that at last gave the British tank parity with the Mark III and Mark IV Panzers.

Churchill, whose request for tanks Roosevelt had so swiftly answered, arrived in Cairo on August 4 to confer with South Africa's Smuts, Australia's Casey, Alan Brooke the C.I.G.S., Wavell, Auchinleck, Admiral Harwood and

Air-Marshal Tedder. Auchinleck was relieved of his Middle East command, along with most of his principal staff officers. General Alexander, hero of Dunkirk and later of the British retreat through Burma, was appointed to overall command of the Middle East theatre and General 'Strafer' Gott to the 8th Army. But returning to Cairo from the front in a lumbering transport plane, Gott was shot down and killed by special long-range Me 109s sent out expressly to destroy Churchill's plane. Brooke, greatly impressed by Lieutenant-General Bernard Montgomery's performance before Dunkirk, persuaded Churchill that 'Monty' was the man the 8th Army needed.

Montgomery arrived in Cairo on August 13 and immediately went to Alexander to demand the formation of a mobile reserve corps on the lines of the Afrika Korps. He was promised such a corps, to comprise the New Zealand Division and two armoured divisions, and it

237

*Top* A Stuka dive-bomber crashes in the no-man's-land beyond El Alamein

*Above* A British gun crew under fire in the desert

was designated 10 Corps. Before dawn on August 15 Montgomery set out into the desert and at Auchinleck's old spartan, fly-ridden forward H.Q. told a commanders' conference there would be no withdrawal from the Alamein line whatever happened. There were to be no more mobile battle groups of tanks and guns such as had fought in the desert for so long, but divisions would fight as divisions.

Latest information clearly indicated that Rommel was about to make a major attack to destroy the 8th Army, probably near the full moon on August 26. It was three days later that, in a special order of the day predicting the 'final annihilation of the enemy', Rommel told his troops they would be in Alexandria in three days' time.

During the bitter battles of July, when Auchinleck was considering his future campaign, he had planned to persuade Rommel to attack prematurely about the third week in August and squander his armour against strong 8th Army defences. The area Auchinleck had chosen was in the Alamein–Qattara Depression –El Hamman triangle. While the line between the sea and Ruweisat Ridge was held strongly, any enemy advance south of that high ground would be powerfully opposed from well-prepared positions on the Alam el Halfa Ridge. The plan Montgomery drew up was basically the same as Auchinleck's, with a few developments made possible by reinforcements. To the north he had the Tel el Eisa salient strongly held by the 9th Australian Division, with the ground between them and Ruweisat Ridge held by the 1st South Africans. The Ridge itself was occupied by 5th Indian Division and south of it the 2nd New Zealand Division faced west and south-west on the high Deir el Munassib feature.

The 8th Army's defence line from there down to the Qattara Depression comprised a series of six minefields. Out of sight, but ready to sweep in to attack any Panzer breakthrough at a moment's notice, the 7th Armoured Division was poised to the south-east. Like Auchinleck, Montgomery anticipated Rommel would strike at El Hamman with the object of bursting through to fall upon the 8th Army's lines of communication. To do this he would have to drive eastwards along the southern edge of the Alam el Halfa Ridge where he would run the

238

Ambulances and infantry carriers silhouetted against the flare of gunfire which preceded the attack

gauntlet between the guns of a British infantry division in prepared positions and dug-down tanks on one side, and a British armoured division on the other. At last the British infantry divisions were equipped with the new and far more powerful tank-killing 6-pounder gun, and of the 713 tanks the 8th Army deployed, 164 were the heavy Americans with 75-mm guns.

Rommel, with no choice but to attack the Alamein line head-on, now staked all on a swift and powerful punch by night direct at the line's southern extremity at Himeimat. Here there appeared to be a soft spot, covered only by minefields. Before first light the combined 15th and 21st Panzer Divisions would blast through to Alam el Halfa, in the 8th Army's rear. At daybreak the Afrika Korps would sweep swiftly north while armoured formations on the left would make a series of short hooks around Ruweisat Ridge. Within hours Rommel reckoned the 8th Army would be surrounded, its supply lines cut, and nothing could then stop the Panzers' onrush to Cairo.

Largely because of difficulties in amassing adequate fuel, Rommel did not attack until August 31. Surprise was absolutely essential for the success of his armoured punch. There were exactly 200 German tanks, half of them the latest type, to deliver the decisive blow. Backing

239

A 4·5-inch gun bombarding enemy tanks concentrated at the southern end of the Alamein line

them up were 243 Italian medium tanks and 38 light tanks. But it was alarmingly apparent early on that he would not achieve surprise. Two hours before the Panzer columns were due to set out, R.A.F. night bombers made a damaging raid on the mass of assembled transport.

When the Panzers rumbled out to the south, and troops advancing forward of them began to lift the British mines, the dug-in troops covering the minefields opened heavy and accurate fire. The pattern of the enemy attack was already becoming obvious to Montgomery and he called on the R.A.F. to deal with the advancing Panzers. Where the Africa Korps had expected a swift drive through after lifting a few mines

they found they were in a death trap. Among the many casualties were General von Bismarck, commander of the 21st Panzer Division, who was killed, and General Nehring, commander of the Afrika Korps, gravely wounded.

Rommel was compelled to modify his plan, making Alam el Halfa the immediate objective, and postponing his dash to Alexandria and Cairo. On a narrow front he sent in both 15 and 21 Panzer divisions, 90 Light Division, and the whole of 20 Italian Corps, including its two armoured divisions, the Ariete and Littoria. An onslaught by 100 Panzers from Himeimat was Rommel's next move. They penetrated two minefields and advanced seven miles but were checked by a third minefield. To add to their difficulties, the Panzers were churning into soft sand they had not expected.

Montgomery's choice as new commander of

units, was not sufficiently welded together to chase headlong after them, and instead concentrated on destroying Rommel's thin-skinned vehicles, to aggravate his already difficult transport problem.

The enemy reacted furiously when the veteran New Zealand Division attempted to close the minefield gap before the Panzers could escape, demonstrating that they intended to hold on to this area of desert between the two British minefields. Montgomery, planning a major offensive in the very near future, let them keep it. It conformed to his plan if the enemy insisted on remaining strong at the southern end of the Alamein line. He called off the battle early on September 7. He was well pleased with the way the 8th Army had fought the battle of Alam el Halfa. There had been a significant cohesion between units, many new to the desert, and effective co-operation between Army and Desert Air Force. Above all, the morale of the 8th Army was once more high.

Montgomery encouraged the enemy to concentrate south with a plan of deception worked out even before the battle of Alam el Halfa. Dummy lorries, dumps and a dummy pipeline were constructed at the rear of the south end of the line, and radio activity was stepped up to suggest an attack was planned for early November.

Meanwhile farther north, where Montgomery really intended to attack, operational transport and guns were moved in by night and carefully camouflaged. By the third week in September the forward slit-trenches from which the infantry would attack had been dug by night out in the desert and effectively camouflaged. Throughout the decisive period of six weeks in which the 8th Army was preparing its offensive, German air reconnaissance only told Rommel what Montgomery wanted him to believe. Increasing activity by the Desert Air Force against enemy airfields and communications effectively grounded the Luftwaffe, as planned, by October 23.

*Top* Australian soldiers take away a wounded German soldier from a captured strongpoint

*Bottom* When the battle appeared to have reached stalemate, General Montgomery addressed officers of his staff to tell them precisely what he was going to do next

From the second week in October Montgomery addressed meetings of senior officers explaining how he intended to fight the forthcoming battle. On October 21 and 22 the officers in turn put the men in the picture. Although the 8th Army veterans admired and had confidence in Auchinleck, there was something very reassuring about their new commander. When he told them 'We'll hit Rommel and his army for six right out of Africa!' they believed him.

Montgomery planned three simultaneous attacks, the main one by 30 Corps in the north on a front of four divisions. This was to tear two corridors through the enemy defences, towards Kidney Ridge and over Miteiriya Ridge, for the mass of the armour of 10 Corps to surge through and give battle. Whether or not the infantry divisions opened up the necessary corridors, the tanks of 10 Corps were to fight through to take up position on the open ground beyond.

To the south, 13 Corps was to make two thrusts, one east of Jebel Kalakh and Qaret el Khadim, the other farther south towards Himeimat and Taqa. Once 30 and 13 Corps had forced their way in among the enemy's defences they were methodically to destroy the troops there. The main role of 13 Corps was to mislead Rommel into believing the major attack would be in the south so that he would keep powerful armoured formations there. In addition to the main, frontal blow in the northern sector, with the traditional attempt to turn the southern flank ruled out, Montgomery was introducing another innovation to the desert war. He was not using his mass of armour, first to destroy the enemy's armour, then to fall upon the unprotected infantry, as heretofore. He aimed to destroy the enemy's unarmoured formations first, meanwhile holding off their armour from intervening.

If the soldiers necessary to hold the ground won by the Panzers were liquidated, Rommel's armour would just not be able to hold territory, Montgomery calculated. Then its supply routes would be in constant jeopardy and the only course would be to withdraw. To destroy the enemy infantry divisions Montgomery decided to employ what he called a 'crumbling process' during the opening break-in battle. This would begin with a massive bombardment, both from

Back beyond the area of devastation wrought by the
British artillery, German gunners crouch round one
of their dreaded 88-mm dual purpose anti-tank,
anti-aircraft guns, waiting for the British tanks
to break through

air and ground, first of the enemy's artillery positions, then of the infantry. While the enemy
soldiers were still dazed the toughest 8th Army
shock-troops would charge from their forward
slit-trenches. Bloody hand-to-hand fighting was
inevitable with such a plan, but Montgomery
reckoned his men would get the better of it, and
when they had remorselessly 'crumbled' away
the defending troops' resistance, the mass of
armour would rumble through. The *corps de
chasse* of 10 Corps would pursue whatever survived of the Afrika Korps and destroy it utterly.
There would also be tanks well forward, on
ground of their own choosing, to halt any
attempt by the Panzers to come to the rescue
of their infantry. Above all else, Montgomery
impressed on his men that the enemy must have
no chance to recover; any sign of weakness
should be pressed hard. Montgomery deemed

a full moon vital for his plan of attack, requiring
as it did the night-time lifting of thousands of
mines and the blasting of a hole through the
enemy's defences. He therefore chose the night
of October 23 for the opening of the battle of
El Alamein.

The enemy minefields, at their most formidable in the north, were 5,000 to 9,000 yards in
depth interwoven with and covered by 'defensive localities' of considerable strength. Rommel
had great faith in his 'Devil's Gardens' of mines,
bombs and barbed-wire entanglements. In the
south the minefields, though less extensive, were
situated so that any attack into them must be
canalized into a massive concentration of Axis
fire power.

The enemy line was held by one German and
five Italian divisions, each of the latter considerably stiffened by detached German formations. The German and Italian infantry were
mixed, battalion by battalion, to strengthen the
Italians' resolve. Ready to deal with a possible
breakthrough were, in the north, the 15th
Panzers and Littoria Armoured Division; to
their rear, near the coast, were the German
90th Light Division, and in the south the 21st

244

GREECE

TURKEY

CYPRUS

CRETE

*Mediterranean    Sea*

Gazala
Tobruk          Mersa          Alexandria
El Adem    Bardia    Matruh    Galal    Nile Delta
*Gulf of Sirte*    Sidi Rezegh    Sollum          El Hammam
Bir Hacheim    Bir Sheferzen    Halfaya    Sidi Raman    Cairo
                    *Libyan Plateau*    Fuka    Alam el Halfa
                    **Libya**    Daba    Tel el Eisa
El Agheila                    Himeimat
                    *Qattara*
                    *Depression*    El Alamein
*Siwa Oasis*    Tel el Aquaqir
                    Assyat

**L I B Y A**

El Ktiarga

●Al Kufrah

**EGYPT**

Wadi Halfa

**Alamein**

Panzer and Ariete Armoured divisions. Farther back, on the Egyptian–Libyan frontier, was the Italian Pistoia Division. Rommel's reinforced army had a three-to-seven proportion of desert veterans. His two Panzer divisions had 220 tanks, mostly Mark 111s, and there were 318 medium Italian tanks and 21 light tanks.

At 9.40 p.m. on October 23, more than a thousand guns, 25-pounders and mediums, opened simultaneous fire upon German artillery positions from the whole British line of El Alamein. In 20 minutes they wrought terrible execution among the German and Italian guns. Then they switched to deluge the enemy's forward positions, and into the towering, choking curtain of dust and smoke that arose over the enemy, the British 13 and 30 Corps advanced to the attack. To the wild skirling of bagpipes, line after line of steel-helmeted infantry moved methodically forward, moonbeams glinting on

*Opposite, top* As the British tanks advanced, infantry were close at hand to deal with enemy infantry and anti-tank gunners

*Opposite, bottom* Truck-borne British infantry in the wake of the tanks come under heavy shellfire as they advance

*Below* A lane through the minefields having been cleared, British tanks advance along the narrow channel leading deep into the enemy lines

bayonets and rifles held menacingly at high port position.

In the northern sector the 9th Australian and 51st Scottish divisions went in with the bayonet, their immediate objective to force a corridor through the minefields. Below them the New Zealanders and South Africans attacked to carve out a southern corridor. Meanwhile, from the dangerous salient on Ruweisat Ridge, the 4th Indian Division began a strong raid into the enemy positions. At the very northern end of the British line an Australian brigade put in a diversionary attack between Tel el Eisa and the sea.

Everywhere the Germans resisted valiantly but by 5.30 a.m. the major objective had been achieved. The two vital corridors were opened up and behind the infantry the divisions of 30 Corps, and 1st and 10th Armoured divisions of 10 Corps, were respectively moving into the northern and southern corridors. But at this point Montgomery's precise timetable went wrong. As the spearheading infantry reached the minefields, an increasingly ferocious fire swept them. Although 9th Armoured Brigade and the 2nd New Zealand Division pushed forward of Miteiriya Ridge, 10th Armoured was checked, and so was 1st Armoured. The British tanks were compelled to remain behind the Miteiriya Ridge, engaging at extreme range and in danger of being jammed up on a

narrow front behind the slowing infantry. However, several small counter-attacks by 15th Panzers were beaten back.

In the south, meanwhile, 7th Armoured Division and 44th Division failed to get through the enemy minefields north of Himeimat and the infantry of 13 Corps embarked, between the minefields, on the bloody fighting necessary to implement Montgomery's 'crumbling' tactics. In the extreme south an advance by the Free French was thrown back before their support could get up. Although the 8th Army's night attack had secured a bridgehead in the enemy positions, when day came the armour had failed to penetrate the minefields, and the main German defence line had not been penetrated. The channels into the enemy defences opened up by the infantry were as yet cul-de-sacs with formidable enemy fire power at the other end. Conditions were precarious indeed for British tanks thrusting into these channels.

The Scots infantry and 1st Armoured Division renewed their attack the following afternoon, and by dusk the 2nd Armoured Brigade had blasted its way through, but 10th Armoured Division, behind a massive artillery barrage, still encountered stern resistance in the southern corridor. At 4 a.m. next morning it was still held up, but Montgomery insisted it must continue attacking despite casualties. This insistence by Montgomery that the closely grouped tanks (set to advance along just three lanes per armoured division, each barely a tank wide) must press on regardless, occasioned a bitter incident destined to have a considerable effect upon the development of the battle.

General Lumsden, commanding 10 Corps, one of the few original desert generals remaining, had from the beginning been critical of Montgomery's proposed employment of armour. He was convinced that to crowd hundreds of tanks in a few restricted corridors, among thick minefields covered by massed enemy guns, was to invite massacre. The leading tanks would inevitably be knocked out and, as the following ones became bogged down behind them, they would be blown to bits by the German 88-mms. As the initial attack lost impetus, Lumsden sought to pull his tanks back from the precarious corridors and regroup them behind Miteiriya Ridge. Montgomery diagnosed 'a certain infirmity of purpose in the mind of 10 Corps com-

*Above* With Churchill tanks equipped with 6-pounder guns, 8th Army armoured formations could at last meet the Afrika Korps Panzers on equal terms

*Opposite, top* The crew of a disabled German tank surrender to British infantry

*Opposite, bottom* Farther back from the battle-front, German heavy artillery bombards the advancing 8th Army

mander' and summoned Lumsden and Oliver Leese, commanding 30 Corps, to his battle H.Q. Lumsden insisted that the planned advance by massed armour would be a tragic calamity and repeated the words of Gatehouse, commander of the spearheading 10th Armoured Division, that even if he succeeded in getting tanks through the minefields and out on to the southern face of Miteiriya Ridge, they would be shot to pieces by the formidable German anti-tank artillery, well dug in and just waiting for such a target.

Gatehouse had fought in tanks during the First World War. In the Second World War he had been in at the start in Europe where, as commander of the only tank regiment with the B.E.F., he had trained with all the infantry divisions, including Montgomery's 3rd. He was the same Alec Gatehouse who, atop his tank, had led the hopelessly outgunned Honeys at

Sidi Rezegh in the Crusader campaign. Montgomery almost accused Gatehouse, four times decorated for valour, of cowardice. 'I discovered to my horror,' Montgomery wrote later, 'that he himself was some 16,000 yards (nearly ten miles) behind his leading armoured brigades. I spoke to him at once in no uncertain voice, and ordered him to go forward at once and take charge of his battle. . .'

This was hardly fair to Gatehouse who, according to his own account, had made his way back from front-line battle headquarters to reach a field telephone and tell Montgomery that he refused to squander his division – the elite force meant to thunder through already cleared minefields to destroy Rommel's Panzers.

After an abrasive exchange of opinions, Montgomery finally ordered Gatehouse to make the advance over the ridge with one armoured regiment instead of the entire division: Complying, under protest, with this amended instruction, Gatehouse despatched the 49 tanks of the Staffordshire Yeomanry. From the holocaust that engulfed them over the ridge 15 scarred tanks limped back. 'If I had committed the whole division it would almost certainly have been annihilated,' commented Gatehouse afterwards.

By daylight on October 25 the leading armoured brigade had managed to fight to a position 2,000 yards through the enemy minefields. Soon afterwards came the good news that the New Zealanders' 9th Armoured Brigade was also through to its objective. The attempts of the Afrika Korps to destroy these salients were beaten off at heavy cost. His armoured spearheads having penetrated into the enemy line and established positions from which they could challenge any counter-attacks, Montgomery now concentrated on the 'crumbling' by the infantry.

The crowded battlefield, befogged by the smoke and towering sand clouds of thousands of exploding shells and bombs, was becoming increasingly confused as formation after formation was sent into the attack. The particularly bitter fighting in which the New Zealanders had become embroiled in the south-west persuaded Montgomery to switch the main crumbling task to the Australians in the north. They attacked on the night of October 25 and were swiftly successful. However, a complementary attack by 1st Armoured Division at Kidney Ridge was held up, although 7 Motor Brigade managed to establish itself on the ridge.

Montgomery had hoped 1st Armoured would break into the open desert to Sidi Rahman, there to menace the enemy's supply routes. In view of the infantry's heavy casualties and the formidable arcs of anti-tank guns confronting the armoured spearheads, which had already lost 200 tanks, Montgomery now had to make a reassessment of the battle. He decided to concentrate on the northern sector, hoping to cut out and destroy a large German force and at the same time open up the way to the vital coastal road. He therefore withdrew the New Zealanders from the south to provide himself with a hard-hitting reserve, and ordered 1st Armoured Division into reserve until the moment when he could smash through his knock-out punch. Gatehouse's 10th Armoured replaced 1st Armoured in the line. The Afrika Korps flung in a succession of savage counter-attacks, led by Rommel in person, upon Kidney Ridge, but all were bloodily repulsed and on October 27 1st Armoured Division alone destroyed 50 Panzers. Finally furious attacks by the Desert Air Force compelled the massed Panzers to disperse.

Next day Montgomery was able to put his plan into good effect. He ordered that 13 Corps in the south should temporarily adopt a defensive role while doing everything possible by

hostile patrolling and artillery fire to continue the deception. When 21st Panzers switched to Kidney Ridge on October 26, Montgomery felt it was time to move 7th Armoured Division from the south to lend its weight to the assault in the north.

There could be no doubt that the whole armoured strength of the Afrika Korps was concentrated opposite the northern corridor. Montgomery completed the regrouping of the 8th Army in readiness for the tremendous all-out punch he intended it should deliver – a blow of such violence that it would burst right through the remaining depth of enemy defences. He put the infantry and artillery in the northern corridor on the defensive and pulled back 24th Armoured Brigade to join 1st Armoured Division in reserve. With the infantry of both armies still interlocked after five days' fighting, he could see there was little hope of breaking through either of the two corridors he had selected for the big punch. His next major attack would be up by the coast.

Rommel, expecting an attempted British breakthrough towards Mersa Matruh and anxious that his army should not be split in two, was concerned with only one question: with the two armies so closely entangled in bitter fighting on such a narrow front, who would become exhausted first? His immediate concern was to throw the British out of his main defence line at all costs and eradicate the ominous 8th Army salient at Kidney Ridge.

The so-called Kidney Ridge was the scene of an epic stand by the Rifle Brigade and tanks of the 1st Armoured Division. There the Afrika Korps tanks and Italian armour made successive massed onslaughts, backed by lorried infantry and machine-gunners, in their efforts to regain this lost ground. But the tanks and the men of the 2nd Rifle Brigade, commanded by Lieutenant-Colonel Vic Turner who earned his V.C. in the battle, halted every charge. The 6-pounder anti-tank guns proved exceptionally effective.

On the night of October 28 the Australians, supported by the 40th Royal Tanks, drove a wedge practically through to the coast road near Tel el Eisa. Calculating that Rommel would be expecting the main 8th Army assault along the parallel road and rail lines by the coast, Montgomery chose to deliver it on a

*Top* Learning their lesson from the Afrika Korps in earlier desert armoured warfare, the 8th Army now had an effective tank recovery service. Here a British recovery crew are seen under fire as they load up a damaged cruiser tank to take it back for repair

*Above* Another surprise for Rommel – Montgomery's 8th Army was equipped with 17-pounder anti-tank guns which could put paid to even the most heavily armoured Panzer

section of defence line, mainly held by Italians, a little to the north of the original northern corridor. While the 9th Australian Division flung in a ferocious new attack towards the coast road, the 2nd New Zealand Division would fall upon the Italians and smash a gap right through the enemy line. Then the full might of 10 Corps armour – the 1st, 7th and 10th Armoured Divisions plus two armoured-car regiments – would hurtle into that gap.

Montgomery gave the code name Supercharge to the operation. And even as the 8th Army clenched its fist to deliver this lethal punch, the unsuspecting Rommel had moved his guard of the 21st Panzer Division up north to join 90th Light Division against the Australians. He had blocked Montgomery's right only to lay himself open to his devastating left. Nearly all German units had been moved up to the north now and Rommel told his commanders that the decisive moment was upon them and every man must be prepared to fight to the death. Already, however, worried by lack of fuel, he was considering withdrawing 50 miles to Fuka.

The first move in Operation Supercharge was made by the Australians to the north on the night of October 30. They arose from their trenches and fought forward against bitter resistance until they reached the coast road and the sea, driving a formidable wedge through the German positions and surrounding a force of Panzer Grenadiers in a strongly fortified feature known as Thompson's Post. Furious attacks were made from the west by Panzer formations, and some succeeding in fighting through to the trapped force. In the bitter encounters that continued for three days and nights the Germans, though encumbered with heavy casualties, managed to extricate the survivors from Thompson's Post.

While this battle was at its height in the north, Montgomery unleashed the full weight of Supercharge farther south. It was directed towards Tel el Aqqaqir on a 4,000-yard front at the point of junction between the Italian force and the Afrika Korps. By drawing all the Germans north, the assault by the Australians had achieved Montgomery's aim of separating Italians and Germans. At 1 a.m. on November 2 two British infantry brigades stormed forward from the New Zealanders' front and on each

*Top* After the ultimate breakthrough, British armoured cars race on through the sand-fogged battlefield, endeavouring to get behind the retreating enemy

*Above* With British armour driving hard to outflank them, these Afrika Korps gunners hasten to bring their 88-mm gun out of action and head for the coast road

side of them ensuing attacks began to expand the base of the salient.

The fighting was exceedingly tough, but they managed to carve out the new corridor required for the Supercharge westwards of the main body of the armour. Spearheading that armour, 9th Armoured Brigade rumbled into the corridor, its objective 2,000 yards ahead on the Rahman track by Tel el Aqqaqir. There they were to destroy the enemy's last line of defences and knock out all anti-tank guns. Then 1st Armoured Division, with 270 tanks, would charge through and after them 7th Armoured Division. The 10th Armoured Division, the powerful *corps de chasse*, would thunder out into the open desert behind the enemy's battered fortress line and the battle would be won. To 9th Armoured Brigade, comprising 123 tanks (Shermans and Crusaders) was assigned the perilous task of destroying the ultimate anti-tank screen, which included ranks of the terrifying 88 mms. Montgomery told their commander, Brigadier John Currie: 'I am prepared to accept 100 per cent casualties'. Currie insisted on leading personally.

As they rumbled out on their perilous charge for the German guns, detonation after detonation, followed by the red eruptions of exploding fuel, told of advancing tanks running on to mines. But the brigade pressed on through the glowering dark, followed by the infantry with bayonets lowered in readiness. As the exquisite desert dawn was devoured by the soaring sun, 9th Armoured Brigade accelerated their advance, but as the day grew hotter triumph was overwhelmed by disaster. Out in the open desert 9th Brigade was swept by an awesome concentration of dug-in German anti-tank guns. Tank after tank burst asunder in crackling flame and boiling black smoke, dooming to hideous death crews not already killed by the impact of high-velocity shell. In the bitter hours that followed, 9th Armoured Brigade lost all but 19 of its tanks, and 230 out of 400 officers and men. Yet it attained its objective and heroically held the vital bridgehead open.

Following 9th Armoured Brigade through the corridor 1st Armoured Division also plunged into a battle near Tel el Aqqaqir. It became embroiled with formations of 21st Panzer Division, now furiously counter-attacking as Rommel realized too late where the 8th Army's main attack was being made. Next day the British tanks were confronted by a formidable screen of anti-tank guns rushed down to plug the gap. Meanwhile, however, 51st Division was extending the salient southwards and 7th Motor Brigade was making ground as it attacked strongly westwards from the Sidi Rahman track.

The tank battle that ensued, with 2nd Armoured Brigade in the forefront astride the Sidi Rahman track, was the most ferocious of the whole battle. More and more German and Italian tanks were flung in, backed by artillery and anti-tank fire, but the British artillery and the bombers of the Desert Air Force struck back and after a desperate two-hour slogging match, Rommel's first counter-attack against the Supercharge salient petered out. Early that afternoon he sent in another, this time with the addition of a large part of the Ariete Armoured Division and artillery from the south, but was again checked, suffering crippling losses (the Afrika Korps now had only 35 tanks left).

Rommel decided to pull back to Fuka before his army was wiped out. He wrote to his wife, 'The battle is going very heavily against us. . . At night I lie open-eyed, racking my brains for a way out of this plight for my poor troops. . . The dead are lucky, it's all over for them.'

Rommel knew that as the British armour poured through the gap it had torn in his line and fanned out behind, his army was doomed unless he withdrew. It was at this moment, on November 3, that he received an urgent order from Hitler: 'The position requires that the El Alamein position be held to the last man. There is to be no retreat, not so much as one millimetre; victory or death!'

Erwin Rommel knew this order was suicidal nonsense, yet he was a soldier whose duty was to obey orders. For the moment he did not know whether to obey and bring certain disaster to his troops, or to disobey and court certain personal disaster. In his desperate predicament he asked General Fritz Bayerlein, his chief of staff, who had been at his right hand in the desert for the past year. Bayerlein's advice was to ignore Hitler's order, but Rommel had it circulated among the troops. He refused the request of General von Thoma, leader of the Afrika Korps, to pull back with his 30 surviving tanks to positions at Fuka and Daba, but when von Thoma, angrily declaring, 'I cannot tolerate this order from Hitler!' set the columns of the Afrika Korps moving westwards Rommel turned a blind eye.

Soon afterwards von Thoma was beyond the reach of any retribution Hitler might have had in store for him. Driving out into the perilous desert to investigate a report that British armour had broken through to the south, he was surrounded by British tanks and forced to surrender.

General Bayerlein now assumed command of the Afrika Korps, or at least what was left of it. The whole desert battlefield was littered with burnt-out tanks, wrecked armoured cars and shattered guns, the graveyard of the once invincible Panzer divisions. Because of the toll taken by the 8th Army and Desert Air Force of the Axis transport, and the critical shortage of fuel, there were only vehicles enough to get the surviving German troops away. The Italian infantry, loath to retreat on foot in the face of relentless strafing and bombing by the Desert Air Force and with little food or water, surrendered in tens of thousands. After 12 days of battle what was left of the Axis army was in full retreat.

Although the Afrika Korps was retreating Rommel had still not given the order. When Bayerlein asked him, 'What can I do in face of this order of Hitler's?' he merely replied, 'I cannot authorize you to disobey it'. Already a sick man, Rommel's spirit was broken. He knew that with his armour largely destroyed he had no chance of suddenly turning upon his pursuers, to transform retreat into victory, as he had done so successfully before. Nevertheless, he was still a dedicated soldier and he conducted a masterly retreat out of the chaos and confusion of the set-piece battle of El Alamein. When on November 8, four days after the battle had ended, news came that Anglo–American forces had landed at the other end of North Africa, Rommel was left in no doubt that retreat had been the right decision.

The 8th Army had achieved a magnificent feat of arms and won a memorable victory. Where they were not coming out with their hands up, the enemy were in full retreat. Inevitably, because of the narrow and heavily fortified front on which it had been fought, it had been a battle of attrition on First World War lines and

quite different from the swift and dramatic war of manoeuvre fought in the desert during the previous two years. There was considerable confusion in such a confined battlefield and it was not easy to organize a swift pursuit from amidst this confusion. Montgomery sought to swing his main armoured force northwards and round the Afrika Korps to block the coastal road at the bottlenecks of Fuka and Mersa Matruh. But despite the apparent completeness of his victory the 8th Army commander was disposed to observe caution, having a healthy respect for Rommel's oft-proven ability to hit back damagingly when all seemed lost. He refused to allow Gatehouse with his formidable 10th Armoured Division to go all out for Sollum and Tobruk. With more mobile desert war experience than any other commander of armour, Gatehouse was convinced he could outflank the Afrika Korps and trap the Germans against the sea. To his dying day Gatehouse remained convinced that if Montgomery had let him go, the Afrika Korps would have been wiped out within 48 hours and the ensuing frustrating pursuit across North Africa would have been unnecessary.

Surging out of the dust and chaos of the battlefield of El Alamein 8th Armoured Brigade did manage to head off a German column at Galal. It destroyed or captured a large number of prisoners, tanks and lorries. But beyond this no considerable enemy force was overhauled, and it was the incessant ferocious bombing and strafing by the Desert Air Force that caused most damage to the fleeing Axis troops.

Even as it had saved Rommel during the Crusader campaign, the rain now came to the rescue of the Africa Korps. The New Zealanders were bearing down on Fuka, and the 1st and 7th Armoured Divisions were converging on Matruh when, within minutes, a blinding deluge turned the firm going into a treacherous quagmire. On November 7 the whole pursuit force was bogged down. Although the Desert Air Force continued to press home damaging attacks, the Germans were able to make good use of the 24 hours' respite, and most of the surviving troops got away along the coast road. Although Rommel had sustained a crushing defeat, and four crack German divisions and eight Italian divisions had been annihilated, he still had a compact and formidable army of tanks, guns and vehicles.

254

Victory has been achieved – the prisoners begin to stream back towards Egypt, and at last there are thousands of Germans among the huge numbers of Italians

The Battle of Alamein cost the 8th Army 13,500 casualties killed and wounded. Some 500 tanks were knocked out, although only 150 of these were damaged beyond repair, and 100 guns were destroyed. The Axis army lost around 20,000 in killed and wounded and 30,000 prisoners were taken, 10,000 of them Germans. On the battlefield afterwards were found 450 destroyed or damaged Axis tanks while the Italians abandoned 75 through lack of fuel. At least 1,000 enemy guns were destroyed or abandoned. There could be no denying that at last the 8th Army had won a complete victory, and in Britain Churchill ordered that the church bells, held silent so long for an invasion alarm, should be rung out joyously. Alamein, together with the Germans' failure to capture Stalingrad at this time, undoubtedly marked the turning of the tide against Germany. 'After Alamein we never had a defeat', Churchill recorded with justification.

It should not be forgotten that when those bells rang out for El Alamein in November, 1942, they were celebrating a victory made possible by two earlier battles. Had not Auchinleck's do-or-die heroes of the apparently shattered 8th Army checked Rommel on the Alamein line in July, Rommel's Afrika Korps must have triumphed. And had not the reinforced 8th Army under Montgomery stopped Rommel's last desperate attack at Alam Halfa, the Afrika Korps would have been much stronger in the ultimate clash that began on 23 October.

255

# 9. Stalingrad

# 9. Stalingrad

The bitter winter which froze the German advance on Moscow to a standstill was the coldest for 140 years. The fierceness of the frost was such that boiling soup ladled out from the German field kitchens was frozen solid within two minutes. Butter had to be sliced with saws, and axe-shafts were broken in attempts to hack slabs of meat into portions. Tanks, guns and vehicles by the thousand were abandoned and silently engulfed by its vast white blanket. Men went mad with cold and many died from it. By the year's end 100,000 cases of frostbite had been reported, of which over 14,000 were so serious that limbs had to be amputated.

While thus afflicted by the elements the Germans before Moscow were struck by the Russian counter-attack. Fortunately for them, the Soviet winter offensive was as clumsy as the counter-attacks of the summer. Everything was directly controlled from the Kremlin, and the Russian generals were inhibited by Stalin and his political commissars breathing down their necks. Their attacks were mostly frontal and aimed at the strongest points in the German lines. They proved costly in the extreme. Under the initial impact the German Army Group Centre was badly shaken, but Hitler's unequivocal 'no retreat' order was followed by a rally which held the Russians. The ground regained by the Red Army amounted to no more than a 40-mile belt before the capital. And although the Russians had fought back into Kalinin, Klin, Kalugo and Mozhaisk and had relieved Tula, the Germans had successfully resisted all attempts to recapture the key salients of Orel, Rzhev and Vyazma. Smolensk, which had been the real objective of the Red Army's winter offensive, was still far away in the German rear.

But the Wehrmacht had sustained a vast loss of experienced commanders. Hitler had sacked all the generals who had protested at his 'no retreat' policy and was dictating the way in which the war should be fought.

By February, 1942, events seemed to have proved the Führer right. The Russian offensive dwindled and, having suffered terrible casualties, the Red Army appeared to be a spent force. Hitler had very positive plans for the renewed onslaught upon Russia. In the coming campaign he was determined that nothing would stop him fulfilling his intention to smash the Soviet Army once and for all.

*Above* German soldiers, their uniforms caked with snow, on the Russian front during the terrible winter of 1941–42, when over 100,000 men suffered from frost-bite

*Opposite, top* Adolf Hitler made himself Commander-in-Chief of all the armed forces after his disagreement with the generals over the conduct of the Moscow campaign. From then onwards he dictated the course of the war almost entirely, and in this picture is seen outlining his plans to some of his senior commanders

*Opposite, bottom* Field-Marshal von Kleist (right), who became Hitler's favourite and was entrusted with the most powerful single armoured force in the 1st Panzer Army

260

In April, with the snows vanished and the ground firm, preparations were completed for the 1942 campaign. Stalingrad was to be attacked and either seized or subjected to such heavy bombardment that its important war industries would have to be abandoned and its function as a vital communications centre between the southern and northern battle-fronts destroyed, thus facilitating the over-running of the important isthmus between the Don and Volga. According to the High Command's plan Stalingrad, along with Voronezh to the north-west and Armavir to the south-west, would be held as bastions in an unbreakable German line across Russia. Hitler's ultimate and more ambitious plan was to follow the capture of Stalingrad with a thrust northwards up the Volga to Kazan, and rapidly to encircle Moscow. Another army would meanwhile move south-east to take the rich Baku oilfields on the shores of the Caspian Sea, occupy the Caucasus and threaten Persia and Turkey into acquiescence, or at least into complete neutrality.

The German Army was split into two groups, Army Group A and Army Group B. Overall command was invested in Field-Marshal Fedor von Bock, with A under Field-Marshal Sigmund List and B under General Freiherr von Weichs. Army Group B was meant to be the main instrument of the final execution of Russia and was accordingly much the stronger of the two. It comprised the exceptionally powerful 6th Army under Field-Marshal Friedrich Paulus, with crack Panzer and infantry divisions, and also the 4th Panzer Army and the 2nd Army. By comparison Army Group A had the appearance of a reserve force, comprising only the crack 1st Panzer Army, the German 17th Infantry Army and a varied collection of satellite formations including Rumanian, Italian and Hungarian troops. The 1st Panzer Army itself had a mercurial leader in Field-Marshal Ewald von Kleist, who was especially admired by Hitler. The Führer had in fact confided in Kleist that he regarded him and his magnificent Panzers as the shining sword that would sever the rich southern oilfields from the Red Army's grasp, immobilizing the enemy armour and assuring the Wehrmacht of all the fuel it was ever likely to require.

The German armies numbered as many men

*Above* Marshal Stalin, whose insistence that Kharkov should be captured at all costs by a Russian Spring offensive, lost the Red Army nearly a quarter of a million men and almost its entire remaining tank force

*Opposite page* This picture found on a German officer shows Germans executing two Russian prisoners of war. Hundreds of thousands of Russian prisoners were either butchered or allowed to freeze or starve to death

as at the beginning of the Russian campaign, but only through the addition of Rumanian and Hungarian divisions, whose fighting prowess could not be rated so high as that of the German soldiers. And although there were 25 Panzer divisions, against 19 the year before, the German soldiers had learned that they were not invincible, that their Führer was not infallible, and that the scorned Russians could produce weapons as good as or better than theirs. The Germans had no tank to equal the formidable Russian T 34, and nothing in the Wehrmacht's huge armoury compared with the Katyusha multiple-rocket projectors.

The German soldiers posted to the Eastern Front went with some foreboding, and the moment they entered the vast overrun territories they were brutally reminded of this campaign's savagery. Murder of Russians by mass-shooting, by burning, by deliberate starvation and exposure – these and other variations of slaughter were practised by the Germans without compunction on men, women and children. By the war's end, 1,981,000 Russian military prisoners alone had died in their cages and a further 1,308,000 died or disappeared in transit. The ordinary, serving soldier might well shudder at the atrocities in which he shared and contemplate with fear possible Russian victory and revenge.

The Russian armies were desperately short of many of the necessities of all-out armoured warfare. The huge tank factories at Orel and Kharkov, and nearly all those manufacturing vital components in the Donets basin, had been overrun by the Panzer tide. The bitter siege of Leningrad had reduced the great tank factory there to virtual impotence. The new factories in the Urals had as yet barely commenced working. In addition, in that disastrous summer and autumn of 1941, the U.S.S.R. had been deprived of well over half the raw materials vital to its war machine, including iron, steel, aluminium and coal, and 40 per cent of all its grain supplies.

Although British and American tanks had begun to arrive in some quantity by way of the hazardous Arctic convoys or the Middle East cross-country route through Persia, the Russians did not consider them good enough for fighting against the more powerful Panzers. They deployed most of them on guard duty in areas where there was little likelihood of a full-scale shooting war. They adopted a stop-gap method, similar in manner to the British in the Desert War, of distributing their available KV and T 34 tanks in so-called armoured brigades along with motorized infantry, machine-gunners, mortars and anti-tank gunners.

There were about 20 of these armoured brigades available by the spring of 1942. But as Stalin was now absolutely certain there would be no trouble from the Japanese, who were heavily committed against Britain and America, he was able to switch the remaining divisions from his eastern frontiers to fight the advancing Germans. There were also available around 500,000 reservists with a basic military training, who had been called up and were being rapidly prepared for battle.

Success in regaining some ground from the Germans had, however, made the Soviet High Command over-optimistic. A series of spring offensives were planned, and the first opened on April 9 in the narrow Kerch Peninsula joining the Crimea to the mainland, where the Russians had made near-successful counter-attacks the previous autumn.

The new attempt, grandiloquently called the Stalin Offensive, was halted inside three days by Field-Marshal Erich von Manstein's southern army, recently reinforced with armour and dive-bombers. They swiftly cleared the entire Kerch Peninsula and brought the Germans to the threshold of Sebastopol, inflicting heavy casualties and taking 100,000 prisoners.

Stalin and his commanders soon learned further lessons. At the northern end of the front a strong Russian force, including two fresh Siberian divisions, appeared to be advancing strongly towards Leningrad when the Germans struck back. Within five days the Russians had been contained and encircled, suffering severe casualties as they attempted to obey orders to continue attacking.

The third and largest Russian spring offensive was also overwhelmed. Timoshenko attacked towards Kharkov with two-thirds of the total tank force still available to the Russians, some 600 in number.

At first the offensive seemed to be progressing spectacularly, for his massed tanks drove straight through the weak Rumanian 6th Army immediately confronting them. Krasnograd swiftly

*Left* Infantry and artillery of the Red Army hastily thrown into the line before Stalingrad in an unsuccessful attempt to stem the German onrush

*Below* A section of Stalingrad, already heavily blitzed and bombarded, with Russian defence positions in factories and other big buildings under heavy artillery attack

*Bottom* A section of Stalingrad under aerial bombardment

fell, and it seemed that Kharkov would be their next great prize. But then the iron jaws of a German trap – Paulus's 6th Army to the north and Kleist to the south – began to close. Timoshenko realized the danger, but Stalin refused permission to slow the offensive until Timoshenko could consolidate his threatened flanks. The Russian tanks continued to rumble westwards even as Kleist's massive counter-offensive crushed the southern flank on May 18 and Paulus's formidable armoured formations swept down from the north the following day. On May 23, these iron pincers closed behind the Soviet Army; the Russians lost nearly a quarter of a million men, killed, wounded and captured, and practically the entire tank force committed so hopefully to battle.

The stage was now set for the great German summer offensive. Within hours of the whole vast front erupting from Kursk down to Rostov on June 28, the Russians were reeling and disintegrating. The Panzers roared on unchecked across the wide open steppes. There were no black sprawling forests such as had

*Above* In the industrial heart of Stalingrad hastily armed factory workers join the Russian regular soldiers as they fall back before the Germans

*Opposite page* House-to-house fighting in the blitzed outer suburbs of the city

checked them before Moscow, there were no mountains, no hills, no ravines, nor even any shallow folds in the ground to hinder their triumphant progress, just hundreds of miles of even plains.

Like a whirlwind the Panzers swept on, their approach signalled by a towering dust pall that could be seen for 40 miles. To the rural towns and villages in their path it marked the approach of doom. In its wake billowing clouds of acrid smoke from burning buildings swelled the dust cloud until it masked the whole horizon.

The mighty advance of armour across the southern steppes indicated a major German assault, but the Russian High Command was still anxious for Moscow and kept the Red Army's main reserves, such as they were, near

General Vasili Chuikov, who arrived in the city with reinforcements in the nick of time

the capital. Timoshenko was under orders to hold the two hinges at either end of his front – Rostov and Voronezh – as, with the forces left at his command, he could not seriously oppose the storming Panzers along the whole vast front. There was nothing to stop them flooding across the basin of the River Donets and into the huge bend of the River Don. Even there, the Russians could barely attempt to stem the iron tide rolling onwards over the 100-mile-wide stretch of flat, featureless land that lay between the parallel courses of the Donets and Don. Within a week of his renewed onslaught, on June 28, Paulus's massed Panzers had swept through to the banks of the Don each side of Voronezh. Fearing that this attack would swing north to envelop Yelets and Tula from behind, the Soviet High Command sought to establish a Voronezh front. Some of the reserve formations from Moscow were committed under Vatutin, who was under the direct orders of the Moscow Command.

Fierce fighting developed in the heavily industrialized district around Voronezh and south of the Donets as von Bock sought to destroy Vatutin's force rather than bypass it and continue the exhilarating rush towards the Volga and to final victory. He did not want to leave it as a future threat to flank and rear. But Hitler felt that victory was imminent if the great summer offensive were maintained, and von Bock was sacked. In an atmosphere of overwhelming optimism, the original plan of attack was altered so that the two Army Groups that had been under Bock's command now became independent.

With this independence Army Group A, commanded by List, was directed to strike across the Don and down south to seize the Caucasus and all the rich oil of that area. Army

Group B, meanwhile, was to be led by Weichs's Panzers straight upon Stalingrad, there to smash the gathering Russian force, capture the city, and seize the isthmus between Don and Volga. It had been Bock's plan to swing Hoth's formidable armoured formations in a swift and devastating hammer blow against Stalingrad, while Paulus's 6th Army was first to participate in the liquidation of the Voronezh pocket and then to follow Hoth's forces to take over Stalingrad from them. This would leave the Panzer army to withdraw into mobile reserve. But the German High Command's new directive sent the 6th Army against Stalingrad unaided, with Hoth's Panzers instead driving south-east to assist with the crossing of the lower Don.

It transpired that Kleist's Panzers and the 17th Army did not need any help in crossing the Don. The Russian resistance faded before them and they took Proletarskaya beyond the river on July 29. In rapid succession they penetrated to Salsk, Stavropol, Armavir and Maikop (on August 9) whence they could almost see the forest of derricks that bestrode the oilfields. Paulus's 6th Army, however, with only one Panzer corps that was fully mobile, began the 200-mile advance to Stalingrad more slowly, and became strung out – in no position to mount a sudden decisive onslaught. At Stalingrad the Russians were massing as fast as troops could be rushed there. The fateful decision had been taken to commit the Moscow reserves.

One of the Russian commanders ordered to hurry with his troops to Stalingrad was General Vasili Chuikov. With four infantry divisions, two armoured brigades and two motorized brigades of the Reserve Army around Tula, he was faced with a desperate race to get to Stalingrad in time to strengthen the resistance.

The German 6th Army, for all its deficiencies in mobility, made a furious attempt to storm Stalingrad before the Russian reinforcements could arrive. Between July 25 and 29 Paulus launched division after division piecemeal against the city. But although he had been encouraged to do this by the weakness of the resistance so far encountered, the fighting became increasingly fierce as the Red Army sent in reinforcements as they arrived.

To strengthen his thrust for Stalingrad against the stiffening opposition Paulus asked for the help of Hoth's 4th Panzer Army, which had crossed the Don practically unopposed on July 29. The Panzers were to charge in upon Stalingrad's virtually undefended southern side. As soon as Hoth's Panzers turned northwards, the recently arrived Russian 64th Army, which had been largely responsible for baulking Paulus's first piecemeal onslaught, was compelled to extend its left flank widely west to contain this new threat. Consequently the opposition to the German 6th Army had weakened by August 10, when Paulus had massed his divisions for a full-scale attack. At the same time Richthofen's powerful 4th Air Corps was switched from the southern front to Stalingrad.

The first really determined attempt to storm Stalingrad began on August 19. With Paulus in overall command, the plan of attack was a text-book one against a convex Russian front some 80 miles long, but less than 50 miles from side to side at its widest. Perhaps because many of the front-line Germans were convinced that victory in the east would soon be total, there was a marked lack of resolution in the initial assault. Soldiers believing they will soon be going home are invariably extra cautious. After three days, however, Panzer formations broke through the Russian perimeter at Vertyachi, into Stalingrad's northern suburbs, and by sunset on August 23 reached the banks of the Volga. Before long they were reinforced by an infantry corps and, with the vital railway bridge across the river within mortar range, it seemed the Russian 62nd Army in this northern sector was fatally outflanked. To seal its fate the Luftwaffe was ordered to deliver an all-out night bombardment upon Stalingrad, to cause panic throughout the city and demoralization among the troops.

Despite the tearing explosions and the incessant, ear-splitting uproar of the bombardment, neither the Russian soldiers nor the remaining civilians panicked. The authorities did start evacuation of the biggest war factories, and a large section of the civilian population fled across the Volga, but the evacuation of the factories was soon halted by Stalin himself.

As a result, the ruined factories remained centres of resistance. Some continued to repair tanks in the very midst of battle, and the tractor plant even contrived to produce new tanks and armoured cars until the Germans were at its very approaches. When the factories came under such heavy bombardment that work was impossible, the men left the remaining lathes and presses to join workers' battalions alongside the regular troops in the desperate fight against the invaders. Women, children and old men sought refuge in deep caverns on the cliffs above the Volga, while others hid in cellars and sewers.

In the fighting that immediately followed the Luftwaffe's terror raid, Weitersheim maintained, but could not widen, his narrow corridor to the Volga. Hoth's Panzers and guns on the flanks did force the Russian 64th Army to yield ground, but at no point did they penetrate the line. The costly German advance ground to a halt. In the brick and stone ruins of the industrial heart of the city, the Russian resistance concentrated and hardened.

Hitler himself emphasized that the great drive along the Volga must achieve complete success. He summoned the two commanding generals to his new headquarters at Vinnitsa and told them that every available man, gun and tank should be concentrated swiftly to capture Stalingrad and the Volga banks. The Führer assured them that their left flank along the Don would be solidly protected by newly arrived satellite armies. Meanwhile three additional infantry divisions were coming up to strengthen the German 6th Army.

Stalin and his commanders had also decided that the war was going to be finally won at Stalingrad. The luckless Timoshenko was moved to command the quiescent north-west front, and the tough team of generals who had halted the Germans before Moscow took over at Stalingrad. These were Zhukov, the only Soviet commander who could boast an undefeated record, Voronov, an artillery expert, and Koikov, chief of the Red Air Force. The stage was set for a brutal and bloody battle of attrition. For the Germans the days of the blitzkrieg were over. They were now committed to man-to-man encounters to envelop the Volga ferries, the precarious lifeline of the desperate garrison of Stalingrad, absolutely vital to the Russians.

The task of the German guns attempting to command all the river crossings was well-nigh impossible so long as the Russians fought, for

*Above* Two German soldiers armed with light automatics prepare to follow up an artillery barrage and assault a Russian-held building

*Opposite, top* In the teeth of vicious enemy fire, Russian soldiers, newly arrived on the scene, charge into the midst of the battle

*Opposite, bottom* Typical of the bitter house-to-house fighting in which both armies became embroiled is this picture of Russian tommy-gunners taking up positions to fight off yet another German attack

behind Stalingrad the wide Volga curves gently and is scattered with a number of small islands. These immovable obstacles across the field of fire prevented them bombarding all the crossings. In fact the German commanders did not appreciate the importance of those supply lines across the Volga early enough, and they failed to realize the size and function of the Russian artillery on the other side. Had they done so, the long-range bombers and dive-bombers of the Luftwaffe would undoubtedly have been concentrated upon both ferries and guns until they were knocked out. But Paulus chose instead to crush the main points of Russian resistance within the smouldering city, hurling high explosive, tanks and men against one block after another. Forced to fight a battle in which speeding tanks, mobile guns, and motorized infantry could not be deployed in dynamic

manoeuvre, the Germans appeared at a loss how to fight it. By contrast, the Russian commanders adapted their tactics skilfully to the conditions.

At the conference with his Führer at Vinnitsa on September 12 Paulus received the go-ahead for his third and heaviest attack upon Stalingrad, launched by three Panzer divisions backed by eight divisions of infantry. It was planned to repeat the success of Hoth's Panzers, which had blasted their way to the Volga and split the Russian 62nd and 64th Armies into two separate entities.

After six weeks of ceaseless fighting against crack Panzer divisions, the main body of the Red Army on the Stalingrad front was now desperately holding out along 12 miles of railway embankment on the Stalingrad–Rostov line. The weary survivors of the 62nd Army had been reduced to a mere three infantry divisions, remnants of four others, and two battered tank brigades. It was upon them that Paulus's blow fell.

In the midst of a nerve-shattering 24-hour German bombardment of Stalingrad, General Vasili Chuikov made the perilous Volga crossing at Krasnaya Sloboda and set up his command H Q in the burning ruins of the city.

To confront the German onslaught Chuikov found he had not more than 40 tanks, most of

them immobile. The only real armoured fighting force that remained for a counter-attack was 19 KVs. There were no infantry reserves because every soldier had been drawn into the the deadly maelstrom. Although the Russians still fought with desperate courage, they felt inevitable doom upon them. In the Kremlin the worst was feared.

Chuikov knew he had to overcome his troops' forebodings before he could attempt to hold the Germans. He determined that he must at all costs prevent the enemy turning his flanks, which were precariously clinging to the Volga's west bank at each end of the battle. The northern one, below Rynok, was the stronger because it incorporated the fortress-like, though blasted, bulk of the tractor factory, and the ruined, but still massive, factories of Barrikady (Barricades) and Kransye Oktyabr (Red October).

With the exception of several towering grain elevators, the southern flank was a waste of scorched earth and smouldering rubble. It

*Above* General Rodimtsev (extreme right) whose Guards Division fought heroically to stem the tide of German conquest. The General's command post here is inside a huge pipe-line once used to supply the city with water

*Opposite page* A German gun crew amidst the rubble in action against a Russian defence post

provided the shortest route to the vital landing stage opposite Krasnaya Sloboda. It also led into the very nerve centre of the Russian defences – the dug-out command post called the Tsaritsyn Bunker from which Chuikov directed the desperate defence. The dug-out was deep down beside the river bed at the entry to the Pushkin Street bridge.

On September 13, the Germans flung in an all-out attack aimed at the very centre of the ten-mile line facing westwards to which the defenders precariously clung. During the following afternoon they broke through and seized the vital high ground of Mamaye Hill, from

270

which they could dominate the vital Volga ferries with concentrated artillery fire.

Troops of the German 76th Infantry Division next overwhelmed all opposition around the ruined hospital that marked the centre of the Russian line, and swarmed on towards the Volga's west bank. Drunk with the certainty of imminent victory, some physically drunk with looted brandy and vodka, they tumbled down from their lorries, dancing, singing and laughing amidst the ruins, disturbed only by a distant sniper's shots.

Then General Chuikov flung in his 19 KV tanks. As they rumbled up from the southern sector the battle started again. It went on into the night, and spread to within 200 yards of Chuikov's bunker where his staff officers emerged to join the defenders. Soon the vital central landing stage was under machine-gun fire from close range. The attackers were rampaging through shell-torn, debris-littered streets, not in definite waves or extended formations, but in

self-contained battle groups each comprising three or four Panzers and a company of infantry.

The defenders' tactics were well ordered. The riflemen and machine-gunners who were hidden in the ruined buildings, among the piles of rubble and in the bomb and shell holes, held their fire as the German tanks came through, saving their ammunition for the infantry. The German tanks ran into the fire of the dug-down Russian tanks and anti-tank guns, or were suddenly confronted by a roving T 34.

Each separate engagement turned into a desperate house-to-house battle, into man-to-man duels with grenades, point-blank automatic fusilades, or stabbing, hacking steel. The German Panzers could do little in attack. Armour-piercing shots fired at a building merely tore comparatively small holes, while in the narrow streets amidst the towering ruins, the Panzers with their main armour and armament in front were terribly vulnerable to the anti tank rifles and grenades directed upon them from

271

immediately above. And the Russian infantrymen were exceedingly well supplied with anti-tank rifles. Against buildings, flame-throwers were more deadly, though hardly less dangerous to the soldiers who carried them.

It took a whole day and many casualties to clear 200 yards or so of ruined buildings. And invariably the Russians infiltrated back during the night. They knocked holes through attic walls so that they could reoccupy buildings literally above the heads of their enemies. They established machine-gun nests and bombing parties on the top floors, and even among the jagged, shrapnel-torn chimney stacks.

But despite the desperate heroism of the Russian soldiers, the end seemed very near amidst the ruins of Stalingrad when General Rodimtsev's Guards were launched into the battle on the night of September 14. There was no time to counter-attack as a cohesive division. They were fed into the fire and fury battalion by battalion as they scrambled ashore from the Volga ferries. Soon they were dispersed in pockets, without any intercommunication, amongst the reeking ruins. As the German tide strengthened in its flow towards the river bank it encountered stiffening opposition.

The Russian Guardsmen were prepared to die, but before doing so they wrought terrible execution amongst the attackers. The Germans had to bring their tanks up to point-blank range and blast the ruined buildings to rubble with high-explosive shells before they could be certain they had overcome each bitterly resisting pocket.

In theory the Germans should already have won, for they had driven a formidable wedge all along the course of the tributary River Tsaritsa down to the Volga itself. Their guns were within yards of the vital central landing stage, and their soldiers occupied an area of ruins about one and a half miles square behind the Stalingrad main station. With German artillery covering his main river crossing at almost point-blank range, Chuikov's only remaining life-

line for reinforcements and supplies was the precarious factory ferries to the north of the city. Meanwhile the Russian commander had been compelled to evacuate the Tsaritsyn Bunker and move into another at Mamyev Kurgan.

Although the Germans had won almost complete control of the southern half of Stalingrad, they were still seriously troubled by the one remaining Russian formation south of the Tsaritsa, the 92nd Infantry Brigade, whose men formed isolated pockets of resistance. The most formidable strongpoints the Russians still held were in a series of towering grain elevators which, though battered and burnt, appeared to be indestructible. Within these elevators, dispersed in unyielding pockets at all levels from base to top, were Russian Marines as well as Guardsmen. They repelled wave after wave one and a half miles square behind the Stalin-close quarters under cover of tanks.

For almost two months now the two armies had been locked in combat among the ruins of Stalingrad. The German propaganda ministry was finding it necessary to explain why this vaunted offensive appeared to have become bogged down. 'Hurling reserves after reserves into the ruins of Stalingrad the Russians are expending their last remaining strength', the anxious German people were told. In fact, General Zhukov was reinforcing his defenders with the smallest formations adequate, while the German commanders were squandering their own men among Stalingrad's ruins.

During September and October no less than 27 newly formed German infantry divisions and 19 armoured brigades — which included many veterans of units reduced by the fighting on the Russian front as well as new drafts — were subjected to the hideous holocaust for 'combat experience'. But although none of these formations was kept there long, inevitably they suffered casualties, hardships and fatigue which sapped their strength. During the same period only five Russian infantry divisions crossed the river to join in the battle, reinforcements which barely made up for the day-to-day wastage of the fighting. With cold calculation General Zhukov was secretly building up a formidable counter-attack force across the Volga which he intended to launch only when he deemed the time was right. Significantly, after the impact of Rodimtsev's Guards upon the battle on

*Top* A trio of German soldiers armed for house-to-house fighting. The one on the left has a flame thrower; the one in the centre a light automatic; and the one on the right a stick grenade

*Bottom* The blazing wreck of a T34 tank on the outskirts of Stalingrad

273

September 15, the inexorable German advance towards the Volga was interrupted. Gains were sporadic, and soon lost again to ferocious counter-attacks.

There was another highly significant aspect in this apparently most desperate hour. For the first time since the establishment of the Army of the Revolution, Red Army officers were issued with gold-braided epaulettes to mark them as a separate class from their men. Regimental traditions were revived, and the stress was now all on the soldiers' duty to Russia, and not to the Communist party. At last the Red Army was a truly professional fighting machine unhampered by political demands.

The German army engaged at Stalingrad was feeling frustrated at having to fight on and on when apparently within an ace of victory. In

the minds of men who had already experienced that terrible winter before Moscow such frustration turned into foreboding. Each succeeding nightfall was noticeably earlier, and each new dawn was that much more grey and chill. Unrest was also disturbingly apparent among some of their commanders. General von Weitersheim was sacked for suggesting his armour should be withdrawn beyond the range of the increasingly heavy fire of the Russian artillery. General von Schwedler, also an armoured-corps commander, was dismissed with ignominy for warning of the dangers of attacks from the flanks which the Panzers risked if concentrated in a forward position. Colonel-General List, commander-in-chief of Army Group A, was relieved of his command soon afterwards.

But Field-Marshal Paulus prepared a fourth 'all-out and final' offensive. He was particularly

*Above* With snow now covering the battlefield, Russian soldiers launch a counter-attack from the Red Oktyabr factory

*Right* The Germans reach the tractor factory, temporarily subdued by ferocious bombardment. This picture was found on the body of a German officer

*Opposite page* Red Army tommy-gunners charge out from a burning building across a rubble-strewn street

eager to win a famous victory because he had just learned that Hitler was considering him for a senior staff post, even as chief of High Command. But however good he may have been as a staff officer, Paulus's thinking as a fighting commander was devoid of inspiration. All he could contrive now for the final victorious onslaught was yet another massive head-on blow at the enemy's main defence line. He even selected as the prime objective the three most formidable Russian bastions amidst the murderous wilderness of ruins and rubble – the fortress-like factories.

Paulus's fourth offensive was planned for October 4. It was destined to rage for almost three weeks. To meet the German street-fighting experts who led the offensive, the Russians, heavily outnumbered, had 'storm groups' of their toughest soldiers. They were small units of mixed arms which included anti-tank guns,

heavy and light machine-guns, sub-machine-guns and grenades and, for the closest quarters, bayonets and daggers. The Russians had also prepared special 'killing grounds' in their battlefield, heavily mining certain houses and even whole blocks and squares. They left a few approach routes to each of these areas where the attackers would come under heavy fire.

The front-line soldiers of the Red Army who had survived the first phase of the battle of Stalingrad were invaluable in the cruel close-combat fighting. Against new waves of raw German reinforcements, two or three of these veteran Russian warriors were worth a whole platoon. They knew every cellar and sewer, manhole and shell crater, that would serve as a strongpoint.

In a moonscape wilderness of blasted buildings, into which no German tank could penetrate, a handful of men armed with light automatics, patiently watching through periscopes from their below-ground hide-outs, could mow down scores of advancing Germans without being detected. Snipers – ruthless, patient fighting men prepared to lie camouflaged and invisible among the ruins for hours on end – also claimed many German lives.

It often happened that the Germans held one half of a shattered building and the Russians the other. Only murderous hand-to-hand combat

275

would determine whose post it should be. But whenever it was the Russians who were liquidated a counter-attack would be made by mobile combat groups specially detailed for such work. Survivors of units who had lost a house to the enemy were sent back with the first counter-attack; even if only one man had survived he would have to go back to help retake the building. In preparing each wrecked house or factory as a strongpoint, the Russians had made each floor independent of the next, so that if the enemy captured the ground floor they would then have to fight additional battles for the floor and roof above and the cellars beneath. The whole disposition of these strongpoints was to ensure that ruined Stalingrad constituted a maze of fire-swept traps for the Germans.

By such methods the Soviet soldiers made the attackers pay a terrible price for any advance they achieved by weight of numbers. Despite the special street-fighting troops of the Germans, the Russians remained the masters in this hideous form of close combat. By far the greater number of the dead were Germans. As one shaken German veteran wrote at the time, 'Imagine Stalingrad – 80 days and nights of hand-to-hand struggles. The streets are no longer measured in metres but in corpses. Stalingrad is no longer a town. By day it is an enormous cloud of burning blinding smoke. It is a vast furnace lit by the reflection of the flames'. Perhaps the most macabre manifestation on many of those nights was the spasmodic exodus of pet dogs that had been trapped in blasted buildings. Yelping with terror they would from time to time go racing through the roaring inferno to leap into the flame-reddened

*Opposite page* Red Army tommy-gunners open fire on the enemy in the ruins of the Red Oktyabr factory

*Right* A German flame-thrower in action. This highly dangerous job was usually given to men detailed from punishment platoons

Volga and swim frantically to the other side.

At September's end the Russians were still firmly entrenched in positions along 25 kilometres of the Volga's west bank that protruded from half a kilometre to two kilometres into the shattered city. They were manned by some 40,000 soldiers, a number exceeded despite constant replacements because of the heavy casualties.

The bulk of the Russian forces were concentrated in the centre of their 25-kilometre strip, holding fortified positions for some 12 kilometres from the city's centre to the tractor factory to the north. Looming above this solid stretch of jagged, fire-blackened masonry were the cliffs that flanked the wide Volga, a background eminence not only excellent for digging in defensive positions and command posts but also sheltering the river crossings.

On September 28 official Russian communiques had admitted that the enemy had penetrated deep into the workers' settlement in the north-west. The Germans had their jumping-off positions for their greatest offensive of all. Hitler left no doubt of the intended conclusive German onslaught by promising publicly 'to capture Stalingrad very shortly'.

On October 4 the Russians put in a fierce counter-attack in the tractor-factory sector. It was designed to throw the Germans off balance before they launched their new offensive, and to a degree it succeeded. Although the ferocious close-quarter fighting for a mere hundred metres of ruins proved inconclusive, it cost the Germans many dead and inevitably blunted their subsequent attack. On October 6 the *Red Star* reported battles of exceptional violence 'under the most powerful artillery and mortar fire and the ceaseless howl of air bombs'. (The Luftwaffe had flung some 800 dive-bombers into the battle.)

On October 14 the Germans finally launched their attack. Five new infantry divisions and two armoured divisions hurled themselves forward on a narrow front of only five kilometres, after the Russian defenders had been subjected to a stunning five-hour bombardment. Even in deep dug-outs glasses were shattered by the vibration. In General Chuikov's headquarters alone 61 men were killed. He was afterwards to write, 'October 14 will go down as the bloodiest and most ferocious day in the whole Battle of Stalingrad. . .'

But although the Germans broke through to the Volga at the tractor factory, which they captured, their casualties were so heavy that the attack lost its impetus. They had not the strength to expand this salient along the river's bank. During the same period, at the Red October Works, the Germans attempted to break through to the Volga in the central sector. Before they could fight through to the river here, however, they first had to overcome Gurtiev's fanatically brave Siberian division, which had moved into the grim Red October sector in the nick of time. The Siberians were ordered to fight to the death amidst a jagged wilderness of wrecked railway waggons, twisted rails and tumbled iron girders, mountainous heaps of coal and rusty red clay, with the huge ruined factory looming above. Immediately behind the defenders swirled the icy waters of the wide Volga, as if to emphasize that there would be no retreat.

The Siberians were soldiers of outstanding courage, and they were also a rigidly disciplined

and splendidly armed and trained division inured to the bitterest conditions. Before the Germans attacked they had just completed a network of inter-connecting trenches, dug-outs and strongpoints in the hard ground in and around the factory. They remained inflexible under a long-sustained bombardment by dive-bombers, guns and mortars. When the uproar abated, presaging the charge of German armour and infantry, a regiment of the Siberians arose from their positions and went into the attack. At the end of 48 hours of frenzied fighting between the two advancing forces hardly a man of the Siberian regiment had survived – but the Germans had been stopped in their tracks!

This was the pattern day after day, night after night. The German onslaught on the Red October factory continued right through October. They made 117 separate attacks on the Siberians; once, 23 attacks in a single day. The Siberians were formidably supported by Russian artillery across the Volga; from well-hidden observation posts within their network of defences the Siberians were able to direct the guns to fire with a terrible accuracy.

Paulus's final great offensive had been bled

*Above* The wreck of a German fighter aircraft in the ruins of Stalingrad

*Opposite page* Russian soldiers fighting in another quarter of the snow-covered city

to a standstill. He had no soldiers left with the will or the ability to get to grips with the un-yielding defenders. Stalemate settled upon the ravaged city. But while the Germans were mustering their strength to try once more to overcome the last enemy strongpoints, the Russians were stealthily completing prepara-tions for a powerful counter-blow. Without raising the Germans' suspicions, General Zhu-kov was massing across the Volga an immense force of 500,000 infantry with 900 brand-new T 34 tanks, 230 artillery regiments, and 115 regiments of the dreaded Katyusha multiple-rocket projectors. Deployed along a front of 40 miles, the new Russian armies possessed fire power far heavier than the Russians or the Germans had so far used in the campaign.

Paulus's 6th Army was reinforced by more battalions of Pioneers, which he planned to use in the van of four thrusts, under cover of a

278

bombardment that would reduce what still remained of the great factories and the ruined enemy-held blocks. Instead of the house-to-house fighting which had cost the Germans so dear, the infantry soldiers were to penetrate through sewers and tunnels and cellars, while battened-down tanks roamed the smoking wilderness above.

Paulus sent in his attack on November 11, concentrated on a front never exceeding 400 metres in width. The German commander was eager to settle things before the Russian winter once more gripped the land. But after two days and nights the offensive disintegrated into an uncontrollable chaos of hand-to-hand combat. The impetus of the first German rush carried many small do-or-die bands through the final 300 yards to the Volga's banks, but the corridors through which they had fought closed in behind them as Soviet soldiers emerged from hidden

*Above* White-clad Russian infantry crawl across the snow to attack German defences north-west of Stalingrad

*Opposite, top* A salvo of Russian rockets streaks across the Volga in the fearsome bombardment which preceded the Red Army counter-attack

*Opposite, bottom* Just a few of the thousands of Russian guns which, lined up almost wheel to wheel, subjected the German positions to a catastrophic bombardment as the Russians went over to the offensive

caverns beneath the rubble. On both sides every soldier knew that prisoners were no longer taken.

The soldiers, both German and Russian, locked in this furious combat were more like beasts of prey than men. Inflamed with alcohol and benzedrene – for no sane sober man, however vicious, could bring himself to fight with such animal ferocity – filthy, red-eyed, bearded and stinking, these wolfmen shot and stabbed, hacked and kicked and battered each other. The fighting went on for four days and nights, until only soldiers of the Red Army were still

alive. A great and terrible silence settled over Stalingrad – the silence of death.

But not for long. At dawn on November 19, the smoke-fogged air suddenly reverberated with distant thunder. It was the opening of a barrage by 2,000 Russian guns immediately to the north of the shattered city. On the next day hundreds more Russian guns began to thunder to the south. Zhukov's great counter-attack had begun. His massed armour and infantry were already sweeping forward.

Paulus had grossly overestimated the toll he had taken of Russian divisions in Stalingrad and was convinced that no worthwhile reserves remained. Moreover, the German High Command had failed to anticipate the Russian intentions, expecting a winter counter-offensive against Army Group Centre in the region of Rzhev. Consequently the north and south flanks of the most advanced German salient at Stalingrad had been left guarded largely by Rumanian troops. These not only had little stomach for fighting what they considered to be the Germans' war, but they were ill-equipped to stand against the Russians. Nearly all their arms were those taken from the defeated French in 1940. They were pitifully short of anti-tank guns, and those they possessed were mostly obsolete. Lacking suitable clothing, they had been more interested in constructing huge dug-outs to live in than digging defences and anti-tank obstacles.

When the Russian onslaught struck them from across the gloomy Kalmuck steppes, the Rumanians crumbled and disintegrated. Between October 19 and 22 the northern flank above Stalingrad, some 50 miles in the big Don loop between Kremenskaya and Kalach, was completely shattered by six Soviet armies. All through those days and weeks when all attention had been focused on the battle for Stalingrad, there had been continuous Russian attacks and counter-attacks along a sector stretching from the Volga to the region of Boguchan, so that German troops there had been too heavily engaged to reinforce the Stalingrad attacks. But the Germans had always been able to repel them, so that their commanders were quite confident they could take care of any offensive the Russians might mount.

A few Panzer groups which Paulus managed to rush up to the northern flank at the last minute remained as defiant pockets amidst the Russian avalanche. But they could not stem the immense tide rolling relentlessly on. In their sudden bewilderment the Germans could not immediately appreciate the scale and direction of the Soviet offensive. What was happening was that one Russian pincer was striking south around Stalingrad from the middle Don and another northwards from among the salt lakes south of Stalingrad.

On November 23, west of Kalach at the huge bridge of the Don which was vital to the supply of the German troops in Stalingrad, tanks appeared. The German engineers were ready to destroy the bridge should it be threatened, but they were relieved to see the insignia of the 22nd Panzer Division upon the tanks. When the troop carriers leading the convoy apparently with reinforcements for Stalingrad, reached the centre of the great bridge, they stopped. The soldiers jumped down and instantly opened fire to mow down all the German engineers. Then the Russians removed the demolition charges and their 25 tanks rumbled on, heading south-east.

Before nightfall, the southern flank of the Germans' Stalingrad salient had been shattered for a length of 30 miles. The place where the two Russian spearheads met was due west of Stalingrad, some 20 miles behind the German 6th Army. It was a meeting of high significance which not only sealed the fate of 250,000 soldiers in Stalingrad, but at the same time signalled the turning point of the Second World War on the Russian front.

Within three days of their dramatic breakthrough to the north the Russians had 34 divisions across the Don. While armoured columns raced south-west disrupting the German rear, infantry divisions swung down and around and were soon digging in behind the German 6th Army in Stalingrad. Heavy guns hidden behind the Volga opened up on Stalingrad itself. Zhukov rushed batteries of anti-tank guns into position north and north-west of Stalingrad until no less than 1,000 of them stood ready to repel any German counter-attack. By the time General Erich von Manstein and General Guderian – nominated by Hitler to retrieve the situation – had arrived on the scene, the position of the 6th Army in Stalingrad was already critical. And the dreaded Russian winter was imminent.

Manstein's urgent instructions to withdraw from Stalingrad and clear the rear areas around the Don crossing at Kalach either did not reach Paulus, or were ignored. Manstein advocated that the 6th Army should break out to the south-west. Such action would almost certainly have been possible for the Panzer divisions at this time, even though the infantry would have suffered heavily on leaving their prepared positions. But then Manstein changed his plan. Under the new plan Paulus's force was to remain in Stalingrad, providing it could be supplied, until a full-scale relief operation was mounted early in December.

The Russians, meanwhile, had set themselves one objective – the utter destruction of the 6th Army in Stalingrad. They had massed seven reserve armies specially formed and trained for the winter offensive. Their theatre of operations was to be concentrated in an area less than 100 square miles in extent, bounded by Stalingrad at one side and the Don bend on the other.

While Zhukov was still training the junior officers who were to play a big part in the

Kazan

Gorky

Kalinin

Klin

Rzhev

Moscow

Mozhaisk

Vyazma

Kaluga

Tula

Orel

Yelets

Saratov

Kursk

*Donets*

Voronezh

Verkhny Mamon

*Volga*

*Don*

Kharkov

Veshenskaya

Kremenskaya

Petrovka

Dniepropetrovsk

*Chir*

Krasnograd

*Dnieper*

Oblivskay    Kalach    Stalingrad

Nizhne-Chirskaya

Krasnaya Slobodska

Rostov

Kotelnikovo

Proletarskaya

Sea of Azov
Kerch
peninsula

Salsk

*Crimea*

Sebastopol

Armavir    Stavropol

Maikop

*Black Sea*

**Stalingrad**

*Above* After the German army in Stalingrad had been surrounded, attempts were made to keep it supplied by air. Here a Junkers Ju 52 transport plane has become frozen into the snow on Stalingrad's airstrip, and soldiers are trying to release it

*Opposite page* A Russian anti-aircraft gun fires tracer bullets into the night sky

offensive, and thus not fully exploiting the sudden dramatic breakthrough, the Germans stood along a line from Veshenskaya on the Don down along the River Chir through Petrovka, Oblivskay, Nizhne and Chirskaya, where the Chir joined the Don, to continue south with the course of the Don once more. Stalingrad, where the 6th Army was surrounded and encircled by 2,000 Soviet guns, was some 20 miles to the east of this line. The Red Army meanwhile was heavily attacking on three definite fronts, the south-western under Vatutin, the Don in the north under Rokossovsky, and the front of Stalingrad itself to the south under Yeremenko.

More Panzer divisions, artillery and infantry were hurried in from the central and Caucasus fronts and from the west to reinforce Manstein's rescue attempt (code-named Winter Tempest). They attacked on December 11, setting out from Kotelnikovo, south of the Don, and driving up north-east along the line of the railway from the Caucasus to Stalingrad. The main thrust was under the command of Hoth, with his revitalized 4th Panzer Army. Following in unwieldy fashion at the rear was an armada of miscellaneous lorries laden with 3,000 tons of supplies for the beleaguered 6th Army. Once Hoth's Panzers had blasted a corridor through, they were to be run in to Stalingrad at top speed. The Russians swarming to the attack on the city itself were having none too easy a time, for clashing ice floes sweeping down the Volga added to the hazards of shells and bombs falling among the ferries.

Hoth's columns steadily rolled forward over terrain that by now was snow-covered. Beneath the snow, the ground was hard frozen. All seemed to be going well for the Panzers. What the Germans could not see was that the apparently wide white wilderness ahead was criss

285

*Above* General Hoth (right) who led a rescue Panzer army up towards Stalingrad from the south. Von Paulus did not attempt to break out to meet him

*Right* Field-Marshal von Paulus (left) is led away into captivity after his army had suffered one of the most terrible defeats in the history of the German army

crossed with gullies in which Russian infantry, armed with anti-tank guns and heavy machine-guns, and cavalry with mortars and machine-guns, lurked in readiness. During the bitter nights of December 14 and 15 the advancing Germans were attacked by the ghost riders of the Russian cavalry. At dawn and at dusk formations of T 34 tanks raced down upon the lorried troops and the supply train following the Panzers. Each attack forced the Germans to halt and call back armour to deal with it. At the same time heavy grey clouds crowding down to 500 feet were denying Hoth air reconnaissance.

On December 17 Hoth's spearhead Panzers reached the 70-foot wide River Aksay, 35 miles from Stalingrad. Although Zhukov was becoming increasingly uneasy at Hoth's advance, the only immediate action he took was to send some 130 tanks and two infantry divisions with their artillery to protect the Aksay bridges. Apparently he was so obsessed with destroying the surrounded 21 divisions of the 6th Army in Stalingrad that he was loath to detach any considerable force to deal with other German formations. But farther north, at the junction of the southern sector with the central sector, which for long had lain dormant, the Russians now launched another major attack by two army groups under Generals Golikov and Vatutin, along a 30-mile front on either side of the bridgehead over the Don at Verkhny Mamon.

Except for one complete division and two battalions of German troops, this sector was occupied predominantly by the Italian 8th Army, with some units of the Hungarian 2nd Army and the Rumanian 3rd Army. Under cover of choking fog, 450 Russian T 34 tanks rumbled across the thick ice covering the Don. The Italians, upon whom the brunt of the attack fell, were soon in a state of confusion, which rapidly turned to panic, and the tough Soviet soldiers tore through their defences in many places virtually unopposed. As this Red Army onslaught punched a great wedge westwards below Voronezh, another determined Russian attack at Nizhne Chirskaya drove the Germans out of their bridgehead there and back across the river. The whole German line along the lower Chir began to disintegrate. So great was the danger in this sector that the Germans had to abandon the plan to launch the powerful 48th Panzer Corps upon Stalingrad in unison with Hoth's drive up from the south. The 48th Panzers were fully occupied trying to contain the new threat not only to the German Don Army Group, but also to all their forces committed to the invasion of the rich Caucasus territory far to the south.

Hoth's force too was imperilled. His northeastern flank appeared to be crumbling along its whole 200-mile length. Manstein realized that the only chance for the trapped quarter million in Stalingrad was to concentrate all their weight to burst through the Russian ring at exactly the moment when Hoth's armour thrust at the same place. But Paulus would have none of it because to effect such an escape would be to admit a disaster to German arms.

Almost airily, he asserted that he and his 6th Army would still be there next Easter; all that was necessary was that they should be supplied effectively by air. 'In any case', insisted Paulus, 'our Führer has forbidden any such surrender as an evacuation'. Paulus further excused himself by asserting that his underfed troops were not physically strong enough for such an effort at that moment and had only enough fuel to advance 20 miles, not the 30 that would be required.

On December 19 Hoth's spearhead finally thrust across the River Aksay and drove on to Mishovka. On December 21 Manstein spoke to Hitler himself on the urgency of an attempt by the 6th Army to break out of Stalingrad. But the Führer sided with Paulus, and Manstein had to accept the ruination of his efforts to save the army trapped in Stalingrad, for which he had risked his crack armour divisions. At that very moment Hoth's Panzer columns, now along the River Mishooka, were far out across the frozen steppes, and their great unwieldy supply train was dangerously encumbering the roads behind them. And while these armoured divisions were in danger at the eastern extremity of the front, the whole 200-mile north-eastern flank of the Don Army Group was disintegrating in headlong retreat.

Manstein grimly ordered Hoth to pull back the 4th Panzer Army gradually towards Rostov. At the same time he was to provide a flank guard while Army Group A was extricated from the growing danger it faced in the Caucasus. Although Hitler and Paulus might not admit it, the German command knew that the 6th Army in Stalingrad was now being left to its fate. It had been relentlessly encircled by 500,000 dug-in Soviet infantrymen, which was half the infantry under Zhukov's command, and was menaced by 30 per cent of Zhukov's available artillery. If nothing else, it could be said that the sacrifice of the 6th Army was depriving Zhukov of the forces he needed if he were to turn the German Don Army retreat into a rout.

On December 23 Manstein's communications were threatened by a Russian advance from the north to the line Millerovo–Tatsunskaya–Morozouskaya. Next day the Russian reserves, including elite Guards divisions, were thrown in by General Malinovsky, to cause heavy losses among the retreating Germans. This set in motion a major offensive destined to culminate in the recapture of Rostov seven weeks later. On Christmas Day the Russian army in the Caucasus captured Nalchik, on January 2 it stormed Mozdok, and suddenly the Germans were in headlong flight from the Caucasus.

On January 8, 1943, Paulus was called on to surrender, being offered 'the honours of war' including sufficient rations, hospitalization of the wounded, officers being permitted to retain their weapons, and guaranteed repatriation for everyone at the war's end. But Paulus would do nothing without Hitler's permission. Meanwhile, in their dank and freezing dug-outs and foxholes amidst the corpse-littered ruins, the German soldiers suffered increasing privations. The bread ration was one slice per man a day; one kilogram of potatoes had to be shared by 15 men, and melted snow supplied the only drinking water. Ammunition too, was desperately short. Thirty cartridges daily per man was the maximum allocation, with orders to use them if attacked.

It had been estimated that the trapped army could be sustained with 550 tons of supplies daily, and that all of this could be flown in. But the round flight from the nearest airfields at Tatsinskaya and Morozovsky took three hours, and each plane could only manage one trip per day. The transport fleet available comprised 225 Junkers Ju 52s, and the whole supply problem had been worked out on the assumption that all of them could make one daily flight. But there were rarely more than 80 serviceable on any one day. Two squadrons of converted Heinkel 111 bombers were brought in to augment them, but each only had a capacity of 1·5 tons. The supply target was never attained. When two airfields had to be abandoned in face of the Russian advance and supplies could only be flown in by night, the average transport fell to 60 tons nightly. During this period the Germans consumed all the horses of the Rumanian cavalry division that was trapped with them, and they were reduced to eating the dogs, cats and crows they could catch in the ruins.

Inevitably the German soldiers became weaker and weaker, until they could no longer dig new emplacements or trenches when driven out of their prepared positions. They lay on the ground, lethargic in numbing cold, sheltering

*Above* Some of the thousands of German prisoners being marched away after suffering defeat at the hands of the Red Army

*Opposite page* A photograph showing the extent of the devastation wrought in Stalingrad by both sides

behind their painfully heaped walls of frozen snow. To be wounded usually meant death, even if they did not die from frostbite, because their comrades were not strong enough to lift and carry them. Suicides were so common that Paulus put out a special order of the day denouncing self-destruction as dishonourable.

The Russians opened their decisive attack upon Stalingrad on the night of January 10. It has been estimated that there were still 250,000 Germans left to give battle. In the midst of an inferno of flame and ear-splitting explosions a rumour spread that the Russians would take no prisoners. Many German soldiers fought to their last round, keeping the very last bullet for themselves.

The Russians sustained their attacks for two days and nights. The German perimeter shrank hourly. By January 24 they had been pressed back to the positions which had constituted the Russian line on September 13. Without cohesion or central command, they fought until they were killed, or collapsed from wounds or exhaustion. The network of first-aid posts and hospitals in cellars soon filled to overflowing. Grievously wounded men still out in the open pleaded with their comrades to shoot them. The airfield and the reserve airstrip which was their only remaining supply source were overrun, ending the last hope, yet for days after this, desperate resistance continued in the great ruined factories, in the labyrinths of cellars and sewers, and in specially constructed underground fortresses. On January 30 the southern pocket in which Paulus had his command post was overrun. The German commander was captured. Two days later the last sporadic resistance died and the 6th Army surrendered. At last the awful battle of Stalingrad was at an end – as were all German hopes of victory in the east.

Of the 21 German divisions ultimately trapped in Stalingrad (besides the Rumanian cavalry division) 91,000 men, including 24 generals, were marched away as captives. In the course of this battle the great city of Stalingrad had been virtually obliterated, and such a multitude of men had met violent death that it was difficult to tread on ground where the flesh, blood and bones of German and Russian dead was not frozen in. In the last stage of the battle alone, 147,200 Germans and 46,700 Russians were slain.

It was with justifiable pride that the *Red Star* reported on February 5, 1943: 'What was destroyed at Stalingrad was the flower of the German Wehrmacht. Hitler was particularly proud of the 6th Army and its great striking power. Under von Reichmann it was the first to invade Belgium. It entered Paris. It took part in the invasion of Yugoslavia and Greece. Before the war it had taken part in the occupation of Czechoslovakia. In 1942 it broke through from Kharkov to Stalingrad.' The Russian victors had indeed settled some bitter scores.

Defeated Germans in the ruins of Stalingrad after the successful Russian counter-attack

# 10. Anzio

# 10. Anzio

By the beginning of 1944, the fortunes of the Allies were definitely in the ascendant. The battle of Africa had been finally won by the Anglo–American armies, with a quarter of a million Axis prisoners and a vast haul of tanks, guns and supplies.

The United States' participation in the North African campaign had come after Roosevelt, in close liaison with Churchill, had overridden his own chiefs of staff, who dismissed it as an unnecessary venture with no direct bearing on their main objective – an attack across the English Channel, directed finally at Berlin. They felt sure they could overwhelm Nazi Germany by weight of numbers and the sheer mass of war machines which their great industries could produce.

The British, however, were desperately short of manpower and were compelled to think strategically. They had to opt for campaigns of manoeuvre in which they were numerically sometimes at a disadvantage. In centuries of European wars the British had been accustomed to exploit their great mobility of sea power. The First World War, a static land war, had produced horrifying casualties which such a small country as Britain could hardly afford. The British intended, and had done ever since the dark days of Dunkirk, to carry the war deep into Germany, but first they aimed to draw off enemy divisions from Hitler's vaunted Atlantic wall. This policy had paid dividends in North Africa, where the Germans had lost 150,000 of their best and most experienced fighting men.

Victory in Africa was swiftly followed by spectacular triumph in Sicily during July and August, 1943, when in only 30 days of fighting the enemy sustained 167,000 casualties, including 37,000 Germans, for the loss of 21,158 Allied troops. But if the Allies imagined that the German collapse in Africa indicated a cracking of morale in Hitler's 'Fortress Europe', they were soon bitterly disappointed. The war hardened once more with the invasion of the Italian mainland. Mussolini was deposed at the end of July. Italy surrendered on September 9, but German divisions occupied the country so swiftly that the first Allied seaborne landing at Salerno on the same day was heavily contested.

Owing to shortage of shipping, which was concentrated elsewhere for the coming Normandy invasion, this assault had to be made with only two British divisions and one American, under the command of the American General Mark Clark. A foothold was established, but costly fighting increased the American determination to limit their commitments in the narrow, mountainous and multi-rivered peninsula of Italy.

*Above* General Lucian K. Truscott, whose appointment as Commander of the beachhead forces infused a new resolution in American and British troops alike

*Opposite page* Snow-covered mountains confront advancing British infrantry. It was to bypass such mountains that the Anzio landing was made behind the enemy line across Italy.

By January, 1944, the most pessimistic American predictions seemed to have come true. The British Army, which had crossed from Sicily and fought up the toe of Italy was on the Adriatic side, and the American Army under Mark Clark, which had captured Naples, was on the Mediterranean side. These two armies were designated the 15th Army Group and were under the overall command of General Sir Harold Alexander.

The opposing German army, under Field-Marshal Kesselring, had made maximum use of the increasingly difficult mountainous countryside as it fought a series of bitter delaying actions back to the immensely strong Gustav Line – a line of massive steel and concrete fortifications and minefields ranging across Italy from the Mediterranean coast 40 miles north of Naples to Ortona on the Adriatic coast. It was the skill with which Kesselring had conducted his delaying campaign while the Gustav Line was still

*Above* The little fishing port of Anzio in more peaceful pre-war days

*Opposite page* Italian women and children welcome American G.I.s to their still peaceful town

being completed that persuaded Hitler to put him in charge of the Italian theatre, even though he was a Luftwaffe general. Rommel, the Führer's original choice, was despatched to north-west Europe to face the threatened Allied invasion.

Sardinia and Corsica had fallen into Allied hands with hardly a struggle, for Hitler saw the Italian invasion as a threat to Greece and the Balkans and strengthened that side of his 'fortress' instead. Of 320 German divisions outside the Reich at this time, 206 were fighting in Russia, and 114 were tied down by the British and Americans – 22 in Italy, 24 in the Balkans, 50 in France and the Low Countries, and 18 in Norway and Denmark.

At this juncture, all that could be said in favour of the Italian campaign was that it had drawn in more than 20 German divisions which could otherwise have been used against Russia, at a moment when the Russians urgently needed relief.

Winter set in early in 1943. As the year declined, the soaring 6,000-foot mountain spine down Italy was thickly blanketed with snow, and the Allied advance became bogged down barely 70 miles north of Salerno, before the Gustav Line. The pivot and dominating feature of the line was the towering, monastery-crowned Monte Cassino, which gave the enemy clear observation of any move which the Allies might make towards their ultimate objective, the Eternal City of Rome. The only valley which gave access to the Allies' goal was the Liri Valley through which ran Route 6, the broad highway to Rome. The swiftly flowing Liri and Rapido, which joined it under full view of Monte Cassino, were an additional barrier to Clark's Anglo–American army. The River Sangro, which rushed down from the central mountains, obstructed the path of the British 8th Army.

The way out of this stalemate seemed fairly obvious – to make a landing in force farther up the coast. But the conquest of Italy was a low-priority operation, and there was a great shortage of landing craft to put the tanks, guns and men ashore. The inadequate fleet that had been allocated for Sicily and Salerno was anyway under orders to return to Britain for the Normandy invasion. By the year's end Operation Overlord had also drawn away seven experienced British and American divisions and the great leaders whose names had featured

British bren-carriers and tanks clank ashore on an
Anzio beachhead

prominently in the African and Sicilian victories
– Eisenhower, Montgomery, Patton, Air-
Marshal Tedder and Admiral Cunningham.

At this point Winston Churchill intervened.
He insisted that a 'wildcat' should be flung
ashore north of the Gustav Line 'to tear out
the heart of the Boche'. And he got his way. A
plan with the code name 'Shingle' was quickly
developed. It prepared for a landing at Anzio,
which lay some 60 miles behind the Gustav Line
and gave easy access to Route 6. A plan of this
kind had been half-heartedly debated before,
but it had been overborne by the American
insistence that resources should be concentrated
for the cross-channel invasion.

The little town of Anzio, nestling amidst a
flat and sandy coastline, was a fishing port and

weekend resort. It now served as a rest centre
for German troops from the Gustav Line. Its
gleaming sands and backdrop of pine woods and
distant hills gave it a pleasant and restful
atmosphere. But in the cold, dim hour just
before dawn on January 22, 1944, there was no
such inviting outlook for the Anglo–American
invasion force.

Meanwhile, the very man who should have
been full of fire to tear through the enemy and
go flat out along the road to Rome was pessimistic. This was the American General John P.
Lucas, commanding 6 Corps of the American
5th Army. On being told of his bold mission
he made the gloomy observation, 'This is going
to be worse than Gallipoli!'

Lucas, who appeared older than his 54 years,
had witnessed the butchery on the beaches at
Salerno and dreaded a repetition. It hardly
helped that Mark Clark had advised him, 'Don't
stick your neck out as I did at Salerno.' The

parting words of the ebullient Patton – 'There is no one in the army I'd hate to see get killed as much as you, but you can't get out of this alive!' – had been no more encouraging. Lucas was already jaded after four months of commanding 6 Corps in the exacting mountain warfare before the Gustav Line, and he was disturbed by his responsibility for a force that was half British and half American.

The Anzio invasion was mounted from an American base, although it had been Churchill's original intention that his 'wildcat' should be an all-British animal. The two divisions selected for the landing were the American 3rd Infantry Division, under General Lucian K. Truscott, and the British 1st Division, under General W. R. C. Penney. The American 3rd Division had fought courageously in Sicily and Italy, after a somewhat anxious baptism of fire in Tunisia. The British 1st Division had taken part in the grim retreat to Dunkirk, where it had been under the command of Alexander, had fought toughly in Tunisia and had since been trained in mountain warfare. Like most British divisions, it comprised English county regiments, a brigade of Guards, and Scots and Irish battalions as well. Their commander was a hard-driving but inspiring general of the Montgomery school who, like the American Truscott, reckoned not to ask his men to go where he personally dared not venture. It was particularly fortunate, in view of what happened at Anzio, that Penney and Truscott admired each other's military prowess and that they were able fully to rely upon each other during the chaos of battle.

The special troops aiding these divisions were also half British and half American. The British were the 2nd Special Service Brigade of two Commandos; the Americans were a formation of Rangers and a parachute regiment. Behind them, at Naples, waited the American 1st Armoured Division and 45th Infantry Division to follow up as soon as the landing had been consolidated.

The plan was straightforward: the British, American and French assailing the Gustav Line were to exert themselves to the utmost to break through and engage the enemy so heavily that any reserves would be drawn into the battle and thus diverted from Anzio. When the enemy was compelled to send back troops

Major-General W. R. C. Penney (right) at Anzio soon after the landing

to seal off the Anzio force, the Allies expected to break through.

The assault on the Gustav Line opened on January 17. That night the British 10th Corps launched a powerful attack across the lower Garigliano River, while the Free French Expeditionary Corps pushed into the mountains north of Cassino. The next day, the American 2nd Corps launched an attack upon the River Rapido. The Allies hoped to force a breach through the enemy fortifications within 48 hours, so that an armoured spearhead could thrust out along the road to Rome. If things went right at Anzio, this spearhead would be met by the advanced guard of the landing force, surging up to the Alban Hills from the beachhead.

The British wrested a small bridgehead from the enemy and after two days had enlarged it into a four-mile salient, but they could go no farther. The French managed to dent the line to a depth of several miles. The Americans, after suffering terrible losses, crossed the Rapido upstream from the planned bridgehead. But

299

nowhere did the Allies seriously breach the Gustav Line or break into the Liri Valley. Thus the Anzio force was on its own from the moment it landed.

The invasion fleet of 253 vessels, carrying 36,000 men with their tanks, guns and supplies, put out from Naples during the afternoon of January 21, swinging southwards past Capri to confuse any enemy spies. At nightfall it turned to head for Anzio, and the first wave of landing craft surged in at 2 a.m. Complete surprise was achieved, and with the dawn the whole landing operation was in full swing.

It was just like the final phase of a fully rehearsed exercise (although there had been time only for the most hasty, and largely chaotic, rehearsal for Anzio). Soon the first British contingents had taken up their allotted positions north of the little harbour, and the American first wave was pushing south, to provide the southern flank guard along the Mussolini Canal. The only Germans in Anzio appeared to be

some engineers ordered to blow up the harbour if the enemy tried to seize it – and they were mostly captured in their pyjamas by American Rangers. The Alban Hills, only 15 miles inland, and the main highway to Rome, were at the invaders' mercy.

The grim mood of the first-wave troops, who had expected to pay dearly for every yard, soon gave way to exhilaration. By midnight on D-Day, a total of 36,000 troops had been landed, along with 3,000 vehicles and considerable supplies. The only real enemy attempt at retaliation had been one or two fleeting air raids, which caused minimal casualties and damage in face of massive anti-aircraft fire from sea and shore.

It had been Alexander's original concept that both the harbour of Anzio and the hills beyond,

Lieutenant-General Mark W. Clark plans an attack by American troops with Brigadier-General John W. O'Daniel

*Above* British infantry, still untroubled by German counter-attacks, march out from the beachhead towards the main road to Rome

*Left* The Germans attached electrically-fused bombs to trees in an abortive attempt to hold up the advance

which commanded both the beachhead and the road to Rome, should be seized. But General Clark, envisaging strong opposition, considered this impossible, and instructed Lucas not to risk his whole corps by a too precipitate thrust for the hills in strength. First and foremost, he required the establishment of a secure beachhead.

Nobody guessed how literally Lucas was taking Mark Clark's instruction to advance 'on' the Alban Hills, but not 'to' them. He would not even contemplate any advance until the 5th Army had breached the Gustav Line and was on the road to Anzio. Lucas was still thinking of defence when his dazzling surprise called for swift and far-reaching exploitation. His orders were for a methodical occupation of a

302

beachhead perimeter in an eight-mile arc around Anzio, from the mouth of the River Moletta in the north-west to the Mussolini Canal in the south-west.

The invaders had another, even greater advantage on their side. On the night they landed, the German commander had finally given in to a request from his staff that a state of permanent stand-to should be cancelled. Kesselring had allowed himself to be persuaded that while the Allies were making an all-out assault on the Gustav Line they would not be able to attempt a landing anywhere north of it.

Kesselring did, however, have a supplementary plan, to rush in reinforcements from farther afield if events so required. He had meticulously drawn up routes down which reserves from northern Italy would advance to envelop any new Allied landing. The routes were thoroughly prepared to take a heavy flow of troops under even the worst winter conditions, with engineers ready to free the ice-bound passes and to span rivers with pontoons within hours of any bridges being destroyed by bombing. Also, hidden fuel-supply points were established in by-roads where they were not likely to be spotted.

Forced to acknowledge the overwhelming air power of the Allies, the Germans had become adept at moving large bodies of troops swiftly by night. Kesselring's 10th Army was confronting the enemy on the Gustav Line; his immediate reserves to oppose a landing were his 14th Army, part reforming in northern Italy and part watching the coast. He could also swiftly draw in additional divisions from the south of France, from the Balkans, and from Germany itself.

At first Kesselring could hardly believe it when, 24 hours after its unopposed landing, the powerful Anglo–American force was reported still fussing around in the beachhead, and making no attempt to exploit the devastating surprise it had achieved. He could not see why strong Allied armoured columns were not already racing out on the road to Rome while their infantry and guns dug in on the strategic Alban Hills. He was painfully aware that the one, under-strength battalion in shooting distance of Anzio had already been shot to pieces. Given this priceless delay, Kesselring quickly put his plans into operation.

Little more than a day after the Allied landing the Germans were in full control of the vital Alban Hills and the main routes out of the beachhead were covered by tank-killing guns. There was no longer easy access to Route 6. On January 23 Kesselring ordered General Schlemmer to strengthen the defence cordon with all speed, and began to think how to smash the invaders back into the sea.

On this same day General von Mackensen, commander of the 14th Army, arrived. Kesselring put him in charge of the imminent battle, already able to assure him that the immediate danger was over. Units of eight different divisions, thrown in higgledy-piggledy as they arrived, had been linked together in a strong ring around Anzio. Meanwhile five complete German divisions were pouring through the mountain passes and along the prepared routes to deliver the massive blow that would end the emergency.

The British and American soldiers in the beachhead became increasingly restless. By now the feeling that they should be out and attacking was prevalent at all levels. They did not yet know that some really formidable foes had moved up in front of them. Opposite the Americans was the crack Hermann Goering Division, barring their way to Cisterna, their immediate objective. Opposite the British, whose immediate objective was Campoleone, were the 3rd Panzer Grenadiers. Beyond the Moletta River, on the British left, the German 65th Infantry Division was digging in. And down in the Gustav Line the 26th Panzers were already under orders to move to Anzio, as Kesselring rightly judged that the Allied attacks on the Gustav Line had been fought to a standstill.

The increasing volume of artillery fire made the growing strength of the German ring round the beachhead hourly more apparent. At dusk on January 23 the Luftwaffe appeared in force for the first time in many months, attacking the

*Top* American infantry push out in their sector, also still free from enemy reaction

*Bottom* The reclaimed Pontine marshes, flooded by the Germans to create a water obstacle, which formed the right flank of the American sector

*Above* British infantrymen march behind a tank towards the vital road that the Anzio landing was meant to seize

*Opposite, top* As Allied troops moved out cautiously from their surprise beachhead the Germans reacted swiftly and drew a cordon of tanks and guns across their path

*Opposite, bottom* German tanks heading south, in accordance with Kesselring's well-laid plan, with orders to drive the Allied soldiers back into the sea

crowded shipping by dive-bombing, with aerial torpedoes, and with a new secret weapon, glider bombs. These were released by bombers circling out of range while the main attack was pressed home, when their pilots spotted gaps through the navy defence screen. Then they guided the bombs in, by radio control, to their selected target. But although the glider bombs scored some initial successes, the British and American navies soon mastered them with jamming teams who bent the attackers' radio beams and diverted the bombs harmlessly into the sea. In the first few days, three major air raids sank a British hospital ship and a destroyer, damaged another hospital ship and forced a transport to be beached. But the Luftwaffe paid dearly; nearly 100 planes were shot down.

On January 25, three days after the invasion, the elements became restless. A 50 mph gale tossed landing craft upon the spray-drenched sands and rocked the anchored shipping. There were also signs of a storm looming in London

German tanks approach the Allied positions through olive groves

from the British sector. It passed through scattered farmhouses and cottages with Italian peasants still in residence and advanced to the hamlet of Carroceto, three miles along the road to Albano, before the enemy opened fire from a stout red-brick wall which looked like a fortress. The patrol, on their hurried return, referred to it as 'the Factory' but in fact it was a big agricultural settlement called Aprilia, which Mussolini had built for peasants brought there to farm the reclaimed Pontine Marshes. The fortress-like wall enclosed a little village complete with church, a town hall and, inevitably, a Fascist headquarters – all set around a square with a row of shops and a wine store. It was clearly an enviable position to hold, because it straddled the highest ground in the immediately surrounding plain.

The presence, so soon, of the 29th Panzer Grenadiers in the Factory boded ill for any British attack. It meant the Germans must be in force much closer than had been imagined possible. But it was obviously better to attack before they were even stronger. So Penney urged his corps commander to let him attack at once. Lucas agreed after some hesitation, and the attack went in next morning. There was bitter house-to-house fighting in the Factory, while the Italian peasants cowered in the cellars. It became all too apparent that the British and Americans would have to fight hard for every yard of advance out of the bridgehead. Apart from the tough German resistance in the Factory, the bombardment covering their first counter-attack was of an ominous ferocity. Nevertheless, the Guards captured this vital objective – though at considerable cost.

At the same time, the Americans were challenged by equally fierce opposition as they advanced towards Cisterna. They had to fight hard for every ditch and bank and cottage. There was not a farmhouse that did not hide a self-propelled gun.

To make matters worse, one of those unpredictable accidents of war which, though apparently small, can effect the whole course

where Churchill, anxiously wondering when his 'wildcat' was going to start clawing and tearing, sent a message to Alexander, tartly inquiring when the Alban Hills, which should have been seized 'with the utmost speed', would be captured.

Though still unwilling to break out, Lucas considered his existing beachhead too small for the forces that had by now landed. He decided to extend the perimeter, to take in the little white-walled town of Cisterna, which lay ahead of the Americans, and the railway station at Campoleone, which was an equivalent distance inland before the British.

Cisterna, on the edge of the Pontine Marshes, was traversed by the Rome–Naples railway and by Route 7, the main coastal road running north to Velletri, where there was a gap through the Alban Hills. Anzio itself was directly connected to Cisterna by a good main road. Campoleone dominated the other road out of Anzio, leading up to Albano on top of the Alban Hills, as vital as Cisterna both for attack and defence. The first probing patrol was sent out

Hitler took time off to discuss 'political, military and economic problems' with Mussolini while the Anzio battle raged. Hitler became obsessed by Anzio, believing that a German victory there would dissuade the Allies from invading France

*Above* Field-Marshal Kesselring (left) inspecting his troops outside the Anzio beachhead

*Opposite page* General Sir Harold Alexander, Commander-in-Chief, Italy, visiting the Anzio front. He was disturbed by the lack of progress made since the initial surprise

of a battle, occurred at the very outset. As the Guards Brigade prepared to capture the road bisecting the main road and railway from Anzio, one and a half miles short of Campoleone, three company commanders carrying marked maps and orders for the attack, ran into a German outpost and were killed. Penney had to ask Lucas for a 24-hour postponement while he made the adjustments this forced upon him.

One of the most daring aspects of Truscott's attack on the right was to be a preliminary night penetration by the crack Rangers assigned to him. The Rangers had already proved their deadly efficiency in Sicily and Italy. Now they were to infiltrate the German positions by night, to seize Cisterna itself and establish strongpoints within the thick walls.

The route along which 767 Rangers were silently to move was a deep and narrow drainage ditch called the Fossa di Pantano. They set out festooned with bandoliers of bullets, pockets full of grenades, and carrying automatics and a few bazookas, but no heavier weapons. Surprise, daring, toughness and courage were their main strength. Creeping below enemy sentries, they snaked along the dark ditch to within half a mile of Cisterna. Then, as the leading formations reached the road and rushed for the nearest houses, terrible fire engulfed them. The Germans had detected their infiltration and had let them get out into the open where every kind of gun opened up at short range. They never stood a chance. Only six of the 767 who had set out managed to struggle back, many being killed and wounded, the remainder captured.

Lucas's divisional commanders were increasingly impatient to attack before it was too late; already Intelligence reported 40,000 Germans facing them. Lucas's superiors felt a similar sense of urgency. Churchill pressed Alexander, and Alexander in turn pressed Clark. On January 28 the American commander made a perilous speedboat trip through shellfire into Anzio harbour. His arrival coincided with the sailing of the main follow-up force from Naples; consequently, he found Lucas feeling more confident. Soon afterwards the American 1st Armoured Division, with its 250 Sherman tanks, and the American 45th Infantry Division landed on the beachhead. Lucas declared himself ready to make a move. He was not aware that by then the Germans were also feeling powerful. Nor did he know that Kesselring had named the day when he would hammer the invaders back into the sea.

In planning his advance Lucas had ruled out the possibility that the enemy might be established in strength at Cisterna and Campoleone; he expected to hit the main force farther inland, along the lower slopes of the Alban Hills. The main effort was assigned to the British. On their left, they were to have the full force of the American armour surging round Campoleone to charge the Alban Hills from that flank. On their right the American infantry were to take Cisterna and advance up Route 7 through the Velletri gap in the hills. The plan was jeopardized by two unknown facts – the terrain, a network of deep intersecting ditches, was almost impossible tank country, and the enemy were already there in great force.

The main attack of the 3rd Division towards Cisterna ground to a halt on February 1. The division had sustained such heavy casualties that it had not strength enough to push farther. The survivors dug in to face the inevitable counter-attacks.

The right-hand punch delivered from the beachhead had been stopped dead. Though close to their objective, the American tanks had been brought to a full stop by the steep railway embankment and enemy artillery fire.

The heavier left-hand punch delivered by the British 1st Division and the American 1st

The shattered town of Cisterna in the British sector, where some of the most ferocious fighting took place

311

Armoured was soon in similar trouble. Only the main Albano road promised swift movement, and that was a mass of roadblocks and covered by the enemy artillery. What appeared to be open country on the left flank was a frustrating network of flooded ditches, slithering banks and rain-sodden soil, which brought the tanks to a standstill. It was perfect defensive countryside of which the Germans had taken full advantage, lining the ditches with men heavily armed to deal with both armour and infantry. It very soon became obvious that any attempt to advance would result in the decimation of the 1st Armoured Division.

The British attack opened with the Irish and Scots Guards advancing from the Factory to establish a start line from which the 3rd Brigade of the 1st Division was to carry on. Before them the road dropped over a low ridge mostly patterned with vineyards. Nobody knew what lay beyond although Intelligence reported enemy concentrating on the other side of Campoleone. In fact, the Germans were in front of Campoleone, and in great strength. As the advancing Scots and Irish Guards were revealed by German Verey lights, they came under heavy fire. On all sides the Guards were mown down, yet the attack penetrated to the given objective and the required start line was seized.

A few supporting tanks followed the Guards, as the survivors of the advance fought desperately to hold off heavy enemy counter-attacks. By morning the Irish Guards had suffered so cruelly that they were called back, the survivors running a gauntlet of fire down the railway track beneath a smoke screen. Only the right half of the start line was still held by the Scots Guards, and an uncommitted company of the Irish Guards had to make another assault on the left. Behind a tumultuous artillery barrage, strengthened by a company of the Shropshires and with British tanks and American tank destroyers thundering along with them, they drove the Germans back. The start line was completed.

The British 1st Division had now thrust 12 miles forward from the landing beaches in a narrowing salient that projected like a rapier into the midst of the enemy. At the very tip on the first slopes of the Alban Hills were the Shropshires. It was absolutely vital that the mass of the American armour should sweep

round on their left, as the enemy around them grew stronger by the hour. But the forward reconnaissance phalanxes of 1st Armoured had already discovered the dangers of the terrain ahead of them; it was obvious that the tanks could only get through to the Alban Hills along the main road. The British infantry they were supposed to support would have to fight that road clear all the way to Campoleone station before this could be done.

The Sherwood Foresters went forward to make this vital attack. Their objective was hidden by a rugged ridge on the right of the main road which was as far as the rapier point had penetrated. As they pushed on past the foremost slit-trenches of the Shropshires and emerged through a tangle of vineyards they came under heavy fire from artillery, mortars, machine-guns, automatics and rifles. Many survived to reach the main Rome–Naples railway, but could not cross the tracks to reach the station on the other side. As they dropped down into the cutting and attempted to scale the far

*Left* German tanks drive towards the bridgehead down a ruined street

*Right* American anti-tank gunners manning a 57-mm gun, about to go into action against advancing Panzers

side they were fatally trapped. Each side was sheer rock, forming a hideous shooting gallery, and the courageous Sherwood Foresters were mown down in swathes. General Harmon, whose tank spearheads had unavailingly tried to assist, said at the end of it all, 'I have never seen so many dead men in one place'. Only 8 officers and 250 men remained of this infantry battalion.

Both Allied attacks had been stopped in their tracks. Nobody realized that they had been on the verge of a breakthrough, for the Germans had also suffered such casualties that their commanders were desperately shuffling depleted formations to try to hold the line. Kesselring and Mackensen abandoned all thought of offensive and went over completely to defence.

The Allied front-line soldiers were bitter, feeling that what might have been the exhilarating adventure of Anzio was going to be a desperate back-to-the-wall fight against total destruction. The beachhead in which they were contained was no more than 10 miles wide and 15 miles deep, and would soon be subjected to the enemy's utmost fury.

Back in Britain, Churchill sourly noted that his wildcat had become a stranded whale. When Alexander reported to him that neither he nor Clark was satisfied with the speed of the advance, Churchill replied, 'It would be unpleasant if your troops were sealed off there and the main army could not advance up from the south'. That, although the prime minister did not know it yet, was precisely what was happening.

Both Alexander and Clark visited Lucas and voiced their discontent. Both also urged that the perilous British thrust into the midst of the Germans should not be withdrawn, because they hoped that a further all-out attack would

advance the line to Campoleone and Cisterna. So the Campoleone salient, only 2,000 yards wide at its tip among the vineyards before the fatal railway cutting, was left as it was.

On February 3 the weather worsened. Lashing rain and low scudding clouds prevented an intervention of the Allied air forces. On that day 6 Corps officially went on to the defensive after Intelligence reports that the blitz on the beachhead was about to begin. Truscott, with his right flank reasonably secured by the treacherous Pontine Marshes, was able to take up a curving front a mile south of Cisterna. But Penney was in an unenviable predicament. The Germans required the ground that his division occupied as their own start line for attack.

The Germans were, in fact, concerned with the Anzio landing at the highest level. Hitler and his High Command had immediately and correctly seen this daring Allied move as an operation to hasten German defeat in Italy, which would set the whole Balkans aflame at a time when the Russian menace was looming large. Above all, it could be regarded as a full-scale rehearsal for the Allied invasion across the Channel.

Hitler followed events at Anzio with anxious but intense interest. In his view, Anzio also gave the Wehrmacht an opportunity for a resounding and morale-boosting victory that might make the Allies think twice about an invasion of northern France. If that invasion were postponed, Germany's new secret weapons, the V1s and V2s and the longe-range U-boats, could well devastate and starve England so that the British would finally give up.

For all their confidence and fast-growing strength, the Germans did not yet consider themselves strong enough to complete the destruction of the Allies at Anzio with a single blow. The resolution with which the British and American soldiers had fought from the very beginning had bred in the Germans considerable respect. Mackensen limited his initial objective to the destruction of the British 3rd

Brigade which was the point of their rapier salient. Zero hour was one hour before midnight, February 3.

Because they were so widely scattered in their precarious salient, the British were particularly vulnerable to a night attack. By day the glaring gaps between their defence positions could be covered by machine-guns, mortar fire and artillery bombardment from the beach; in the dark, however, considerable bodies of enemy infantry could infiltrate with comparative ease. It was simple for the enemy to mass unseen in the deep ditches and woodlands just over the ridge ahead of 3rd Brigade.

The German attack opened with a tremendous bombardment upon positions held by the Irish Guards. Immediately afterwards waves of shouting German infantry rushed in from all sides. Next, the Gordons were subjected to a ferocious attack and their positions were deeply penetrated. Within 12 hours German Panzers were in command of a stretch of the main road and 3rd Brigade were cut off, as the enemy pressed in from all sides. Penney requested reinforcements, but Lucas told him to withdraw – easier said than done. The smoke of the battlefield and the icy rain that began pouring down made the use of air power impossible, and only the beachhead guns held back the German reinforcements. At nightfall those guns would become ineffective.

It was at this dangerous moment that the British 168 Infantry Brigade disembarked at Anzio, close on the heels of the 1st Special Service Force of 1,800 crack Americans and Canadians. While the latter strengthened Truscott's flank along the Mussolini Canal, 168 Brigade went to reinforce Penney. They had come from weeks of hard fighting around Cassino, but were ordered straight into battle, with a battalion of the London Scottish in the forefront. At 4 p.m. they counter-attacked supported by tanks. The Germans were driven from their newly won ground, and 3rd Brigade could be extricated behind a covering bombardment. The withdrawal continued into the night, amidst erupting shells, burning vehicles, and savage machine-gun fire. But the majority of the men of 3rd Brigade did get back, bringing their wounded with them.

Miraculously, the British line was still intact, though it was now over two miles back towards

*Top* An American medium bomber taking part in an attack on German armour and transport

*Bottom* Burnt out armoured vehicles after a clash between Allied and enemy patrols on the Anzio front

Anzio, curving around the Factory and the railway embankment behind. Lucas ordered construction of a final beachhead-defence line behind the British 1st Division, leading from the River Moletta to the flyover bridge across railway and road three miles to the 1st Division's rear and thence to the Mussolini Canal.

But while this line was strengthened, the British 1st Division was in a nasty predicament beyond it. The chief danger points were a stretch of flat land on their right and a ridge named Buonriposo on their left, thinly held by British troops and overlooking the British

The obliteration of the town of Cassino by massive Allied aerial bombardment was the curtain-raiser to synchronised attacks at Anzio and on the main Italian front

positions. There were not sufficient men to do more than patrol the flat land, beyond which the Germans were massed in the woods and ditches no more than 300 yards distant. It had not been possible to prepare any minefields or defences or even to dig slit-trenches.

With its network of deep ditches the terrain was ideal for night infiltration. Unease pervaded the front-line troops. The tension between Penney and Lucas increased. The British general was annoyed with the American commander for his lack of concern for the British troops. To Lucas it seemed that Penney's division could not be relied on; he failed to appreciate how difficult it was to defend the hazardous terrain of the British salient, which he had not himself inspected, with so few men.

The immediate objective of the Germans was the crossing place over the Fossa di Carocetto where the Grenadiers' battalion H.Q. was established. Attacks were repulsed by Grenadiers and American parachutists, and although the western pincer of the German offensive gained the important Buonriposo Ridge, it failed to penetrate the defence positions below.

The enemy's powerful eastern pincer, however, had by dawn pushed back the British on the right and smashed through to reach a track leading to the Factory area.

The ridge of Buonriposo had to be recaptured, because it dominated the main road down which a fatal blow could be delivered upon the Factory and Carocetto. Throughout February 8 the battle-scarred 1st Division fought bitterly but in vain to take this high ground. By dusk, after sustaining brutal casualties including all their officers, the remnant retreated in the pouring rain to the dubious haven of the Fossa di Carocetto.

Weakened as they were by days and nights of furious fighting in which they had suffered grievously, the British 1st Division was in no shape to repel an all-out enemy attack. Lucas still seemed ignorant of their desperate need, and on the night of February 8, after a pulverizing bombardment, the line was breached. At first light the enemy swarmed through the gap torn on the right of the Factory. Furious fighting ensued for this vital stronghold, and the warships off Anzio, including one American and two British cruisers, thundered upon the advancing Germans. Even that failed to halt them.

By dusk the Germans had the Factory, or what was left of it, and the key bastion in the British line had gone. The enemy now concentrated their full strength with yet more fresh reserves upon the Scots Guards who continued their fierce resistance in the ruins of Carocetto. By dawn on February 10 the survivors were driven out, although they continued their defiance from the earth rampart of the embankment.

Penney persuaded the corps commander to mount a counter-attack to recapture the vital ground of the Factory and beyond at dawn on February 11. Lucas committed one American infantry battalion, with two companies of tanks together with the last British formation in reserve, an infantry battalion – hardly sufficient in Penney's view.

As Penney had feared, the American attack withered away beneath the enemy artillery and machine-gun fire. It was the old sad story of too little and too late. The British line was shortened further, and the troops were pulled back from the embankment.

With the Factory and Buonriposo Ridge in their hands, the enemy had the start line for their all-out assault down the Anzio–Albano road to the beachhead. But things had not gone altogether according to the German plan. The British 1st Division had inflicted heavy casualties and disrupted the German timetable.

As the front line daily came closer, and as the shelling and air raids on the beachhead increased, feelings of doom pervaded the 120,000 men crowded there. But there was also a grim resolution, particularly among those who had already been at grips with the enemy. By radio and leaflets, the Germans tried to impress upon the Allies the hopelessness of their cause, and to drive a wedge between them. Propaganda aimed at the British soldiers suggested that rich, girl-crazy Americans were pouring into Britain and seducing their womenfolk. Other propaganda sought to scare the Americans with the vision of another Dunkirk in which they would be the victims. To add to the Allies' problems, there were some 20,000 Italian refugees living in the labyrinth of cellars beneath the ruins and as the situation worsened their evacuation was commenced. In Britain and America disturbing rumours began to circulate that Anzio was a monumental Anglo–American mess-up and that the blow that should have led to the capture of Rome was more likely to result in an ignominious evacuation.

On February 14 General Alexander arrived at the beachhead. After touring the front, he called a press conference. He assured the correspondents that there was not going to be any Dunkirk at Anzio, but for all his confidence he knew there were precious few British reserves to come to the aid of the beleaguered beachhead. Britain had been at war at full stretch for four years now. Its manpower was committed world-wide on land, sea and in the air and at home in the factories, to its absolute limit. There were simply not enough men to meet all the nation's commitments.

The one division which was brought in for the Anzio battle as the crisis approached had itself been plucked from the main Italian front. The 56th (London) Division, commanded by General Gerald Templer, had been embroiled in bitter fighting for several months, particularly at the River Garigliano and at Cassino. The 168th Brigade was already in action at Anzio and a third brigade was scheduled to arrive on February 21.

As the German onslaught was about to descend upon the beachhead, another all-out Allied effort was made against the Gustav Line. It was hoped that the enemy would be compelled to call on some of the troops that were concentrating for the attack on Anzio. The Anzio landing was originally meant to solve the problems of the Gustav Line: ironically the troops struggling against these fortifications were asked to come to the aid of their would-be rescuers. In turn, crack 8th Army divisions from the Adriatic end of the front were brought across to strengthen the blow at Monte Cassino. British, New Zealand and Indian troops successively assaulted the mountain with the utmost determination.

The heavily armed German paratroops were secure in the defence positions of this immense fortress of rock. Not even a massive Allied air raid on February 15, which blasted the crowning monastery into ruins, could strike home at the German defences. If anything, it made it even more hazardous for the attackers to climb the precipitous wilderness and to get at the German defenders. The veteran British infantrymen who assailed the heights behind this bombardment were mown down from hidden strongpoints among the ruins. At the end of the second assault the enemy still held their own, observing every move of the Allies and directing a fierce fire upon them.

These attacks on the Gustav Line had no effect whatsoever on the Germans at Anzio.

They barely bothered to look over their shoulders to note what was happening. After the months of disaster in Russia, Africa and Sicily, they were obsessed with the idea of at last achieving a glorious victory.

The German force had grown more powerful daily, while the nights resounded with the clank and mutter of the massing tanks and shuttling troop-transport lorries. Despite the Allied warships, whose guns posed an ever-present threat from the sea, despite the overwhelming Allied air power dominating the battlefield whenever weather permitted, the Germans were confident that nothing could now stop them.

Kesselring and von Mackensen were of course aware that the Allies would be expecting an attack down the road from Albano, yet they never seriously considered any alternative. To have attacked from each side at the base of the beachhead would have exposed their men to the great guns of the waiting warships. They did make a half-hearted attempt to bluff the Allies into expecting an assault on the front at Cisterna, but they hardly expected them to be deceived.

The road to Anzio and the flanking countryside were wide open to German observation, and the Germans liked what they saw. The area of open fields which bounded the road's eastern edge, though rain-drenched, was still suitable for tanks to attack in strength. This terrain continued as far as the road flyover, running parallel with the sea behind the Allies' line over the main Albano–Anzio road and railway line. Not far behind were the straggling pine woods of Padiglione which covered the mass of the Allied artillery and armour. The scrubby woodlands along their immediate line of advance were ideal for the favourite German form of attack, infiltration by night.

It seemed that all the Germans had to do was to penetrate those woodlands in order to throw all the Allied defences in this sector into confusion. The Panzers would burst through in the wake of the infantry. After battering

through three miles of overstretched Allied defences, they would be in the Padiglione woods. The next thing would be to surge forward another three miles to the seashore, to fan out right and left in the Allied rear.

The vital flat ground over which the knock-out blow would be delivered was pimpled with shallow slit-trenches, newly dug by the men driven out from the Factory. These soldiers themselves were weary and shaken after many days of bitter and unsuccessful fighting.

The German 14th Army now numbered over 125,000 against the Allies' 100,000. Mackensen massed almost six divisions behind the Factory area. To follow up their punch, he could rely on

two armoured divisions, the 26th Panzers and the 29th Panzer Grenadiers, including two battalions of Panther and Tiger tanks. Once the infantry with their close-support tanks had torn the Allied front wide open, the armoured columns would roar down the Albano–Anzio road and across the flanking flat land and deliver the *coup de grâce*.

In detail, the German plan was for one force of infantry and parachutists to thrust forward along the deep ditches west of the road, while two infantry divisions with one expanded Panzer division, blasted through over the flat terrain east of the road. The infantry were to go in waves. If the first were stopped, another

Although the monastery was destroyed, ample cover was left for German machine-gunners, who still exacted a terrible toll of attacking Allied troops

would follow. They were to keep going whatever their casualties, until they and their supporting armour had shattered the overstretched Allied defences, and had rolled down to the Allied line at the flyover road which, in its turn, would soon be overwhelmed.

Hitler insisted on inspecting and 'improving' the plan, because he was obsessed with shaping the expected victory at Anzio himself. He overruled von Mackensen's instructions that any unexpected success west of the road, in the difficult terrain of deep ditches, should be exploited and widened as events dictated. There was to be no such flexibility in the plan, the Führer insisted. He wanted the attack to be one massive irresistible punch over the flat fields east of the road. It was to be symbolic of the terrible power which Nazi Germany still possessed, even though temporary setbacks in Russia and Africa might have fooled the world into thinking otherwise. To underline this point,

Hitler insisted that the attack should be led by a crack regiment of fanatical young Nazi troops – the Infantry Lehr Regiment – a magnificently drilled demonstration unit which had not yet been given a chance to prove itself on the field of battle.

Hitler's interventions made a change of strategy advisable. As the new formations had no experience of the terrain, the German command decided not to begin the offensive with night infiltration, but to attack at dawn behind a bombardment. Hitler had called for a 'creeping barrage' such as he had known when serving on the Western Front in the First World War, but the Germans did not have the ammunition to permit such prodigious expenditure. The

320

*Above* A wrecked bridge and tank amidst the devastation at Monte Cassino

*Below* An American painting of the Anzio landings

*D-Day*, painted by Terence Cuneo

Rocket-firing Typhoons at the Falaise Gap, 1944

The battle of the Sittang bend. Men of the Queen's
Own (Royal West Kent) Regiment on an armed patrol,
painted by Leslie Cole

Men of the Royal Berkshire Regiment cut through the jungle on the Toungoo-Manchi road, painted by Leslie Cole

Luftwaffe had managed to gather a formidable force for the assault, so that once more the fighting men on the ground would be heartened to see the enemy strafed, bombed, and his warplanes challenged over the battlefield. Furthermore, Kesselring and von Mackensen were confident of offsetting the weight of Allied naval bombardment and air power with concentrated heavy artillery behind the German lines, out of the range of the Allied guns.

To boost their morale further, the German fighting men were told that new secret weapons were available and that the British and Americans at Anzio were already reeling and about to attempt another Dunkirk. Consequently, when the German army went into the attack at dawn on February 16 it was confident of victory.

As the hour of their doom, so gloatingly forecast by enemy propaganda, drew nearer, the Allies made a feverish attempt to reinforce and strengthen their last-ditch defences. From the start, they had been desperately restricted by lack of landing craft in bringing in what they needed; and the British and American navies which had provided the warships with their formidable weight of long-range guns also had their anxieties, because the Luftwaffe was in greater strength than the Allies had encountered for a long while. There were also attacks by the new secret weapons, such as midget submarines and glider bombs, not to mention the constant bombardment by the German long-range shore guns including Anzio Annie, a huge railway gun firing from a hidden tunnel in the Alban Hills. Some of the merchant ships were deterred from going close to unload. Nevertheless, the 5th Army did their best to hurry in reinforcements, ammunition and vital supplies.

The Allied front line was manned on the left of the Albano–Anzio road by the British 56th Division under General Templer and by 157 Regimental Combat Team (equivalent to a British brigade) of the American 45th Division. On the right of the road it was held by the 179 and 180 R.C.Ts of 45th Division. The British 1st Division had been withdrawn behind the road which crossed the Albano–Anzio road by way of the flyover bridge. The Allied line on the right of the Albano-Anzio road was completed by the American 3rd Division and the Special Service Force. It curved round in

A geyser of water towers among American amphibious trucks shuttling between off-shore cargo ships as a German long-range gun fires from the Alban hills

the bulge towards Cisterna to the line of the Mussolini Canal.

The German onslaught erupted with a thunderous barrage at 6 a.m. on February 15. As the British and American guns replied, the artillery duel became deafening. Soon the whole front line, particularly in the crucial sector around the main road, was a towering, choking smoke pall. The enemy infantry swarmed upon the thinly held Allied line. Tank spearheads clanked forward when the ground permitted.

321

Under constant bombardment by German long-range artillery the harbour of Anzio became a mass of ruins – but still reinforcements came in

But obviously most of the attacks were diversionary. The main assault, as expected, came along the Albano–Anzio road. Tanks, hull-down behind the ruins of the Factory, armour, artillery and infantry now blasted the 179th R.C.T. on the right of the road. Although the Americans, from ruined farmhouses and foxholes, mowed down the attacking enemy infantry, the Germans still came on in wave after wave over ground thickly strewn with the bodies of their comrades. The American positions were liquidated one after the other. It seemed that by sheer weight of numbers the Germans must burst the line and pour through to the seashore.

Then the Allied guns on the beachhead opened fire. Ground over which the enemy was attacking had been registered by Allied artillery observers to a fine degree of accuracy. As hundreds of American soldiers, surrounded in their foxholes, continued their defiance, the enemy was slaughtered before and around them by a hurricane of shrieking steel amidst shattering explosions and reeking smoke. The Infantry Lehr Regiment, which spearheaded the German attack, disintegrated. Most of the officers were killed, and the young soldiers tumbled back whence they had come, refusing to go forward again.

The Germans were more successful down the main road and farther west amongst the network of ditches. They achieved some penetration of the American defences across the road and managed to get through the British positions to reach the lateral road behind the Allied line. There, however, Allied tanks stopped them and a determined counter-attack restored the position. At the end of the first day the Allied line still resolutely held.

Despite their awful losses, however, the Germans had a considerable reserve of manpower. They used it to good effect during the night. Infiltration under cover of darkness and an ability to take advantage of the gaps in the Allied line had always been their strong point.

The Germans launched a massive night attack at the junction of the 157 and 179 R.C.Ts and achieved a breakthrough to the Albano–Anzio road. At first light they exploited this breach to the full. A low-level air attack was followed by phalanxes of Panzers and swarming infantry. One after another, American positions each side of the road were overwhelmed as powerful enemy formations wheeled right and left to fall upon them. Daylight revealed that the enemy had smashed a two-mile breach in the Allied line at its most dangerous point. Lucas sent an urgent S.O.S. to 5th Army for air retaliation against the German salient. Clark in his turn persuaded the Mediterranean-based Strategic Air Force to switch their long-range bombers from their raids on German war industries to Anzio.

There was a significant development at high level among the Allies. Mark Clark appointed Truscott 'Deputy Commander of 6 Corps' – a move that made it all too apparent to Lucas that he was about to be sacked as commander of the beachhead. It was equally apparent that the next major decision might have to be evacuation, for the Germans would obviously exploit the breach they had made in the Allied line.

Some German tanks had already raced down the main road as far as the flyover bridge before being blasted by anti-tank guns.

The British 1st Division prepared to hold the ultimate defensible line, running along the lateral road that crossed the flyover, while the 1st Armoured Division launched a counter-attack up the main road. The American tanks did not get very far, and were forced to fall back by the concentrated enemy guns.

That night American infantry launched a counter-attack to recover the ground they had lost during the day. But the only troops available were already wearied and depressed by the hours of fighting on the retreat. They got no farther than 1,000 yards beyond the flyover line. There they became embroiled with, and eventually surrounded by, powerful German formations preparing for an all-out onslaught at dawn. As this fateful zero hour neared, the predicament of the Allies seemed precarious indeed.

On each side of the German bulge, however, there were still strongly held positions. By their resolute resistance they were constricting the flow of the enemy's attack to a two-mile-wide corridor. To use their armour and infantry to maximum effect, the Germans needed more room in which to deploy it. Therefore they now turned their full fury upon the battalions of the 180 and 157 R.C.Ts which respectively held the right and left shoulders of the salient.

All through the night powerful enemy formations infiltrated from all sides to destroy the Americans section by section and foxhole by foxhole. But although many positions were liquidated, the network of American defence posts continued to fight on grimly.

The German drive to the sea began at dawn on February 18. It was aimed straight ahead and had only 1,000 yards to cover before it smashed into the battle-weary company of the American 157 R.C.T. in front of the flyover, and then into the thin line of British infantry behind it. It would also engulf the widely stretched formations of 179 R.C.T. to their right. Mackensen had concentrated an overwhelming force. The first wave consisted of three complete infantry regiments. Two regiments of Panzer Grenadiers were to follow. For the final punch there were two whole divisions of Panzer Grenadiers.

In the first hours that morning strong German tank formations blasted their way down the main road and along its eastern flank to swarm over the American advance positions almost to the flyover bridge. With and behind the Panzers, wave upon wave, came German infantry. They were soon among the last-ditch American and British troops before and behind the flyover. But though many Allied soldiers were slain in their foxholes, the survivors stood fast, with machine-guns and automatics glowing red-hot. Terrible execution was done by the Allied artillery and by the deep-throated guns of the watchdog warships standing off the beachhead. Thousands of German soldiers were slaughtered in the last 1,000 yards before the thin line of American and British who barred their way to the beachhead.

At this portentous moment the determination of Truscott, in his new role, impressed itself upon the wavering Lucas. Truscott insisted on a counter-attack while the enemy was at full stretch yet failing to break through. With the backing of Clark, he persuaded the reluctant Lucas that the American 1st Armoured Division, which had been kept back for a long time, should finally be thrown into the attack. The counter-attack force also included the survivors of the British 1st Division, the British 169 Infantry Brigade, newly arrived and still disembarking, and an American infantry regiment plus a battalion. A plan was swiftly worked out. One blow was to be struck northwards from the left of the flyover by Force T under Templer. A second blow would be struck on the right from the Padiglione area by Force H under Harmon. Force T was the British 169 Brigade. Harmon's Force H, by far the more powerful, was made up of his 1st Armoured Division plus the American 6th Armoured Infantry and 30th Infantry.

As the Allied commanders were completing their plans, the Germans, sent in their Panzers and their last reserves. The Panzers rumbled towards the positions of the 180th R.C.T. which had so gallantly prevented the widening of the salient on the right. But a blown road bridge prevented them from getting to close quarters. After the Panzers came more waves of infantry, flinging themselves forward with a wild desperation. But the Americans held them, despite suffering heavily.

As might have been expected, the most ferocious attack came straight down the Albano–Anzio road. Wave after wave of German infantry broke upon the last line of defence. So desperate did the position become that non-combatant British troops took up arms and prepared to join the line.

When night enveloped the battlefield, the Allied line was still unbroken, and through the hours of darkness the British and American guns continued to blast the ground over which the enemy had to charge. The Germans kept on attacking. There was brutal hand-to-hand fighting all along the Allied line. In stark awareness that after many desperate weeks this was the decisive moment, the British and Americans armed cooks, storemen, drivers and even the men who worked the dockside cranes.

But the Germans cracked first. When the bitter grey dawn of February 19 broke, the hollow-eyed British and American soldiers looked incredulously at the corpse-strewn fields beyond. The Germans were disappearing into the distant smoke.

Although the Allies did not yet know it, the battle of Anzio had been finally won during those 24 hours of fury and despair. From this time it became apparent to the German front-line soldiers that they could not destroy the Allied beachhead. Their last reserves had been committed, their resources of courage and human endurance had been expended, yet they had failed to break the Anglo–American line. More than 3,500 Germans had been killed or wounded during the awful hours of their last great attack – all to no avail.

Barely pausing to draw breath, the Allies flung themselves into the counter-attack. The British infantry launched themselves upon the German rearguards which were still in the scattered farmsteads beyond the flyover. Harmon's American tanks, over to the right, soared out from Padiglione to strike up towards the Factory area and the main Albano–Anzio road. A pulverizing artillery barrage obliterated the ground ahead of the American tanks.

The tanks and supporting infantry were soon among a considerable enemy force – a conglomeration of units, many of them survivors from the holocaust before the flyover who were in the process of being formed into a cohesive force for another attack in that direction.

CORSICA

ITALY

SARDINIA

Valmontone
Rome
*Alban Hills*
*Moletta*
Campoleone
Carocetto
Anzio
Albano
*Pontine Marshes*
Terracina
Gaeta
Ischia
Capri

*Garigliano*
*Rapido*
Velletri
*Liri*
Nettuno
*Lepini Mountains*
Cisterna
*Monte Cassino*

Pescara
Ortona
*Sangro*

Naples
Salerno

Tunis

TUNISIA

Palermo
Messina

SICILY

**Anzio**

When conditions were suitable for bombing, Allied air superiority proved to be a vital factor in the Anzio battle – as can be seen from these wrecked German tanks and armoured vehicles caught by an attack

Already shaken, they were now thrown into confusion and had soon recoiled a mile before the attacking Americans.

Because of delays in unloading the necessary heavy and support weapons and moving them up to the front the British Force T had not yet launched its complementing counter-attack up the main road. Harmon's Force H therefore withdrew that night to establish itself in strong positions. But its success suggested that the Germans' iron resolution was failing. Significantly, a white flag of surrender was run up over a ruined farmstead beyond the flyover and, in the sudden silence, the British troops were amazed to see hundreds of German soldiers emerge from the ruins and from surrounding slit-trenches to shamble dazedly forward with their hands up.

The waning of morale among their troops was not lost on the German commanders.

Without a shadow of doubt, they realized that unless they were massively reinforced the battle of Anzio could not be won. General Westphal, Kesselring's chief of staff, went to Berchtesgaden and tried to impress this fact upon the disbelieving Führer. It took considerable courage, for Hitler raged at 'this man who slanders my brave troops'. Then he acted as in no other case, not even when events on the Russian front were at their worst. He had 20 front-line soldiers flown up from the battlefield so that he could personally question them. Afterwards he listened to Westphal's plea that the troops at Anzio should not again be called upon to try to liquidate the beachhead, because it was a

British infantrymen in a foxhole typical of the positions in which they were repeatedly attacked by German artillery, machine-guns and infantry

human impossibility. And Hitler, suddenly weary, accepted the position, hinting mysteriously at the secret weapons which would soon be available to set the Wehrmacht once more on the road to victory.

Although the Germans never again attacked that thin line that had so heroically held them at the flyover, ugly and costly fighting continued for many more weeks amongst the sodden fields that were criss-crossed by the deep ditches that the British called wadis.

Lucas was replaced by Truscott as corps commander. A new resolution filled the troops at once, for Truscott was admired and trusted by both Americans and British. But although Truscott's first commitment was to ensure that any new enemy attack on the beachhead was repelled, attack rather than defence became the main Allied concern.

The last really determined attempt against the beachhead was made on February 29, from the Cisterna area against the American 3rd Division. But Truscott had anticipated this attempt and saw to it that this splendid division, which he himself had fashioned, was at full strength to meet it.

When the sky suddenly cleared on March 2 the Allied air power struck at the Germans. Hundreds of bombers and waves of fighters bombarded the Germans and lashed them with low-level fire. This ordeal of the German fighting men went on for hour after hour. Even the British and American soldiers who had been in deadly combat with them shortly before pitied the enemy.

Kesselring became convinced that after the immense losses sustained at Stalingrad and in Tunisia the Wehrmacht could not afford the destruction of two more armies and began to concentrate on preserving his 14th and 10th Armies for a long defensive war in Italy. On the other hand, the Allied chiefs of staff were increasingly obsessed with preparations for Overlord and a complementary invasion of southern France, so that the forces in Italy could expect neither reinforcements nor additional equipment and shipping. As a consequence, both sides dug in for a long defensive war. The one concession that Churchill was able to wring from the disenchanted American military chiefs was that no more troops or equipment would be withdrawn from Italy until Rome had fallen.

In mid-March the front at the Gustav Line briefly flared up as British, New Zealand and Indian troops once more attempted to storm Cassino behind a bombardment by 500 bombers which obliterated the town. But the mountain remained in German hands, and the road to Rome was as firmly barred as ever. From then on the Italian front relapsed into an ugly defensive war of raids and bombardments that exacted a steady toll on both sides. At Anzio in particular, it resembled the trench warfare of the First World War.

The long, bitter winter finally came to an end. With April the air was full of birdsong and the fields and hillsides became bright with flowers. But the tranquility that settled upon the battlefield was only temporary. It merely meant that on both sides fighting men were being rearmed and trained for another decisive battle.

The Allied troops in the beachhead were able to enjoy such peaceful delights as sea bathing, despite the interminable and deadly attention of Anzio Annie and other long-range guns. There was no indication that the stalemate would be ended, but all the time the ships that sailed in and out of Anzio harbour unloaded supplies that totalled half a million tons before the campaign's end. And down south, along the Cassino front, Alexander made an important, highly secret readjustment of forces, withdrawing the British 10th Corps from Clark's 5th Army and concentrating the 8th Army in the Cassino area to make the main attack into the Liri Valley. He planned that the 8th Army should punch right through along Route 6 towards Rome, whereupon Truscott's 6th Corps was to break out of the beachhead at Anzio and block Route 6 at Valmontone, so that the retreating German 10th Army would be trapped.

While Alexander secretly massed his strength on the western side of the mountains, the Allied air forces stepped up their attacks on the routes over which the German supplies and reinforcements must come. This was an effective overture to the Allied offensive, which opened an hour before midnight on May 11.

The Germans fought back as bitterly as ever. Polish troops who battled bravely up Monte Cassino were beaten back. A British assault

British infantry search a partly demolished building in the ruins of Cassino, looking for any remaining enemy snipers who have stayed behind to pick off Allied troops

across the River Rapido failed to break into the Liri Valley. At the Garigliano's mouth, the Americans could make no appreciable penetration.

The Gustav Line *was* breached, however – by the French under General Juin. Spearheaded by specialized colonial mountain troops from North Africa, they brilliantly penetrated the enemy's sky-high rocky fastness behind the Garigliano. After two days of hard fighting they reached heights overlooking the Liri Valley west of Cassino, and compelled the Germans to withdraw from positions by the Garigliano's mouth, whereupon the Americans advanced, heading for Route 7, the coastal road which led to Anzio and the Alban Hills.

By May 15 the British 8th Army had exploited the Rapido bridgehead and was thrusting out

328

Fighting on the Anzio front opened once more on the night of May 22, when the British 1st Division launched a diversionary attack west of the Albano road. The British 5th Division joined in at 2.15 a.m. with an artillery barrage. At dawn, over 500 guns in the beachhead added to the uproar by bombarding enemy positions opposite the American front. Minutes later 60 light bombers made a concerted attack upon the ruins of Cisterna.

Despite the advantage of surprise, the American attack was soon slowed down. Bitter resistance was offered everywhere to the 45th Division on the left, and to the American 1st Armoured and 3rd Divisions and the American–Canadian Special Force in front of their main objective of Cisterna. At the day's end the Americans had sustained heavy casualties and lost about a hundred tanks and tank destroyers; though they had killed many Germans and taken 1,500 prisoners, they had advanced no farther than the Cisterna–Rome rail.

There was no indication of a possible breakout from the beachhead. Neither had the simultaneous onslaught of the British 8th Army in the Liri Valley made much headway. However, important happenings had taken place elsewhere. The American 11th Corps had swarmed across the Garigliano and assailed the Germans before Terracina. Driven from the left of the Gustav Line the enemy was being steadily hammered back. Kesselring was compelled to readjust his dispositions. He ordered his troops back to the so-called Caesar Line. This was yet another series of defensive positions across Italy, from the Tiber's mouth to Pescara on the opposite coast.

As the German 10th Army began to stream back behind toughly resisting rearguards to join their comrades of the 14th Army in the Caesar Line, the British and Americans on the southern front flung themselves forward. On May 24 the Americans took Terracina and were 30 miles from Cisterna. At the same time the French Expeditionary Force, spearheaded by their amazing Moroccan Goumiers high amongst the icy peaks, were tearing through the Lepini Mountains towards the Alban Hills.

On the Anzio front the American 3rd Division fought its way to the outskirts of Cisterna, and tank spearheads of the 1st Armoured Division crossed Route 7 north of the ruined town. South

into the Liri Valley. The gallant Poles resumed the battle for Monte Cassino, and finally captured those significant heights. In desperation and too late, Kesselring ordered the 26th Panzer Division down from Anzio to stem the out-flooding of Allied armour and troops. He thereby improved the chances of an American breakout from the beachhead.

On May 17 Alexander conferred with Clark. They agreed that an attack out of the Anzio beachhead should begin soon, but while Alexander thought of an all-American thrust towards Valmontone, Clark was more interested in reaching Rome. When the advancing Allies were within 40 miles of Anzio, Clark ordered Truscott to attack towards Valmontone, but added that he must be prepared to divert his main strength swiftly towards Rome after Cisterna had fallen. Clark was determined that American troops should take Rome and that history should record him as saviour of the Eternal City. And he wanted this to be before the headlines were stolen by the great Allied cross-channel invasion of north-western Europe.

of Cisterna this main coastal thoroughfare had also been reached by advanced units of the Special Service Force. One of the main roads vital to the retreating German 10th Army had been cut. A wedge had been driven between them and the German 14th Army.

Soon after dawn on May 26 Anzio, after four months of bitter siege, was no longer a beleaguered beachhead. An advanced unit of the American 11th Corps, picking its way northwards through the Pontine Marshes, was suddenly confronted across the coast road by a probing formation of the British Reconnaissance Regiment and American 36th Engineers.

General Clark ordered Truscott, to his surprise, to leave only the American 3rd Division and Special Force to block Route 6, and to mount an all-out assault towards Rome without further delay.

Truscott's surprise was understandable. He seemed to be on the verge of accomplishing his role in Alexander's plan for the destruction of the German forces in Italy. It seemed that the two German armies had no chance of escaping along the highway which was their only way out of this tangled countryside of mountains, rivers, ditches, vineyards and marshes. But Mark Clark's sudden switch of the main attack towards Rome changed all this. It enabled the Hermann Goering Division, which was rushing south in an attempt to hold the escape route open, to reach Valmontone in force before any sufficiently strong Allied formations could intervene.

Truscott's thrust for Rome proved to be no dramatic dash, for his men had to overcome the bitter resistance of German defences south of the city before they finally broke in on June 4. The Germans had begun to withdraw two days earlier. When Clark entered Rome, he had a hero's welcome, but he had permitted the German 10th and 14th Armies to live to fight another day. Years later, Alexander commented somewhat sourly, 'I always assured General Clark that Rome would be entered by his army, and I can only assume that publicity rather than military considerations dictated his decision'.

General Mark Clark talks to a priest in front of St Peter's Cathedral, Rome, after making his dash north, which did not exactly conform to Alexander's overall plan

# 11. Imphal

# 11. Imphal

One ominous day in May, 1942, Lieutenant-General William Slim stood watching his emaciated, rain-soaked men straggle in at the end of one of the longest and most disastrous retreats in the history of British arms. It was the culmination of a 900-mile retreat through Burma to the Indian borders, with ferocious Japanese always close behind.

The torrential rain that for some days had driven down unceasingly upon the fever-ridden remnants of Slim's corps was a blessing in disguise. In the haunted green gloom of this unfamiliar world it turned the tortuous jungle tracks into ribbons of sucking mud and steep slopes into treacherous glissades, for victor and vanquished alike. The Japanese finally halted at the monsoon-swollen Chindwin. The retreating Burma Corps stopped when they reached Imphal, high in the Assam hills of north-east India. They had expected that once they had crossed into India strong formations of the Indian Army would be waiting to man the frontiers. Instead, there was only a single brigade of scarcely trained Indian infantry. The Burma Corps were ordered to provide their own covering force.

The invasion of Burma had become inevitable once the Japanese had overwhelmed Malaya and Singapore. With complete air superiority and control of the seas, and freedom to move in Vichy-French Indo-China, they were able to pour troops into Burma through supposedly neutral Thailand even as they had been able to invade Malaya and storm Singapore's unfortified 'back door'. Within a fortnight the invaders had reached the River Salween, although furiously fought all the way by the 17th Indian Division, comprising three hastily amalgamated British-Indian brigades.

Because it was believed that the retreating British force must have been annihilated, the Salween bridge was blown and the 17th Division was stranded. But the men determined to save themselves to continue the fight. Although many were drowned or shot while attempting to cross on bamboo rafts, improvised floats and petrol cans, 3,300 men with 1,400 rifles and a few machine-guns took up the fight again from the other side.

The 17th Indian Division was joined by three British battalions and the 7th Armoured Brigade, plucked straight from the African desert after its valiant part in the Crusader offensive. The 1st Burma Division, the morale of whose Burmese riflemen had already disastrously slumped, moved south of Toungoo to guard the road to Mandalay. But in face of such a powerful

*Above* General Slim during a B.B.C. recording in Burma

*Opposite page* Japanese soldiers landing on a Malayan beach to begin an invasion that was to take them to the very threshold of India

Japanese invasion it was obvious that Rangoon, Burma's principal port and city, was already doomed. On March 5 General Sir Harold Alexander, hero of Dunkirk's rearguard, was flown in to take command. Slim flew in to Prome eight days later and 1st Burma Corps was hastily formed. Alexander then set out to lead his men in a desperate fight to cut through the encircling Japanese. There was nothing left but to conduct a fighting retreat all the way to India.

There ensued a desperate race to reach India before the monsoon broke. On March 31 the Japanese captured Toungoo, and a month later were at Mandalay. A strong Japanese column was marching fast up the river to break into India which, the Japanese hoped, would rise against its British rulers.

The ravaged British and Indian remnants who staggered out of the steaming jungle into the doubtful security of the Imphal plain, felt a horror of their foe (whose advance had been marked by inhuman savagery) amounting perhaps to fear. Revenge, fortunately for morale, was stronger among the fighting men who had actually got to grips with the Japanese. The British and Indian casualties were 13,000 killed, wounded and missing; thousands more were in hospital with raging malaria, dysentery and other diseases of the mosquito-ridden rain forests. Of the 150 guns with which Burma Corps had started there were 28 left, and only 80 vehicles out of several hundred. It was to transpire that in achieving their remarkable conquest of Burma the Japanese had lost only 4,600 killed and wounded.

'To our men, British or Indian, the jungle was a strange, fearsome place; moving and fighting in it was a nightmare', noted Slim. 'We were too ready to classify jungle as "impenetrable", as indeed it was to us with our motor transport, bulky supplies and inexperience. To us it appeared only as an obstacle to movement and to vision; to the Japanese it was the welcome means of concealed manoeuvre and surprise. The Japanese used formations specially trained and equipped for a country of jungles and rivers, while we used troops whose training and equipment, as far as they had been completed, were for the open desert. The Japanese reaped the deserved reward for their foresight and thorough preparation; we paid the penalty for our lack of both.'

British soldiers go into captivity, which many thousand were not to survive, after the catastrophe of Singapore

The most telling form of attack employed by the Japanese all through Burma had been flanking movements through the jungle around the road-bound British columns. While fiercely engaging frontally, they would despatch a mobile force on foot to emerge on the precarious British line of communications and there establish a roadblock. Armed principally with automatics and light machine-guns, sometimes with pack artillery and anti-tank guns, they would rapidly create havoc and confusion. Because practically every British soldier was in the front line, men would have to be detached from the formations heavily engaged at the front to deal with the roadblocks behind them. The Japanese would then increase the fury of their frontal attacks and inevitably the British positions would crumble. The necessary swift withdrawal would meet further roadblocks.

By the time they had been driven out of Burma the British had acquired a definite inferiority complex over what seemed the inevitability of defeat at each roadblock. The enemy infiltrators did not carry out their deadly moves with any particular speed or subtlety – they tramped, crowded together, chattering volubly, along the jungle trails, halting when they felt like it. But without reconnaissance screens or local knowledge, the British were constantly out-manoeuvred.

By June, with the monsoons swamping the battlefront, the British had somehow to pull themselves together for the next brutal round. With the Japanese pressing up to the 700-mile

Another village goes up in flames as the Japanese invaders continue their spectacular advance

border of Burma with India, this was likely to be the full-scale invasion of the sub-continent. Responsible for the defence of the border was the Eastern Army, with Headquarters in Ranchi, Bihar, itself answerable to G.H.Q. New Delhi. Such forces as it had – the 70th British Division and 50th Armoured Brigade – were hardly adequate reinforcements for the two, under-strength forward corps facing Burma and guarding hundreds of miles of Bengal–Orissa coast. Yet they were required for internal security as well, guarding the vital railway and road links with the front in a land simmering with strife and verging on open rebellion.

When General Wavell, commander-in-chief, India, decided the internal unrest had subsided sufficiently to permit counter-attack in Burma, an ill-fated campaign was mounted in the Arakan. It had only a limited objective, to re-

capture the Mayu Peninsula and Akyab Island beyond Eastern Bengal. This narrow peninsula, 90 miles long and 20 wide, sandwiched between the Mayu River and Bay of Bengal, was densely forested, and much of it was deemed impenetrable. A 2,000-foot mountain range ran from end to end. Wavell had intended the overland advance to be diversionary, with the main attack a landing behind the enemy. But his 'Forgotten Army' (as it became known) was bottom priority and even the few landing craft allocated were withdrawn for Europe.

The attack started in a blaze of publicity suggesting the reinvasion of Burma. It was hoped that it would prove the disgrace of Singapore,

Malaya and Burma a huge mischance. Rapidly the issue became one of national honour.

Wavell planned the attack to synchronize with one by a Chinese force from the Yunnan mountains on the far side of Burma. Also there was to be a daring deep-penetration raid by a specially trained brigade, called Chindits, under Brigadier Orde Wingate. His 3,000 men were to *march* on a round trip of 1,000 miles, taking in their stride three mountain ranges, three large rivers, and hundreds of miles of jungle shown on the map as impenetrable.

Deliberately Wingate had chosen a 'typical cross-section' of the British race, mostly townsmen of the King's Liverpool Regiment and made up with odds and ends from a dozen other regiments. Many were married men between 28 and 35, wartime soldiers fresh from garrison duty at home. The British comprised half the force, the rest being predominantly Gurkhas.

The Mayu attack opened in December, 1942, and by the month's end the British were within ten miles of Donbaik, at the peninsula's tip. Then the advance paused. Japanese reinforcements were coming up fast, and successive frontal attacks on Donbaik were bloodily repulsed.

Further troops were brought in from India, and soon four full Indian brigades and one British brigade had been added, making a total of nine brigades. The Japanese, in their wellnigh impregnable bunkers, comprised little more than one ferociously fighting battalion, but they were so deeply dug in that they could safely bring down massive artillery, mortar and machine-gun fire on and around them. Determined but unsuccessful attacks were pressed home by Punjabis, Rajputs, Lancashire Fusiliers, Royal Welsh Fusiliers, Royal Scots, Royal Berkshires, Durham Light Infantry, and Lincolns.

By March there were signs that morale was cracking. Amidst the ghostly, muttering jungle where the enemy, lurking unseen, had already slaughtered so many of their comrades, the British and Indian soldiers were becoming jittery and trigger-happy. Increasingly, sinister rumours seeped back to the troops behind, to India, and to troops and civilians in Britain. Could it be that the stories about the Japanese were true and that they could not be beaten?

What happened next seemed to confirm the worst forebodings. A powerful Japanese force,

stealthily brought up from central Burma, fell upon the British flank guard in the steaming jungle of the Kaladan Valley, beyond the Mayu River, and scattered it. At the same time a fanatical fighter named Colonel Tanahashi burst through the jungle around Rathedaung with a picked force and fell upon the rear of 55 Brigade. The Japanese attacked with demoniacal fury and the brigade, badly shaken and savagely mauled, barely managed to fight clear.

Tanahashi's force crossed the Mayu River by night and took in their stride the Mayu Range itself. En route they burst among the utterly surprised and dismayed 47 Brigade, completely shattering them. Brooking no obstacle, they passed through the 'impenetrable' jungle, climbed the 'insurmountable' hills, and fell upon 6 Brigade on the other side. Practically the entire brigade headquarters, including the brigadier,

*Opposite page* While the British, tied to road transport, were always vulnerable to Japanese roadblocks set up behind them, the jungle trained Japanese moved swiftly through the forests on either side, improvising brilliantly, as can be seen from this half-bamboo, half-human bridge used in their advance

*Below* As they thrust swiftly up through Burma, the Japanese capture oilfields, one of the many objectives of their drive in south-east Asia

were slain in a horrifying night attack. Now the Japanese stood triumphantly astride the vital Maungdaw–Buthidaung road. The British troops in Buthidaung were trapped.

For the British it was ignominious defeat with every worst aspect of the previous year's retreat through Burma repeated. On May 11, 1943, they withdrew to a new line in eastern Bengal, covering the vital port of Chittagong. Then again the monsoon burst, and even the Japanese could advance no farther.

The demoralized survivors of the Mayu offensive were withdrawn. But not without significance, in this desperate and distressing hour, was the reappearance from the jungles across the Chindwin of Wingate and his Chindits. True, a third of them were missing, but these gaunt, bearded scarecrows who returned with their fabulous leader had proved his point. The

average British civilian soldier *could* overcome the jungle, and outwit and outfight the Japanese in the sweltering domain of their supremacy.

Nor did defeat dominate the mind of so grimly determined a leader as Slim, whose 15 Corps would certainly be heavily committed in the next fighting. From his battlefield experience of British and Indian troops, he believed the Japanese could be held and finally broken and driven out. Some redoubtable reinforcements were arriving for 15 Corps, chief among them the 5th Indian Division which had covered itself with glory at Keren and on El Alamein's Ruweisat Ridge. Also there was the newly formed 7th Indian Division and 81st West African Division, jungle-trained African soldiers whom some believed would be the answer to the Japanese in the jungle. To 4 Corps at Imphal went the 20th Division. As the monsoon waned,

339

the rivers fell, and the sun hardened the mud, the 5th and 7th Indian Divisions quietly took over the Arakan front.

There were also significant developments in the High Command. Auchinleck was now commander-in-chief, India, Wavell being appointed Viceroy, and a whole new command called South-East Asia Command had been formed by the British and American governments to control all forces in the planned reconquest of South-East Asia. Admiral Lord Louis Mountbatten was appointed supreme commander, and Slim was given command of the newly constituted 14th Army in October, 1943.

This strengthened British army in Burma had some new and redoubtable divisional commanders, not the least being General Frank Messervy, hero of Fort Dologorodoc at Keren. He brought with him to the Burma theatre an insistence that heavy tanks could be used in the jungle. This had been ruled out because existing roads and bridges would not support their weight, but Messervy maintained that big tanks would win the war in the dry zones of sandy plain and baked paddy fields around and south of Mandalay. In the so-called impenetrable jungle, he said, they would both blast the Japanese bunkers at point-blank range and operate as mobile pillboxes from dominating jungle hill tops. In the end an order went out for 300 Sherman tanks to equip the Indian Armoured Corps for imminent battle.

Because Mountbatten's previous command had been Combined Operations, and Burma's vast jungle territories cried out for a series of hook assaults down the coastline, it was believed that the reconquest would be carried out by amphibious operations. But the shortage of landing craft ruled out this method. The 14th Army would have to recapture Burma by hard and bloody slogging through jungle and swamp, across scorched plains and wide, racing rivers. Mountbatten promised that if lines of communication were cut again he would fly in all supplies required.

*Above* British infantry advance continuously along a flooding chaung. As their khaki shorts and shirts indicate, they were equipped for desert warfare. Later, jungle green battledress was adopted

*Right* General Orde Wingate, whose first daring Chindit expedition deep into the jungle behind the Japanese lines inspired the revival of the British morale.

*Opposite page* Japanese infantrymen under fire from a British rearguard during the first weeks of the war in Burma

The opening move of the new campaign was begun by the 7th Indian Division, with the 5th Indian at their right. They were to carry the fight to the enemy down that same Mayu Peninsula where, but a few months earlier, the Japanese seemed to have put the final conclusive stamp on their reputation as jungle fighters. They were now strongly established on the general line Maungdaw–Buthidaung, and they had developed a fantastic fortress dominating it which they called the Golden Fortress of the Mayu Range. Meanwhile they were gathering their strength for an all-out attack to smash the British once and for all and submerge the great subcontinent of India itself.

As his troops pushed forward into the Mayu Peninsula, Messervy increasingly showed himself among his forward fighting men. Before this unruffled, English figure, who in the jungle gloom chatted amiably about the weather and one's home-town, the vast and frightening shadow of the Japanese superman seemed to fade. On the night of November 30, in the ghostly moonlight, they stole forward silently, trigger fingers itching, each one keyed up, expecting the eerie night to awaken abruptly to the stabbing flame and staccato hammer of Japanese automatics.

Yet surprisingly they had almost reached their objective before the enemy did react. They became embroiled in savage hand-to-hand fighting, and casualties were heavy on both sides. Then all three brigades advanced determinedly but with caution, and night after night for a week fought back strong Japanese counter-attacks. They even took a prisoner, the division's first live Japanese because the enemy soldiers had been taught that to become a prisoner was the most shameful thing that could happen to a fighting man.

By mid-December the enemy's outposts had been driven in, and their main fortified position around the tunnels and Buthidaung were reached. At the end of December, thanks to immense efforts of engineering and road making, the Ngakyedauk ('Okeydoke' to the British soldiers) Pass was opened to give a link with 5th Division across the Mayu Range. All set now to launch his offensive, Messervy established his headquarters at Laung Chaung, a narrow steep-sided valley some five miles from Sinzweya. On a jungle-clad hillock amidst dense cover the men

erected camouflaged tents and dug slit-trenches.

The planned offensive was to synchronize with attacks by 5th Indian on the other side of the range, culminating in a joint assault on the vaunted Golden Fortress. This formidable defensive position stretched 15 miles from the thick jungle and precipitous slopes of the Arakan Hills, through tortuous jungle terrain to the mango swamps and crumbling inlets of the coast at Maungdaw. At its core were deep fortified tunnels.

While Messervy was manoeuvring his fighting formations to shatter the enemy, the Japanese were preparing to smash his division utterly. And the planned destruction of 7th Indian was in fact only to be the beginning of things; a few days later 5th Indian would meet a similar fate. Then the whole fury of the Japanese in Burma would fall upon the main bases of the 14th Army in Assam and scatter the British, whereupon the Indian formations would melt away. With the Japanese would be the Indian National Army (the 'Jiffs'), mostly subverted Indian soldier prisoners, and the 'subjugated' population of Bengal and Bihar would arise in bloody revolt. And that would be the end of the British in India.

Thanks largely to the cold-blooded courage of intelligence operatives behind the Japanese lines, and to the persistence of Messervy's jungle patrols, the enemy's intentions had become known to 14th Army. Slim and his planners were well aware that Japanese forces in Burma had been greatly increased. Throughout the monsoon of 1943 the Japanese strength had been four divisions plus a considerable number of communications troops. A fifth division, the

*Top* Wide, deep rivers were only one of the hazards with which the Chindits had to contend on their hazardous march, from which no wounded man could expect to be brought back. Mostly, they had to swim the rivers, or steal native boats, but there were a few rubber boats provided for ferrying across radio sets and similar vital equipment

*Bottom* The great awakening of British morale came when Lord Louis Mountbatten, newly appointed Supreme Allied Commander South-East Asia, visited combat troops to assure them that they would be supplied by air if they were cut off in the jungle.
The 14th Army in Burma had become known as the 'Forgotten Army'

*Above* Another morale booster was the wresting of aerial supremacy over Burma from the Japanese by fighters of the R.A.F. Here a Hurribomber (a Hurricane fighter equipped with bombs), being prepared for blasting a Japanese jungle stronghold, is passed by a native bullock cart

*Left* One of the Japanese objectives in attacking Burma was to close the supply route which ran across the north of the country from India to China. This had been further developed by the Americans, who named it the Stilwell Road (after General 'Vinegar Joe' Stilwell, who commanded a Chinese-American force in the far north). It zig-zagged miraculously through almost impossible terrain until it reached Konming in China

54th from Java, had since begun to move into Arakan and a sixth, the 31st, had arrived from Malaya. In November there was news of a seventh marching in from Thailand. In addition there were indications of other formations being transferred from the Pacific. These increases were satisfactory from the point of view of global strategy, as they drew off Japanese forces from the Americans' Pacific theatre.

The Japanese invasion plan, known to the High Command as Operation C, was a grand design. It was first to split the British Arakan front, cutting both divisions' lines of communication and liquidating them separately. The road into India through Chittagong would then be laid open. The second phase, the capture of the British northern bases of Imphal and Dimapur, was to commence precisely one month later, when all Slim's reserves would have been drawn down to the Arakan.

The Japanese were completing their build-up in Burma to two armies totalling 200,000 men. The formidable Colonel Tanahashi, who had turned the last British thrust in the Arakan into bloody defeat, was given command of the main striking force. General Sakurai was in command of the immediate attacking force (the 55th Japanese Division plus formations of the Indian National Army) which was organized into three task forces.

Tanahashi was to lead his men swiftly and secretly through the jungle between 7th Indian and their outer flank guard of West Africans in the Kaladan Valley. They were to take Taung Bazaar from the rear, seize the Kalapanzin River crossing, sweep right round behind and march south to cut the Ngakyedauk Pass. Messervy's division would then be completely trapped. Another Japanese formation, known as Kubo Force, was to march northwards through the jungle and seize the Goppe Pass, the only other possible way out for 7th Indian. Elements would then cross the Mayu Range, get behind 5th Indian Division on the far side, and thus cut the communications of the whole of 15 Corps. A third force, Doi Force, was to attack 7th Indian from the south to complete their destruction. A vital feature of Tanahashi's onslaught was his planned seizure of the British main supply base, being rapidly developed as the administrative area for the whole corps at Sinzweya near the eastern entrance to the Ngakyedauk Pass. This would solve the immediate supply problem for the Japanese.

During the first seven days there would be maximum support by the Japanese air force, significantly unobtrusive since R.A.F. Spitfires had appeared over Burma. Seven days were considered enough to destroy 7th Indian and for the three Japanese forces to combine to decimate 5th Indian, also expected to be trapped across the range. The Japanese had no doubts that 5th Indian, in their turn, would seek escape in panic-stricken flight across the River Naf. The overall timing of the plan decreed that the battle should commence on February 4, and that 7th Indian would cease to exist by February 10.

Mountbatten's promise to send air supply to cut-off formations looked shaky when over a hundred Japanese aircraft roared over to sweep the skies clear of British and American transport planes. In the forefront were squadrons of a new fighter, the Tojo, whose manoeuvrability offset somewhat the advantage of speed enjoyed by the Spitfire. From their forward airfields three squadrons of Spitfires took off to join battle, while the ageing Hurricanes arose to give them airfield cover during refuelling and rearming.

Just how near the enemy were to Messervy's divisional H.Q. became apparent on the afternoon of February 5. Gurkhas, supported by tanks of the 25th Dragoons, having just arrived for 7th Indian's attack, clashed with them on a jungle ridge barely two miles away. The Japanese were closing in, and in large numbers. As night fell the Gurkhas dug in, and the tanks clanked back through the jungle to the administrative area at Sinzweya. With the Japanese closing in all around him, Messervy decided that he and his divisional H.Q. would stand and fight where they were – to the last bayonet and the last man if needs be. Meanwhile, he changed into pyjamas and climbed into bed. 'No bloody Japanese is going to spoil my sleep', he explained.

Shortly before dawn, as the mists began to writhe up through the jungle, the Japanese came charging in with their high-pitched shouts of 'Banzai!' The British and Indian soldiers killed scores of men who came bounding into divisional H.Q. from all sides. So determined was their resistance that the Japanese were compelled to halt their attack while they brought up mortars and infantry guns and deployed heavy machine

345

guns on high ground around. It began to rain heavily, and soon the jungle tracks were treacherously slippery, while the mists decreased visibility.

At about 10.30 a.m., when shells and heavy mortars began to explode among them, Messervy decided his H.Q.'s determined stand had served its purpose. After destroying all documents and radio sets, the defenders slipped away in small parties, making for the Admin. Box at Sinzweya. For five vital hours they had held off the frenzied attacks of a whole Japanese battalion.

With the grim news that Messervy's H.Q. had been overrun and that he was almost certainly slain, things looked desperate indeed. The Japanese attack had come earlier than expected by South-East Asia Command. About to assault the Japanese Golden Fortress, the British Arakan force was too widely deployed and at a grave disadvantage among the thick jungle and hills. And 7th Indian's very nerve centre had apparently been destroyed with the first blow struck.

Brigadier Geoffrey Evans, who had arrived only that day to command 9 Brigade of 5th

*Above* Once R.A.F. Spitfires ranged the skies over Burma the Japanese Zeros were no longer supreme and the Japanese air-force played no further significant part in the campaign. These Spitfire pilots have just returned from a sortie after the first rains of the monsoon

*Opposite page* Admiral Mountbatten, the 'Supremo', confers with General Stilwell on his front in north Burma

Indian Division, took over 7th Indian's Admin. Box to stand against the enemy, and ordered 25th Dragoons with their Lee-Grant tanks to join him. He had arrived to find few fighting troops available, but two battalions of 9 Brigade had come through the tortuous pass to join 7th Indian. One of these Evans called into the Admin. Box.

The area of the Admin. Box at Sinzweya was really a large clearing of jungle-surrounded paddy fields. It was some 1,200 yards square, and about the size of a large football stadium. It was ringed all around with steep hills covered with jungle so dense that attackers could creep through right to the paddy's edge without being

seen. In the centre was a small scrub-covered hill, 200 yards long and 150 feet high. A force caught within this arena by a superior and resolute enemy was in a deathtrap.

With the Japanese no more than two miles away, Evans set about forming a perimeter defence as fast as possible, allocating a part of the perimeter to each small unit, whether it was a supply issue section, ordnance field park, or officers' shop. There were still not enough soldiers, so the eastern and north-eastern edges had to be left open. The commanders were told to begin digging in at once, to run out barbed wire and put up such obstacles in the jungle as they could. Evans ordered that each unit should be responsible for its own little box within the Box. They were to fight until help came, or to the death. All units were ordered to concentrate their fire on any Japanese coming over the rim of the hills in the unguarded north-east quarter. Across the flat paddy fields, in the very centre of the Box, Evans deployed the tanks and dug in between them two companies of infantry – his counter-attack force to be hurled at any Japanese breakthrough.

*Above* Men of the 14th Army follow a tank through thick undergrowth

*Opposite page* A British Lee Grant tank crosses a shallow river to attack a Japanese strongpoint near Imphal. Although the big gun had little traverse, it was ideal for 'bunker busting', always necessary before enemy positions could be overcome

While the troops were digging furiously, the bedraggled but upright figure of a tall, hatless man walked out of the jungle. It was General Messervy, with the survivors of his staff. During ensuing days many more stragglers were to find their way in through the jungle. Messervy approved Evans's measures and told him to carry on, while he planned the next fight. Taking an armoured car as his tactical H.Q. he radioed his three embattled brigades, still sad at his death. The effect on the troops everywhere was electric.

The general had been in the Admin. Box barely 30 minutes when the Japanese opened their attack, fighters roaring down low to flay the wide-open paddy fields with bullets. Caught

still digging in, the troops sustained a number of casualties.

With the encirclement of 7th Indian completed, the remarkable Tanahashi had executed the first phase on schedule. The Japanese press and radio went wild. 'The March on Delhi Has Begun!' 'New British 14th Army Destroyed In One Thrust!' 'Tanahashi, Victor of Arakan!' The notorious Tokyo Rose added her seductive tones to tell the troops in the Pacific, 'Why don't you go home? It's all over in Burma.' The Japanese High Command arrogantly marked up their war maps to show Tanahashi would be in Chittagong within the week. But Mountbatten faithfully implemented his promise to supply by air any British force that stood and fought it out when surrounded in the jungle, and the Admin. Box defenders were also joined by a battalion of Gurkhas who fought their way across from 89 Brigade Box.

Each Japanese attack was furiously blasted back by the concentrated fire power of the tanks and guns. Soon the once tree-crowded slopes were a wilderness of splintered wood, shredded vegetation and butchered Japanese. Time and again the infantry followed up the artillery with determined bayonet charges. By night the orders were that no man should move from his foxhole and that anything that moved in the darkness must be shot.

With 7th Division apparently doomed, the Japanese attack increased in fury as more and more reinforcements came up through the jungle. But always they were beaten back, were outfought in snarling, hand-to-hand encounters with British, Indian and Gurkha soldiers. When by night they broke into the main dressing station of the Admin. Box, the merciless Japanese killed doctors, orderlies and wounded alike.

The attacks continued with unabated ferocity. The Japanese had never expected to meet heavy tanks in the jungle and were determined to destroy them. They repeatedly attacked them with artillery fire and infantry – even with bayonet charges.

Night attacks were the worst, when men awaited unseen attackers, hardly daring to breathe, until suddenly they were fighting hand-to-hand. The 72 hours from first light on February 10 were among the most hideous. The

hitherto confident Japanese were at last aware that things were *not* going according to plan. The British had *not* lost their nerve and tried to escape but were hitting back with fierce determination.

The Japanese commander realized that unless he destroyed 7th Indian's jungle boxes – the brigade boxes were being assailed as well – and most of all the Admin. Box with its vital stores, his attack must fail. In an all-out assault he flung the whole of his Arakan force, excluding only one cavalry regiment containing the Africans in the Kaladan Valley, upon the thin ring of defence positions around the rim of the Sinzweya arena. The bulk of the Japanese 54th Division was moved up to reinforce or exploit success.

Attack after attack, with increasingly ferocious desperation, was hurled upon the Admin. Box from all sides. A tornado of fire was poured in, while planes bombed and strafed until the arena became a choking inferno. By February 11

For the invasion of India the Japanese massed the biggest army they employed anywhere in the whole of the Far East and south-east Asia. These soldiers are presenting arms to the Rising Sun before launching an attack on the British stronghold in north Burma

the Admin. Box had been fighting for five furious days and nights. According to the Japanese master plan 7th Indian was to have been finished in five days, but already seven days had passed. The magnificent stand of 7th Indian had actually defeated the enemy's plan even before the air supply promised could come to their aid with food and drink, fuel, ammunition, weapon replacements, medical supplies, rum, clothing, everything the heroic defenders were likely to require. Meanwhile the Japanese task forces, carrying only seven days' rations, were in a precarious predicament.

The Japanese had been so certain of victory

that Radio Tokyo carried on according to plan. Day by day it described the latest phase of the destruction of the British in the Arakan. As Messervy played liar dice in his tent during a lull, he heard a remarkable broadcast telling in blood-curdling detail of the destruction of the 7th Indian Division and how the divisional commander had flown out and deserted his troops!

On February 13 a brigade of 5th Indian Division began to fight up into the Ngakyedauk Pass. To the north, patrols of the 26th Division, held in reserve at Chittagong for just such an eventuality, were coming into action through the Goppe Pass. Messervy ordered his brigades to begin counter-attacking from their boxes towards the Admin. Box. Tanks actually rumbled up into the pass and made brief contact with a 5th Indian forward patrol, in itself hearteningly significant. Although news reaching the outside world was still hazy, it had become evident that a major Japanese land offensive had for once gone seriously wrong.

To strengthen his dwindling counter-attack force Messervy called a Scots battalion in from the 89 Brigade Box in the Awlanbyin area. On the same day a tank patrol, pushing cautiously past the smoke-blackened shambles of Messervy's overrun divisional H.Q., met a patrol from 26th Division, and a growing rumble of gun-fire from north and west told that both this division and 5th Indian were on the offensive. The ominous message for the Japanese in that distant thunder became apparent next day, February 17, 1944 – the most significant date in the Burma war. It was the day when the Japanese Imperial Army admitted defeat for the first time and began, hardly perceptibly at first, to pull back.

The 5th Indian Division finally broke through the Ngakyedauk Pass and raised the siege on February 24. Sakurai Force had broken up into small detachments trying to escape through the jungle. Kubo Force, caught between out-thrusting 7th Division and the southwards-driving 26th and 36th Divisions, was slaughtered to the last man. Of Sakurai's 7,000 soldiers who had hurled themselves upon the Admin. Box no less than 5,000 were found dead in the jungle. Hundreds more were killed and never discovered, and more still undoubtedly died of starvation and disease. Very few could have survived.

Half a world away, when the tremendous news was made known in a tensely waiting Britain, Winston Churchill jubilantly prepared a message of congratulation. 'I congratulate you and the 14th Army heartily upon the successful outcome of the series of fierce encounters with the Japanese in Arakan', he telegraphed Mountbatten. 'It must be a great satisfaction to all ranks and races engaged in our common effort that the Japanese have been challenged and beaten in jungle warfare in Burma, and that their boastfulness should have received a salutary exposure.'

With the ending of the battle of the Admin. Box, on which the desperate enemy had finally staked their all, the battle of Arakan was virtually at an end. General Slim's 14th Army had gloriously triumphed in its first great battle, and had set a pattern of heroism that, before the war's end, won 30 Victoria Crosses for the men of the 'Forgotten Army', more than in any other theatre of the Second World War.

In shattering the Japanese in the Arakan, 7th Indian had suffered casualties totalling 500 dead and missing, and 1,500 wounded. But they had killed nearly 7,000 Japanese and, above all, had shaken Japanese morale. The fact that they had taken 50 Japanese prisoners, something previously unheard of in Burma, proved this point emphatically. But even as the fighting lulled in the Arakan, there were dramatic and alarming developments far away to the north. The second, and major, all-out assault of the Japanese March on Delhi suddenly erupted out of the jungle, and again British and Indian soldiers stood back to back desperately fighting for survival. But this time 14th Army knew that the Japanese were not invincible.

It had been ominously apparent for some weeks that an enemy offensive bigger than that in the Arakan was to be made in Assam. Because Slim had been compelled to commit his reserve 26th and 36th divisions to the Arakan he now withdrew 5th and 7th Indian with the intention that they should briefly rest before moving up to Imphal. To the now quiescent Arakan he sent the 25th Division from India. During ensuing weeks, as the battle swelled in the north, the line was shortened in the Arakan to make it more defensible should there be an unexpected Japanese resurgence.

Even before the Japanese northern offensive

opened there had been dramatic developments in far north-east Burma. The American General 'Vinegar Joe' Stilwell had begun to advance towards the Mogaung–Myitkyina area to cover the Ledo road, with three American-trained Chinese divisions, some Chinese-manned tanks, and Merril's Marauders, an American long-range penetration regiment. After some progress, Japanese resistance stiffened and Stilwell was having difficulty in moving. Then, by night, between March 5 and 10, a special shock force of nearly 12,000 British and Gurkha troops under Wingate was flown in by 100 gliders and 600 Dakota sorties to establish fortified jungle boxes across the Japanese lines of communications. Meanwhile, marching through the jungle to join them was another Chindit brigade led by Bernard Ferguson, commander of a column in

Two British Chindits, with a Gurkha soldier who fought alongside them, after being flown out from the bitter fighting 200 miles behind the Japanese front line

*Opposite, left* The Tiddim-Imphal road snakes through the hills. All along this vital thoroughfare there was bitter fighting between the British 14th Army and the Japanese

*Opposite, right* Even as the great battle was joined, Wingate led an airborne Chindit force across the Japanese lines of communication. This time they were far better armed and equipped – even taking blood plasma to give transfusions to the wounded (as seen here), who could expect to be airlifted from the battlefield to a base hospital in a matter of hours

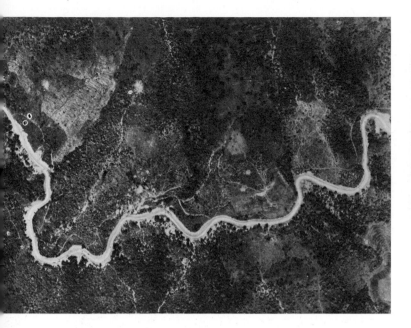

the first Chindit expedition. Wingate's objectives were to aid Stilwell's advance by harassing the Japanese rear and preventing their reinforcement, also to encourage a Chinese force in the Yunnan mountains to attack across the River Salween.

Although the Japanese army closing in through the jungle upon Imphal heard the planes flying over night after night, no troops were detached to deal with the airborne force. Instead a scratch, but nevertheless belligerent, force from scattered garrisons and communications troops was sent against them. The powerful Chindits were fully ready for them. Within 11 days of their dramatic sortie, Wingate's force had achieved its first objective (although its spectacular leader had been killed in an air crash). It had cut rail and road communications to the Japanese divisions fighting Stilwell's troops. The Japanese could ignore this threat no longer and a force from the 53rd Japanese division, then arriving in Burma, was sent north against them. Soon they were locked in hand-to-hand fighting of the utmost ferocity, both by day and by night.

The forces of the Imperial Japanese Army that swarmed across the Chindwin to fall upon Kohima and Imphal numbered 100,000 of the toughest, most highly trained Japanese fighting men. Complete victory in Burma and the invasion of India had become an utter necessity for the Japanese High Command. Already the resurgent Allied sea and air power in the Far East

was beginning to interfere with the supply of the far-flung territories which the Japanese had snatched in their hour of triumph. It was for this reason that the Japanese High Command had withdrawn crack troops from other Asian battlefronts to launch the greatest army they ever deployed in South-East Asia in the twin onslaughts on the Arakan and the northern Imphal Plain. Meanwhile, to the Allies, as they built up for the pending invasion of Europe,

Burma remained the least important front.

General Slim was prepared for the Japanese attack in the north. Determined patrol activity across the Chindwin had brought in evidence of enemy intentions in the form of captured operation orders, marked maps and diaries. To meet it he planned to withdraw his frontier troops to the remote uplands of the Imphal Plain. There the enemy would not only be committed to fighting with a broad river immediately behind them, but would also be dependent on precarious jungle lines of communication. In addition, Allied air superiority not only ensured the supply of any beleaguered British force, but would deny the Japanese their supplies. With the monsoon about to transform parched riverbeds into raging torrents and jungle tracks into slimy glissades, the Japanese had to achieve swift and crushing victory before its onset, or face calamity.

Although the 40 by 20 miles of the Imphal Plain lie within the borders of India, the Manipur Mountains, amid which it forms a 3,000-foot-high plateau, are the natural barrier between India and Burma. Of all the inaccessible fronts in Burma – and every one was a nightmare to supply – this northern one was the most isolated. Through all the hundreds of hazardous miles of gloomy forest and serried ranks of jungle-clad mountains there was only one supply route, a railway. There was no road at all, only tracks and rails suitable for bullock carts.

During the two years since the British had been driven from Burma, a great base had been constructed there, from which, one day, a counter-offensive would spring. The Imphal Plain was now a very different place from the monsoon-drenched morass into which the defeated Burma Corps had dragged itself after its disastrous 900 miles of retreat. It was spread over with great camps of *bashas* (huts of plaited bamboo and reeds), hospitals, rest camps, ordnance depots, artillery magazines, arms dumps, workshops, engineering parks and all the vast requirements of a major military base. Through them all ran a network of tarmac roads, and a wide motor road connecting Imphal with the main railhead at Dimapur had been constructed from virgin jungle since 1942.

The presence of a strong British force in this remote region was also necessary to cover the construction of the Ledo road to China, to which the Americans were now lending their considerable skills and energy. It was the dream of General Stilwell, the tough and effective American commander of the small Chinese army in north Burma, that one day he would strike up into China with a Chinese army of 30 divisions. This, supplied by way of the Ledo road, would drive right across the continent to the Pacific and there join the United States Navy in the invasion of Japan. In retrospect, the forces guarding and supplying this road might have been better employed building up the British offensive in Burma. The most natural, easiest, and most fruitful supply route to China had always been through Burma from the deep-water port of Rangoon, so the sooner Burma was recaptured the better. But the Anglo–American chiefs of staff wanted the Ledo road built – and it was.

At Imphal all was as well ordered and organized as a base for an attacking army should be. Indeed, the three divisions of 4 Corps were already tentatively pushing out into north Burma towards the Kabaw Valley and the Chin Hills 150 miles south. But Imphal was anything but well laid out to withstand an invasion, because the plain was entirely overlooked by steep, jungle-clad hills. The great *basha* encampments, most thickly clustered around the villages of Imphal and Palel, 25 miles farther south, had been sited with air attacks in mind. It was no place to fight a defensive battle and amongst its immediate embarrassments was the presence of a 70,000-strong Indian non-combatant labour force.

When it became obvious that the Japanese offensive was imminent, Slim ordered back to Imphal his 4 Corps troops just beginning to advance. Meanwhile all administrative troops and R.A.F. ground personnel were told to construct wired-in boxes on the Admin. Box pattern within the Imphal Plain.

Marching against them were the Japanese 33rd Division, from the south; the 15th, ordered to encircle Imphal and attack from the north; and the 31st, moving farther north to mop up

*Opposite page* Covered by a Bren gun, British troops probe the tall elephant grass for Japanese

the insignificant garrison at Kohima before falling upon the vital railway and base at Dimapur.

On March 17 Japanese columns crossed the broad Chindwin on rafts and boats. These Asiatic storm-troopers were, as marching infantrymen, probably the world's toughest. The distances they could cover in a day, through jungle, were phenomenal, and they emerged around Kohima earlier than expected. For the first time, the Rising Sun of Imperial Japan flew over Indian soil.

The furious battle now joined was necessarily confused, for much was hidden in the gloomy depths of the jungle. It was to surge backwards and forwards, erupt into deep Japanese penetrations, sway back and forth with attack and counter-attack until, over a vast tangled area, British, Indians and Gurkhas were locked in bloody combat with the Japanese, sometimes by brigades, sometimes by divisions, sometimes by battalions, but often by companies and sections and little groups. The first major Japanese attack was at Tonzang on the Tiddim road south of Imphal. A powerful force swarmed through thick jungle to bypass a 14th Army defence post and seize high ground to cut the road. Another enemy force fell upon a camp at Milestone 109, some miles farther north, and established itself in strength. The 17th Indian's way back to Imphal was barred. There were also ominous signs farther north that the Japanese were massing in great strength for over 100 miles along the Chindwin from Tanga up to Tamanthi.

During the next night the two powerful enemy divisions here began to surge out of the jungle. The crack 15th Division had the heroic order to 'advance through the hills like a ball of fire' and seize Imphal. It was to sweep round north of the town, surround it, and then storm in. Travelling light, assured of all the supplies they could require when they had taken Imphal, the division's separate columns marched through jungle and crossed waterways with incredible speed. On March 18 one was assailing the flank of the British 20th Division near Myothit while others were attacking just south of Ukhrul. The Japanese 31st Division had split into eight strong columns and crossed the Chindwin on a 40-mile front from Homalin northwards. Because of the thick jungle it was not possible to determine the main thrust or the strength of each column. It seemed that one main column was heading for Ukhrul, with Kohima its chief objective, while another was swinging west on Imphal.

The Japanese plan was, in fact, for the advancing columns to cut the main Kohima road, north of Imphal, and swarm through the Somra Hills towards Jessami. Then the whole force was to converge upon the little garrison at Kohima. The garrison was warned by Naga hillmen, and defence positions were hastily constructed on a series of hillocks along a mile-long ridge, 5,000 feet above sea level. At the centre of the defences in this pleasant little hill station was the Assistant District Commissioner's bungalow, his pretty garden and his tennis court.

If nothing else was clear in the increasingly confused state of the swelling battle, with its continual reports of more and more Japanese thrusts developing, it was obvious that this was the biggest attack yet made in South-East Asia. By March 19 powerful Japanese formations were ferociously attacking the Indian Parachute Brigade and a British battalion covering Ukhrul. Desperate fighting ensued for two days and nights, with heavy casualties on both sides, before the defenders were forced back – but not far, for they held again nine miles south at Sangshak and withstood six days and hideous nights of relentless assaults. Whenever possible, R.A.F. planes plunged to bomb and strafe the Japanese, and to drop badly needed containers of water to the British. But by the night of March 26, the defenders were desperate with thirst, too few air drops having reached them. They were ordered to fall back into the main positions at Imphal, but not before they and the R.A.F. had inflicted such casualties in this bitter ten days' battle that the enemy's future operations were to be seriously affected.

Another savage battle was joined at Litan, on the Ukhrul road, some ten miles south-west.

There a 5th Indian battalion had just been flown up in the nick of time from the Arakan to join dug-in detachments of the Parachute Brigade. Furious counter-attacks drove the enemy back, and by the time more Japanese had been hurled into the battle, another 5th Indian brigade had been flown up. There ensued five days and nights of savage fighting at the end of which the Japanese thrust on Imphal along the road from Ukhrul was decisively held. To the north, however, they met with more success, on March 30 strongly blocking the Kohima–Imphal road 30 miles north of Imphal and blowing a vital bridge. All main roads into Imphal were now effectively blocked. The only supply route was a track connecting to the west with the railhead at Silchar.

Troops of the 23rd Indian Division were meanwhile fighting strongly down the Tiddim

*Left* Gurkhas and men of the West Yorkshire Regiment advance along the Kohima-Imphal road, now cleared of Japanese

*Below* Lee-Grant tanks and Gurkhas on the Kohima-Imphal road

road to the still cut-off 17th Indian Division. The most formidable obstacle ahead was the camp at Milestone 109, which the Japanese had finally seized with its considerable stores. Powerful infantry detachments advanced along the ridges flanking the road up which the main force marched towards the camp. On the right the enemy was beaten down from the crests and a formidable road block south of Milestone 109 was stormed. Supported by close attacking R.A.F. fighter-bombers the enemy was routed and in the following bitter battle the camp recaptured.

As they marched on towards Imphal, 17th Indian took with them most of the stores, recovered intact. Increasingly heavy attacks, some with medium tanks, were launched by the Japanese upon the division's rearguard, and every one was bloodily repulsed. Then the advance guards of the two converging divisions met and 17th Indian finally entered Imphal on April 5. Towards the end of their epic fighting march, during which the Japanese never ceased harrying them from the jungle, they had been supplied entirely by air.

The 20th Division had also made a successful fighting withdrawal to the Imphal Plain from Tamu and the head of the Kabaw Valley. On April 2, two brigades stood before Palel to block the south-east approach to Imphal while the third brigade was pulled back into reserve.

As these moves were taken to counter the growing menace to Imphal, the threat to Kohima developed more swiftly than Slim had anticipated. So precipitous were the hills, and so thick the jungle, it was not believed the enemy could send in more than a lightly armed regiment. But it was becoming increasingly apparent that the Japanese had committed almost the entire 31st Division. Hilltop Kohima, with its scratch garrison, and the vital base at Dimapur, virtually undefended, were in dire peril, as were the string of giant American air bases which had recently been constructed along the

Brahmaputra Valley.

Slim urgently ordered 5th Indian Division and 3rd Special Service Brigade of Commandos to be flown in, and 7th Indian to be airlifted immediately from the Arakan. Additionally, he had Wingate's 23 Long Range Penetration Brigade, still in India, despatched by rail to cover Ledo, and ordered up the 2nd British Division from India. The question was, would the reserves arrive in time to stem the Japanese onslaught upon Kohima?

The first shots of this battle were fired by the Assam Regiment and Assam armed police some 30 miles east of Kohima. In action for the first time, these British-officered Assamese fought furiously in their own homeland as they fell back slowly from position to position. They sustained and inflicted heavy casualties and gained vital time by slowing the crack Japanese 31st Division. Meanwhile desperate efforts were being made to convert the leisurely hill station of Kohima into a redoubt strong enough to stem the tide sweeping towards Dimapur. After non-combatants and hospital patients had been hurried away, the 500 soldiers convalescing there were armed. With every available man, some from administrative units, pressed into service, Kohima's garrison numbered 1,000. No less than 15,000 crack Japanese fighting men were closing in upon them.

At this fateful moment, as clerks and storemen helped dig trenches and weapon pits, Colonel H. U. Richards, in command, called in every soldier in the immediate area. Soon he had a battalion of Gurkha recruits, two equally in-experienced Burma Regiment independent companies and one trained combat battalion of the Burma Regiment. Meanwhile at Dimapur, the huge railhead base only 30 miles to the rear, there were no more than 500 among 45,000 on the ration strength who could even handle a rifle. As the Japanese hourly neared Kohima, 161 Brigade of 5th Indian Division was flown in and deployed to hold the Nichugard Pass, eight miles before Dimapur. Slim estimated that the enemy could be attacking there in force, having overrun Kohima, within five days. Still

British infantrymen fire mortar bombs at an invisible enemy position during the confused fighting around Imphal

359

fighting bitterly and sustaining heavy casualties, the gallant Assam battalion which alone stood between the Japanese and Kohima, was now almost exhausted. On April 4 some 200 of the Assamese fell back into Kohima's defences; the remainder managed to retire behind 161 Brigade.

Major-General Sato, commanding the Japanese 31st Division, was in some ways a typical Japanese professional soldier – tough, pitiless and brave, but he was markedly inflexible. His orders were to take Kohima and hold it. He could have easily masked it with a fraction of his force, while his division mopped up the almost helpless main base at Dimapur. As Slim said later, 'Sato was without exception the most un-enterprising of all the Japanese generals I encountered. He had been ordered to take Kohima and dig in. His bullet head was filled with one idea only – to take Kohima.' Sato was just poised to hurl his division in, wave upon wave, at the scantily defended Kohima when Major-General Monty Stopford, commanding 33 Corps, took over direction of the battle.

During the night of April 4 the Japanese charged from the jungle. Bravely though the outposts fought, some of the hill-top positions were overrun. Already the enemy had a foothold upon this frail fortress. But before they could mount a main attack the leading battalion of 161 Brigade, the 4th Royal West Kents, ordered up by Stopford, marched into Kohima. A few hours later, under cover of darkness, a company of Rajputs got in, one platoon returning as escort to 200 walking wounded and non-combatants. They had barely slipped away before the Japanese completed their encirclement of Kohima, whose garrison now numbered 3,500, and cut the Kohima–Imphal road. The greater part of 161 Brigade was prevented from fighting through.

It was indeed fortunate that the R.A.F. had absolute air mastery. All through the daylight hours fighters and fighter-bombers roared down almost to the jungle roof to augment the defenders' fire power. Also they dropped ammunition, medical supplies, food and water to the hard-pressed garrison. Sato was soon deterred from flinging in wave after wave of daylight attacks. So heavy were his casualties that he sent in his reckless infantry only by night; by day he lashed the British positions almost ceaselessly with shells, mortars and machine-gun fire.

The defenders' casualties were also mounting, and they suffered from increasing exhaustion amidst a battlefield where they never dared relax and could not sleep for the unceasing uproar. By April 6 they had fought their way back to the main positions on Garrison Hill. The Japanese had captured their only water supply so that they were completely dependent on the R.A.F.'s low-level drops of water-filled inner tubes. At the beginning they had held an area roughly 1,000 yards square, but now they were fighting desperately from an area half that size. Everywhere around them, on the slopes below and in the jungle-fringed valleys, the Japanese dead lay in swathes. But still they came on.

Little by little, the heroic garrison was forced backwards and inward. The hand-to-hand fighting became constricted to a blood-stained mound known as Summerhouse Hill on the central Garrison Hill. The enemy were so close now that the British fought from one side of the assistant district commissioner's once-immaculate tennis court and the Japanese from the other, lobbing short-fused grenades at each other rather than tennis balls. Yard by yard, each one paid for with scores of dead, the Japanese fought in across the commissioner's garden. As they dug their foxholes, earth scattered into the British trenches. The plight of the wounded was pitiable; their only cover was in hastily dug pits where many were hit again and again. In the British dressing station doctors and orderlies carried on regardless despite three direct hits and the dismembered limbs that littered the floor.

For 16 terrible days the siege of Kohima's reeking hilltop continued with unabated fury. Then strong relief forces began to close in. A brigade of 2nd Division fought up the road against bitter resistance, to break through to 161 Brigade on April 15. When a second brigade followed, a powerful attack with tanks, artillery and air support was made along the road and upon the main dominating ridge. On April 18 it broke through, for a Punjabi battalion to wriggle up through a gulley to join Kohima's

defenders. Next day food and water was taken in to the wild-eyed, bearded survivors who had fought so long against such odds. Two days later men of 2nd Division fought up to the smoking, blasted hilltop to relieve the rest of the garrison.

But although the siege had ended, much bitter fighting was required before the enemy's defeat was complete. They still held deep bunker positions on a dominating jungle-clad ridge 7,000 yards in extent, a forest fortress, whose sides were unscaleable green cliffs of closely crowded trees and undergrowth. Despite determined attacks by formations of 2nd Division, still arriving piecemeal and as yet unaccustomed to jungle warfare, the enemy could not be moved. So long as they held this position they were a constant threat to Dimapur–Imphal communications. A brigade of 7th Indian had now arrived to cover Dimapur, and the Chindit Brigade had been despatched south-east towards Jessami to block

Japanese reinforcements and supplies from the Chindwin.

Bitter and bloody fighting ensued as the 2nd Division endeavoured to drive the Japanese from the ridge and fought off ferocious night counter-attacks upon ravaged Garrison Hill. Both sides had fought nearly to a standstill by April 30, and a lull ensued in which the British gathered themselves for a final assault. Heavy rain now rendered the steep terrain so treacherous that a full divisional attack by 2nd Division could not be put in until May 3. Artillery was massed and tanks brought up to add weight to the attack.

The steaming jungle-clad hills of Kohima trembled to a new frenzy of battle as Japanese bunkers and gunpits were stormed. Everywhere the panting attackers were lashed by a murderous crossfire from scores of hidden hilltop positions. By nightfall only a section of one dominating ridge had been attained and the British soldiers grimly clung on cheek-by-jowl

with Japanese. But the enemy had also sustained grievous casualties. On May 7 Stopford sent in his corps reserve, 7th Indian's 33 Brigade, to attack a bunker-riddled eminence called Jail Hill. This attack was repelled. Three nights later, 33 Brigade again stormed Jail Hill, while the British 2nd Division attacked enfilading ridges, and finally, at considerable cost, a large part of the hill was captured. Next day, reinforcements clambered up under cover of a smokescreen, a Japanese minefield was cleared and, as the hot sun crusted the mud that had hitherto precluded their use, tanks began to crawl up.

Early on May 13 the surviving enemy finally gave way and fell back leaving the smoking air stinking with their dead. Soon the remaining heights of Kohima, including the whole blood-soaked area that had been elegant bungalow, garden and tennis court, were cleared of the enemy. Many who would not surrender were despatched deep down in their bunkers by point-blank tank guns, or by high-explosive charges thrust down on the end of bamboo poles. Others who broke cover at close quarters were shot or bayonetted. None tried to surrender. But the Japanese had reached the farthest point on their triumphant March on Delhi.

While victory was being snatched from near-disaster at Kohima, the siege of Imphal had been building up to formidable proportions. To the nervous viewing this swelling battle from afar it seemed that yet again a British force was being ominously enveloped by Japanese attackers – this time a whole army hell-bent on the invasion of India.

There were six obvious routes through which the enemy could burst into the wide plain of Imphal. Two were from the north, one of these down the broad road from Kohima and the other along a track that followed the valley of the River Iril. A third was down the Ukhrul road in the north-east; a fourth from the west along the Silchar–Bishenpur track; a fifth from the south-east along the well metalled Tamu–Palel road and the sixth was up the broad, undulating Tiddim jungle highway. The Japanese decided to advance along all of these and to reinforce success as soon as achieved.

Although the main Japanese onslaughts were made through these entries, which admitted tanks, guns and vehicles, fighting flared furiously all around the perimeter. When a headlong assault down a road was halted, then the Japanese spread out into the jungle each side and continued to try to fight and ferret through. Time and again suicidally aggressive attacks forced bulges in the defences, some up to two miles in depth, but always a determined counter-attack drove them back. No quarter was expected, or given, by either side.

Despite the superficial pattern imposed by the six roads, the overall battle of Imphal was one of the greatest confusion. Each time a massive Japanese blow appeared to threaten a breakthrough, it was immediately countered by massed artillery and squadrons of tanks swiftly switched to the danger area. And always each and every emergence of the Japanese from jungle to plain brought down upon them the bombs and bullets of the R.A.F.

During the first week of April soldiers of 5th Indian Division, who had leaped straight from air transports into action on the Ukhrul road,

*Above* Japanese soldiers retreating from Imphal as the 14th Army goes over to attack are seen crossing a river. Those in the foreground have commandeered a native boat

*Opposite page* Although this Japanese tank was only a miniature one, it was ideal for fighting in the thick jungle. This was one of a number abandoned by the enemy as they withdrew from Imphal

had with the aid of formations of 23rd Division battered an encroaching Japanese column back to Litan. But though held there, the enemy increased pressure in the north so that the victors of Ukhrul road were threatened in the rear. On April 6 the Japanese captured one of the peaks of the twin-peaked hill at Nungshigum. This was of the greatest value for it gave them artillery observation of the R.A.F.'s main airstrip. They gained the other peak five days later, and swiftly constructed formidable bunkers on each. But bombers clipping the tree tops bombed and strafed both peaks; tanks were somehow winched up to blast the bunkers point-blank, while infantry plunged in with great determination. By the end of the battle every single Japanese soldier was a corpse because not one would surrender.

Having cleared the Nungshigum peaks, 5th Indian hurried to deal with a mounting danger from the north along the Iril Valley. Meanwhile the savage battle they had just fought was being repeated time and again all around the perimeter.

Admiral Mountbatten decreed that the counter-attack
should be pressed home even though the monsoon had
begun, something which had not been done before in
the Burma campaign. Here a British patrol crosses
flooded paddy-fields as the 14th Army inexorably
keeps the enemy in retreat

In their initial assault the Japanese had occupied in force a jungle-covered spur thrusting between the Iril Valley and the Imphal–Kohima road and dominating the north-western area of the plain. This dangerous salient was the scene of heavy fighting from mid-April until the end of the first week of May. The Japanese were eventually beaten back from the southern end of the spur, which had given them observation over the plain. During the same period a British brigade fought through the hills south of the Ukhrul road, driving the enemy before it, while another brigade hammered up the road to meet them. By mid-May the enemy onslaughts both up the Ukhrul road and down the Iril Valley had been met, held, and savagely battered back. At the same time men of the 20th Division had obtained the ascendancy over crack Japanese jungle troops along the Palel road approach, a most difficult front of alternate abrupt ridges and deep folds enshrouded in a green gloom of jungle.

To hold this 25-mile stretch of tortuous terrain only two brigades were available, so there could be no continuous line. The British therefore dug in across the approach tracks and trails and the Palel road itself, at the same time manning all the commanding heights. In between they maintained continuous fighting patrols to challenge all Japanese infiltrations, and from the beginning of April there was ceaseless hand-to-hand combat amidst the jungle. General Mutaguchi had marked the Sheam Pass on the Palel road on his war map as the place for a decisive breakthrough and concentrated armour and heavy artillery to blast through. By April 11 the British had been forced back at Tengoupal immediately overlooking the main road. Although a furious counter-attack flung the enemy out, five days later a considerably reinforced Japanese counter-blow drove through at a weak point held by an inexperienced Indian unit.

Sensing a success to exploit, the enemy attack mounted to a crescendo. During the night of April 19 three successive onslaughts, in which medium tanks were used, were all smashed. But continuous Japanese attacks on April 22 finally penetrated dangerously, though at such cost that they could not push on any farther.

The Japanese encroachments into the hills around the Palel road entry were successively liquidated by May 8 by a brigade of 17th Indian.

But General Yamamoto, the Japanese commander immediately responsible, believing he was on the verge of success, had already called up heavy reinforcements to blast through at Tengoupal. A series of ferocious night attacks finally achieved a measure of success, and the British line was drawn back. Undeniably, the Japanese were on the point of a breakthrough, but on May 12 a counter-attack regained most of the ground. During an ensuing lull General Scoones withdrew the 20th Division formations who had held the Palel front and replaced them with the full-strength 23 Division. The crisis was over; the front was secure once more.

During this same period the fighting along and around the Tiddim road and the Silchar–Bishenpur track reached its highest pitch. In a courageous night foray some Japanese managed to blow a 100-yard-long suspension bridge carrying the track over an 80-foot-deep chasm to cut the main line of supply. This was followed by a succession of strong Japanese raids converging upon Bishenpur and, with the danger obviously mounting, General Scoones switched 17th Indian from north of Imphal. They arrived in the nick of time on April 19 to engage a powerful enemy force north-west of Bishenpur, and held it.

The Japanese next flung in a strong attack south of Bishenpur, and achieved some penetration. A succession of British counter-attacks resulted in some of the bloodiest fighting of the battle. The Japanese used every man and every weapon they could bring to bear, including waves of strafing Zeroes – half of them shot down by anti-aircraft fire – and for the first time batteries of 10-inch mortars. On this sector now occurred something of great significance – several deserters, the first known, came in from the Japanese lines. They revealed that one spearheading regiment of the formidable 33rd Division had lost over 2,000 of its 3,000 men. However, there were also signs of considerable Japanese reinforcements to this particular battle so that British anxiety continued.

While fighting raged at Bishenpur, strong enemy formations detached from the original Kohima attack force had swung south down the Kohima–Imphal road towards a 14th Army supply depot at Kanglatongbi. There they were attacked by a brigade of 17th Indian supported by tanks. By the end of the first week in May the brigade was beginning to invest Kanglatongbi, when it was relieved by 5th Indian and switched to the Bishenpur fighting. Strengthened by a brigade of 7th Indian, 5th Indian mounted a purposeful assault and by May 21 recaptured the depot almost intact.

The monsoon's first thunder was muttering among the hills, and increasingly frequent, heavy, rain showers were making the going treacherous. Unless the Japanese could achieve victory in a final all-out assault these ominous rumblings foretold their failure. From Slim's point of view the great battle of attrition that had frustrated the enemy's intent was nearing its close. Along every possible axis of advance the Japanese had been checked, and even in the still anxious Bishenpur sector they were staunchly held. Slim began to plan his own offensive, intending not only to relieve Imphal but to annihilate the invading Japanese 15th Army.

The first move of the British offensive was actually made on May 15, when 48 Brigade of 17th Indian struck into the rear of the Japanese 33rd Division and dug in at Milestone 33 on the Tiddim–Imphal road. The enemy reacted angrily and flung in piecemeal attacks with every available formation, including administrative troops. After four days the Japanese 15th Division mounted a furious assault, but this too was blasted back. The British brigade then advanced northwards to Moirang and after fierce fighting established another roadblock, but failed to trap the Japanese 33rd Division.

The 14th Army offensive was next stepped up on the Ukhrul road and down the Iril Valley, coinciding with yet another enemy attempt to batter into the plain from Sangshak along the Ukhrul road. The monsoon had started in earnest, and everywhere cascading rain was turning tracks into slithering ribbons of mud and the jungle into a steaming green hell. Through the foetid, corpse-littered undergrowth Japanese fighting men pressed forward, with all available transport, including pack-mules, lined behind them right back to the Chindwin. The British 20th Division clashed head-on with this force, and yet again savage fighting swayed back and forth, both on the Ukhrul road and in the surrounding jungle. But by June 13 the British had mastered the enemy and they were disintegrating everywhere. Other 14th Army men sloshing from Nungshigum up the muddy Iril

Valley were striking into the Japanese lines of communication, and by June 20 had blocked their main supply route. The Japanese were now in a desperate predicament because all subsidiary tracks were impassable.

To the north, around Kohima, the almost ceaseless fighting since the raising of the siege had reached a point where the enemy were surrounded but defiant in well-nigh impregnable hilltop bunker fortresses. Beneath the downpour, the precipitous jungle-shrouded hills, rising almost sheer for 3,000 feet or more, had become so slippery as to be almost unclimbable. Concentrated against the Japanese skyline fortifications were troops of the 5th and 7th Indian Divisions and the Chindit 23rd Long Range Penetration Brigade.

The Chindits, despite the awful conditions, had circled through the trackless Naga Hills to cut the Japanese communications and threaten them from the rear. They had received invaluable aid from the Naga hillmen, led by British political officers of the Indian Civil Service. The key to the battle here was Naga Village, a cluster of deep bunkers on the crest of a steep, slippery eminence strongly held by Japanese soldiers prepared to fight to the death.

The 7th Indian set out to capture this key position in thick dawn mists. Explosive charges thrust in on long poles, and the searing inrush of flame throwers, liquidated the Japanese bunkers one by one. The final desperate resistance on a hillock known as Church Knoll was overcome by Gurkhas in a tremendous night attack up a precipitous jungle track. The enemy's communications were now irreparably cut: their own tactics had been turned against them. They withdrew without further resistance.

It was apparent that the Japanese retreat down the main road from Kohima was planned to keep pace with the force falling back down the Chakabana–Mao–Songsang track, a tortuous jungle way along the crest of the watershed between Kohima and Imphal. With this realization, forward troops of the 2nd Division advanced to reach Mao simultaneously with a brigade of 7th Indian on June 19.

Ukhrul was the focal point of the British drive, for it was the Japanese army's great mountain base between Chindwin and Imphal, rapidly developed there after battle was joined. The strong surge of the British forces down from

CHINA

Yunnan

Dimapur

Laung Chaung

Kohima

Myitkyina

Assam

Ukhrul

Tonzang

Mogaung

*Chindwin*

Homalin

Imphal

Silchar

Palel

Pinlebu

*Irrawaddy*

Bishenpur

Tamu

Mawlaik

Eastern
Bengal

Tiddim

Kalewa

Thabeikkyin

Myinmu

Ye-U-

Lashio

Chittagong

Monywa

Shwebo

Gangaw

Myingyan

Mandalay

Maymyo

Pagan

BURMA

Pauk

Meiktila

Buthidaung

Thazi

Pakokku

Chauk

Pyawbwe

Maungdaw

Seikpyu

Yamethin

Akyab Island

Pyinmana

Yenanyaung

Myothit

*Arakan*

Toungoo

Prome

Penwegan

*Salween*

Pegu

Bay of Bengal

Rangoon

Moulmein

THAILAND

*Gulf of Siam*

**Imphal and Rangoon**

Kohima was timed to synchronize with and meet a powerful thrust out from Imphal itself. Each was one jaw of a steel trap which on June 22 shut at Milestone 109. Caught in it was the 15th Japanese Division and, in Ukhrul itself, a brigade of the Indian National Army. Along the approaches to their main base, various Japanese columns straggled, and from the north, dragging their agonized way along a slimy jeep track to Ukhrul, came the starving, sick and dying men who had once been the crack Japanese 31st Division. Also converging, strongly and inexorably, on Ukhrul was a brigade of 7th Indian, bypassing the enemy to attack from the south-west, while Messervy's 33 Brigade made an amazing march through the cloud-swathed peaks of Mao Songsang to attack from the north.

Colonel Lewis Pugh of 33 Brigade afterwards wrote:

'The brigade had placed itself between the Japanese garrisons retreating with their large attendant bodies of sick and dying and their immediate goal, Ukhrul. No hope remained, no food, no medicine, nothing could now reach them. Too weak to struggle onwards, their mouths filled with the grass with which they tried to keep alive the last sparks of life. . . they died now in thousands. The brigade and its artillery marched slowly and painfully on, digging its way uphill step by step, and sliding down the muddy slopes. Six mountain ranges had been crossed, each entailing an ascent and descent of more than 4,000 feet in under ten miles. . .

The brigade crossed the Ganjan Lok Gorge and moved cautiously forward along the Ukhrul ridge itself. Here they met the first sights of the destruction wrought on the Japanese. A fighter-bomber strike had evidently caught a Japanese column moving up the track. The road was thick with dead Japanese, animals, and littered with arms and equipment, its surface pock-marked with the strike of machine-gun and cannon fire from the attacking aircraft. The brigade passed through and round deserted camps of leafy huts, concealed strongpoints, living accommodation for thousands. Unburied dead lay everywhere, many untouched, some fat and well-looking, others emaciated, filthy skeletons. Typhus, that scourge of armies, had done its worst. The miscalculations of the administrative requirements, under-estimation of the fighting qualities of the troops seasoned in

While the shattered Japanese army was pulling back to try to re-group to fight another big battle, air attacks were intensified on the enemy's vital supply bases. These Liberator bombers are heading for the major port of Rangoon in the south

the bitter winter's fighting in the Arakan and on the beaches of Dunkirk, in North Africa and Madagascar, had led to the Japanese undoing.

Naga tribesmen started bringing in Japanese prisoners too sick to move, filthy skeletons, raving, weeping and jibbering in their madness, the ultimate resistance of their minds broken by the unspeakable hardships to which their bodies had been subjected. . . From the jungle camps

lining the road, from nullahs, and valleys lived in by the Japanese, rose the stench of putrefaction. At the side of the road, or fallen down the hillsides, lay lorries and cars, their drivers dead at the wheel or lying in the mud beside their vehicles.

In the foot-deep mud of the track floated dead Japanese and the carcasses of animals. Equipment lay everywhere, the unseemly evidence of the rout. A field-gun was found buried, a tank stuck in the mud, its crew dead inside it. Shells, mines, small-arms and the inevitable gas masks lay everywhere in innumerable quantities. Along a thousand jungle paths the sick and battered remnants of the would-be conquerors

of India struggled painfully southwards, dying in thousands at the sides of the dank and uncharted jungle tracks, the victims of the greatest defeat of the war suffered by the Japanese.'

While 7th Indian pressed the enemy back towards the now raging River Chindwin, 23rd Division determinedly attacked to the south. At the same time 17th Division closed in. Guns were massed to blast with tumultuous connonades trees and bushes, wet earth and mangled Japanese. For weeks the killing went on, until the last Japanese bunkers had been shattered and 50,000 Japanese dead had been counted on the battlefield. How many more thousands rotted in the jungle no one will ever know.

# 12. Normandy

# 12. Normandy

On the restless, blustery night of June 5, 1944 – four years almost to the day after the last British soldier had escaped across the Channel from Dunkirk – the mightiest invasion armada the world had ever known put out from the southern shores of England.

This Anglo–American fleet that was to seal the doom of Nazi Germany had been organized by that same admiral, Sir Bertram Ramsay, who had so brilliantly contrived the evacuation of Dunkirk. It numbered 5,000 vessels, many designed specially for this day, and was spearheaded by hundreds of heavy R.A.F. bombers and 23,000 paratroopers and glider-borne shocktroops to seize vital bridges and roads. Close behind were assault troops numbering 176,000, with 20,000 vehicles, all to be landed on the coast of Normandy within 48 hours.

This invasion across the English Channel was an extremely hazardous operation. Apart from the risks run in the actual assault upon Hitler's Fortress Europe, the crossing of almost 100 miles of treacherous sea was in itself fraught with danger. At the end of that crossing the assault craft bearing the troops which were to seize the beachhead, and the amphibious 'swimming' tanks with them, had to come in on a tide attaining half-flood 40 minutes after first light. Such a tide provided the very minimum period required by the attendant warships and warplanes to blast the bristling coast defences. Moonlight in the hours immediately before this full tide was also required so that the airborne troops could identify their targets. A combination of such

conditions only occurred for three days in each lunar month. In June, 1944, those days were the fifth to the seventh. If the Allies did not launch a successful invasion of the continent then they were not likely to have sufficient time to exploit a landing before winter's onset. In addition, they would be too late to prevent the massive bombardment of London and the invasion ports by Hitler's devilish secret weapons called V1 and V2.

It had been estimated by the Allied planners that within the first week the Germans would be able to move against the beachhead at least 18 divisions, including 6 armoured. Within a month they would be likely to concentrate around 40 of the 59 divisions stationed in France and the Low Countries, while the Allies were expecting to have only 37 divisions in action inside seven weeks. The main restrictions on the rapid reinforcing of the invasion were of course logistical. Until the Allies had captured a usable port everything would have to be landed

*Above* General Montgomery, Lieutenant-General Miles Dempsey and General Omar Bradley in Normandy. General Dempsey commanded the British 2nd Army in the invasion

*Top* Rommel inspecting the defences of the Atlantic wall early in 1944. Under his command they were made much more formidable

*Bottom* The Allied chiefs pictured in invasion headquarters shortly before D-Day. Front Row: Tedder, Eisenhower, Montgomery. Back Row: Bradley, Ramsey, Leigh-Mallory, Bodell Smith

on the open beaches. Even with the two brilliantly contrived, artificial, Mulberry harbours, secretly prefabricated in sections all over England, it was touch and go whether the invading force could be built up fast enough to hold, let alone smash the inevitable counter-attacks.

As the hour of invasion loomed the Germans had massed 41 divisions in northern France and the Low Countries; 18 further divisions were poised south of the Loire to surge northwards. The 15th Army, with 19 divisions, was positioned around Calais and Boulogne, where the invasion was expected. The 7th Army, of 10 divisions, was in Normandy. They had a further 56 divisions in southern Europe, and 18 on guard in Scandinavia. Thus, of all their divisions in the field, the Germans had 133 confronting the Allies to the 165 engaged against the Russians. Of their 32 Panzer divisions, 18 still faced the Russians while 12 were committed against any Anglo–American invasion of France. Curiously, in view of the bitter lessons they had taught their adversaries about the power of massed armour, the Panzer divisions in the west were scattered from Belgium to Bordeaux.

However unpopular with the American chiefs of staff, the British strategy of attacking Europe's 'soft underbelly' had compelled the Germans to maintain strategic reserves south of the Alpine mountain ranges instead of within Germany, where the splendid autobahns – built for just this purpose – permitted the swift switching of forces eastwards or westwards as events dictated. And on the eve of the cross-channel invasion, Hitler had ordered a crack Panzer division from Normandy to Italy, to shore up the disintegrating German front there.

Developments at sea and in the air during the preceding months had made invasion possible. The Battle of the Atlantic had been won and the U-boats cleared from the sea lanes across which troops, arms and supplies were pouring in from the New World. The Allied air forces had won command of the air and smashed many of the factories that supplied the Luftwaffe. During April and May, 1944, they had shattered the road and rail routes which the Germans required to bring in forces for counter-attacks. No less than 1,500 of the 2,000 railway locomotives available had been knocked out. Many bridges – including 18 of the 24 over the Seine between Paris and the sea, and most bridges across the Loire – had been destroyed. Crossings, marshalling yards and other installations had been effectively bombed. Allied bombers and rocket-firing fighters had knocked out nearly all the German radar stations along the Channel coast from Calais to Guernsey to prevent them giving warning of an approaching invasion.

The Allies had achieved their objective of creating a 'railway desert' in northern France, while ensuring that the pattern of destruction gave no clue to where the invasion might strike. Indeed at this time, and for seven weeks after the Normandy landings, the German High Command believed that the main invasion would come across the narrow Straits of Dover. On the assumption that the Normandy assault was a diversion, the highly trained 15th Army was kept up along the Pas de Calais.

For many weeks before D-Day (and for more than six weeks afterwards) the British mounted an elaborate and successful plan of deception, which included the massing of a dummy invasion fleet, and radio messages simulating the assembling of an invasion H.Q. in Kent. The dashing American general, George Patton, whom German Intelligence had identified as the man chosen to lead the main Allied armoured onslaught, appeared conspicuously in Kent. In fact, the transports were massing in Southampton and ports along the south-west coast. On the very night of the Normandy invasion the R.A.F. deceived the few surviving German coastal radar stations by simulating an eastward-bound convoy off Dieppe with scattered streams of tin-foil strips known as 'window'.

The German troops massed along France's northern coast were backed by the formidable fortifications of Hitler's vaunted Atlantic Wall. The energetic Field-Marshal Rommel, switched to this front in January under Field-Marshal von Rundstedt, the supreme commander in the west, had lost no time in preparing a hostile reception for his vanquishers in Africa. With a work force of half a million slave labourers he had constructed a forest of steel-and-concrete wrecking devices under water and along the heavily mined beaches. Beyond them were deep-dug gun emplacements covering every conceivable landing place, tank traps, festoons of barbed wire, fortified weapon pits and thick-walled pillboxes. Behind the coast lay minefields, and still farther back forests of posts had been planted

A German picture of part of the Atlantic wall

across the flat fields to wreck any airborne landings. To add to the difficulties of airborne assault, the flat, marshy lands behind the Normandy coast had been extensively flooded, particularly around the base of the Cotentin peninsula, below the major port of Cherbourg.

Rommel aimed to defeat any Allied invasion on the beaches; as Montgomery put it, 'He'll do his best to Dunkirk us'. Montgomery, commanding the Anglo–American invasion force, drew upon the Allies' bitter lessons at Salerno and Anzio when he briefed his com-

manders. 'Armoured columns must penetrate deep inland and quickly on D-Day. . . We must gain space rapidly and peg claims well inland'. But however brilliant the Allied invasion plan, the final intangible of the weather on the chosen day was an uncontrollable yet vital factor.

As D-Day, for which June 5 had been named, drew nearer, the fine, sunny days of May gave place to dull, rainy weather. Weatherships and aircraft out in the Atlantic reported depressions approaching, with accompanying high winds and low cloud. The experts predicted that these depressions would envelop the Channel area all

through June 5 to 7, and that the sailing of the invasion fleet would be highly dangerous. When the first-wave troops had already embarked on June 4, the weather worsened to a storm, and General Dwight D. Eisenhower, the supreme commander, had no option but to postpone the invasion. Nevertheless, with the wind-lashed Channel still turbulent, that night the meteorologists gave reason to hope the storm might decrease sufficiently for landings next day. On the strength of this forecast, Eisenhower ordered the invasion fleet to sail.

As the vast and varied fleet pitched and yawed out into the broad channels which had been cleared by navy minesweepers from the Isle of Wight to the Normandy coast, the heavy bombers of the R.A.F. thundered over to blast the enemy coastal guns and defences with 5,200 tons of bombs. When the grey, blustery dawn of June 6 broke, American medium bom-

Anti-aircraft guns on the Atlantic wall open fire

bers and fighter-bombers continued the pounding. Meanwhile Allied fighting men had already landed in north-west Europe, one British and two American airborne divisions being launched behind the Atlantic Wall between midnight and 3 a.m. The British 6th Airborne Division went down east of Caen, on the eastern flank of the invasion front, and the Americans dropped out of the sky upon the Cotentin peninsula at the western end.

The British were to seize vital bridgeheads over the River Orne between Caen and the coast. The Americans were to engage enemy troops on the peninsula, prevent them counterattacking the American landing beaches and secure causeways through the floods north of Carentan to admit the seaborne invaders.

British paratroops photographed just before they took off to spearhead the Normandy invasion

The beaches chosen for the American landings were from half-way down the eastern coast of the Cotentin peninsula eastwards to Port-en-Bessin. From west to east they were called Utah and Omaha beaches. The beaches selected for the British extended eastwards from Port-en-Bessin to Ouistreham and were called Gold, Juno and Sword beaches. Each front was approximately 25 miles long. The American assault was by their 1st Army under Lieutenant General Omar Bradley; the British by their 2nd Army under Lieutenant-General Miles Dempsey.

First of all, and even before the enemy realized what was happening, the flanks of the beachhead had to be secured by the British 6th Airborne Division and the American 82nd and 101st Airborne Divisions. The eastern flank was the most vital, because it was near the main counter-attack force of Panzers. Unless the armoured divisions were held off until the invaders had landed in considerable force with tanks and guns, the bridgehead could be swiftly wiped out. There was a natural barrier against Panzers on this left flank in the River

377

Gliders used by British and American airborne troops who landed in Normandy during the dark hours before D-Day dawned

Orne and the canal that ran parallel with it for eight miles from the historic town of Caen to the sea. If the bridges over the Orne and the canal could be seized at the outset and barred to the enemy, then that flank would be reasonably secure and there would be an outlet for British armour from the beachhead to Caen and the open ground beyond. Additionally, six miles east of the Orne, the River Dives flowed through a valley deliberately flooded by the Germans: if the five bridges across the Dives were blown up those inundations could be turned against the enemy as a barrier to their Panzers.

Similarly, the American sky troops were to disrupt counter-attacks on the right flank. The Germans had created a lake, over a mile wide, from the River Vire and Carentan Canal, behind their defences amidst the dunes beyond Utah beach. Ten miles west and south-west of Utah there were more extensive inundations in the valleys of the Merderet and Douve, forming a wide water barrier almost to the west coast of the Cotentin peninsula. Unless the American

airborne troops captured the five narrow causeways that led out from Utah beach the landing force was in grave danger of being trapped and destroyed between sea and inland floods. The danger increased when a crack German division, trained to deal with airborne landings, moved into the area two weeks before D-Day.

This called for a revision of Montgomery's original plan for the American airborne division to be dropped right across the neck of the Cotentin peninsula, to isolate Cherbourg. Bradley now ordered that formations of 101st Division should concentrate on seizing the exits of the causeway from Utah beach, silence a heavy battery there, and destroy road and rail bridges over the Douve to hold a line along that river and the Carentan Canal. The 82nd Division was to drop south and west of Sainte-Mère-Eglise on both sides of the Merderet River, to blow two bridges over the Douve and continue the southern flank protection afforded by the 101st farther west. They were also to hold bridges across the Merderet until the main force was ready to break out southwards.

Shortly before midnight on June 5 the windy skies over southern England reverberated to the roar of 1,100 transport planes which had risen from 20 different airfields. Two hours later scores of gliders behind their growling aircraft tugs winged south with shock-troops specially trained to seize vital objectives. They took with them the anti-tank guns which would be needed to hold the captured bridges against the Panzers.

Although many paratroopers were blown eastwards of the dropping zones, the assault from the sky by the leading British parachute brigades achieved both surprise and success. They drove the enemy from the village of Ranville, near the river and canal bridges, and secured the main landing area for the gliders with the anti-tank guns. The gliders crash-landed almost upon the bridges, which were quickly seized and, all but one, destroyed. The bridge they missed was the most important one at Troarn. But a major and seven men of the Royal Engineers who had landed some miles from their objective drove hell-for-leather with automatics blazing through enemy strongpoints and Troarn itself to blow the bridge.

While all this was going on, 150 paratroopers stormed a coastal battery at Merville covering

As British paratroops hold their precarious bridgehead against mounting German attacks, supplies are dropped to them from Stirling bombers

Sword beach. After a hand-to-hand fight with 180 German defenders in surrounding fortifications they destroyed the guns, though at the cost of half their numbers. On the American flank, mass parachute drops through scudding clouds in the teeth of the driving wind went less well. Heavy flak caused many pilots to fly too high, too fast and too erratically for accurate jumping. Only 20 of the 805 American transport planes were lost, but the 101st Division was scattered over an area 25 miles by 15. At first light little more than 1,000 of the division's 6,600 fighting men had reached their rendezvous. The 82nd Division had better luck, swiftly concentrating on the ground to capture Sainte-Mère-Eglise within two hours and bestraddle the main Cherbourg–Carentan road. However,

only 22 of the 52 gliders with the anti-tank guns, vehicles and signals equipment came down within the selected landing zone. Consequently, the troops were short of the heavier weapons to hold off enemy armour. They failed to capture the bridges across the Merderet and the division was split into two by the floods.

The vast majority of the paratroops dropped west of the Merderet were widely scattered over terrain bristling with strongpoints manned by the German 91st Infantry Division. They were immediately engaged in brutal fighting in which they were necessarily concerned more with their very survival than attaining their objective. As a result the bridges across the Douve remained unblown and no bridgehead was formed west of the Merderet to guard the crossings. Nevertheless, although 82nd Division failed in these objectives, its scattered formations attacked so resolutely that the German 91st Division became fully engaged where it stood.

It was lucky for 101st Airborne that the countryside of orchards, little fields and high hedges over which they were so widely distributed was not heavily defended. They had time to find each other, often as individuals, until in little groups and squads they converged upon the rendezvous. By dawn they had concentrated sufficiently to seize all the western causeway exits from Utah beach. To the south, however, they had not been able to blow the river and canal bridge.

Although the Germans had known that an invasion was imminent, they were taken by surprise. The stormy weather had proved to be a blessing in disguise. Certain that no landings could be attempted with such high seas running, three of the senior commanders were away from their headquarters, including Rommel himself.

American paratroopers, some of them mounted on farm horses they have 'borrowed', enter Sainte-Mère-Eglise, one of their main objectives

Only von Rundstedt and General Geyr von Schweppenburg, commander of Panzer Group West, were where they should have been, and both were hamstrung by higher authority. Rundstedt was not permitted to commit strategic reserves without High Command's authority, and Geyr had no direct operational command. As a result, when Major-General Feuchtinger, commanding 21st Panzer Division, reported to Rommel's Army Group B headquarters at 1 a.m. on June 6 that paratroops were landing around Troarn, he received no orders to move his tanks forward from Falaise where they were concentrated. All Feuchtinger could do in the event was obey standing orders and send his two most forward infantry battalions against the invaders. It was not until about 6.30 a.m. that sanction was given for the Panzers to move. Another two hours elapsed – bombing had interrupted communications – before permission was given to Feuchtinger to attack. Meanwhile, on his own initiative, he had despatched battle groups including tanks against the paratroops.

The first intimation of a seaborne landing reached von Rundstedt's H.Q. at 2.45 a.m. with a report, 'Engine noises audible from the sea on east coast of Cotentin'. The response to this was, 'Commander-in-Chief West does not consider this to be a major operation'. The Germans felt certain that they would be forewarned by radar stations of any Allied invasion attempt, but the few that were not already knocked out were nearly all effectively jammed. Thus when the Germans first became aware of the proximity of the invading force the troops were already taking to the landing craft 12 miles from the shore.

The confusion of the German Command was so great during those dark early hours of June 6 that when Hitler was asked by Rundstedt's chief of staff for authority to launch 21st S.S. Panzers and the Panzer Lehr divisions against the airborne landings, he forbade any move of this strategic reserve until daylight reconnaissance had clarified the position. He believed that the assault from the skies upon Normandy was a diversion to draw down the reserves while a main sea invasion was attempted north of the Seine.

This view was held not only by Hitler, but at High Command and at Rommel's H.Q., even while the Allies were bombarding the Normandy coast from 143 British and Canadian warships, including 4 battleships, 21 cruisers, 116 destroyers and 2 monitors; and 46 American vessels including 3 battleships, 3 cruisers and 40 destroyers; plus 3 cruisers and 8 destroyers from other Allied navies.

The Allies were short of landing craft for the Normandy invasion, partly because the U.S. Navy was giving priority to the Pacific theatre, and also because British shipyards had been working on the Mulberry harbours. This brilliant conception had first been considered for the Indian Ocean after the loss of Singapore, and the disastrous assault on Dieppe in 1942

had proved that no Channel port could be seized and immediately used to land a powerful invasion force. Churchill had suggested a prefabricated harbour as early as 1917, for seizing the German Frisian Islands. Afterwards Mountbatten's experts had developed the idea. It was brought to spectacular fruition in readiness for the Normandy invasion, with two prefabricated harbours each the size of that of Dover. They comprised concrete caissons which, when put together, formed outer and inner breakwaters, and four floating piers to run right into the beaches. They provided facilities for the direct unloading at the pierheads of everything the invaders were likely to need to maintain their attack.

The Allies had plenty more surprises for the Germans on D-Day, not the least being a variety of specialized tanks designed to overcome minefields, obstacles and concrete fortifications. Since 1943 the British 79th Armoured Division had been an experimental formation working out ideas for all kinds of ingenious armoured vehicles: amphibious tanks, flame-throwing tanks, bull-dozing tanks, and many others. While the swimming tanks and the first infantry went ashore, the Allies were equipped with multiple rocket vessels, and artillery and mortars at the bows of landing craft. This was to give them close fire-cover throughout the dangerous period when the enemy would be manning their guns again in the lull after the naval bombardment.

The sea was heaving sickeningly, a cold wind lashing the invaders with spray, as they went in soon after dawn. The German soldiers had been prepared for a preliminary massive bombardment by sea and air. The immensely thick concrete fortifications gave them confidence to face it. But they had expected to be confronted next with invading troops at their most vulnerable – struggling in through the surf and stumbling ashore. They had not reckoned with tanks actually swimming in from the sea, nor on a furious barrage of shells and rockets from the landing craft themselves, nor yet on such armoured engines of war as now came at them, exploding minefields and destroying gun emplacements and defence positions point-blank. The invaders were swiftly on the firm beaches, without the German artillery or anti tank and machine-guns being able to fire upon them.

*Above* American troops going ashore under fire on one of their invasion beaches

*Opposite, top* British Commandos swarm ashore from landing craft on D-Day

*Opposite, bottom* Some of the first wave of the British invasion force – a number have already been wounded – landing on D-Day

The defenders were prevented by the thickness of their protective concrete from traversing their guns. They had been designed to deal with an invasion at high tide, and the attacking troops had landed at half-tide. By the time the charging infantry had reached the high-water mark, where they should have been helplessly slaughtered, the German defences were already hotly engaged by armour.

The immediate task confronting the 1st British Corps, commanded by Lieutenant-General J. T. Crocker, was formidable. It was – and the whole success of the invasion depended on it – to fight through to join the 6th Airborne Division beyond the River Orne, and there to hold on at all costs against the 21st Panzers known to be in and around Caen, and the 12th S.S. Panzer Division, between Evreux and Gacé.

It was Montgomery's plan for the British sector to engage, hold and destroy the bulk of the German armoured divisions while the Americans overran the Cotentin peninsula. They were to capture Cherbourg, build up their strength, and finally break out to deliver a devastating hook around the Germans across the excellent tank country south and south-east.

The British 3rd Division came in on Sword beach, near the mouth of the Orne, behind a concentrated bombardment that made the ground shudder three miles inland, where the airborne troops were holding the eastern flank. Behind armoured assault units and amphibious tanks, the first infantry assault crossed the foreshore on which so many had expected to die, and within an hour was through exits opened up for tanks to push inland at their head.

They were nearly two miles in before they were halted by infantry and self-propelled 88-mms of 21st Panzer. After the impetus which had taken them clear of the dreaded beaches, the 3rd Division did not thrust on as swiftly as it might. The men had been thoroughly trained for the assault landing on a fire-swept beach, but were less sure what to do if they survived it. They dug in to meet the expected counter-attack, and consequently lost momentum. Eight hours were to elapse before the 3rd Division linked up with the paratroops. More dash was shown, however, by 1st Special Service Brigade of Commandos and Royal Engineer bridging tanks. They plunged forward through Colleville, to join the 6th Airborne on the Orne by 1.30 p.m. Behind them, on the beaches and the roads immediately beyond the shore, an increasing traffic jam of arriving troops and vehicles hampered the armour trying to thrust towards Caen.

Farther west on the British sector the assault was made by 30 Corps comprising 50th, 51st and 7th Armoured Divisions – all of them battle-proven in North Africa. The 50th Division and 8th Armoured Brigade went in on Gold Beach and fought through the enemy defences within an hour. Renewed impetus was given by the follow-up brigade at 11 a.m. By noon the beachhead was two and a half miles deep and three miles wide. By last light the British infantry and tanks, behind a thundering barrage from destroyers and support craft, had cleared two miles of coastal fortifications towards Arromanches and had seized this village and anchorage.

They now had the selected site for one of the Mulberry harbours. Word was sent to begin towing its giant sections across. Troops of 30 Corps continued heavy pressure inland to

American infantry file out of their beachhead

Bayeux; the enemy were already hastily evacuating this historic little town and important road junction. British patrols probed its northeast outskirts before dark, by which time 50th Division's beachhead was six miles deep and six miles wide. Splendid progress had also been made by Royal Marine Commandos who had fought their way through behind the enemy defences almost to Port-en-Bessin.

To the Canadians at Juno beach, meanwhile, the difficulties presented by the breaking, windswept seas were accentuated by a dangerous reef off shore. This delayed their landing for half an hour, and many of the amphibious and obstacle-clearing tanks that should have gone in ahead could not be risked in the rocky shallows, but were put ashore afterwards from landing craft. Those Canadians who did go in with tanks by the mouth of the Seulles disposed of the major enemy strongpoints within the hour. Without their specialized armour, however, they could not prepare exits for vehicles from the beaches. So the sands were soon choked with tanks, guns and transport. The following assault wave was caught up in this jam and the initial impetus lost.

Farther east of Juno beach, where it was too rough for amphibious tanks, the assaulting infantry suffered heavy casualties in a 100-yard dash for the sea wall. But after an anti-aircraft ship had almost beached herself to blast the German defences, the Canadians also broke through here. Exits were made for the following armour. By dusk the little town of Bernières had fallen, spearheading Canadian troops had penetrated seven miles inland, and their tanks were probing the main road between Bayeux and Caen. In fact, the Canadians made more progress than any other Allied division on D-Day, their foremost troops advancing to within three miles of Caen's outskirts. When, on their right, they linked up with the British 50th Division, an Anglo–Canadian beachhead twelve miles long and nearly seven miles deep had been created.

Behind a terrifying bombardment from two battleships, two cruisers and twelve destroyers,

As the invasion gets under way more and more troops pour ashore, while barrage balloons are flown from the beachhead to deter low-flying enemy planes

387

American troops keep watch from foxholes on a
Normandy beach

on defences already battered by hundreds of
night and dawn bombers, the Americans went
in on the Utah sector. The 32 amphibious
tanks for this assault were launched under the
protection of the Cotentin peninsula; 28 completed their two-mile voyage to go in with the
first assault wave. To their amazement and
relief the attackers were only met by spasmodic
fire as they stumbled up 500 yards of foreshore.
Many of the defenders, paralysed by the ear-
splitting bombardment, were still crouching
under cover. Those who stood to their guns
were petrified by the unexpected sight of tanks
emerging from the foaming breakers, coughing
flame and high explosive. These German
soldiers were not, it so happened, the resolute,
well-drilled fighting men manning most of the
other defences, because a fortunate navigation
mistake had brought the Americans in on the
wrong beach. They had landed in an area
where the flooding behind was so extensive that
the Germans had considered an attack most
unlikely. Within three hours the first wave of
Americans had broken through the Atlantic
Wall, and assault engineers were clearing
avenues through the mines and beach obstacles
for the follow-up troops to surge in. Although
German guns covering the beach on which the

Americans should have landed had by now been
swung to shell this one, the flood of invading
infantry, artillery, tanks and vehicles continued
to pour in. Accompanied by amphibious tanks
they hurried across the causeways spanning the
inundations, whose exits had overnight been
captured by the paratroops.

At Omaha beach, however, it was a far less
happy story. There the firm 300 yards of sandy
foreshore culminated in a steep shingle bank,
most of it backed by a sea wall. The four miles
of beach were overlooked not only by sheer
100-foot cliffs at each end, but also by a 150-
foot plateau inland. There were only four ways
for vehicles up into the plateau, each a narrow
valley cut by a stream discharging into the sea.
Where the shingle bank was not backed by the
sea wall there were soft sand dunes, equally
impassable to vehicles. Beyond these barriers
was marshy ground traversed by one paved
road and some cart tracks. First the invaders
had to penetrate belts of minefields, anti-tank
ditches and concrete dragon's teeth, festoons
of barbed wire and serried ranks of mutually
covering strongpoints. The defences were

manned by a crack German mobile division, which had recently moved in. There were more defence posts on the plateau above, and the scattered villages along the immediate coast were strongly fortified. Behind all of this lay the wide wastes of the floods.

In addition, the sea was even rougher in this most exposed sector; only two of the tanks, launched four miles out, escaped the waves; and the first groups of infantry were weak and wretched from sea-sickness. The preliminary bombardment had failed to neutralize the defences because of bad visibility, and anxiety on the rocket ships caused their terrifying salvoes to erupt in the shallows ahead of the assault troops, not upon the enemy.

As the landing craft lurched in among the breakers, and the heavily weighted infantry came tumbling out, they were caught by a terrible fire. Swiftly the sea was jumbled with dead, dying, and wounded – the survivors only remained alive because they managed to hide behind beach obstacles. The next assault wave suffered a similar fate, with the exception of some men whose landing crafts grounded somewhat wide on a smoke-enveloped stretch of beach. Eventually, almost a whole infantry company, whose craft had been blown east of the chosen landing place, managed to reach the sea wall and find a way through the mines. They were soon strengthened by a formation of Rangers who came in behind them, and some 200 men reached the plateau just in time to repel a German counter-attack on the beach.

A mile to the east, two battalions landed under cover of heavy smoke from burning buildings and undergrowth ignited by naval bombardment; some men got through before heavy enemy artillery fire closed the gap. Down on the beach where landing craft with troops, guns and vehicles continued to come in, bewilderment spread among the men. Amidst exploding shells, murderous machine-gun fire, burning landing craft and vehicles, and exploding ammunition, there seemed no chance of escape.

However, resolute men rose above the paralysing terror. In small parties, often suffering heavily, they wove their way through fire-swept minefields to attack the nearest defences. Some, aided by fire from destroyers, clambered up the cliffs on the left, overcame the defences

and began to move towards Port-en-Bessin and the British Gold beach beyond. But the armour and guns which were needed to make a really decisive incursion could still not get through because of the terrible chaos on the bare hundred yards of beachhead they had been able to snatch. As a desperate measure, General Huebner, commanding the 1st Infantry Division, called on destroyers to shell German guns and strong points point-blank at the risk of killing his own men as well.

The destroyers did their job so effectively that German soldiers came out with their hands up. Supported by amphibious tanks put ashore by landing craft, American infantry now began to advance inland. Engineers were at last able to concentrate on the minefields. But there was still no way out for the vehicles until 7 p.m. when a few tanks and tank-destroyer self-propelled guns clanked through to join the infantry attacking the fortified villages just inland. By nightfall the American beachhead of Omaha was no more than 1,200 yards deep, and already the enemy was massing for a counter-attack.

However, the Germans had been compelled to rush all their available armour towards Caen where the British and the Canadians had penetrated more dangerously. Satisfied with the slaughter they had effected at Omaha beach, the Germans even switched a mobile brigade from Omaha to join a counter-attack against the British near Bayeux.

One battalion of the German 352 Division had been detailed to deal with the American airborne troops further into the Cotentin peninsula; another was switched to counter-attack the British. As a result, only one battalion of that tough division was left to engage the Americans at Omaha. Even then, it was largely drawn away to the extreme western end of the beach where 130 Rangers, with great daring, had scaled a sheer cliff with rocket-propelled grappling hooks and rope ladders.

During the afternoon the unnerved troops penned in amidst the butchery and wreckage of Omaha beach received a boost from the commander of the apparently broken first-wave regiment, Colonel G. A. Tayler, 'Two kinds of people are staying on this beach' he said, 'the dead and those who are going to die now let's get the hell out of here!' There

followed determined breakouts by a number of small parties, culminating in a fight out to Colleville and beyond. The attack was soon strengthened as the main force of the American 1st Division, many of them veterans of North Africa and Sicily, filed up from the narrow beachhead.

On the British front the problem next morning was whether to drive all out for Caen with the 3rd Division, or to battle through to the Canadians and consolidate their joint beachhead. General Crocker chose the second course, because he wished to consolidate the beachhead before hurrying to the aid of the airborne troops fighting against increasingly heavy odds to hold the vital left flank. Towards evening on D-Day plus one, the last resisting enemy strongpoints between British and Canadians were overcome and the beachheads joined.

It was not so easy to reach Caen, which was part of the Atlantic Wall defences. This Normandy *bocage* country was excellent for defence. Down the centuries, the Norman

*Above* As they thrust inland, American jeep-borne troops are compelled to make a detour round a street in which one of their light tanks has already struck a mine

*Left* Pushing inland from the British beachhead, infantry and an armoured 'tank destroyer' come under enemy fire

peasants had divided the land up into individual smallholdings with steep banks, ditches and hedges, and the hundreds of square miles over which the Allies had to fight were an intricate patchwork of natural obstacles. Hundreds of tanks and 88-mm guns were dug down out of sight, and the whole area was a warren of interconnecting and mutually covering defence posts, brilliantly camouflaged. Obviously there would be much bloody infantry fighting, field by field and farmstead by farmstead, before the enemy could be overcome.

That day Montgomery established his advance H.Q. within the beachhead, and was soon visited by Churchill. All through June 7

Within two days of the Allied landings General
Montgomery took a drive towards the front line – to
the astonishment of the young German prisoners on the
left of this picture

and for many days to come, the guardian
warships off the coast and the never-ending
streams of Allied warplanes kept the enemy
under bombardment. The Germans were
shaken by the immensity and accuracy of the
naval shelling which included battleships
capable of devastating targets 16 miles inland
around Caen. The British artillery exhibited
both flexibility and accuracy. Time and again
it was turned upon threatening enemy moves,
undoubtedly helping the airborne forces east
of the Orne to continue defying repeated and
savage German attacks.

The devastating effects of the Allied warplanes occurred farther away. Among their
early successes was the thwarting of an attempt
by 260 tanks of the formidable Panzer Lehr
Division to smash into the beachhead. 'This

division alone will throw the Anglo-Americans
into the sea!' tank expert 'Fast Heinz' Guderian
had vainly boasted. An S.S. Division sent to
the front on D plus one soon disintegrated
under closely pressed bomb and rocket attacks,
and the shaken troops were compelled to shelter
in the woods until dark. The Allied warplanes
bombed troop trains and transport columns
30 miles and more from the battlefield.

On the American front, on D plus one, many
of the widely scattered airborne troops had
meanwhile amalgamated into active battle
groups. Apart from preventing the German
troops concentrated inland on the peninsula
from falling upon the precarious Omaha beachhead, they had achieved a major success in
capturing Sainte-Mère-Eglise, the most vital
crossroads on the Cotentin front. Omaha was
divided by ten miles of strongly held enemy
coast from Utah; on its other flank it was
isolated from the British Gold beach, with
which it should have joined by now. All
through D plus one, the little fishing port of

Port-en-Bessin, which separated the beachhead, was subjected to determined attacks by Royal Marines, backed by naval bombardment and Typhoons. The Germans finally surrendered, and the British and American beaches linked next day.

For the next twelve days, until June 19, the Allied strength steadily increased. By then the skilfully organized transport across the Channel had put some 20 divisions ashore. With around 500,000 men in Normandy the Allies had achieved a faster build-up than the Germans, as relentless Allied air attacks and the previous destruction of communications made it impossible for Rommel to bring in fresh divisions as battle-ready formations. They had to break up and make their way to the front by night in scattered units, often on foot or by bicycle. Much of their heavy fighting equipment was destroyed en route. Rommel, who in the desert had been a master of massing his armour to deliver devastating knock-out blows, had to commit his tanks in handfuls to plug the German line.

So far and wide did Allied warplanes range that two S.S. Panzer divisions which Hitler switched from the Russian front were in trouble long before they neared Normandy. The first one did not arrive until early July, having taken longer to cross the last 400 miles than the 1,300 miles from the Eastern Front to the French border. With his avowed intention of keeping the enemy off balance, Montgomery mounted constant attacks. Though bloody and costly to the British troops, they were equally costly to the Germans, compelling them to use more and more of their tanks as dug-down artillery rather than as an iron hammer with which to batter the Allies back into the sea. The German High Command, still duped by the Allied deception plan, continued to believe that the Normandy landings were a diversion while General Patton waited in south-east England to launch his major invasion upon the Pas de Calais, and held the German 15th Army, with its heavily armed and battle-proven divisions, north of the Seine.

Rommel had two main tasks in Normandy – to contain the Allied bridgehead, and to gather a powerful armoured force that would finally drive the Allies back out of Europe. He appeared to be achieving the first objective, but only at the expense of the second, because he constantly had to plug his defences with his Panzers. So long as Allied air power dominated the battlefield, it was impossible to mass the armour.

On the American front, where the Germans had comparatively few tanks, progress was slow but steady. After some particularly savage fighting the Americans entered Carentan on June 12; Utah and Omaha were finally joined. Once Omaha was no longer isolated the German front against this beachhead cracked. The Americans surged out to push a salient 20 miles long to the threshold of Caumont. Another dramatic American thrust took them almost simultaneously across the Cotentin peninsula to Barneville on the west coast. With the top half of the peninsula cut off, Cherbourg was directly threatened – and Rommel had emphasized that Cherbourg must be held against the Allies at all costs.

Compared with such spectacular territorial gains the British front had little to show, although the 6th Airborne Division, which had hardly ceased fighting since landing, achieved one notable success. It captured the key village of Breville with a daring attack in which the 160 men suffered 141 casualties – but after that the dangerous eastern flank was never again in jeopardy.

On June 19 catastrophe almost overwhelmed the Anglo–American beachhead. The worst June gale for nearly half a century raged unbated for three days and nights. It drove 800 vessels ashore, sank dozens out at sea, wrecked most of the great concrete caissons of the Mulberry harbour off Omaha beach and severely damaged others off Arromanches in the British sector.

The sudden grave curtailment of supplies, particularly of ammunition, forced Montgomery to postpone an imminent attack. For the Germans it was an obvious opportunity to unleash the armoured counter-attack, and Rommel's inability to do so was conclusive

*Top* On June 10, four days after D-Day, Winston Churchill once more set foot on the soil of France. 'General Montgomery reported that he was sufficiently established ashore to receive a visit,' Churchill noted

*Bottom* A German Tiger tank rumbles towards the battle front with orders to blast the invaders back into the sea

*Above* British medium artillery bombards German positions near Caen

*Opposite, top* British infantry of the Green Howards attacking an enemy strongpoint in the difficult *bocage* country

*Opposite, bottom* American soldiers advance through a pine-wood on the Cotentin peninsula

proof of how desperately the Germans were committed in defence.

Thanks to ceaseless day-and-night efforts by the crews of scores of DUKWs (amphibious trucks) which had crawled clear of the sea as the storm broke, a growing stream of supplies was brought in from the big off-shore transports. By the end of June the daily tonnage was back to its previous level and by the next high tide on July 15 most of the vessels driven ashore had been repaired and refloated. Mulberry sections salvaged from the wreckage at Omaha were used to complete one great artificial harbour off Arromanches by the first week of July. By this time the Americans had overrun the entire top half of the Cotentin peninsula

and captured Cherbourg. Though the Germans had wrecked the port so completely that it could not be used for several weeks, the capture of Cherbourg did remove a major worry concerning long-term supplies.

The first great British offensive, which had been delayed by the storm, was launched on June 26 to take Caen and suck in most of the enemy armour continuing to arrive on the battlefield, thus facilitating an American breakout on their flank. It began with a monstrous barrage of land and sea guns that warned the Germans where to send reinforcements. By June 28 British infantry and armour had fought to a dominating height known as Hill 112. The expected German counter-attack came next day – a day of sunshine and clear visibility. Hundreds of German tanks, drawn in to hold the British attack, clanked forward on the offensive. They included Panzer divisions just arrived from Russia and from the South of France and sent in without detailed briefing.

The Panzers had barely moved from the cover of assembly areas when the Allied air forces fell upon them with terrible intensity,

395

particular execution being done by rocket-firing Typhoons of the R.A.F. Of all the Panzers massed for this counter-attack not many more than 200 joined battle with the British. The remainder, and many times their number of vital fuel lorries, littered the road behind with smouldering wreckage.

The surviving Panzers came in from three sides upon the British salient. Many were knocked out by aircraft and artillery. Many more were stopped by the infantry's un-complicated Piat anti-tank weapons, for in this close *bocage* country the German tanks, for all their thickness of armour and their heavier guns, were just as vulnerable to determined close-quarters attack as the British tanks. Yet the battle developed into a bloody deadlock, with Hill 112 under such heavy fire that neither side could occupy it. Signs of the most dreadful butchery were everywhere around; the little River Odon was dammed by human bodies. There had been nothing in Normandy so far to equal the intense fighting during the five days and nights of this short offensive. Hitler was gravely concerned, and on July 3 he replaced von Rundstedt with Field-Marshal von Kluge, who arrived from the Russian front expecting war in the west to be easy by comparison. He was soon disillusioned.

July brought lashing rain and enshrouding clouds. It was to be a thwarting and costly month for the Allies. In both England and America an increasingly impatient public and press criticized the lack of achievement and heavy losses since the brilliant success of D-Day. To the pessimists of both nations the invasion of Normandy seemed to be bogged down into brutal trench warfare as unending as in the First World War.

But Bradley, although disappointed that his American army had made little progress after capturing Cherbourg, resolutely maintained the pressure on the enemy. For three weeks the Americans fought grimly forward in the face of bitter enemy defence amongst the lethal little fields and marshes until, at a cost of 11,000 casualties, they reached the smouldering ruins of St-Lô. This once-pleasant market-town was the gateway to the fine road that led towards the Loire Valley. It was the vital objective the Americans needed for launching the great armoured offensive which Montgomery had

The Mulberry harbour off the Normandy coast. In all their elaborate anti-invasion plans the Germans never envisaged such a thing, feeling certain that the Allies would have to capture a Channel port if they were to sustain an army

planned. Code-named Cobra, this offensive was to be led by that tearaway tank specialist, George Patton.

While the Americans battled through to St Lo, the Canadians suffered grievous casualties in their gallant attempt to seize the airfield at Carpiquet, north-east of Hill 112. This was followed by another all-out British onslaught on Caen after British bombers had dropped 2,500 tons of bombs. After two days of relentless fighting, parts of Caen north of the Orne, as well as Carpiquet airfield, were captured. But the enemy was still dug in on the hills across the

Orne, barring the way to Falaise and its surrounding wide plain.

With hardly a pause, Montgomery sent a powerful attack towards Hill 112 from the salient across the Odon, and on July 15 and July 17, all the British formations west of Caen became embroiled in savage fighting that soon cost them 3,500 casualties. Montgomery's intention was to divert the enemy here while he mounted a massive attack, code-named Goodwood, east and south of Caen to suck in the maximum German armour against the British and enable Patton to burst through with his blitz army from St-Lô to Brittany and the Loire.

Although it was not known at the time, the aggressive 12th S.S. Panzer Division had by now sustained 70 per cent losses and another Panzer division had lost 75 per cent of its men. Many others had been almost as badly savaged

during the unrelenting attacks of the 2nd Army on this front, yet nevertheless they continued fighting as reserves were fed into the maelstrom immediately on arrival.

The Goodwood offensive went in behind a mighty aerial bombardment of the German defences. But Rommel had anticipated it. He packed the defence belt – ten miles deep and formidably fortified – with hundreds of the dreaded 88-mms and six-barrelled *Nebelwerfer* in addition to tanks and other artillery. His army stood on dominating ground which he had, many months earlier, chosen as the place to meet and destroy the enemy if he did not hurl them back into the sea at the outset. Fate, in the shape of a ranging R.A.F. fighter, decreed that he should not conduct the battle. As he drove away from inspecting the defences on the afternoon of July 17, his car was raked by fire and overturned. He was taken to hospital

ENGLAND

London ●

Dover ●

BELGIUM

Calais ●

Southampton ●

Merville ●
Boulogne ●

Isle of Wight

Dieppe ●

Carentan Canal

Port en Bessin
Bayeux
Cherbourg ●
Bernières
Ste Mère Eglise ●
Colleville
Carentan
Ouistreham
Arromanches ●
Seine
St Lo ●
Caen
Coutances ●
Caumont
Troarn
Evreux ●
Paris ●
Vire ●
Falaise ●
Avranches ●
Gace ●
Conde ●
Orne
Dreux ●
St Hilaire
Argentan ●
Sees
Mortain
Chartres ●
Carrouges
Fougère ●
Mayenne ●
Alençon ●
Orleans ●
Laval ●
Ecouche
Le Mans ●

Loire River
Angers ●
Nantes ●
Tours ●

FRANCE

Normandy

unconscious and gravely wounded, and never fought again. (Rommel committed suicide in October, 1944, when implicated in the plot on Hitler's life.)

At the end of the first day of the Goodwood battle, 200 tanks and 1,500 men had been lost by the British. There seemed no ending to the hidden screens of 88-mms that stood between the attackers and the wide plain of Falaise. At awful cost, both in armour and infantry, the British kept attacking for 72 brutal hours; but when a violent thunderstorm with torrential rains turned the battlefield into a mudbath Montgomery called the offensive off. For a loss of over 400 tanks and heavy infantry casualties, the great British offensive that he had been expecting to smash clean through the German defences had achieved no more than a seven-mile penetration on a precariously narrow salient.

But although the Germans had managed to hold the Goodwood offensive, it caused considerable alarm and finally convinced Hitler and his High Command that the Normandy landing was the main invasion after all. Urgent orders were given for the 250,000 soldiers of the highly trained 15th Army guarding the Pas de Calais to join the Normandy battle. However, with the widespread devastation of communications up to the Seine it took another month for the 15th Army to reach Normandy – much too late. By July 5, the Allies had landed 1,000,000 men in Normandy while Rommel had less than half this number committed to the battle.

Eisenhower and other Allied senior commanders lost confidence in Montgomery after the Goodwood failure, although Bradley appreciated his strategy as did Brooke, chief of the imperial general staff, who pointed out that the 2nd Army had not only drawn in the bulk of the armour against them, but were destroying it much faster than it could be replaced. The Allies, he felt, did not have sufficient superiority for the attack on all fronts that Eisenhower favoured.

The British were now fighting on a 40-mile front from the Orne to Caumont, where the Americans continued the front 40 miles westwards across the Cotentin peninsula to the sea. At Caumont and Caen, the two significant bulges in their line, the Germans had massed the bulk of their armour and guns. But despite

the outward appearance of stalemate on both fronts, the Allies had reached the required position for the break out. General Patton, the most spectacular of all the Allied generals, was soon to deliver that punch with his splendidly equipped 3rd Army, an ultra-mobile, armoured force that even the Germans never equalled.

In preparation for Operation Cobra, the assault which was to culminate in Patton's blitz, Montgomery stepped up his diversionary attacks at Caen. Bradley commented later, 'We desperately wanted the Germans to believe this attack on Caen was a main Allied effort . . . For another four weeks it fell to the British to pin down superior enemy forces in that sector while we manoeuvred into position for the U.S. breakout. With the Allied world crying for blitzkrieg the first week after we landed the British endured their passive role with patience and forbearance'.

For American and British alike the fighting during July was increasingly savage and bloody. As the Americans fought yard by yard down the Cotentin peninsula they entered a still more difficult terrain of streams and swamps. By mid-July, however, they had established a line from which it would be possible to deliver the planned punch to convert the warfare into a fluid state permitting the Allies to send their tanks racing deep into Europe.

That vital line was from the ancient fortress town of St-Lô across to the west coast. Caen was to be held by the British as the pivot while the whole Allied line across to the Cotentin coast wheeled eastwards into the attack. Then one powerful thrust would be launched down to Nantes on the Loire, to cut off Brittany and its ports, while another thrust would punch eastwards and race parallel with the Loire to the Orléans gap south of Paris. The whole Allied line would then pivot swiftly and surge eastwards to the Seine.

Patton crossed the Channel on July 6 to go into well-camouflaged bivouac on the Cotentin peninsula, while the first formations of the American 3rd Army (though not yet so designated) began to land on Utah beach. The front line was 20 miles away. There was no opposition, no shots were fired at them, no bombs were dropped, only a few even got their feet wet. Patton told war correspondents he would burst through the enemy in the western sector and project one armoured spearhead at Brest to cut off the Brittany peninsula and another eastwards to encircle and destroy the German 7th Army. 'I shall be ready to go in two weeks and will win the war by the 11th November, my birthday', he added as an afterthought.

Just before Operation Cobra began the Germans switched two Panzer divisions from Caen to the U.S. front, where they now had nine divisions – largely made-up remnants from other shattered formations. Despite the tremendous Allied air assault and consequent transport difficulties, the Germans had increased their 58 divisions in the west to 65. Operation Cobra, designed to tear open the hole through which Patton's blitz army would hurtle, opened on July 25.

To a massive artillery bombardment nearly 3,000 U.S.A.F. bombers added 4,000 tons of high-explosive, fragmentation and napalm bombs on a small rectangle of the enemy's defences, five miles long by one mile wide west of St-Lo. According to the German General Bayerlein, they turned the area into a *Mondlandschaft* – a moon landscape, all craters and death. Bayerlein estimated that 70 per cent of the troops were put out of action – either dead, wounded, crazed or stupefied. This was the gap for Patton's army.

Through difficult countryside of streams and marshlands up to and around the gap, three tough American infantry divisions, veterans of Africa and Sicily, fought their way forward. Slowly, bitterly they won ground over which tanks could deploy. They were breaking out of the *bocage* country, the fatal terrain where the fighting was called by the GIs 'the Gethsemane of the hedgerows'. Fighter bombers of the 9th American Air Force supported the grumbling tanks and warily advancing infantry. There were visual control posts in leading tanks in verbal communication with bombers constantly overhead ready to attack any target to which they were directed.

The fighting of July 27 proved decisive. The Germans gave way: Coutances was captured. The German 7th Army responsible for this front began a retreat which rapidly degenerated into a rout. On July 30 Avranches was entered and the breakout was finally achieved.

Patton's instructions were to overrun Brittany and capture the main ports. Meanwhile Montgomery continued to draw in the mass of enemy armour and guns by setting the British 2nd Army to attack on a front between Caen and St-Lo, and the Canadians to attack south of Caen towards Falaise. Montgomery was beginning to shift his weight from Caen to Caumont, to drive for the high ground between Vire and the Orne. Bradley, with his 12th Army Group, was hoping swiftly to encircle the Germans from the south while the mass of their armour and fire power faced northwards against the British and Canadians. As the enemy threw in their full strength to hold the British attack, with tanks, machine-guns, mortars and the dreaded 88s covering the fields in successive lines, the American thrust on the right rapidly gained impetus.

Hitler saw the danger too late. He ordered von Kluge to switch four armoured divisions from the British–Canadian front to cut off the columns of the American 3rd Army, but von Kluge could not disengage his counter-attack force before August 7. By then the four Allied armies were wheeling east for their 100-mile advance to the Seine, while a tremendous air assault completed the destruction of all bridges between Paris and the coast.

For Patton's 3rd Army the beginning was almost ridiculously easy: it was delirious, thrilling and magnificent, with hardly any danger to mar the triumphant progress. They roared along the Lessay–Coutances road, hurtled pell-mell through the Lessay Gap down along the splendid coastal highway through Coutances and Avranches, and burst out through this gateway into the heart of France.

Fine, broad, metalled roads, wide green countryside, a splendid area practically devoid of natural obstacles stretched before them. It seemed that nothing could stop them until the German frontier. General Leclerc, who was attached to Patton's army as commander of the 2nd Free French Armoured Division, had the impression of 'reliving the 1940 situation, but in reverse – total chaos among the enemy, complete surprise of his columns'.

Patton was hurling his whole army through a bottleneck which, according to the book, was far too narrow and dangerous, but he knew that the Luftwaffe had been practically swept from the skies and that the bulk of the enemy

armour was inextricably engaged elsewhere. He, perhaps more than any other commander, knew exactly what to do in such circumstances: 'If I had worried about flanks I could never have fought the war.'

By August 6 Patton's tanks had made spectacular progress. Formations driving south and

*Top* A British infantry officer leads his men in an assault on a German strongpoint in a farmhouse that is now a burning ruin

*Bottom* Churchill tanks moving into position to attack towards Caen

British infantry dug in at the foot of a hedgerow
during the bitter fighting for Hill 112

south-east captured Mayenne and Laval,
while others raced westwards to drive the
Germans across the Brittany peninsula and
invest them in the ports. The particularly
tough French Resistance in Brittany gave
invaluable assistance, harrying the retreating
Germans and preventing them from destroying
installations of value to the Americans.

When the counter-attack was finally begun
from Le Mans in the early hours of August 7 it
ran into dogged American resistance. It had
been Hitler's idea to launch an armoured
assault upon Avranches, with the intention of
cutting Patton's supply lines and then swinging
north to spread chaos and destruction among
the Americans in the Cotentin peninsula. All
the German commanders in touch with the
disastrous events in Normandy were against it.
They all realized that the battle of Normandy
was lost, and that the only thing to do was to
conduct a quick and orderly retreat, to get the
Seine between themselves and the converging
Anglo–American armies.

Four fresh divisions of the German 15th

Army had just arrived from the Pas de Calais.
But instead of using them to cover a retreat,
Hitler insisted on launching them towards
Avranches. They were part of a force of five
Panzer and two infantry divisions which delivered a formidable blow upon the American
1st Army at Mortain. One American division
alone took the first shock but it held firm until
other Allied troops were rushed to its aid.

Powerful formations of the American 1st
Army pressed down from Vire, the British 2nd
Army attacked towards Condé, and Patton
swung a whole corps at them from the south
through Alenson to Argentan. Meanwhile the
Canadian army finally smashed its way into the
long-disputed Falaise. The counter-attacking
German troops were disastrously compressed
into a narrow pocket between Falaise and
Mortain which the Allied artillery, bombers
and fighters soon turned into a hideous
slaughter-house.

Although Patton had received reports that
several Panzer divisions might attack he saw
these as a German bluff, actually to cover their
withdrawal. Nevertheless, he stopped the 80th
and 35th Infantry Divisions and the French
2nd Armoured in the vicinity of St-Hilaire as a
precaution. Then he ordered Leclerc to con-

General George Patton, Commander of the American 3rd Army, the blitz army that was to deliver the knockout blow in Normandy

battlefield was in a state of chaos and confusion. Neither side knew when or where they would be suddenly confronted by the enemy.

By August 13, 20 Corps was meeting only scattered opposition, so Patton ordered the main force to advance north-east of Le Mans, while combat teams raced down to Angers and Nantes on the Loire. Meanwhile Haislip's 15 Corps was sweeping northwards, headed by the 5th American and French 2nd Armoured divisions, striking up at the rear of the main German force which was desperately battling against the British and Canadians.

The American 1st Army, which had played the major role in defeating the counter-attack, was meanwhile remorselessly destroying what remained of the enemy salient. Bradley and Montgomery decided that the time had come for an assault from all sides, to close in on the main German force. As the Canadians battled onwards from the north, the American 1st Army pressed in from the north-west and west, and the American armour and infantry of the 3rd Army swarmed up from the south.

The only way out to the east was the gap between the Canadians and Patton's foremost French and American troops on the line Alencon–Sées–Argentan. By the early hours of August 14 this gap had been ground down to a width of 18 miles. Bitterly contesting every river, stream, ditch and hedgerow, the mass of the German 7th and 5th Panzer armies gave way only slowly before the unceasing attacks of the British and Canadians.

Nobody, not even Patton, knew where all the various formations of the 3rd Army were at that time. 'Go where you can as fast as you can' had been the American general's order. Patton's army might have lost its cohesion, but it was achieving amazing results. Complete German units were throwing down their arms and surrendering to solitary tank squadrons, afraid of being killed in the woods by the ruthless French Resistance fighters. One combat team of the American 6th Armoured Division defeated the remnants of an entire German division for the loss of two men killed.

Patton was champing at the bit to hurl his armour on Falaise from the south to close the gap. But Bradley had ordered him to halt. The apparent missing of a golden opportunity to trap and annihilate the huge German force in

centrate at Fougères, with its important road junctions, to safeguard gaps in his flanks. When the clouds lifted about mid-day rocket-firing Typhoons fell ferociously upon the Panzers.

Columns of Panzers caught at a standstill in the narrow lanes were blasted to destruction. By early afternoon the intended German onslaught on Avranches, to cut off and destroy Patton's daring army, had been halted within a few miles of its starting point, but several days and nights of confused and bitter fighting ensued before Patton's army resumed its progress. The 3rd Army tactics were for groups of tanks to race on regardless, firing on any enemy formations they encountered. The whole

such mortal danger remains a contentious issue. Patton vehemently maintained that Haislip's 15 Corps could easily have reached Falaise, but the stiffening German resistance south of Argentan, particularly within the Forest of Ecouves, decided Bradley not to persevere with the attack from the south.

Instead he ordered Leclerc's force, plus one of the American infantry divisions, to hold the position at Carrouges and south and east of Argentan, while the rest of Patton's army continued its blitz and conformed to Montgomery's original plan. They were to drive eastwards to the Seine, to cut off the Germans before they could reach the river. American armoured columns now raced on through open countryside practically unopposed, heading for Orléans, Chartres and Dreux. Omar Bradley's precise order to Patton was, 'Shoot the works and rush east with everything you've got.'

The task given Haislip's 15 Corps was to form the American southern pincer of the trap closing around the German 7th Army; for this purpose it was to seize the important road junction of Argentan and block the enemy's main withdrawal route.

The gap was still 18 miles wide when Haislip's men consolidated their objectives on August 13. 'George (Patton) was doubly irritated for having been forbidden to close it (the gap) himself', Bradley later wrote, 'but Monty had never prohibited and I had never proposed that U.S. forces close the gap from Argentan to Falaise. I was quite content with our original objectives and reluctant to take on another. Although Patton might have spun a line across the narrow neck I doubted his ability to hold it. Nineteen German divisions were now stampeding to escape the trap. Meanwhile with four divisions George was already blocking three principal escape routes through Alencon, Sées and Argentan. Had he extended his road block a distance of 40 miles, the enemy could not only have broken through but he might have trampled Patton's position in the onrush. I much preferred a solid shoulder at Argentan to the possibility of a broken neck at Falaise.'

While the American 3rd Army thundered across France to the Seine, an American–French Army, with some Canadians and British, under the command of the American General Jacob Devers, landed in southern France on August 15 against comparatively slight opposition. Hitler is said to have called August 15 the worst day of his life. While the new invasion was launched in the south, the Germans around Falaise were making their final desperate stand against British, Canadians and Poles.

At Ecouché, meanwhile, the Free French surged forward to close the gap to 11 miles. The German troops in the Falaise pocket, hammered from all sides, were disintegrating and running out of ammunition; their commander, General von Kluge, was reported missing. Heavy air attacks had put his radio network out of action and created utter confusion, but he was back and in communication two days later. (Shortly afterwards he was relieved of his command and committed suicide.)

By August 17 the defeated Germans were streaming eastwards behind still bitterly resisting rearguards. Bad weather and the confusion of closely joined battle had kept the air forces out of the picture for a while, but now the clouds rolled away to open up easy targets for the Typhoons and Spitfires of 2nd Tactical Air Force.

Although desperate last-ditch German resistance against British, American, Canadian, French and Polish attacks was still holding open a six-mile gap, on August 18 Allied warplanes and artillery wrought such terrible execution that they practically closed it. As the enemy troops were compressed into a fast-dwindling pocket they were killed in their thousands while desperately swarming eastwards along roads and across fields. Eisenhower said of this hideous slaughter: 'The battlefield at Falaise was unquestionably one of the greatest killing grounds of any of the war areas. Roads, highways and fields were so choked with destroyed equipment and with dead men and animals that passage through the area was extremely difficult. Forty-eight hours after the closing of the gap I was conducted through it on foot, to encounter scenes that could be described only by Dante. It was literally possible to walk for hundreds of yards at a time, stepping on nothing but dead and decaying flesh.'

In addition to the terrible slaughter of some 10,000 Germans during the six days when they tried to escape through the gap, 50,000 prisoners were taken. Of the 20,000 to 50,000 who escaped, many more were killed before they

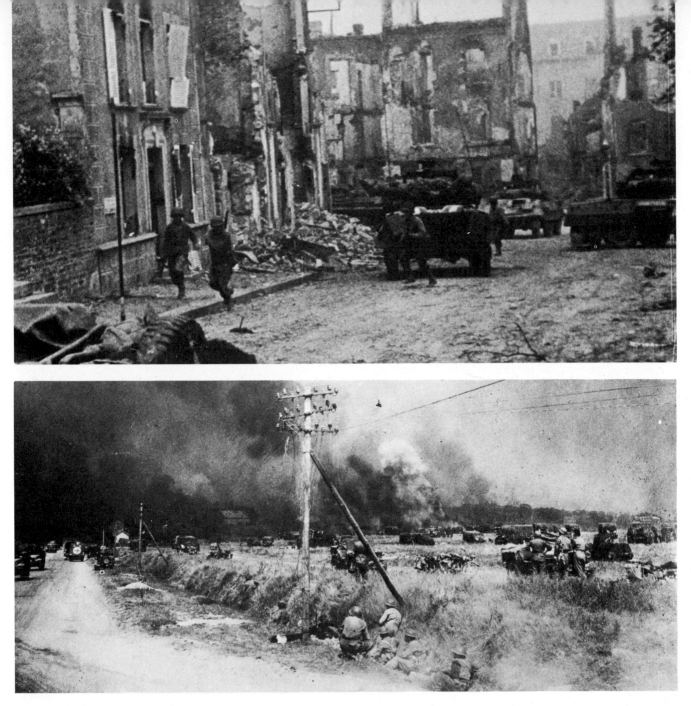

reached the Seine. Thousands more, cut off elsewhere by this devastating defeat, also surrendered. Eight divisions of infantry and two Panzer divisions were captured almost complete. The armies to which Hitler had entrusted the destruction of the Allies in the west had been smashed and routed. Their total casualties in Normandy were over 400,000 (half of them prisoners) 1,300 tanks, 20,000 vehicles and 1,500 guns. Against this, the Allies lost 209,672 men, of whom 36,976 were killed.

The Germans' last hope of holding a line in France had been destroyed in one of the costliest battles in Western Europe. They had set out on a headlong flight from which they were not to recover until behind the German frontier, 325 miles east.

*Top* American troops driving the last of the enemy from St-Lô, after which the way was clear for Patton's spectacular advances

*Above* A holocaust of explosive erupting among the Germans in the Falaise pocket. They were encircled by British, Canadians, Poles, Americans and Free French

# 13. Rangoon

# 13. Rangoon

Although the double battle of Imphal-Kohima was the biggest disaster in the history of the Japanese Imperial Army, the Japanese still believed they could win in Burma. They had lost 50,000 dead actually counted on the battlefield, and must have lost double that number in the whole campaign. The British 14th Army had lost only 15,000 dead, and most of its wounded and sick were in due course nursed back to full fighting fitness.

Reinforcing as fast as they could, south of the flooded Chindwin, the Japanese were grimly determined to take revenge. Their military leaders were convinced that they would achieve their March on Delhi when they had met the British again in a pitched battle on ground of their own choosing. And there was no doubt that the Japanese soldiers were as determined as ever: for all the tens of thousands killed, the British had taken more than 600 prisoners, and most of them were so terribly wounded or enfeebled by malnutrition and disease that they did not have sufficient strength to commit suicide. That the Japanese soldiers would rather die by their own hands than surrender was brought home to the 14th Army time and again as they drove the enemy before them through the streaming jungle. In hideous field hospitals they came upon neat lines of dead Japanese on stretchers, each with a bullet hole through his head. Their composed attitudes indicated they had willingly endured death at a comrade's hand rather than be captured. In the depths of the jungle advancing patrols came across lorry-loads of dead Japanese soldiers sitting stiffly to attention, every one shot through the back of the head by an officer who, dead by his own hand, was stretched beside them. The 14th Army still had to contend with growing numbers of such fearless and fanatical warriors before total victory could be gained in Burma.

On August 6, 1944, General Slim named the objectives required before the next great battle. He intended to strike before the enemy could reassume the offensive, and to keep up relentless pressure, however hard the rains and however impossible the terrain, just as his army had continued to pursue the enemy from Imphal despite the monsoon. Even the tough Japanese had always reckoned that the monsoon season ruled out campaigning, but the British never let up. It was of the utmost importance to seize the bridgeheads across the Chindwin before

*Above* General 'Vinegar Joe' Stilwell serenely observes his American trained Chinese troops crossing a river in North Central Burma to get to grips with the enemy on the other side

*Opposite, top* Soldiers with flame throwers liquidate Japanese suicide squads in bunkers impervious to shell fire

*Opposite, bottom* Their transport almost entirely destroyed during the decisive battle at Imphal, Japanese soldiers used horses and mules where they could find them to expedite their retreat from the battlefield. Here Burmese villagers appear more interested in the photographer than in the departure of the erstwhile conquerors from their midst

A Japanese 150-mm gun knocked out by a 14th Army tank lies in the mud of the monsoon beside a jungle track beyond Imphal

The 14th Army was ready and eager to drive the enemy out of Burma before he had a chance to recover, but the Anglo–American chiefs of staff in London were more concerned with supplying China, in support of Pacific operations. The ground and air forces available to Mountbatten were directed to protect the air link to China and to 'exert maximum effort ... to exploit the development of overland communications to China'. The Americans were still eager to arm and train the Chinese divisions and send them up the Ledo road, which led through North Burma into China, to fight across to the Pacific and participate in the invasion of Japan. They did not seem to appreciate the significance of recapturing Rangoon and tying up the Japanese army in Burma. While Mountbatten was thinking in terms of 'Rangoon before the monsoon' (the next monsoon would start in May), the American objective for the 14th Army was only to keep the Japanese out of northern Burma. In their view, the very ultimate of any British offensive was to be the capture of Mandalay.

Leaders of the calibre of Mountbatten and Slim could not be content with such a modest role. They soon developed an unofficial 14th Army plan, known as Operation Sob, short for 'Sea Or Bust'. And 'Sea' meant Rangoon! This ambitious plan was worked out on the assumption that considerable reinforcements would be available during 1945. Mountbatten had been given assurances that ample resources would be sent to South-East Asia immediately after the defeat of Germany, expected *before* the winter of 1944. The despatch of a further six divisions and a considerable amphibious fleet to Burma was discussed at the Quebec Conference, in September, 1944. But then came the failure of Arnhem and von Rundstedt's Ardennes offensive, followed by an unexpected Japanese push

the enemy could seriously contest them, and to stop them from using this great waterway for reinforcements. On September 4 East African troops hacked through desperate Japanese rearguards and seized Sittang. They swiftly established a bridgehead. But a week later another East African formation was fought to a standstill at the approaches to Mawlaik, some 50 miles south, where another bridgehead was sought.

*Opposite, top* Steadily driving back the Japanese who threatened the Ledo road to China in the extreme north of Burma, these American troops are seen crossing the Shweli river

*Opposite, bottom* So precipitate was the Japanese retreat after their defeat at Imphal that they failed to destroy some important bridges. This one on the Palel-Tamu road has only been slightly damaged by explosive charges and 14th Army soldiers are seen pressing on across it

British infantrymen, with fixed bayonets, move in on a
Japanese position in a banana grove

into China. This demanded a drastic re-
allocation of forces. Mountbatten was not only
denied the promised reinforcements, but also
lost two Chinese divisions from the northern
combat area and three U.S.A.F. supply squadrons.

As the monsoon of 1944 petered out, the 14th
Army sought to wrest two more bridgeheads
across the Chindwin from the enemy – one at
Mawlaik, 50 miles farther south, and one at
Kalewa, some 30 miles south again. It was
Slim's intention to fight a major and decisive
battle on terrain where the British superiority
in armour and air power could be fully
exploited. There was one place that was
eminently suitable, although this must have

been equally obvious to the enemy – the sandy
Shwebo Plain. It was an extensive loop of land
immediately north-west of Mandalay, bounded
on each side by two great rivers, the Irrawaddy
and Chindwin. The Shwebo Plain was part of
Burma's dry central plain. It was closely
patterned with paddy fields, criss-crossed with
irrigation ditches, dirt roads and tracks, and
thickly scattered with villages and extensive
areas of scrub.

Slim had no illusions about the still
considerable Japanese army which faced him.
According to Intelligence reports, which proved
extremely accurate, it consisted of ten infantry
divisions, two independent mixed brigades, one
tank regiment, 100,000 communications troops,
two Indian National Army divisions of about
6,000 each, and seven battalions of the renegade
Burma National Army. Although some Japanese
divisions were naturally understrength because

Another view of the Imphal-Tiddim road – by now
completely clear of enemy – winding through steep,
jungle-covered hills, tiered paddy-fields and occasional
villages of bamboo and reed huts

of their heavy losses, they normally varied
between 20,000 and 25,000, much larger than
an equivalent British formation. In addition,
the Japanese had for several months rushed in
7,000 reinforcements a month from the Pacific
theatre.

The crux of the British plan was that four
and two thirds British and Indian divisions
should attack five and one third entrenched
Japanese divisions in the main 'killing ground'
of the Shwebo Plain. Slim reckoned that two
Japanese divisions would be contained in the
northern area by the five divisions of Chinese
and Americans, plus a Chinese tank brigade

under the American General Dan Sultan and
the Chinese troops threatening from the Yunnan
mountains. Formations of the British 15 Corps
would meanwhile engage an estimated one
and one third Japanese divisions in the Arakan.
Deception schemes, including a constant threat
of amphibious attacks down Burma's long
coast, would keep an additional one and one
third divisions out of the main battle. Above all,
if the 14th Army was to fight its way down
Burma as fast as Slim intended, it would have
to rely almost completely on air supply.

Slim chose General Frank Messervy to lead
the daring drive down Burma which was
intended to win the war. Promoting Messervy
to command 4 Corps Slim told the planning
conference, 'I want a man who will throw his
hat over the Chindwin and then lead his troops
after it   and Messervy's that man!'

Mountbatten's proposal for reorganization

413

of the command in this theatre had finally been approved by the combined chiefs of staff. On November 12 Lieutenant-General Oliver Leese, fresh from commanding the 8th Army in Italy, became commander-in-chief of Allied Land Forces South-East Asia (A.L.F.S.E.A.), and a number of U.S. Army staff officers, headed by Brigadier-General Ray Maddocks, were appointed to his staff. The 14th Army now comprised 4 Corps and 33 Corps, with 15 Corps separately responsible for the Arakan so that the 14th Army could concentrate on its central Burma offensive. Meanwhile 36 Division under General Festing was placed under operational control of Northern Combat Area Command.

Messervy's 4 Corps comprised his own magnificent 7th Indian Division, now commanded by Evans, and the splendidly trained but as yet untried 19th Indian, commanded by the ebullient General Pete Rees, another veteran of Keren and the desert. His armour comprised the 25th Tank Brigade. Messervy's orders were to cross the Chindwin and advance into the Shwebo Plain. Then, by airborne assault if necessary, the vital Japanese airfields in the Ye-U-Shwebo area were to be seized. The blow was to be swift and violent.

The fighting for a second bridgehead at Mawlaik had continued, and by November 10 a battalion of the Assam Regiment were over the Chindwin. The first move of the 14th Army offensive was made on December 3 when a brigade of 20 Division crossed at Mawlaik and cautiously pushed south-east. Helped by accurate R.A.F. air strikes, the East Africans meanwhile fought down the gloomy Kabaw Valley west of the Chindwin toward Kalewa. They overcame the resistance of a strongly dug-in enemy force at Kalemyo on November 12 and entered Kalewa on December 2, the day before the 14th Army offensive was scheduled to begin. Troops of the 11th East African Division, who had crossed the Chindwin 12 miles farther north on tarpaulin rafts, heavily attacked the strong Japanese force on the east bank. By December 10 the bridgehead was secure and the longest Bailey bridge in the world – 1,154 feet of prefabricated sections and spans – was erected across the Chindwin in rapid time. All was ready for the 14th Army to attack the main enemy force farther south beyond the river.

During the next two weeks the East Africans

extended the Kalewa bridgehead so that the rest of 20 Division could thrust forward beyond the river. Next to cross were 2nd Division, forging east towards Pyingaing, and Stopford's 33 Corps. Messervy's 4 Corps also went into the attack. His 19th Division had made surprising progress: by December 12 it had advanced 45 miles. Four days later they stormed Banmauk, which lay 40 miles further east, and soon afterwards met up with the British 36 Division thrusting down from the northern combat area. Within hours Rees's men had taken Pinlebu, obviously aiming at the Shwebo Plain. The enemy was immediately threatened.

The fact that 19 Division had fought this far without arousing major Japanese reaction, however, now caused Slim to think again. General Kimura, who had replaced General Kawaba after Imphal, was one of Japan's best military brains. As he had permitted 19 Division to take Pinlebu so easily, the inference was that he did not intend fighting in the Shwebo Plain.

Here, obviously, was a Japanese commander of outstanding intelligence. Kimura was prepared to 'lose face' and withdraw behind the immense obstacle of the Irrawaddy. In fact, his intention was so to shatter the 14th Army as it attempted to cross the vast river that his revitalized army would be able to fall upon them as they sought to escape across the Chindwin.

Slim swiftly made a new plan: to attack and destroy the main Japanese force in the Mandalay–Thazi–Chouk–Myingyan area. Strengthened by 19th Indian which was already committed across the Chindwin, 33 Corps was to force bridgeheads over the Irrawaddy north and west of Mandalay to draw the bulk of the enemy troops. In the meantime Messervy's reduced 4 Corps was to carry out the swiftest and most daring thrust yet attempted by either side in the Burma war. It was to move secretly through the jungle-cloaked Gangaw Valley and force a surprise crossing of the Irrawaddy at Pakokku. Then it was to smash swiftly through, using armour and airborne troops, to the vital Japanese base of Meiktila to the south-east.

Meiktila, with Thazi 12 miles farther east, was the administrative centre and stores depot of the Japanese 15th and 33rd Armies. There were also six important airfields in the area.

Meiktila supplied all the Japanese front-line troops from the River Salween in the east to the Irrawaddy. If captured, the whole arc-shaped enemy front before the advancing 14th Army would be imperilled from behind, and the Japanese commander would have to detach a considerable force from the arc to preserve it. If Messervy's men held out, then the Japanese would be caught between the hammer of 33 Corps from the north and the anvil of 4 Corps

*Top* Now clear of the hills of North Burma (seen faintly on the horizon) this British patrol presses on across flooded paddy-fields hot on the heels of the retreating enemy. Meanwhile a Burmese villager methodically prepares for the next rice crop

*Bottom* Soldiers of the 14th Army advance through a Burmese village captured from the Japanese

All the time the British and Indian troops were thrusting southwards through the monsoon the Japanese were pouring reinforcements into central Burma to fight what they believed would be 'the decisive battle of the Irrawaddy shore'. Because of the increasing bombing of their main sea and overland routes, many of the Japanese reinforcements came in through the jungle from Thailand – some equipped with bicycles

in the south. Messervy's eagerness was increased by Slim's assertion that, when the Meiktila battle was won, 4 Corps was to make an all-out dash to take Rangoon and finish the war before the next monsoon.

Slim's new strategy meant that Messervy had to remake his plans completely. First, Kimura would have to be deceived into believing that 4 Corps was pushing on in full strength behind Rees's 19th Indian towards Shwebo. A dummy corps H.Q. was set up at Tamu, using the same radio channels as the real one which meanwhile slipped secretly away. All signals from 33 Corps to 19th Indian continued to be passed via the dummy H.Q., while 4 Corps's real H.Q. maintained silence as long as possible. Minor 'breaches of security' were contrived by staff officers talking en clair, and news broadcasts made similarly misleading references. Numbers of vehicles made dummy runs to and from Tamu, simulating the traffic flow of two corps H.Qs.

With all set to go, 75 American Dakotas were

abruptly diverted to China, where a resurgence of Japanese military activity was suddenly threatening advanced American airfields. Slim justly felt that he might at least have been forewarned, as the planes were already loaded with supplies for his forward troops. He was now faced with a crisis, for the planned Meiktila thrust had been based on air supply. The big attack had to be postponed for nearly three weeks, giving the enemy more time to repair his defences, and reducing the critical period before the monsoon started. Messervy's corps had to move the hazardous 328 miles between Tamu and Pakokku along a rough dirt road which was impassable during the monsoon. Built for bullock carts, it was to be used by up to three divisions with heavy tanks, guns and full mechanical transport. At the road's end, where all the troops and supplies had to be at exactly the right time, a broad, swift river had to be crossed which was certain to be bitterly contested. Only after that would come the breath-stopping dash for Meiktila, right into the hornets' nest.

Compared with the huge Anglo-American fleets of powered craft which were available for the river crossings in the West, Messervy's boats for crossing the far wider and more difficult Irrawaddy were absurd – 'a couple of bamboos and a boot-lace', was Slim's description. As Slim later recorded, 'the only equipment my Army had in full supply was, as ever, brains, hardihood, and courage.'

The 'armada' comprised a number of assault boats and bamboo rafts driven by outboard motors, as well as clumsy Burmese country boats and captured enemy pontoons. The bulk of the 14th Army's supply fleet was built by the army itself from the teak forest a few miles upstream of Kalewa. The chief trouble was getting the assault boats to the water. Much

*Opposite, top* American long range Superfortress bombers made a number of devastating attacks on and around the main Japanese supply port of Rangoon. They operated from airfields in Northern India near the beginning of the Ledo road

*Opposite, bottom* Japanese ingenuity: having laid a railway track on the one remaining girder of a destroyed bridge, they fitted railway wheels to their lorries and pulled railway wagons across

*Above, left* Amphibious DUKW of the 14th Army taking supplies down the Chindwin river, the first great water barrier they had to cross as they advanced southwards. Because the 14th Army was 'bottom priority' of all the Allied war fronts, they did not possess many DUKW but had to manufacture their own boats and rafts from trees felled in the great Burmese forests

*Above, right* British troops about to enter the jungle after crossing the Chindwin

*Opposite page* As the Japanese re-formed and were reinforced around Mandalay, their defence stiffened. Here artillery men are seen firing a light howitzer behind a tree-clad slope

digging into the hillsides was necessary, and innumerable improvements had to be carried out to the tortuous track before the five-ton lorries and the tanks could pass. Despite every effort and every risk taken, it was obviously going to be impossible to put more than one division across the Irrawaddy at once.

The first 180 miles of the road, from Tamu to Gangaw, were constructed by 7th Indian's engineers in 15 days, so that the 25-pounders could move up secretly for a barrage on Gangaw on January 10. But the real weight of high explosives was an 'earthquake' bombardment by a powerful force of British and American warplanes. Behind it, Messervy deliberately sent in East African troops, instead of 4 Corps infantry, to make the Japanese consider them

the dominant force in that sector.

The other part of Slim's plan, the feint for Mandalay, progressed well. On December 19, the spearhead of 19th Indian burst out from the hills to seize Wuntho. Four days later they had completed an advance of 200 miles in 20 days across atrocious country traversed only by monsoon-ruined tracks. At the same time, 2nd and 20th Divisions continued to thrust eastwards from Kalewa and Mawlaik. By the beginning of January the Ye-U airfield had been captured, the Mu River crossed, and on January 5 the 2nd Division and 19th Indian met at Kabo. Both these divisions then thrust swiftly for Shwebo. By January 5, 19th Indian had smashed through the Japanese rearguards, to enter the town and destroy the garrison. Two days later the 2nd Division fought in from the north-east while 20th Division marched fast through thick forest and closed on Monywa after some hard fighting. The formation of 33 Corps cleared the Shwebo Plain in preparation for the attack on Mandalay.

While the Japanese armies were massing for the conclusive battle of the Irrawaddy shore, Messervy's 4 Corps was preparing the thrust that was to wound them mortally. The final dramatic advance began on January 19, when the East Africans pushed on down toward Pauk. The 7th Indian's 114 Brigade was 'hiding' sufficiently far behind to avoid being given away by becoming embroiled in any minor

Tanks of the 14th Army move along a dried-up chaung
in the dramatic advance that took Mandalay and
Rangoon, nearly 400 miles apart, in 43 days

fighting. Meanwhile 89 Brigade moved secretly
on a long, curving, eastward swing to seize
Pauk and force a bridgehead over the Irrawaddy between Chauk and Pakokku. Through
this Cowan's 17th Indian Division, rushing up
at the last moment, was to drive for Meiktila.

The men of 7th Indian had already overcome
most of Burma's formidable hazards – the
frightening jungle, the dread diseases, the
stupefying climate, and the horror of the
Japanese. Now they were confronted with
another great natural hazard, the mighty

Irrawaddy river.

Running for 1,300 miles north to south down
Burma, the Irrawaddy is navigable from the
sea by quite big steamers for 1,000 miles. In the
months of the monsoon it is a seething torrent,
varying from one to five miles wide. In that
January, it was a full 500 yards wide at its
narrowest and 4,000 yards at its widest.
Although the levels were at their lowest, wide,
soft sandbanks presented an additional hazard.
Vehicles were liable to sink suddenly axle-deep
at the river's edge, and even shallow-draft boats
were in constant danger of stranding.

While 4 Corps marched secretly through the
jungle towards their crossing-point, away up
north at Imphal, whence the tide of war had

420

far receded, Cowan's supremely confident veteran 17th Indian Division had been re-equipping on a fully mechanized and airborne establishment. It was being prepared as the iron fist that would shatter the Japanese. General Kimura was, during these same portentous days, regrouping his divisions before Mandalay to stand against the British, Indian, Chinese and American troops advancing from the north. He was not unduly worried, for the positions he had chosen were naturally strong, his troops resolute, his bases secure, and he was receiving a steady flow of seasoned reinforcements from the east.

General Honda's 33rd Army faced the Chinese threat. General Katamura's 15th Army, nearly twice the strength of the 33rd, kept the line of the Irrawaddy. The Japanese 15th and 53rd divisions barred the way of Pete Rees's division. Their 31st Division stood in the Sagaing Hills and on the Irrawaddy line to the west. Their 54th and 55th divisions confronted the British troops in the Arakan, and formations of their 18th and 56th divisions opposed Festing's 36th Division. The bulk of the Japanese 2nd and 49th divisions plus two strong independent brigades and such Jiffs as survived, were manning the Irrawaddy banks west of Mandalay.

The Japanese were well aware there were some 200 miles of the Irrawaddy along which the 14th Army might try to cross. Kimura had taken the militarily correct action of strongly covering the more easy crossings and holding a powerful mobile reserve of picked shock-troops, tanks and massed guns ready to fall upon any other crossing point. The troops still on the western bank around Kabwet had the dual role of impeding the British advance and retaining bridgeheads for Japanese counter-attacks. Some were suicide squads, to raid and spread confusion among 14th Army concentrations.

Of the likely crossing-places on his front Messervy chose the most obvious, at Nyaungu, where on February 5 he ordered 7th Indian to establish a bridgehead. The reason for his choice was the weight of build-up on the other side. The crossing at Nyaungu was the narrowest, though a sandbank in midstream, enforcing a diagonal course, increased the distance to about one mile. Not only would it permit the

Japanese field artillery, significantly horse-drawn, hurries towards the battleground where their High Command intended that the final great victory of Japanese arms in Burma should be achieved

fastest turn-round of rafts and boats, but it led directly on to the junction of roads leading east and south on the other side.

Messervy also planned a fake crossing at Seikpyu, 40 miles down-river from Pakokku and opposite the important oil town of Chauk. The 28th African Brigade was to make this feint, coinciding with dummy paratroop landings and supply drops by night across the river. A marked map was also judiciously planted, which showed an intended advance on Yenangyaung. Simultaneously a crossing was to be launched at Pakokku; it was to include tanks, used for the first time in this part of the country, to persuade the enemy that it was the real thing. Another, smaller, feint was to be made six miles south of Nyaungu at Pagan, the ancient capital of Burma. There a Sikh battalion was to demonstrate, and cross if possible.

Understandably, the Japanese discounted the likelihood of a crossing at Nyaungu; for, except where the town itself flanked the river, the east banks were high cliffs cleft by occasional dry chaungs. They overlooked the flat banks of the other side and were topped by pagodas which provided excellent observation posts. Though the attackers did not know it at the time, they had one fact in their favour; Nyaungu was actually the boundary between two Japanese divisions, and therefore not within such easy reach of reserves as the main positions.

British soldiers on the look-out for Japanese beside the Bahe pagoda

Messervy ordered the crossing for 4 a.m. on February 14. There would be no moon that night, which was advantageous for concentrating unseen on the west bank, although some light was needed because of the sand bars. Immediate objectives were four beaches on a 1,500-yard front, slightly upstream from Nyaungu town, which gave access to high ground through dry chaungs. There was to be no preliminary bombardment, no bombing, no covering fire. The first wave of infantry were to go in entirely on their own, swiftly, silently. Complete and utter surprise was essential.

The advance of 114 Brigade on Pakokku, which opened the attack, soon met the ferocious opposition anticipated, yet drove the strongly entrenched Japanese out. While 89 Brigade covered in the west and launched the feint crossing at Pagan, and while 114 Brigade mopped up at Pakokku, the men of 33 Brigade moved up for the decisive crossing. In little more than 48 hours all the available boats, rafts, equipment and stores were rushed secretly into the concentration area. In the darkness shortly before H hour, Special Boat Section detachments and a Sea Reconnaissance unit made

a daring final reconnaissance of the selected landing beaches. As their craft crept back, they had the misfortune to run across two Japanese out swimming. They had no option but to shoot them. This possibly alerted the enemy. The beaches were still clear a little later, however, when other detachments crossed and shone hooded guidelights. The first wave got across without a shot fired, shrouded by the white mists of dawn. At 5 a.m. all had gone according to plan, but this smooth progress was soon interrupted.

Partly through lack of rehearsal, partly through over-confidence, the following companies set out in some confusion; the confusion was increased as some of the motors did not start and some boats began to leak. As a result, when the sun's first golden light suddenly bathed the scene in sparkling clarity, the reserve company was leading. It was decided to get into correct order out there on the fast-flowing Irrawaddy – but then the circling boats were suddenly raked with the fire of Japanese machine-guns from the far cliff. The swift current swept them past the beaches on which they should have landed and the fire intensified. There were many casualties.

With the element of surprise gone, guns and tanks now fired across at the enemy positions, and aircraft were called up to attack them. Under this cover the surviving boats struggled back, leaving one company on the enemy side in danger of total destruction. Messervy ordered

*Above, left* Gurkha troops of the 14th Army pressing on to join battle with the enemy along the road to Mandalay

*Above* Beneath the inscrutable gaze of a Buddha on Pagoda Hill, British and Indian soldiers charge an enemy strongpoint in the heart of Mandalay

his alternative plan to be put into action forthwith. Tanks were already lined up along the west bank. Behind them the artillery was deployed to give support in greater depth, so that devastating fire could be directed on to any beach showing Japanese resistance. Punjabis crossed in precarious little boats under cover of a considerable barrage, which forced the Japanese to keep their heads down, and swarmed safely up the chaungs on the other side to the higher ground. Successive waves were soon

423

chugging across to thicken up the bridgehead. Three battalions had been put across by nightfall.

Next day the little armada was again shuttling back and forth. Cumbersome rafts bearing Sherman tanks sailed in majestic serenity across on a diagonal course to land on the appointed beaches. At the end of the second day, February 16, a strong defensive box had been established to meet the expected counter-attacks. Yet, surprisingly, only Japanese jitter-raids had so far materialized, and the bridgehead, 6,000 yards by 4,000 yards in depth, contained two whole brigades. Messervy ordered 17th Indian down to commence crossing the Irrawaddy and concentrate beyond the 7th Division bridgehead. He was determined to strike hard for Meiktila without delay. Still misled by the feints at Pakokku and Seikpyu, and threatened up north by bridgeheads which 19th and 20th Divisions had just forced to menace Mandalay, the Japanese commander reacted slowly. It was not until February 19 that 89 Brigade, pushing strongly southwards beyond Pagan, was suddenly counter-attacked fiercely. This was the start of a whole series of headlong counter-attacks, thrown in piecemeal and intended to annihilate the intruders at all costs. But the soldiers of 4 Corps pushed on determinedly.

On the Mandalay front Rees's 19th Division had stealthily slipped patrols over the Irrawaddy near Thabeikkyin by night, to reconnoitre for a major crossing. The division began to cross in strength some 20 miles farther south during the night of January 14. The enemy counter-attacked heavily behind a considerable artillery barrage on January 20, but the British repulsed them, captured dominant high ground three miles inland, and continued to expand the bridgehead. General Katamura, commanding the Japanese 15th Army, was persuaded that this was a major crossing intended to link up with Festing's 36th Division, pushing down from the north, preparatory to an assault on Mandalay by the whole of 4 Corps.

Kimura was convinced that this was the beginning of the offensive by Messervy's Corps, which he was quite certain was up there on the left of the British line. He therefore rushed up two divisions plus the artillery from two other divisions, and as many tanks as he could immediately muster. For the stout troops

of 19th Indian, there ensued three weeks of ferocious non-stop fighting and subjection to the heaviest artillery bombardment yet encountered in Burma. But although they suffered heavy casualties, they grimly fought off a succession of furious attacks. Finally the fury began to go out of the enemy attacks; Sherman tanks were ferried across the Irrawaddy, and 19 Division went over to the offensive. All the time, so long as there was light to see, the bombers and fighters of 221 Group R.A.F. pressed home devastating attacks upon the enemy.

While Rees's Division was thus engaging the enemy north of Mandalay, Gracey's 20th Division loomed as a growing threat from the west. It took Monywa, the strongly fortified main supply and administrative centre of the Japanese on the Chindwin, on January 22 and in the following three weeks probed for crossing places along the river. On the night of February 12, it began to slip across at a point near Myinmu, which a captured map showed to be the boundary between the Japanese 31st and 33rd divisions. Two brigades were firmly established before the enemy reacted in strength, then Japanese reinforcements were rushed up and, as usual, thrown in piecemeal. They included waves of suicide charges by infantry supported by tanks, the infantry being slain to a man and the tanks blasted to destruction, most of them by Hurricanes. By February 15 the 20th Division bridgehead was six miles by two and, with the R.A.F. dominating the skies and mercilessly attacking enemy artillery positions, it was possible to build up swiftly in broad daylight. Still the Japanese flung themselves forward in wave after wave, and there was particularly severe fighting between February 21 and 26. But by the end of the month 20th Division had expanded its bridgehead to two and a half miles in depth by eight miles long.

There was reason indeed for Kimura to expect that the all-out British drive from the north was about to begin. Confident that he was going to fight – and win – the great battle on the ground of his own choosing, the Japanese commander-in-chief began to dispose his forces accordingly. Assuming that his 15th Division could contain the 19th Division where it was, and that his 33rd Division would stop the 20th

With the enemy routed in and around the city, British and Gurkha soldiers enter Fort Dufferin, one of the strongholds in the city

Division, he brought up troops from Pakokku and Meiktila to reinforce his Mandalay army and instructed his 10th Division, up near Lashio, to prepare to move down.

Meanwhile, much farther south, the really decisive battle was already being fought. Yet although the 4 Corps bridgehead was firmly established and Cowan's division was storming through, Kimura was not unduly worried. His opinion still was that the crossing at Nyaungu

was a distraction. Had it not been for his underestimation of Messervy's force, Kimura could hardly have been faulted. He recognized the threat of Sultan's three Chinese divisions, with the American Mars Brigade and the British 36th Division, fighting down from the far north-east to menace Lashio, but banked on the Japanese 56th Division holding them until he had fought the decisive battle. He felt the same about the fighting retreat of his 54th Division, in the Arakan, before the British 15 Corps. There were only two passes from the wild Arakan hills to central Burma, and Kimura reckoned that his men could hold

*Top* With Mandalay won, a British artillery observer notes the strike of his guns on enemy rearguard positions beyond the city

*Bottom* Indian soldiers fire 3-inch mortars over the advancing tanks as the decisive battle for Meiktila begins

to Meiktila was taken by Cowan's 48 Brigade, with Sherman tanks pushing out on a parallel course to the south. The first Japanese road-block crumbled when the tanks suddenly swung in towards its rear. The attacking force now divided, 64 Brigade Group to thrust for Seiktein to the south, while another formation raced to seize vital high ground preparatory to a pincers movement on Taungtha. Although Japanese delaying parties fought to the death, 63 Brigade were within two miles of Welaung by February 23. Meanwhile the main force of 17th Indian advanced powerfully on Kamye.

Next day the pincers closed on Taungtha. Increasing enemy resistance compelled 63 Brigade to fight hard, but 48 Brigade's tanks burst through from the south, and Taungtha fell. Maintaining the tempo, the now concentrated division swept forward on a broad front. That night, after destroying many suicide squads and snipers, it was poised astride both main road and railway for the final surge upon Meiktila. Next morning, while 48 Brigade remained to confront Japanese reinforcements from the north, the main force of 17th Indian, with its formidable tank force, continued the race for Meiktila. Thabuthon airfield was taken and 99 Brigade commenced flying in at first light on February 26, while 63 Brigade pushed on along the road. Eight miles from Meiktila, they were met by a fury of fire from the first really strong enemy defence positions, but a two-way attack seemed to mesmerize the Japanese, who were swiftly overrun. That night patrols went in to test Meiktila's defences.

Despite the movement of troops towards Mandalay there were still some 12,000 Japanese in the Meiktila area, spread out in the defence of the vital airfields and dumps. There were also 1,500 base troops, and several hundred patients in the hospital. Every man, even the wounded, was now put into the firing line, with orders to fight to the death, as Cowan's formations converged.

them until he was ready to deal with that British force. Around Mandalay, he felt certain that he would destroy the main strength of the 14th Army. There he had a total of nine Japanese divisions, massing on the battlefield of his own choosing, to meet five British divisions. There was good reason for confidence.

This picture of the war in Burma as the Japanese saw it was about to be shattered by Messervy. Without waiting for 17th Indian to complete crossing, he ordered the attack to commence. On February 21 his armoured spearhead plunged forward. The dusty road

*Above* Mules making the long haul across the Irawaddy. Tons of supplies were rushed across the river to sustain the attack on Meiktila

*Above, right* Near Pagan, where a feint crossing of the Irrawaddy was made, British and Indian troops advance past ancient tombs

There was no shortage of weapons and ammunition, nor any lack of food. Meiktila was packed with stores of every kind. Nearly every Japanese soldier was armed with an automatic of some sort, with liberal ammunition, and burrowed down into formidable bunkers and strongpoints, under houses, shops, warehouses, pagodas, even into the banks of the lake which spread out around the approaches from west and south. The entrenched garrison received last-minute reinforcements when a Japanese regiment en route from Thailand to Mandalay was detained in Meiktila by Major-General Kasuya, the Japanese commander, who also pulled in anti-aircraft units from the surrounding airfields to serve as anti-tank guns. Also at his disposal was considerable reserve artillery parked in Meiktila. The 14th Army was using up its petrol and straining to the limit the air

supply squadrons, as every division except the reserve 5th Indian simultaneously plunged into the battles around Mandalay and Meiktila. A speedy conquest was essential.

On February 28 17th Indian launched an all-out attack. While one formation established a roadblock to bar the road to Chauk, 63 Brigade stormed forward to assail the western defences, and 48 Brigade fell upon the northern defences. Sherman tanks, backed by self-propelled 25-pounders and two battalions of infantry, swung to the north, north-east and east. Cowan now called down the supporting bombers and fighter-bombers of the R.A.F. and U.S.A.F. and ordered the full concentration of his divisional artillery, together to project a crashing curtain of high explosive ahead of the troops. The tremendous support of the two American Air Combat Groups was particularly effective. Each had a Dakota squadron to carry the air-transported brigades, two fighter squadrons of Lightnings and Thunderbolts, and a bomber squadron of Mitchells, plus two L5 squadrons for air evacuation of sick and wounded. They had their own main radio communications with 4

427

Indian soldiers waiting to deal with Japanese suicide squads which they anticipate will be flushed out of Meiktila by the tanks and flame throwers

Corps H.Q., and liaison officers with the leading division. Their fighters had much longer range than the R.A.F.'s, so that they could keep up continuous patrols over the leading troops, ready to be directed on any enemy opposition.

From their dug-down fortifications, the Japanese fought back with ferocity. They had to be sought out and slain, man by man. When the brief sunset flared there were considerable areas to be mopped up, and Cowan pulled back his tanks and infantry from the night-time perils of the burning ruins. The men, whose blood was up, were loath to withdraw, but the tanks could not be risked. Fighting patrols remained behind and the night was full of the sound of shattering, point-blank exchanges of fire, as the Japanese came creeping back into the flame-flushed chaos to try to recover lost ground.

From the moment when 17th Indian's airborne brigade was flown in, there had been a continuous shuttle service of combat cargo planes between Meiktila and the airfields around Chittagong. From first to last light the air was loud with the roar of Dakotas and Commandos wheeling in with vital supplies. On March 1 Slim himself flew in to put himself in the picture and complement this great drive with his attack in the north. There the 2nd Division had joined 19th and 20th divisions after crossing the Irrawaddy at Ngazun, ten miles east of 20th Division's bridgehead. After a shaky start, when the leading battalions were swept by machine-gun and mortar fire in midstream, two brigades of 2nd Division, with some tanks, were securely across by February 26. Surprisingly, after the initial resistance had been overcome, the division was little troubled by the enemy. Kimura was gathering his strength for the great battle north of Mandalay.

The name the Japanese had earned for courage they doubly proved at Meiktila during the fighting that raged through the ruins and chaos. A Japanese soldier had to be really dead before he could be discounted from the battle. If a wounded Japanese could crawl to a machine-gun to fire it, in the face of certain death, he would do so; if a dying Japanese had just sufficient strength left to press his trigger, he would press it. Not until the last 50 living Japanese had jumped into the lake and drowned themselves was Meiktila subdued.

Messervy's men had dealt a shattering and, as it proved, decisive blow at the very heart of the Japanese army in Burma. General Kimura reacted swiftly as he appreciated its grave implication. New orders were rushed out to all Japanese reinforcements that were hurrying to give battle before Mandalay. At Mandalay troops closing in on the Irrawaddy bridgeheads were halted, and every available man was ordered to rush to Meiktila. The tough and capable Lieutenant-General Honda was instructed to retake Meiktila at all costs. For the task he had two full divisions, with tanks and artillery, all of them crack troops. His main objective was the airstrip, for it was essential to prevent the landing of more Allied troops. The Japanese flung themselves ferociously upon it, while other formations marched with desperate speed in an effort to seize both banks of the Nyaungu bridgehead to trap Cowan's men. On March 15, with the smoke of battle streaming across the airfield, the airborne brigade of the redoubtable 5th Indian Division was flown in. Shells were bursting around the transports as they touched down, and the troops leaped straight into battle. In a desperate surge the enemy fought up to the airfield's edge, and for a time no plane could land. The Japanese tried every ruse they knew, even destroying tanks with 'human mines'. Volunteers slipped down into fox-holes, each dragging with him a 100-kilo aerial bomb. There he would crouch, holding the bomb fused to 'instantaneous' between his knees, to be struck at the moment a tank loomed over the hole. Few tanks were destroyed by these desperate methods, but numbers of Japanese were.

All arms of Messervy's forces worked brilliantly together. Liaison was so good that aircraft safely blasted enemy positions only 100 yards ahead of the attacking infantry. By March 29, the scorched countryside was littered far and wide with the Japanese dead and large numbers of enemy guns were in British hands.

While the fighting raged around Meiktila itself, Japanese formations succeeded in recapturing the dominating high ground around Taungtha to cut off 17th Indian's supplies from

As their troops rush on towards Rangoon, Generals 'Punch' Cowan (left) and Frank Messervy, the Corps Commander, watch them go by. Note the carbine slung over General Messervy's shoulder – it was given to him by an American soldier

the Irrawaddy bridgehead. Messervy set about reopening the road to Meiktila and at the same time he pushed out to capture Myingyan to provide a new riverhead that would alleviate the supply problem. Using air supply daringly, he sent out powerful fighting columns from 7th

Indian across the arid, dusty plain, towards Myingyan. In a week the hills were recaptured and a link-up affected with an armoured column from Meiktila. At an opportune moment, a brigade of 5th Indian, who had made the long trek south by road, arrived to complete mopping-up at Taungtha, which permitted Messervy to swing the 7th Indian formations around and back upon Myingyan. After four more days of ferocious fighting, the town fell. Quays were swiftly built for the fleet of wooden boats, constructed far up north, to commence ferrying supplies across the river.

Honda sent in a sweeping attack upon Nyaungu from the south, only to be obliterated by a strong formation of 7th Indian. Another 7th Indian column, pushing down the Irrawaddy's east bank towards Chauk, clashed with a Japanese force which pulled back on to high ground and stood at bay. Messervy had to leave them for the moment to deal with more enemy formations around Mount Popa and with a dangerous situation near Letse, where the Japanese had pushed back the East Africans. But the Nyaungu bridgehead and the road to Meiktila were finally secured. The battle of Meiktila was won.

When Kimura had at last realized that Messervy's thrust was much more than a feint, and desperately switched his strength to Meiktila, Slim reacted by flinging his full available strength at Mandalay.

The hill which dominated Mandalay to the north-east was formidably fortified with dug-down machine-gun nests and held in strength. Yet British and Gurkha infantry assailed the enemy with such determination that at the end of three days and nights of savage fighting they stood triumphant. The 14th Army men closed in on Fort Dufferin, and surrounded it on March 15. But parties who rafted across the 200-foot moat, in a series of attempts to obtain it, were beaten back, and continued bombardment of the high earth-banked walls made little impression, even when medium artillery was brought up to point-blank range and shuttling aircraft dropped masses of bombs. But just as

From a forward airstrip, Thunderbolt fighters of the R.A.F. take off to blast the enemy still offering resistance to the fantastic 14th Army advance

During the time when they held sway in Burma, the Japanese formed a 'Burmese National Army', which in the end turned upon them to complete their rout at the hands of the 14th Army

Slim decided to bypass Fort Dufferin and deal with it later, the Japanese slipped away through drains from the moat during the night of March 19. Most of them were intercepted and killed during the next few days.

Maymyo was next to fall, to 19th Indian again, and with Maymyo's capture the road and railway supplying the Japanese farther north were cut. Stopford marshalled the full strength of 33 Corps for a devastating drive south, and the 2nd and 20th divisions surged forward on a wide front. The 14th Army was established in strength on both banks of the

Irrawaddy from Mandalay down to Chauk and had seized the main road and railway to Rangoon as far south as Wundwin. It remained to destroy all Japanese resistance and capture the vital supply port of Rangoon before the monsoon. A race against time was on, in which every day and night counted.

Messervy's 4 Corps – consisting of three divisions and a tank brigade, with strong air support – was to charge straight through the enemy and throw them into confusion. But there were still tens of thousands of Japanese soldiers in the hills and jungles between the British troops and their goal, and Messervy's line of advance was restricted to one dusty road crowded in by jungle-clad hills crawling with enemy troops.

'It was very plain to me – and if it had not been, plenty of people were willing to enlighten me – that this dash for Rangoon for a mechanized force confined to one road, thrusting against time through superior numbers, was a most hazardous and possibly rather un-British operation', Slim afterwards wrote. 'I knew the risks and the penalties of failure, but I was ready to accept them . . . the exhilaration running through the Army was a tangible thing that could be seen and felt. I shared it.'

Kimura strove desperately to parry the blow. The shattered Japanese 15th Army was ordered to move to Toungoo, to reform and re-equip. He determined to use the 56th Division from the north, which was still in good order, as the nucleus of a reserve force. The Japanese 28th and 33rd armies, though both of them had been terribly battered, also remained integrated fighting forces.

There were only two main routes from north to south on which the 14th Army could advance. One was down the axis of the railway and the other down the line of the Irrawaddy itself. Slim knew that he must thrust home swiftly down one or other route before both were barred. General Honda's 33rd Army was ordered to bestride the road and railway to Toungoo near Pyawbwe, while General Sakurai's 28th Army was ordered to block the Irrawaddy route at Yenangyaung and hold the passes to pen back the British divisions now triumphant in the Arakan. Meanwhile the reserve force which was built up around the Japanese 56th Division was to threaten, and if necessary counter-attack from the flanks, any British advance down the railway corridor.

At this stage Slim received good news. Mountbatten had decided on a supporting amphibious and airborne assault on Rangoon. But the requirements of the European and Pacific theatres robbed Burma yet again of the aircraft carriers, reinforcement troops and landing craft that had been promised, and even this small-scale and hastily organized amphibious assault depended on Messervy's men. Messervy's Corps would first of all have to capture the extensive Japanese airfields at Toungoo, 150 miles north of Rangoon, so that adequate air cover could be given from inland to compensate for the lacking cover from the aircraft carriers.

The chosen date, May 5, was less than a week before the expected beginning of the monsoon. If the rains came before Rangoon

British and Indian paratroops being dropped near Rangoon

fell, the 14th Army would be left floundering in the morass of the flooded plain while the Japanese recovered their strength. The monsoon's heralding thunder already rumbled in the distant hills. Messervy led 4 Corps into the fray once more, with Cowan in tactical control. Cowan ordered his 99 Brigade to strike out east and capture Thazi, and immediately to swing south and seize the range of hills south-east of Pyawbwe. Around Pyawbwe on the west 63 Brigade were to fight up to high ground, while

48 Brigade were to thrust directly down the main road from Meiktila. Still wider out to the west, designed to cut the Rangoon road south of Pyawbwe, Messervy sent a motorized infantry force spearheaded by tanks. As soon as all four forces had gained their objectives they were to launch an assault from all sides.

In villages, on hillocks, in chaungs, in hastily constructed bunkers, everywhere the Japanese resisted desperately, to the last man. It was not

*Right* A Japanese machine-gun and its crew silenced by the paratroops

*Below* A British patrol trudges through the monsoon mud close to the Pegu canal

434

until April 10 that the core of the Japanese defences at Pyawbwe were reached.

As the Japanese retreated, they left 2,000 dead around Pyawbwe alone, and many more around Thazi, besides 31 guns, 8 tanks, scores of vehicles and considerable ammunition and stores. The Japanese 49th Division ceased to exist. Their 18th Division was completely shattered. The iron men of 4 Corps had destroyed the main barrier across the road and railway routes to Rangoon.

The road to Rangoon was wide open for the final dash, with 300 miles to go in a maximum 30 days before the monsoon. As the soldiers of 17th Indian hunted down and slew the last of their desperate enemies around Pyawbwe, Messervy gave the order that sent 5th Indian

hurtling for Rangoon. An armoured and motorized infantry group spearheaded the leading division to seize an enemy airstrip. If none were available, they were to seize the necessary flat ground for constructing one. Airfield-construction parties, including glider-borne American specialists, with bulldozers and other equipment, could convert the scorched ricefields into adequate Dakota landing-strips very quickly.

The transport planes would then land an airborne brigade, which would liquidate any surrounding points of opposition, and, if called

Members of the R.A.F. Regiment manhandling light ack-ack guns on the landing beaches off the Rangoon river

A British Sherman tank rumbles through the outskirts of burning Pegu, the last battle the 14th Army fought before Rangoon and the whole of Burma was theirs

upon, lend weight to any attack already under way. By this time the main body of the division would be up and ready to thrust forward again. First one division would deliver its punch and consolidate, then the next division would sweep through it, punch, and consolidate. And so they would drive on, punch by punch. The controlling factor would be the speed with which airstrips could be brought into use. One was needed every 50 miles.

The 5th Indian Division was the first to encounter a check, after 12 miles, at Yamethin. Although the armoured group rumbled spectacularly through this small, thatched town, a strong Japanese suicide force slipped back by night and dug in. By dawn their anti-tank guns covered the exit road. They had to be killed to the last man. Time was made up in the next surge forward, to Shwemyo, 30 miles on, beyond which the road cut through a dark and

ominous gorge. Even as the advancing column sighted it, strong Japanese reinforcements were digging in above. But as one brigade pressed on to engage the enemy, a second brigade was secretly despatched to assail them in their lofty lair. The Japanese were still digging when the warriors of 5th Indian fell upon them from behind. The road to Rangoon, now 240 miles away, was clear again. Twenty miles farther on they ran into strong opposition again, at Pyinmana, but found a way round and, before the bewildered Japanese realized what had happened, seized Lewe airfield ten miles beyond. Soon the Dakotas and Commandos put down and disgorged an airborne brigade.

A large proportion of the Japanese army which had struggled clear of the Meiktila–Mandalay pincers was now behind 4 Corps. Heading south to join up with their own troops, they strove to outrace the British to Toungoo. The group of five airfields at Toungoo was within fighter range of Rangoon, and the Japanese had to get there first if they were to hold Rangoon.

If the Japanese did succeed in reaching Toungoo first, the British would lose more than

When an invasion force came in at the Rangoon river to complete the capture of Burma's great seaport it was to find that the garrison had moved out to fight the advancing 14th Army at Pegu, and had been defeated there

just the opportunity to seize the airfields. The date of the planned amphibious assault on Rangoon had been advanced to May 2, because conditions at sea would almost certainly be impossible for landing troops after that date. Messervy's men had only 11 days left and 200 miles still to go! Kimura ordered all his troops in the Shan Hills to drive flat out for Toungoo, stopping for nothing, by night or by day. The Japanese 15th Division, which had been re-organized and was once more a force to be reckoned with, led the way. Soon its route lay parallel to that of Messervy's Corps, so that from the air the two dust storms could be seen pushing forward almost side by side with only a narrow barrier of jungle-covered hills separating them.

It was at this juncture that Slim played an as yet undeclared card    the British officered Karen guerrillas, who had been secretly raised, armed and trained in the very midst of the enemy. On the word to rise and attack, the tough Karen tribesmen ambushed and slew, blew bridges, blocked roads, and cut off staff cars. At the same time, their British officers called down air strikes to blast Japanese columns and disrupt headquarters. The desperately hurrying Japanese were hamstrung. Messervy's men pulled into the lead and thundered on triumphant for Toungoo.

On April 22, the armoured spearhead of 5th Indian Division smashed its way into the town. The Japanese could not believe their eyes. A military policeman on point duty angrily held up his hand to halt a column of tanks – and was overrun. For the first time there were signs of panic among the Japanese under orders to die fighting. They fled before the rampaging tanks as though they were supernatural engines of war. It meant further indignity for Honda, whose Army H.Q., was in Toungoo. He made a dash for it, but he was destined to remain a fugitive, with no control over events, until very near the end.

After their shattering impact on the Japanese at Toungoo, 5th Indian never paused. They burst straight through and next day were 30 miles farther south at Pyu. There a big bridge had been demolished, but the 14th Army was by now used to bridging impossible rivers and chasms. The division was soon on its way again, thrusting on with such enthusiasm that 17th Indian, which should have pushed through on April 24 to take the lead for the next 50 miles, was still to the rear. Twenty miles farther on, at Penwegan, an armoured car actually came across a Japanese demolition party sleeping at the entry to the bridge. The exuberant troops rolled on over the bridge – seven days left and 114 miles to go.

At this juncture Kimura stepped in. He had lost touch with Honda and was under direct orders from General Taruchi, the Japanese supreme commander, to hold southern Burma at all costs. As the monsoon was so close Kimura thought that the British would not attempt a seaborne assault on Rangoon and, considering the great port indefensible from the land, he decided to stand and fight the decisive battle at Pegu. He brought up the 24th Independent Mixed Brigade from Moulmein and formed two new brigades from the Rangoon garrison, from lines-of-communication troops, shore-based naval units, and even from fishermen and civilians. His artillery was reinforced by anti-aircraft guns brought out from Rangoon, which were to be used in an anti-tank role.

Cowan's 17th Division had stormed into the lead. On April 26 it was 80 miles from Rangoon, with five days remaining and Pegu yet to be attacked. After overcoming a determined Japanese stand around a defile, they reached the outskirts of Pegu on April 28. Their armoured patrols drew heavy firing, proving that the town was strongly held. But as Cowan's armour probed Pegu, another column with armoured support swung around to cut the escape road east of the Moyingyi reservoir. The Japanese were forced to abandon most of their remaining vehicles and scatter into the foothills and scrub.

Pegu was a considerable town standing athwart the winding River Pegu. The Japanese had blown the railway bridges, covered the approaches with minefields, and dug in under and among the houses with all their customary skill.

Cowan opened the attack with twin thrusts, from the north by one brigade and from the east

and south-east with his armoured formations. They went in early on April 29. The northern brigade succeeded in battling through the houses nearly to the road bridge. The area was difficult for tanks, and they could not be exploited fully. The accompanying infantry stormed the approaches to the wrecked railway bridges in desperate house-to-house and bunker fighting. Indian infantrymen crawled across the twisted girders under heavy fire and slew the nearest Japanese defenders. Then they gave covering fire while more of their comrades ran the gauntlet by scrambling, on rafts, and by swimming. When night fell on April 30, the day's fighting had achieved this small bridgehead and the occupation of the northern residential area of the town.

While 17th Indian held a large part of the town on the west bank, the bridgehead across the river was expanded in the dark. The smoking dawn revealed a skeleton town from which the enemy was obviously withdrawing, leaving only mines and boobytraps.

Cowan marshalled his forces for the final dash. There were two full days left, only a broken and retreating enemy in his path, and barely 40 miles to go. But even as the forward troops surged out on to the Rangoon road the skies blackened and burst asunder, and torrents of rain cascaded down. The monsoon they had been racing had arrived 14 days early. In a few hours the flat fields they needed for airstrips were inundated, the roads were treacherous morasses, the ditches and chaungs had become wild torrents. The Pegu River was beginning to mutter, a mutter that would soon become a roar.

But if 4 Corps had lost the race against the monsoon, it had won Rangoon. A reconnaissance pilot for the sea-borne invasion noticed a rooftop inscribed with the message, 'Japs gone. Extract digit'. Only a genuine R.A.F. type could have thought that one up. The message was no Japanese trap! The Japanese had indeed abandoned Rangoon to go out and fight the great menace that had raced down upon them from the north.

The loss of Rangoon had been the beginning of the end for the British in the desperate days of 1942. So it was now for the Japanese. The immediate task of the British troops was to destroy all the Japanese who remained in pockets and groups over huge areas. West of the

Rangoon burns

Salween alone it was estimated that 70,000 starving men still survived, short of weapons and ammunition, kept alive by a vague hope of escaping eastwards through the trackless jungle. But the monsoon was lashing the land from end to end. The jungle was dank and sodden and wreathed in the chill mists that were drummed up by the driving rain. Disease stalked along with hunger. Men were reduced to tottering skeletons, until they crawled and raved and died.

The 14th Army, comprising the bulk of the remaining forces which had fought in Burma plus one new formation, went back to India to rehearse the invasion of Malaya. A new British army, designated the 12th, was formed to 'clear up' Burma during the monsoon. This army was destined to exist for no more than three months, but during that period the British and Indian soldiers fought a savage and beastly mopping-up operation in which 20,000 Japanese soldiers were slaughtered. Many thousands more died unseen and unrecorded, some at the hands of the Burmese, to whom they had promised equal participation in 'Greater Asian Co-Prosperity'.

At last, Japanese soldiers began to surrender. There could be no doubt at all that their fighting spirit was at last collapsing. All over Burma, remnants of shattered formations, left far behind by the onrush of the war, were dying in hundreds from starvation and disease. Soon the warlike sounds receded from the depths of the endless jungle and the haunted green silence returned. Only the scattered bones and hollow skulls of the Japanese dead marked the scene of their defeat.

439

# Bibliography

*Fourth Indian Division* by Lt. Colonel G. R. Stevens; *Ball of Fire* (history of 5th Indian Division) and *Report My Signals*, by Anthony Brett-James; *Golden Arrow* (history of the 7th Indian Division), by Brigadier Michael Roberts; *The Tiger Strikes* and *The Tiger Kills*, H.M. Stationery Office; *Take These Men* by Cyril Joly; *The Desert and the Jungle*, by Lt. General Sir Geoffrey Evans; *Burmese Outpost*, by Anthony Irwin; *The Sidi Rezegh Battles 1941* and *Crisis in the Desert, May–July 1942*, by J. A. I. Agar-Hamilton and L. C. F. Turner; *Official History of the Indian Armed Forces in the Second World War*, Historical Section (India and Pakistan); *Report of the Supreme Allied Commander South-East Asia, 1943–45*, and Supplement 1943–46, by Earl Mountbatten of Burma; *Defeat into Victory*, by Field-Marshal the Viscount Slim; *The History of the Fourth Armoured Brigade*, by Brigadier R. M. P. Carver; *Eastern Epic*, by Sir Compton Mackenzie; *The Desert Rats*, by Major General G. L. Verney; *Rommel*, by Desmond Young; *Auchinleck*, by John Connell; *African Trilogy*, by Alan Moorehead; *Safer Than a Known Way*, by Ian MacHorton and Henry Maule; *The Campaign in Burma*, by Frank Owen; *The Second World War* by Sir Winston Churchill; *Alamein to the River Sangro*, by Field-Marshal Viscount Montgomery; *Diplomat Among Warriors*, by Robert Murphy; *North-West Europe 1944–45*, by John North; *Crusade in Europe*, by General Dwight Eisenhower; *Victory in the West*, by Major L. F. Ellis; *A Soldier's Story*, by General Omar Bradley; *War As I knew It*, by General George S. Patton; *The Man in the Helmet*, by James Wellard; *The Struggle for Europe*, by Chester Wilmot; *Brazen Chariots*, by Robert Crisp; *The First and the Last* by Adolf Galland; *Anzio, the Gamble that Failed*, by M. Blumenson; *History of 2nd World War*, U.K. Military Series; *The Mediterranean and the Middle East*, Vol. 2, by I. S. Mayfair; *El Alamein*, by R. M. P. Carver; *Desert Generals*, by Corelli Barnett; *Anzio*, by W. Vaughan-Thomas; *Battle for Normandy*, by E. M. G. Belfield and J. Esseme; *Triumph in the West*, by Sir Arthur Bryant; *The Year of Stalingrad*, by Alexander Werth; *Barbarossa*, by Alan Clark; *Challenge for the Pacific: Guadalcanal, the First Turning Point of the War*, by R. H. Leckie; *The Battle for the Pacific*, by D. G. F. W. Macintyre; *Midway*, by M. Fuchida and M. Okumiya.

# Index

# *Acknowledgements*

**Black and white photographs were provided by the following:**
Associated Press: 144T; 155B; 159; 161; 189T; 211B; 216; 221; 363;
380; 390R; 417T.
Camera Press: 34–35; 38L; 43B; 48; 52; 60; 152; 174; 230–231; 239;
240; 246T; 255; 276; 281; 284; 301T; 308; 322; 337; 358–359; 370–371;
384–385; 388.
Central Press Photos: 44C; 176T; 196–197; 208B; 256–257.
Fox Photos: 27T; 40; 42; 44B; 49T; 51; 65.
Freelance Photographers Guild: 200; 206; 302T; 368–369; 394B; 405T;
432.
Heinrich Hoffmann: 138.
United Press International (U.K.): 313.
Imperial War Museum: 8–9; 18–19; 29T; 29C; 29B; 31; 39B; 47T; 50;
72–73; 82; 83; 88; 93T; 97; 101T; 101B; 104; 105; 108; 110; 111; 113T;
113B; 131T; 132; 133; 135; 151T; 156; 162T; 162B; 175; 186; 188;
190R; 192T; 194; 195; 199T; 201; 202B; 214–215; 227; 234; 235; 236;
237; 238T; 241T; 241B; 248–249; 252T; 262–263; 280T; 288–289; 295;
298; 299; 301B; 316; 321; 328–329; 332–333; 334; 341T; 348; 349; 355;
356–357; 357; 372; 378; 390L; 394T; 395; 396–397; 401T; 401B; 402;
405B; 406–407; 411T; 412; 415B; 419L; 420; 422; 433; 434T; 434B;
435; 437.
Keystone Press Agency: 10; 13; 14T; 24; 26TL; 27B; 30; 36–37; 59; 75;
86T; 90–91; 98; 102–103; 120T; 124T; 124B; 125T; 126B; 150; 173B;
176B; 177; 178–179; 179T; 180; 182T; 183B; 185; 190L; 192B; 198;
202T; 204; 205; 207; 209; 211T; 213; 220L; 220R; 222; 223; 229;
238B; 249B; 261; 268; 271; 294; 300; 309; 340; 350; 352; 353L; 353R;
363; 364; 403; 408; 409B; 410; 411B; 413; 415T; 417B; 421; 423L;
426B; 428; 429; 436; 439.
Novosti Press Agency: 151B; 167; 169; 266; 269T; 269B; 270; 275L;
275R; 278; 279; 280B; 286B; 290–291.
Photoworld: 173T; 189B; 208T; 226; 242B; 272T; 277; 292–293; 297;
347; 383; 386–387.
Pictorial Press: 183T.
Popperfoto: 19T; 44T; 49B; 53; 56; 62; 80; 85; 96T; 106–107; 109;
126T; 129; 131B; 134T; 170–171; 179B; 181; 199B; 212; 233; 242T;
246B; 247; 249T; 251T; 251B; 296; 304; 327; 330–331; 336; 341B;
343T; 343B; 344T; 344B; 346; 373B; 376; 377; 379; 382T; 382B; 391;
392T; 416; 419R; 427L; 430–431.
The late General Denys Reid's Collection: 86B; 89; 93B; 95; 96B.
Society for Cultural Relations with U.S.S.R.: 136–137; 260; 265; 274;
289.
Staatsbibliothek, Berlin: 39T; 142; 157B; 158T; 166; 314T.
Syndication International: 20–21; 55; 68–69; 71; 302B; 310–311; 314B;
361; 409T; 423R; 425; 426T; 427.
Ullstein: 11; 14B; 16; 17; 18T; 21T; 21B; 26TR; 26B; 32; 38R; 41;
43T; 47B; 74; 77; 79T; 79B; 94; 112; 115; 116; 117; 118; 119T; 119B;
120B; 122; 123; 125B; 134B; 139T; 139B; 140; 143; 144B; 146; 147;
148; 149; 154; 155T; 157T; 158B; 172; 182B; 217; 218; 232; 233T;
244; 252B; 258; 259T; 259B; 263C; 263B; 264; 272B; 285; 286T; 305T;
305B; 306; 307; 312–313; 319; 320; 326; 335; 338–339; 339; 373T;
375; 393B; 418.

**Colour photographs were provided by the following:**
Australian War Memorial: Ivor Hele painting of Australian troops at
Tel el Eisa (between pages 224–225).
Department of Defense, U.S.A.: Midway (between pages 128–129) and
Anzio (between pages 320–321).
Fox Photos: Spitfires (between pages 128–129).
Imperial War Museum: Paul Nash painting 'The Battle of Britain' and
Roy Nockolds painting 'Stalking The Night Raider' (between pages
128–129); Aircraft Carrier, General Montgomery, Crashed Junkers and
25-Pounder gun (between pages 224–225); Wrecked bridge at Cassino.
Rocket-firing Typhoons, 'Battle of the Sittang Bend' and 'Burma 14th
Army Patrol' (between pages 320–321).
Keystone Press Agency: Charles Cundall painting 'The Withdrawal
from Dunkirk' (between pages 128–129).
Novosti Press Agency: 'Anti-tank rifleman', 'Battle for Krukovo
Station' and 'After the Battle' (between pages 224–225).
Soldier Magazine: 'D-Day' commissioned from Terence Cuneo by
SOLDIER magazine.